ENCYCLOPAEDIA OF MOLECULAR BIOLOGY - I

MOLECULAR BIOLOGY OF CELL

By

Dr. M.Prakash

Dept. of Zoology
M.M.H. Post Graduate College
Ghaziabad
(U.P.)

DPH

DISCOVERY
PUBLISHING HOUSE

First Published – 2008

Reprinted – 2025

ISBN: 978-93-5056-572-8 (Set)
978-81-8356-266-9

Molecular Biology of Cell

Published by:

DISCOVERY PUBLISHING HOUSE
4383/4B, Ansari Road, Darya Ganj
New Delhi-110 002 (India)
Phone: +91-11-23279245; 23253475; 43596065
Mobile: +91 9811179893 / +91 9871656464
E-mail: discoverybooksindia@gmail.com
orderdphbooks@gmail.com
namitwasan9@gmail.com
web: www.discoverypublishinggroup.com

Printed at:
Infinity Imaging Systems
Delhi

Preface

The Present title **Molecular Biology of Cell** is a fast growing area of research from majors or careers in physics, chemistry, mathematics and engineering as well as animal, plant, cell biology and medicine. The overall objective of this publication is to provide a professional level reference work with comprehensive coverage of the molecular basis of life and the application of that knowledge in genetics, evolution, medicine, and agriculture. It deals with the life processes at a molecular level genetic disease diagnosis and genetic therapy; the theory and techniques for understanding manipulating, and synthesizing biological molecules and their aggregates; and the application of biological process to make or modify products to improve plants or animals or to develop microorganisms for specific uses.

Teachers and professors in schools and universities will use this publication for course preparation, and members of the press will find useful background information on new development in biotechnology and genetic medicine. Efforts have been made to prevent a concise treatment of their field of expertise at a level useful to both colleagues and researchers who are experts in related fields, as well as to university students requiring an introduction to a specific molecular biology discipline.

There can be no claim to originality except in the manner of treatment and much of the information has been obtained from the books and scientific journals available in the different libraries.

The author expresses his thanks to his friends and colleagues whose continue inspirations have initiated him to bring out this book.

The author expresses his gratitude to Mr. Wasan and staff of M/s Discovery Publishing House for their whole hearted co-operation in the publication of this book.

Author

Contents

1

INTRODUCTION

The myriad different species of living cells, plants, animals, or protist, microbic or human, are obviously variations on a single basic theme—the cell theme. Some cells, like different makes of bicycles, have features not possessed by all, but all are obviously derived from the same fundamental patterns.

All cells, however they may different in physical and physiological characteristics, are composed of essentially identical elements combined in similar or identical compounds which, with small modifications from species to species, constitute similar or homologous cellular structures. Chemical reactions of the same general (often identical) types underlie the processes by which foodstuffs are utilized in different species of cells as sources of energy and of cell substance. And, finally, it is now known that all of the variations in structure and physiology, including enzymic activities, that characterize different species an be ascribed to relatively small variations in the structure of certain complex molecular groups that are common to all cells; i.e., the heredity-determining nucleic acids. Thus virtually all the phenomena of life may be explained in terms of molecular biology and referred ultimately to the molecular structure of nucleic acids: deoxyribonucleic acid (DNA) and ribonucleic acid (RNA).

STRUCTURE OF ATOMS

From the foregoing it is obvious that a knowledge of molecular structure is essential to a modern appreciation of biology, especially microbiology. Therefore we shall, for the convenience of the reader, recapitulate some basic concepts concerning atoms, molecules, their structure and their roles in the phenomenon that we call life. It is assumed that the reader has at least a speaking acquaintance with physics and chemistry.

Molecules, as the reader will doubtless remember, are made up of atoms. Each atoms, in turn, consists of a heavy, central nucleus surrounding by one or more negatively charged, weightless particles called *electrons* that encircle the nucleus in various inner and outer orbits. Both nucleus and electrons are minute, yet the distance between them is so vast, relative to their sizes, that the spatial relationship of nucleus to orbiting electrons suggests the relationship of the sun to the orbiting plants.

The *atomic nucleus* consists of several kinds of particles, of which protons and neutrons are the most important in this discussion. Each *proton* has a positive electrical charge. *Neutrons* have no electrical charge; they represent a combined proton and electron. Each uncombined proton and each uncombined neutron is assigned an arbitrary weight of 1 unit. The electron weights about 1/1848 of this unit—not

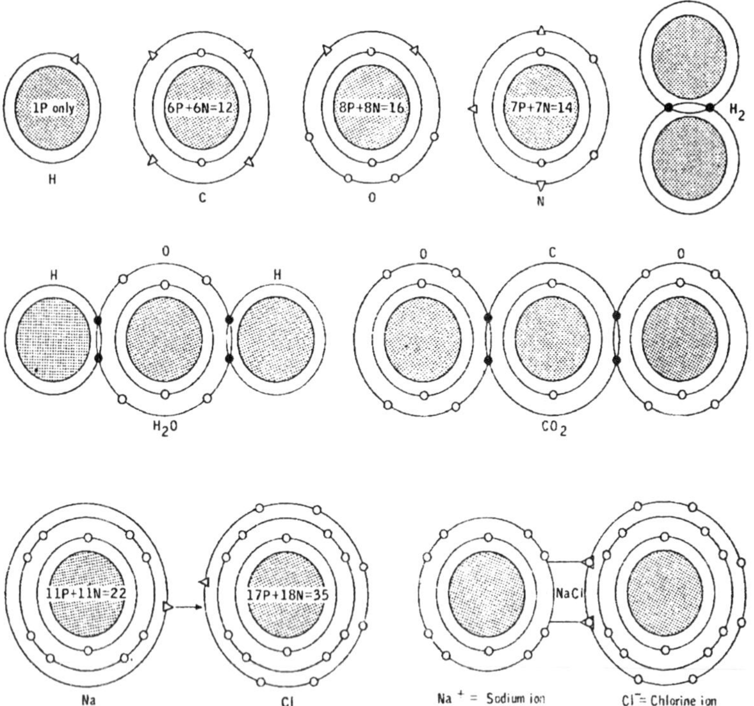

Fig. 1.1. Diagrammatic structures of atoms of hydrogen, carbon, oxygen and nitrogen, the hydrogen molecule and the molecules of H_2O and CO_2.

very heavy! Atoms of different substances have different numbers of protons and neutrons and of orbiting electrons. It is these differences, and especially the differences in number and arrangement of the electrons, that create the differences between substances.

Under usual conditions the negative charges on the electrons of an atom are balanced by the positive charges of the protons in the nucleus of the atom: i.e., the numbers of protons and of electrons are alike. Such atoms are electrically neutral. The number of electrons (or of protons, since their numbers are equal) is any given type of atom is called the *atomic number* of that atom. The number of protons plus the number of neutrons is the *atomic weight* of the atom. Atomic weight is a relative quantity. It is usually expressed as the number of times heavier a given atom is than an atom of some other substance taken as a standard. This is now commonly carbon (6 protons + 6 neutrons = at. wt. 12; 6 electrons = at. no. 6).

The hydrogen atoms is unique in having in its nucleus only one proton; atomic weight = 1.00^+. A single electron, spinning on its own axis like the earth, orbits the nucleus with extreme rapidly, always at nearly the same distance from the nucleus. The centrifugal force of this whirling motion might cause the electron to fly off into space, were it not balanced by the constant attraction of the positively charged proton. So rapid is the motion and so strong and generalized is the influence of the electron around the proton that it forms a continuous spherical shell, or cloud, around the nucleus. The continuous zone of distribution of an electron around its nucleus is called a *shell* or *orbital*. Spherical orbitals are designated *s* orbitals; orbitals with patterns other than spherical (commonly figure-eight patterns) are called patterned or *p* orbitals. Depending on the element there may be one or several shells, the series of shells from within outward being designated by the letters *k* to *p*. Carbon, for example, has two shells, an inner or *k* shell containing two *paired* electrons in an *s* orbital close to the nucleus, and an outer or *l* shell with four electrons in modified (hybrid) *p* orbitals.

The six protons in the nucleus of the carbon atom balance the six electrons. The six electrons give it an atomic number of 6. The two electron shells give it a position in the periodic table of the elements in period 2.

The Periodic Table of the Elements

This is a descriptive tabulation of all elements according to atomic structure. Arrangements vary, but in all tables the numbers of the *periods* represents the numbers of electron shells per atom. The *group* numbers represents numbers of electrons in the outermost shell. Of these outermost electrons all or, depending on patterns and arrangements of the orbitals, only certain outermost electrons can enter into the formation of compounds with other atoms. The outermost electrons available for the formation of bonds with other atoms or radicals are called *valence electrons* and their number is the valence number (*valance*) of that atom or element.

Elements with one, two or three electrons in the outermost shell tend to become stabilized by giving these electrons up, elements with five, six or seven outermost electrons tends to achieve stability by accepting electrons. Thus the elements of Group I, II or III have a tendency to combine in particular with elements of Group V, VI or VII. The readiness of an element to lose or gain electrons is expressed as *activity*, and the degree of activity is dependent in great part of the distance of the electrons from the nucleus. In general, those changes in electronic structure which achieve greater stability tend to occur and usually release energy.

The outermost shells of elements in Group O are "saturated" with electrons; helium with two, the others with eight, the maximum for any outermost shell. This is a condition of complete stability; there is no tendency either to give up or to accept electrons. These are the *inter elements*: helium, neon, argon, krypton, xenon, and radon. The transitional elements are subgroups of Period 4, 5 and 6 and generally have two valence electrons, except Cu, Ag, Pt and Au, which have only one. The rare earth elements (lanthanide series, Period 6, and actinide series, Period 7) concern us but little in biology. Indeed of over 100 known elements, only about 19 are of demonstrated importance in biology: Ca, *C*, Cl, Co, Cu, *H*, I, *Fe*, *Mg*, Mn, Mo, *N*, *O*, *P*, K, Na, Rb, *S*, Si. Those italicized are most abundant in living cells, although several of the others are absolutely essential in minute amounts. Some of those not listed may be essential, although present only in trace amounts.

Valence and Compounds

It is clear that the numbers of outermost electrons and their positions in regard to combinations of any element with other elements, i.e., in the formation of compounds. Electrons in the inner or *k* shell are generally very strongly held by the nucleus and, except for the hydrogen electron, are not involved in chemical reactions. Outer-shell structures are least stable because outer electrons are less strongly

Table 1.1. Long form of the Periodic Table of the elements.

Period	IA	IIA	IIIB	IVB	VB	VIB	VIIB	VIII			IB	IIB	IIIA	IVA	VA	VIA	VIIA	O Inert Gases
			Transition Elements															
1	1 H 1.008																1 H 1.008	2 He 4.003
2	3 Li 6.939	4 Be 9.012											5 B 10.81	6 C 12.011	7 N 14.007	8 O 15.999	9 F 19.00	10 Ne 20.183
3	11 Na 22.990	12 Mg 24.31											13 Al 26.98	14 Si 28.086	15 P 30.974	16 S 32.064	17 Cl 35.453	18 Ar 39.948
4	19 K 39.12	20 Ca 40.08	21 Sc 44.956	22 Ti 47.90	23 V 50.94	24 Cr 51.996	25 Mn 54.94	26 Fe 55.85	27 Co 58.93	28 Ni 58.71	29 Cu 63.54	30 Zn 65.37	31 Ga 69.72	32 Ge 72.59	33 As 74.92	34 Se 78.96	35 Br 79.909	36 Kr 83.80
5	37 Rb 85.47	38 Sr 87.62	39 Y 88.91	40 Zr 91.22	41 Nb 92.91	42 Mo 95.94	43 Tc 99	44 Ru 101.07	45 Rh 102.91	46 Pd 106.4	47 Ag 107.870	48 Cd 112.40	49 In 114.82	50 Sn 118.69	51 Sb 121.75	52 Te 127.60	53 I 126.90	54 Xe 131.30
6	55 Cs 132.91	56 Ba 137.34	57-71 La-Lu Rare Earths	72 Hf 178.49	73 Ta 180.95	74 W 183.85	75 Re 186.2	76 Os 190.2	77 Ir 192.2	78 Pt 195.09	79 Au 196.97	80 Hg 200.59	81 Tl 204.37	82 Pb 207.19	83 Bi 208.98	84 Po 210	85 At 210	86 Rn 222
7	87 Fr 223	88 Ra 226.05	89-103 Ac-Lw Actinides															
Rare Earths			57 La 138.91	58 Ce 140.12	59 Pr 140.91	60 Nd 144.24	61 Pm 145	62 Sm 150.35	63 Eu 151.96	64 Gd 157.25	65 Tb 158.92	66 Dy 162.50	67 Ho 164.93	68 Er 167.26	69 Tm 168.93	70 Yb 173.04	71 Lu 174.97	
Actinides			89 Ac 227	90 Th 232.04	91 Pa 231	92 U 238.03	93 Np 237	94 Pu 242	95 Am 243	96 Cm 247	97 Bk 249	98 Cf 251	99 Es 254	100 Fm 253	101 Md 256	102 No 253	103 Lw 257	

attracted to the nucleus. The strength of the attraction decreases in proportion to the distance of the electron from the nucleus; the outermost electrons are therefore more easily removed and the outermost shells are most readily added to. Although the outermost electrons of atoms are those farthest removed from the strong attraction of the nuclear protons and therefore most involved in combinations between atoms, as a general rule only those outer electrons that are *unpaired* tend to form bonds. For example, oxygen has six outer electrons and is therefore in Group VI of the periodic table; but only two of these six electrons are unpaired, giving oxygen a valence of 2. Similarly, nitrogen has five outer electrons but only three are unpaired. Nitrogen therefore has a valence of 3. Under some circumstances it may exhibit a valence of 4 or 5. Some others elements show this variation of valency.

In general, atoms tend to enter into combinations by which they can approach the stability that, for still obscure reasons, results from the presence of eight (four pairs) outer electrons. This is the structure of most inert elements of Group O. Hydrogen is an exception in that it has only one shell that requires only one more electron to saturate it. It then achieves the stability (and identity) of the inert helium atom with a pair of electrons. Because of its single electron, hydrogen is extremely active. It even reacts with itself to form H_2, a diatomic molecule. The halogens, nitrogen and oxygen also generally occur as diatomic molecules.

The capacity of each shell to contain electrons is limited, varying from the *k* shell (capacity two electron) to the outermost shell (eight electrons). Intermediate shells may have up to 32 electrons. The outermost shell never contains more than eight electrons. A shell with eight electrons is a very stable structure and strongly resists alternation: i.e., it is an inert element (Group O).

Valence electrons cannot long be free or floating in the air, as it were, they tend to be attached to something else. For example carbon, with a valence of 4, cannot form such a compound as CH as a distinct and stable compound because three of the carbon valences would be left free; the simplest stable compound of carbon with hydrogen is CH_4 or methane, the principal constituent of marsh and sewer gas.

Among the elements carbon, the basis of all organic compounds and therefore the key to life as we know it, is unique and most versatile. In the first place, carbon atoms are ambivalent, i.e., they can combine with positive or negative ions or groups simultaneously. They also have the rare property of combining with other carbon atoms. They thus can form almost indefinitely long chains of lined carbon atoms—straight, bent, branched or cyclic. This property is the basis of the large group of aliphatic compounds that underlie many structural parts of living cells. There will be mentioned later.

Ionization

Some properties of aqueous suspensions of large molecules (e.g., proteins) or groups of molecules such as *colloids* are already mentioned. Colloids conduct relatively little electricity.

Electrolytes

Substances whose aqueous solutions readily conduct electricity are called *electrolytes*. If they are very active in this respect they are said to be strong electrolytes. Generally these are inorganic compounds: salts like sodium chloride, acids like sulfuric acid, bases like potassium hydroxide. Except carbon monoxide, carbon dioxide, carbonates and cyanides, *inorganic* compounds characteristically lack carbon, carbon-to-carbon or carbon-to-hydrogen bonds. These bonds are always found in *organic* compounds, which typically are not strong electrolytes.

Substances whose aqueous solutions do not readily conduct electricity are called *nonelectrolytes*. They are generally organic compounds. Organic colloids like protein and fat emulsions are virtually nonelectrolytes. Organic acids like citric (of lemons), acetic (of vinegar) and lactic (of sour milk) are weak electrolytes, that is, their aqueous solutions conduct electricity to a slight degree.

Electrolytes have several other properties that distinguish them from nonelectrolytes. Compared with nonelectrolytes, electrolytes markedly after the colligative properties of water: i.e., they (a) lower the freezing point, (b) raise the boiling point, (c) increase the osmotic pressure and (d) lower the vapour pressure of their aqueous solutions.

Dissociation

Electrolytes are electrically conductive because their molecules in aqueous solution split (*dissociate*) into positively and negatively charged particles called *ions*. They dissociate in this way because: (a) pure water has a high dielectric constant; i.e., it has practically no conductance for electricity and (if pure!) is therefore a very good insulating material; (b) water molecules are *polar* because in each molecule the oxygen has attracted the electrons of the hydrogen unequally, giving it unbalanced negativity. These seemingly unrelated facts are easily integrated as follows.

If an electrolyte, for example HCl, (H^+Cl^-) is dissolve in water (H_2O) the positively charged hydrogen ion (H^+) (a *cation*) attracts around itself swarms of water molecules, each with its negative pole

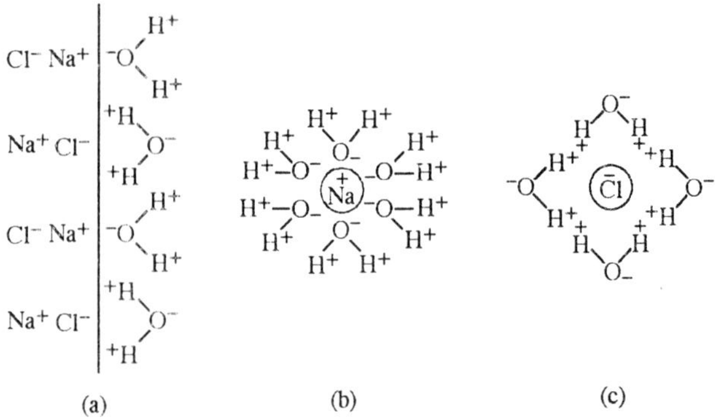

(a) (b) (c)

Fig. 1.2. Dissociation of sodium chloride in water.

(oxygen) nearest the H^+. In a like manner, or electrolytic dissociation the negatively charged chlorine ion (Cl^-) (an *anion*) attracts other water molecules with their positive poles (hydrogen) nearest the Cl^-. The two ions (H^+ and Cl^-) are thus well insulated from each other by the dielectric action of the water molecules. The H^+ and Cl^- move about freely in the water. If two oppositely charged, chemically inert electrodes from a battery (e.g., platinum electrodes) are immersed in the solution at opposite side of the vessel, any cations in the solution migrate to the negative electrode (the *cathode*), accepting electrons therefrom, any anions in the solution migrate to the positive electrode (the *node*), yielding electrons thereto and thus demonstrating the conductivity of the solution. Each pair of H^+ ions, accepting electrons, becomes a hydrogen molecule, and passes off in hydrogen bubbles at the cathode. Each pair of Cl^- ions, yielding electrons, becomes a chlorine molecule, and passes off in bubbles at the anode: an example of *electrolysis*. Various other reactions may occur at the electrodes, depending on the electrolyte in solution, the nature of the electrodes, the solvent, the voltage applied and other factors. The water itself is concomitantly decomposed into $2H_2$ and O_2. If the forces of attraction between ions in aqueous solution are great enough to overcome the insulating effect of the water molecules, then those ions will combine or react together.

Radicals (Groups)

A *radical* is a group of atoms held together by strong bonds but containing an excess (or deficiency) of electrons. The group commonly acts as an ion, the valence number of which depends on the net charge of the group; e.g., ammonium, valence = +1 (NH_4^+); hydrogen, valence = −1 (OH^-); nitrate, valence, −3 (PO_4^{---}).

Hydrogen and Hydroxyl Ions

Hydrogen and hydroxyl ions (H^+ and OH^-) are extremely important in biology because they are the constituents of water and the basis of the properties of acidity and alkalinity. These influence all aspects of cell life. Degree of *acidity* is commonly expressed as pH, with a number representing the concentration of hydrogen ions, since it is ionized hydrogen that determines the immediate acidic activity of any solution. *Alkalinity* of solutions may be expressed as concentration of hydroxyl ions (pOH) (not hydroxyl groups attached to C). However, since concentrations of hydrogen ions and of hydroxyl ions are reciprocally related, as will be shown, degrees of either are commonly given in terms of pH only.

pH

Since H ions determine acidity, acids or alkalies may be strong or weak, depending on their degree of dissociation. This is always a fixed value for any given electrolyte and is generally expressed as the *dissociation constant*.

Strong acids are those which, when dissolved in water, dissociate largely into positively charged hydrogen ions and negatively charged ions. For example, sulfuric acid dissociates into two hydrogen ions and a sulfate ion. Weak acids like acetic or citric also dissociate, but to a lesser degree. The acidic activity of any acid solution depends upon the concentration of ions of hydrogen, and this is obviously dependent upon the ability of the acid to give them off into the solution or to dissociate. Thus, two acid solutions may be of the same concentration with respect to the total amounts of hydrogen available, yet have widely differing activity due to differences in the amount of active or ionized or dissociate hydrogen. Hence we deal with a capacity effect, i.e., total available (dissociated plus undissociated) acid, as contrasted with an intensity or activity effect (dissociated acid or hydrogen ions alone).

As an example, let us compare acetic acid and hydrochloric acid. A liter of a normal solution of each contains exactly 1 gm of total available hydrogen, yet the activity of the N/1 acetic acid is slight while that of the N/1 hydrochloric acid is great. Of the gram of available hydrogen in the acetic acid solution only 1.36 percent is in an ionized state, so that there is, in the liter of solution, only 0.0136 gm. of hydrogen ions. The gram of hydrogen in the liter of N/1 HCl solution, therefore, is about 67 times as active or "strong" as the N/1 acetic acid.

If one were to titrate the solutions, i.e., add N/1 NaOH solution until each became neutral, the total amount of alkali required would be the same in each case. This is due to the fact that, as the alkali combines with the hydrogen ions, more hydrogen ions take their place from the undissociated acid, which strives to maintain a constant hydrogen ion concentration consistent with its dissociation constant. Each acid finally give up all its available hydrogen and, since each of the solution by definition (N/1) contained exactly 1 gm. of available hydrogen to start with, each requires the same amount of alkali for its neutralization.

A measurement of hydrogen ion concentration differs from such a titration, in that the former determines the actual concentration of ionized hydrogen at the moment, without calling out any of the reserve, undissociated acid.

In acidimetry the term "normal" refers to the presence of 1 gm. of *total available* hydrogen per liter (dissociated plus undissociated). By contrast, a solution normal only with respect to *ionized*, hydrogen contains 1 gm. of hydrogen ions per liter. This implies the presence of 1 gm. equivalent of a completely (100 percent) dissociated acid; a N/10 solution would contain 0.1 gm. equivalent of a completely dissociated acid, and so on.

Table 1.2. Relationships of hydrogen ion concentration expressed in various ways.

Reaction	*Fraction of normality (grams)*	*Hydrogen ions per liter*	*Logarithms of H ion*	*Expressed as pH*
Acid	N/1	1.0	–0	0.0
Acid	N/10	0.1	–1	1.0
Acid	N/100	0.01	–2	2.0
Acid	N/1,000	0.001	–3	3.0
Acid	N/10,000	0.000,1	–4	4.0
Acid	N/100,000	0.000,01	–5	5.0
Acid	N/1,000,000	0.000,001	–6	6.0
Neutral	Pure water	0.000,000,1	–7	7.0
Alkaline	N/1,000,000	0.000,000,01	–8	8.0
Alkaline	N/100,000	0.000,000,001	–9	9.0
Alkaline	N/10,000	0.000,000,000,1	–10	10.0
Alkaline	N/1,000	0.000,000,000,01	–11	11.0
Alkaline	N/100	0.000,000,000,001	–12	12.0
Alkaline	N/10	0.000,000,000,000,1	–13	13.0
Alkaline	N/1	0.000,000,000,000,01	–14	14.0

As shown in Table 1.2, if we were to express hydrogen ion concentrations or normality in terms of grams of hydrogen ions per liter we should have to deal with long words and long rows of zeros; a confusing and laborious system of nomenclature. In 1909 Sorensen devised a simpler system based on the fact that water is itself a very weak electrolyte. As noted previously the extent of dissociation of any electrolyte is a physical constant (K) for that electrolyte under standard conditions. A liter of pure, neutral water of 20°C always contains 0.0000001 gm. (1×10^{7} moles) of OH^-. In Sorensen's system, the term "grams of hydrogen ions per liter" is replaced by the symbol pH, while the number of moles of H^+ per liter (1×10^{-7} in the neutral water under discussion) is expressed as the logarithm of the reciprocal of the fraction, i.e., the positive number 7. The reaction of neutral water, and of any neutral solution, is therefore expressed as pH 7.

Now the product of the concentration of H^+ and of OH^- in neutral water is always 10^{-14} ($H^+ \times OH^- = K_w = 10^{-7} \times 10^{-7} = 10^{-14}$). Since the product of the two is always the same (i.e., since the two are reciprocally related), the term pH is commonly used to express either. For example, the pH of a solution containing 1 gm. of H^+ per liter (i.e., normal [N/1] with respect to hydrogen ions or 1 gm.-equivalent of a completely dissociated acid) is 0 (log 1 = 0). Reciprocally, this is also pOH 14; the smallest fraction of a gram of OH^- per liter possible on the Sorensen scale. Similarly, pH 6 implies pOH 8; pH 2 implies pOH 12, and so on.

Since the number representing pH is derived from a fraction, the larger the fraction the smaller the pH number. Therefore pH numbers between 7 and 0 represent increasing degrees of acidity, and numbers between 7 and 14, increasing degrees of alkalinity. Unless one is familiar with the numbers they can at first be misleading. For example, a change in pH from 7 to 6 represents a 10-fold increase in concentration of hydrogen ions since the 7 and 6 are logarithms; a change from pH 7.0 to 7.3 represents a 50 percent decrease in the concentration of hydrogen ions ($1/2 \times 10^{-7}$ = log 2 + 7 = 0.3 + 7 = pH 7.3).

Isotopes

All atoms of a given element have the same number of electrons and the same number of protons to balance those electrons. Atoms thus remain electrically neutral. But not all atoms of a given element necessarily have the same number of neutrons; i.e. different toms of a given element may have different numbers of neutrons and therefore different atomic weights. Such atoms are called *isotopes*.

In any given samples of an element there is usually a mixture of isotopes. The international atomic weight of any element is listed as an average of the weights of all the various isotopes normally (commonly) present. For example, the weight of a single atom of normal (the most common isotope) chlorine is 35. But any considerable quantity of the element also contains about 25 percent of heavy chlorine, Cl^{37}. The international atomic weight of chlorine as an element is therefore given as 35.457. Similarly, the atomic weight of normal hydrogen is 1 bout the international atomic weight is 1.00814. Three isotopes of hydrogen are known: H^1, mass (at. wt.) 1.00814; deuterium (H^2), mass 2.01474; tritium (H^3), mass 3.01701. Tritium is radioactive; it is so designated by the asterisk (*).

There are isotopes of nearly every element; not all are radioactive. Chlorine has two principal (most common) isotopes with atomic weights of 35 to 37. The atomic weight of an isotope is generally indicated by a superscript number (Cl^{35}, Cl^{37}). Lead has at least 16 isotopes, carbon five or six, and so on. In the periodic table all of the isotopes of an element are placed together, since the position of each element in the table depends only on the number of its *electrons* (at. no.), not its nuclear structure (at. wt.). Isotopes of an element are *chemically* similar since it is mainly the electrons that determine the chemical properties. However, since isotopes have different numbers of neutrons, they may differ markedly in *physical* properties because these are affected by their atomic weights. For example, of the four principal carbon isotopes C^{11*}, C^{12}, C^{13} and C^{14*} one (C^{11*}) is lighter and two are heavier (C^{13} and C^{14*}) than the "normal" C^{12} carbon atom. The radioactive isotopes may be detected by means of a Geiger counter.

Radioactivity and Transmutations of Substance

Radioactivity is the emanation of various atomic particles and rays (energy) from certain elements that have unstable atomic structures (e.g., isotopes). The emanations of radium (chiefly Ra^{226*}), for example, are (1) alpha rays (particles) that are actually helium nuclei ($2P^{++}$ plus $2N^{00}$) traveling at about one fifth the speed of light; (2) beta rays or particles (actually stream of electrons) moving at nearly the speed of light; and (3) gamma rays. The last are nonparticulate radiant energy somewhat like hard (i.e., short and penetrating) X-rays. They move at the speed of light (186,000 mi/sec.). Radioactivity is isotopes is derived from instability of their nuclei only, and is fully manifested and detectable with a Geiger counter whether the isotopes are free or combined in compounds.

Stability of an atomic nucleus is greatest when the numbers of protons and neutrons are equal; a ratio of 1:1. If too great a discrepancy exists in this ratio, in either direction, the nucleus is unstable and tend to adjust the ratio to greater stability by giving off energy in the form of various radioactive emanations.

Adjustments are made toward greater stability by alterations in structure of the nucleus such as transformation of neutrons into protons by splitting off electrons from the neutrons. For example, the unstable (radioactive) carbon isotope $_6C^{14}$, with 6 protons and 8 neutrons (a proton : neutron ratio of 3:4), loses an electron from one neutron and thus gains one proton, becoming the stable form of nitrogen ($_7N^{14}$) with 7 each of protons and neutrons. The electron escapes with its energy; a beta particle. Transmutation of one element into another has occurred.

Radioactive isotopes of a number of elements are commonly manufactured by shooting their nuclei with high-velocity atomic particles; neutrons, protons, alpha particles or gamma rays. For example, bombarding normal nitrogen atoms (at. wt. 14) with neutrons made to travel at extremely high speeds by means of an *accelerator* (*cyclotron* or *synchrotron*) splits the nitrogen nucleus, yielding radioactive heavy carbon (C^{14*}).

C^{14*} is produced in considerable amounts in atomic bomb explosions. Because carbon enters into organic compounds, C^{14*} eventually gains entrance into the cells and tissue of living human beings. As will be detailed later, radioactivity is an important cause of genetic mutations (altered inherited characteristics) and of cancer, hence isotopes in fallout are of intense interest not only to biologists but to everyone else.

Since the nuclei of radioactive isotopes constantly give off nuclear particles and energy, the nuclei eventually become altered: i.e., they decay. The element finally changes into another element of lower atomic number. For example, the nucleus of uranium (at. no = 92; or $_{92}U^{238}$) becomes a thorium nucleus (at. no = 90; i.e. $_{90}Th^{232}$) by losing an alpha particle; the radium nucleus (at. no. = 88) becomes a radon nucleus (at. no = 86) in the same way.

When a beta particle is given off in radioactivity, a neutron (an electron combined with a proton) splits, permitting the electron to leave the decomposing nucleus. The neutron residue remains in the nucleus as a proton. The atomic number (number of orbital electron) is thus increased and the element changes into another; for example, uranium (at. no 92) becomes first neptunium (at. no 93) and then plutonium (at. no. 94).

The emanation of gamma rays involves only loss of energy, which does not cause alteration in either atomic weight or number although it occurs during both alpha and beta radiations.

All of these nuclear modifications result in the transmutation of substances—the mysterious change that medieval alchemists, wholly ignorant of atomic structure or the true nature of matter, tried so long and so hard to achieve with the aid of abracadabra and other incantations in order to make gold from lead! Many an ambitious prince of bygone centuries subsidized at court alchemist who never in his life came nearer to the secrete of "the philosopher's stone" than the causing of weird light and horrible odors! Often, instead of gaining a fortune, he lost his head.

Uses of isotopes

Isotopes are of special interest to the biologist because he can use them to study many biological phenomena, such as determining exactly what a living cell does with any given element or compound that it takes in with its food; for example, carbon assimilation. By the use of carbon dioxide made with $C^{14*}O_2$) it has been shown that, in photosynthesis, carbon dioxide is not combined directly with any organic compound in the cell. It is first reduced by transfer of electrons of hydrogen split from water. The carbon (C^{14*}) is then found in a number of compounds formed during the synthetic process: e.g., phosphoglyceric acid:

$$C^{14}O_2 \xrightarrow[\text{synthesis}]{\text{Photo-}} \begin{array}{l} H_2C-O-PO_3H_2 \\ \quad | \\ HC-OH \\ \quad | \\ C^{14}OOH \end{array}$$

3-Phosphoglyceric acid

If H_2O^{18} is provided in photosynthesis, all of the free oxygen given off is O_2^{18}. No O^{18} is found in the synthesized products. In many species of chemosynthetic bacteria carbon dioxide combines directly with already formed organic molecules. For example, Werkman, Wood, and their colleagues have "fed" carbon dioxide made with C^{14*} to propionic acid bacteria. The radioactive carbon can be followed, like a tracer bullet, through its course in the synthetic processes of the bacterial cell. For each molecule of C^{14*} one molecule of succinic acid or propionic acid is formed, probably from pyruvic acid via oxalacetic acid, or from glycerol:

$$\begin{array}{c} H_2COH \\ | \\ HCOH \\ | \\ H_2COH \end{array} + C^{14}O_2 \rightleftharpoons \begin{array}{c} COOH \\ | \\ CH_2 \\ | \\ CH_2 \\ | \\ C^{14}OOH \end{array} + H_2O$$

Glycerol *Succinic acid*

A common soil saprophyte, *Aerobacter indologenes*, produces acetic, lactic and succinic acids as waste products of glucose utilization. When $C^{14*}O_2$ is added, C^{14*} is found in these acids. *Proteus vulgaris*, another common saprophyte of soil and water, produces lactic and succinic acids. The $C^{14*}O_2$ is found mainly in the carboxyl group of the acids. The pathway to the formation of these acids is via pyruvic acid according to the *Wood-Werkman reaction*:

$$\begin{array}{c} CH_3 \\ | \\ C{=}O \\ | \\ COOH \end{array} + C^{14}O_2 \rightleftharpoons \begin{array}{c} C^{14}OOH \\ | \\ CH_2 \\ | \\ C{=}O \\ | \\ COOH \end{array}$$

Pyruvic acid *Oxalacetic acid*

2

Basis of Life in Cell

Protoplasm is a highly complex mixture of some elements and compounds found in the bodies of living beings. The protoplasm is variously known as the *living matter*, *living substance* or *physical basis of life*. It is the basic fundamental substance exhibiting all the vital processes of the cell. The protoplasm was first observed by *Corti* in 1772. In 1835 *Dujardin* a Frenchman described it as a soft and gumy substance and named it as *scarcode* i.e. *flesh*. *Purkinje*, a Bohemian physiologist (1839), was the first biologist, who gave the name *protoplasm* to this living substance. *Hugo von Mohl,* a German botanist, in 1839, also suggested the name *protoplasm* for the granular and viscous substance found in plants similar to that found in the animals. The above-mentioned German botanist popularized the word protoplasm as a name given to the living matter found in plants and animals. Protoplasm is the most complex and interesting substance. It is not to be thought of a chemical compound but rather as very complex organized system. Protoplasm varies somewhat in its nature from cell to cell and from organism to organism, but basically it must be the same, as evidenced by its common manifestations of metabolism, growth, reproduction and by some other peculiarities.

Physical Nature of Protoplasm

Different workers have proposed different theories to explain the physical nature of protoplasm as given under the following heads:

Granular Theory

This theory was propounded by *Altmann* in 1893. According to this theory, protoplasm consists of numerous tiny granules as shown in *Amoeba*. *Henle, Maggi,* etc., considered these proto-plasmic granules

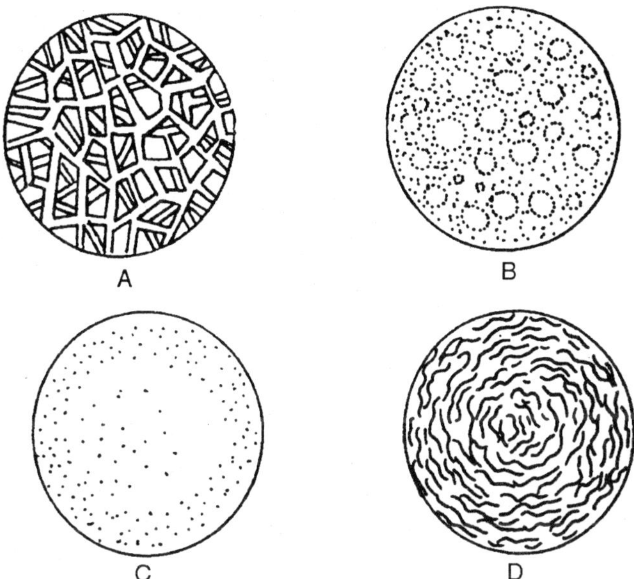

Fig. 2.1. Physical appearance of protoplasm. A—Reticular, B—Alveolar, C—Granular, D—Fibrillar.

plastidules. Altmann reconginzed them as "elementary organisms," or *bioplasts* (or cytoplasts).

Alveolar Theory

The alveolar nature of protoplasm was suggested by *Butschilli* in 1892. According to him, protoplasm consists of many suspended droplets or alveoli or minute bubbles, resembling to foam of emulsion.

Fibrillar Theory

This theory was put forward by *Flemming*. According to him, protoplasm consists of fibres embedded in the inner mass of matrix. The fibrillae are called mitome or spongioplasm and ground substance is termed paramitome or hyaloplasm.

Reticulate Theory

This theory was proposed by *Klein, Cornoy* etc., suggesting that the protoplasm consists of a network or reticulum of fibres in the ground substance.

Colloidal Theory

Proposed by *Wilson* in 1925. According to this theory the protoplasm having any of the aforesaid appearances is always a fluid-colloidal system having various chemical inclusions in *gel phase*. A gel is a semi-solid condition which presents jelly-like appearance. Here the molecules are held together by various bonds depends upon the imature and strength. By absorbing water the gel changes to more liquid-like phase. This is known as *sol* and the process is termed as *solation.* The sol can stream easily and by losing water again changes into gel-state. Both these states of colloidal matrix are interchangeable according to the various physiological, mechanical and biochemical activities of the cell. This represents phase reversal in the colloidal system. These sol-gel conditions of colloidal system are the basis for the mechanical behaviour of protolplasm.

Properties of Protoplasm

Cohesiveness

The various particles or molecules of protoplasm are adhered with each other by forces, such as Van der Waal's bonds, that hold long chains of molecules together. These Van der Waal's bonds are weak and non-specific forces between non-polar groups of atoms. This property varies with the strength of these forces.

Contractility

This property is significant in various stomatal operations in plants. The contractility of protoplasm is important for the absorption and removal of water as they generally occur in protoplasm.

Electrical Charge

Protein molecules repel each other because their overall charge is similar. All molecules are either positively charged or negatively charged. However, if the molecules approach one another close enough so that valency forces can act, then they may be attracted to each other.

Precipitation

Addition of certain amount of electrolyte in a colloidal suspension causes its dispersed particles to colloide, aggregate and finally to precipitate as suspension. For example, the addition of HCl to a colloidal system of arsenic sulphide causes precipitation.

Viscosity

The viscosity of the ground substance of the cell varies greatly. It may be as low as that of water, or may be very high in the gelating cytoplasm of pseudopodia of *Amoeba.*

Streaming Movement or Cyclosis

The protoplasm exhibits various sorts of streaming movements inside the cell. These have been studied in *Amoeba, Paramecium* etc. The movement involves only the localized portions with no visible changes in the protoplasm. No complete explanation of this has been given as yet. But it is seen that its rate depends upon the rate of cell metabolism. It is due to the fact that the energy is supplied by respiration.

Amoeboid Movement

The amoeboid movement as exhibited by *Amoeba* and other protozoans involves the movement of entire protoplasm of the cell, where the cytoplasm moves as one mass carrying the various inclusion with it. It is due to the continuous change of gel to sol and sol to gel.

Brownian Movement

It is characterized by the zigzag motion of suspended colloidal particles, occurring due to the bombardment of one particle or molecule by other. This type of movement of particles was first of all observed by *Robert Brown* in 1827 in the colloidal solution and hence such movements are known as Brownian movements. The higher the temperature, more rapid the movement and thus viscosity of cell is decreased. This means that high viscosity indicates a more gel-like state of protoplasm and low viscosity, a more sol-like condition.

Tyndall Effect

Colloidal particles of protoplasm have the property of scattering light. When a beam of light is passed through a colloidal solution it becomes visible. This is the Tyndall effect. A colloidal solution of proteins in water shows a typical Tyndall cone.

Adsorption

The tendency of particles, molecules or ions to adhere to the surface of certain solids or liquids is known as adsorption and is exhibited by the particles of colloidal system. The phenomenon helps the matrix to form protein boundaries.

Biological Properties

Protoplasm has all the biological properties of a living organism. It is capable of nutrition, respiration, excertion, metabolism, growth and reproduction. It has the property of irritability, e.g., it responds to stimuli like heat, light and chemicals. It also has the property of conductivity, i.e., of conducting impulses produced by stimuli.

Chemical Nature of Protoplasm

For the detailed study the chemical components of the cell can be classified as inorganic (mineral salts) and organic (proteins, carbohydrates, nucleic acids, lipids and so forth) substance. Although the most prominent constitutent of protoplasm is water—the substance which gives protoplasm its characteristic structure is protein. Lipids are important in all membranes and carbohydrates serve as nutrient stores. The protoplasm of a plant or animal cell contains 75 to 85% water, 10-20% protein, 2-3% lipids, 1% carbohydrates and 1% inorganic material. The following Table 2.1. gives approximate active protoplasm.

Table 2.1. Chemical Analysis of Protoplasm

Substance	*Percent*	*Average molecules weight*	*Number of molecues in relation to protein*
Water	85	18	180
Protein	10	36000	1
DNA	0.4	10	—
RNA	0.7	4.0×10^4	—
Lipid	2	700.	10
Other Organic matter	0.4	250	20
Inorganic substances	1.5	55	100

Water

Water is a substance that is justifiably called the *fluid of life*. It comprises over 90% of the chemical content of most organisms. In human body about 55% of the water (20-22 litres) is intracellular water and remains confined to the cells and the rest is found in extracellular fluids such as blood, tissue fluid and lymph. Water participates directly or indirectly in all metabolic reactions. The biologically active conformations of macromolecules and arrangement of phospholipids in the lipid bilayer of membranes are dependent on water. Water helps to keep minerals ionised in body fluids. It ionises itself to provide hydrogen ion (H^+) concentration to body fluids. It also helps in maintaining the constancy of the internal environment of an organism.

Water is a remarkable compound with unique properties that result from its molecular configuration and hydrogen bonding. Some important properties of water are as follows.

Polarity

The water molecule is composed of two hydrogen atoms covalently bonded to one side of an oxygen atom. Since the mean angle (105°) between the hydrogen atoms is not rigid, water can absorb large quantities of heat and be subject to other physical stresses without breakage of the bonds. Water is a polar molecule and as with other polar molecules it has a surface charge. Water is a dipolar substance in that the hydrogen pole is positively charged and the other pole is negatively charged due to electrophilic (electron attracting) properties of oxygen. The polar nature of the water molecule causes salts to be held in solution through charge interaction (ionization; salt dissolved in water exist in the form of positive and negative charges).

Cohesion and adhesion

Because of the asymmetrical distribution water molecules associate with each other (cohesion) and 'wet' other substances (adhesion). The attraction of the positive hydrogen atom of one water molecule for the negative oxygen atom of another water molecule results in a *hydrogen bond.* Hydrogen bonding of water produces a dipolar molecule and favours the formation of a lattice-like structure that enables the packing of many atoms into a small area and stabilizes the molecular structure of water. Fluidity of water is maintained by very rapid formation and dissociation of hydrogen bonds between water molecules.

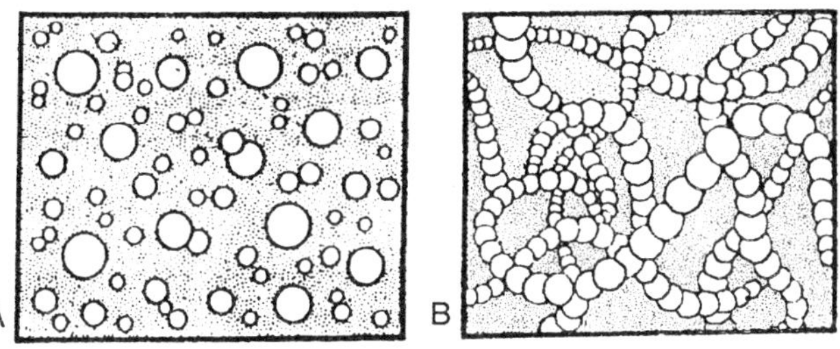

Fig. 2.2. Two water molecules showing polarity and formation of a hydrogen bond between them.

Latent heat and specific heat

The presence of hydrogen bonds is directly responsible for the high heat of fusion, high specific heat, and high heat of vaporization of water. The energy required to break hydrogen bonds for melting of ice, heating of water, and evaporation of water is considerably greater than the energy needed to overcome the Van der Waal's forces that are normally found in the weak association of molecules of ethane, ether and benzene. Due to high specific heat, water affords protection against sudden temperature changes in living organisms. High latent heat of evaporation of water causes elimination of excess heat through evaporation of sweat. This maintains a constant body temperature.

Density of freezing properties

The density of water decreases below 4°C and ice therefore tends to float. It is the only substance whose solid form is less dense than its liquid form. The fact that water below 4°C tends to rise helps to maintain circulation in large bodies of water. This may result in nutrient cycling and colonisation of water to greater depths.

Solvent action

A property of water that is very important to the living cell is its solvent action. Because it forms a solution with a vast array of compounds, water is sometimes referred to as the *universal solvent.* The solvent action of water is an effect of its ability to form hydrogen bonds due to the asymmetrical distribution of its charges. In solution with water, compounds like sugars, alcohols, and amino acids—which contain oxygen atoms, hydroxyl (-OH) groups, amino (–NH_2) groups—form hydrogen bonds with the molecules of water.

The solvent action of water is of tremendous importance for the living system. The essential elements necessary for normal growth, the compounds necessary for energy transfer and storage, and the components of structural compounds all require water as a translocation and reaction medium. Indeed, physiological processes in dilute solutions and suspensions; and the reactions are, therefore, under control of the physical and chemical laws that govern the activities of dilute solutions and suspensions.

INORGANIC COMPOUNDS

A number of inorganic salts occur both in free as well as in the ionised state. The elements that occur in quantity in protoplasm are oxygen, carbon, hydrogen and nitrogen. Always present but in much smaller amounts are potassium, phosphorus, calcium, sulphur, magnesium and iron. These ten are generally referred to as *essential elements.* Chlorine and sodium are necessary components of most animal protoplasm but are apparently not essential for plant protoplasm. Copper, boron, iodine, maganese, zinc and several other elements which are present in all protoplasm but only in minute quantities, are called *trace elements.* This term must be used with care, because these elements are still important even though they are present only in very small quantities. The essential elements found in human protoplasm are listed in table 2.2.

The elements are almost always present in protoplasm in the form of chemical compounds rather than elements. Many of these compounds inorganic salts, which are usually in solution. These salts have numerous functions. They serve as source of elements to be built into other compounds, and some act as *buffer* in maintaining the proper acidity or alkalinity in the protoplasm. Because salts in solutions are electrical conductors, they also function in some way in connection with the electrical properties of protoplasm, however, this is not well understood at present.

Table 2.2. Showing Percentage by Weight to the Element in Protoplasm

Elements	*Symbol*	*Percent*
Oxygen	O	65.04
Carbon	C	18.24
Hydrogen	H	10.05
Nitrogen	N	3.15
Potassium	K	1.60
Phosphorus	P	0.84
Calcium	Ca	0.25
Sulphur	S	0.20
Magnesium	Mg	0.04
Iron	Fe	0.01
Chlorine	Cl	0.27
Sodium	Na	0.26

Organic Compounds

Proteins

Protein is an indispensable constituent of the diet because it is the only source of the amino acids. Amino acids are needed to built up new tissue during he period of growth; to maintain the structure of every tissue cell including its content of protein—containing enzyme systems; to provide raw material for the manufacturing of digestive enzymes and certain hormones; and to maintain the normal concentrations of plasma proteins and haemoglobin.

The proteins are macromolecules of very high molecular weight. The polymer molecules of protein are formed by linking together of a number of amino acids. About 20 odd different kinds of amino acids are known. Each amino acid has an amino (NH_2) and a carboxyl (COOH) group. A bond is formed between the amino group of one amino acid with the carboxyl group of another amino acid. The bond is called peptide bond. With the help of such peptide bonds a variety of amino acids can form a long chain molecule called polypeptide.

The nutritional value of a protein depends upon its amino acid composition. Synthesis of amino acids from organic keto-acids is of common occurrence in bacteria and plants. Animals can synthesize only about half of the naturally occurring amino acids (20). Thus there are two categories of amino acids:

Essential amino acids

The amino acids which cannot synthesized by an organisms i.e. they must be obtained from the dietary proteins are called essential amino acids. These are *arginine*, *histidine*, *isoleucine*, *leucine*, *lysine*, *methconine*, *theronine*, *phenylalanine*, *tryptophan* and *valine*.

Non-essential amino acids

Although these amino acids are required by the animal as they are found in the protein of the tissues, but they can apparently be synthesized from alpha-keto acids, by the process of amination. These amino acids are *tyrosine*, *serine*, *alanine*, *asparagine*, *proline*, *hydroxyproline*, *asparatic acid*, *glycine*, *glautamine*, *glutamic acid* and *cystine*.

People who eat diets lacking only one of the essential amino acids are unable to synthesize normal body proteins and become protein deficient, despite having a normal nitrogen intake.

Most animal proteins, are *complete or first class proteins;* that is they contain all the necessary amino acids in appropriate proportions for ultilization by man as eggs, meat, kidney, fish, liver, poultry, milk etc.

Plant proteins are *incomplete* or *second class proteins,* since they lack certain essential amino acids. as. cereals, nuts, legumes etc. Thus people living on a strict vegetarian diet may become protein deficient.

Associated with protein deficiency is *Kwashiorker,* which affects millions of children in developing countries. It must commonly occurs in infants after weaning and particularly when given an inadequate and predominantly carbohydrate diet. Many of the children also have an inadequate energy intake and the disorder is known as *protein-energy malnutrition* (PEM). The affected child stops growing and loses weight. The skin and hair may become depigmented, and oedema associated with low plasma levels of albumin often develop. Untreated Kwashiorker is often fatal.

Structure of Protein

The critical determination of biological function of a protein is its conformation, which is defined as the three-dimensional arrangement of the atoms of a molecule. Four basic structural levels are assigned to proteins. These are:

Primary Structure

Arrangement of amino acid in a polypeptids chain is the primary structure of a protein. Amino acid sequence of the smallest protein known, that is of insulin, was studied by *F. Sanger* (1954). Insulin consists of two chains,. A and B, joined together by two disulplide bonds (A chain contains 21 and B chain 30 amino acids). Normal human haemoglobin consists of four polypeptide chains (2α and 2β) to be held together by non-covalent forces. Each α-chain is composed of 141 amino acids, and each β chains 146 amino acids.

Fig. 2.3. Structure of haemoglobin; the molecule consists of four chains: two α-chains and two β-chains.

Secondary Structure

The polypeptides are held together to give rise a definite shape (helical pattern) of the protein molecules by hydrogen bonds. Hydrogen bonds can be broken by many physical and chemical treatments, for example, by excessive heat, pressure, *pH*, electricity, heavy metals and other agents that changes the environment of protein.

The most common type of secondary structure is α-helix. This is formed by the bending of polypeptide chain to form hydrogen bonds in the same chain. The bending of the chain is very regular and chain assumes the shape of a helix.

Pauling and *Corey* have considered an alternate type of secondary structure. In this case the polypeptide chains are lead linearly either parallel or antiparallel with respect to one another. This is called β-structure of β-helix.

Tertiary Structure

The arrangement and inter-relationship of the twisted chains of protein into specific loops and bends in called the tertiary structure. Such a structure enables the proteins to form specific layers, crystals or fibres. The tertiary structures is maintained by hydrogen bonds disulphide bonds, Van der Waals interaction, hydrophobic interactions and ionic bonds. The tertiary structure is important and found in globular proteins. If this structure is disrupted, the biological activity of protein would be lost.

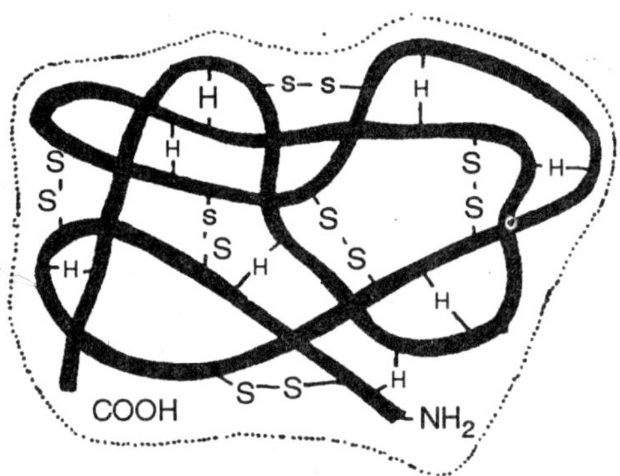

Fig. 2.4. Tertiary structure of a hypothetical protein molecule; note the extensive folding of the secondary structure which imparts a globular shape to the protein.

Quaternary Structure

This defines the degree of polymerisation of a protein unit. This structure is found in only oligomeric proteins. They are composed of

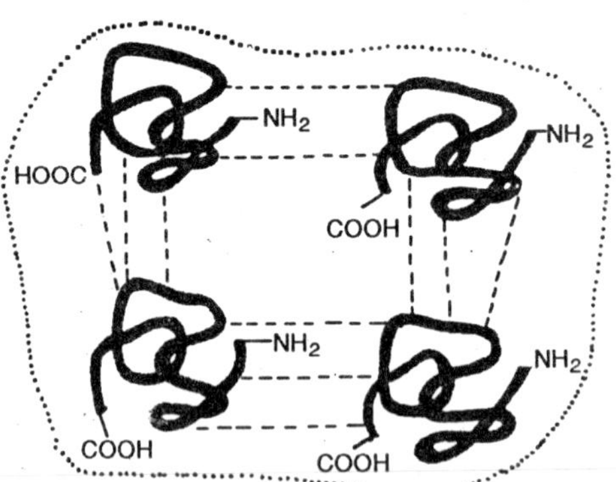

Fig. 2.5. Quaternary level of protein structure; note a diagrammatic representation showing four sub-units which are polymerized in the functional protein molecule.

subunit peptide chains linked together by any or all of the forces that can act between amino acid side chains. Haemoglobin is a fine example of quaternary structure and was studied by *Kendrew* and *Perutz* (1963).

Classification of Protein

The proteins are mainly classified into two—simple and conjugated proteins.

Simple Proteins

These are consisting mainly of peptide chains. On hydrolyses they yield only amino acids. These are of two types:

(A) Fibrous or insoluble proteins.

(B) Globular or soluble proteins.

Fibrous (insoluble) proteins

Fibrous proteins (scleroproteins) comprise all insoluble proteins which have a supporting or protective function in the animals. Secondary structure is the final structure of these proteins. The fibrous proteins can be subdivided into following types:

1. *Collagens*. Approximately 30% of the total protein in mammalian body is collagen. They are the principle proteins of skin, tendon and bones and are resistant to peptic and tryptic digestion. They contain large amounts of hydroxy-proline. They can be converted into soluble gelatin by boiling with water, dilute acids or alkalies.
2. *Elastins*. They are present in ligament, arteries and other elastic tissue. They cannot be converted into gelatin.
3. *Keratins*. They are present in animal skin, nails, hairs, horns, hooves, claws, feathers etc. they are derived from ectoderm.
4. *Myosin*. The major protein of muscles is also a fibrous protein.

Globular or Soluble proteins

These are soluble simple proteins with more or less definite molecular weight. These are speherical or ovoid in shape. They are generally soluble in water. This group includes enzymes, oxygen carrying protcins (globulins), hormones like oxytocin, vassopressin, insulin, glucogon etc.

1. *Albumins*. They are soluble in water, dilute acids and bases. They coagulate when heated. Common examples are albumins of egg white, blood serum and lactalbumin.
2. *Globulins*. They are insoluble in water but soluble in dilute salt solution. They are also coagulated when heated. Examples are serum globulin, fibrinogen, ovoglobulin in egg-yolk etc.

3. *Glutelins.* These are insoluble in water but soluble in dilute acids or base solution. They are commonly found in various plant seeds. Examples are wheat, cereals etc.
4. *Protamins.* These are basic proteins. They are very soluble, small, stable proteins and cannot be coagulated by heating. They are exceptionally rich in arginine amino acid. They are found in the ripe sperm cells of certain fishes.
5. *Histones.* These are water-soluble basic proteins. They coagulate on heating. These are found associated with nucleic acids in nucleoproteins. They are obtainable from the thymus, spleen and nucleated erythrocytes of birds.

Conjugated Proteins

The conjugated proteins differ from the simple proteins in that they consist of proteins combined with some non-protein substances. The term *prosthetic group* is generally used to designate such substances (non-proteinous).. They are classified according to the nature of prosthetic group as follows:

1. *Nucleoprotins.* These are formed by the combination of nucleic acids with protein.
2. *Mucoproteins.* They contain carbohydrate bound to protein molecules. The protein components of *mucoids* are combined with large amount (more than 4%) of carbohydrate. Examples are ovomucoid-β from egg white; or osomucoid from blood serum.
3. *Glycoproteins.* The carbohydrate percentage is less than 4% in glycoproteins. The carbonhdrate in these is usually the mucopolysaccharids. Mucin of saliva, chorionic gonadotropins and some other hormones of pituitary such as follicle stimulating hormone and luteinizing hormones are glycoproteins.
4. *Lipoproteins.* They are compounds of lipid and protein. The protein part is water soluble and lipid unsoluble. Examples are cholesterol, phosphatidylglycerides, lipovitelline of egg-yolk and serum lipoporteins.
5. *Chromoproteins.* These are the proteins which have a matelloprophyrin or some similar substance. Examples are haemoglobin which contains a basic protein globin with an iron porphyrin as Heme. Haemocyanin, haemoerythrin, erythrocuorins are other examples.
6. *Phosphoproteins.* In these the protein molecule is linked to phosphoric acid when treated with dilute sodium hydroxide yield inorganic

phosphate. Examples are casein of milk, vitellin of egg-yolk and pepsin.

7. *Metalloproteins.* These proteins contain metals as an inherent part of their molecules. They include tyrosinase (Cu), carbonic anhydrase (Zn), arginase (Mn or Mg) etc.
8. *Flavoproteins.* The prosthetic group of flavin component remains permanently attached to the protein. Flavoproteins act as coenzymes which catalyze oxidation-reduction reactions.

Derived Proteins

These include the products obtained from proteins by the action of heat and other physical agents or by hydrolysis.

Denatured and Coagulated proteins

Upon treatment with certain chemical agents or heat treatment the proteins become insoluble on account of some sort of intramolecular rearrangement and it is said to have denatured and when it gets separated in the form of precipitate, it is said to have undergone coagulation.

Peptides

These include the various fragments of the proteins which are broken off during hydrolysis of the big protein molecules either the presence of the acids or enzymes. The larger fragments had previously been named as the proteoses and the smaller fragments as peptones. This terminology is being abandoned now.

Properties of Proteins

1. ***Colour and Taste.*** Proteins are colourless and usually tasteless. These are homogenous and crystalline.
2. ***Molecular weight.*** The proteins generally have large molecular weights ranging between 5×10^3 and 1×10^6. It might be noted that the values of molecular weights of many proteins lie close to or multiples of 35,000 and 70,000.
3. ***Colloidal nature.*** Because of their giant size the proteins exhibit many colloial propertis such as (a) their diffusion rates are extremely slow, (b) they may produce considerable light— scattering in solution, thus resulting in visible turbidity (Tyndall effect).
4. ***Denaturation.*** In refers to the changes in the properties of a protein. The process of denaturation is followed by coagulation. Denaturation may be brought by a variety of agents. The physical agents, include mechanical action, heat treatment, cooling and freezing operations, ultraviolet rays etc. The chemical agents include X-rays, acetone, alcohol (solvents), salicyclates etc.

5. ***Amphoteric nature.*** The proteins are amphoteric i.e., they act as acids and alkalies both. These migrates in an electric field and the direction of migration depends upon the net charge possessed by the molecule. The net charge is influenced by the *pH* value. Each portion has a fixed value of isoelectric point (pl) at which it will move in an electric field.
6. ***Solubility.*** It is influenced by *pH* solubility is lowest at isoelectric point and increases with increasing acidity or alkalinity.
7. ***Hydrolysis.*** The proteins are hydrolyzed by a variety of hydrolytic agents.

(a) *By acidic agents.* Proteins, upon hydrolysis which come HCl (6-12 N) at 100-110°C for 6-20 hrs yields amino acids in the form of their hydrochlorides.

(b) *By alkaline agents.* Proteins may be hydrolyzed with 2N NaOH. This process is less used as it is highly disadvantageous.

(c) *By proteolytic enzymes.* Under relatively mild conditions of temperature and acidity, certain proteolytc enzymes such as pepsin and trypsin hydrolyze the proteins. Enzyme hydrolysis is used for the tryptophan.

8. ***Reactions involving—COOH group***

(a) *Reaction with alkalies* (salt formation). The carboxylic group of amino acids release a H^+ ion and forms carboxylae (COO^-) ions. These may be neutralized by cations like Na^+ and Ca^{++} to form salts.

(b) *Reaction with alcohols* (*esterification*). With alcohols, corresponding esters are produced.

$$\text{R—}\underset{\substack{|\\ NH_2}}{\overset{\substack{H\\ |}}{\text{C}}}\text{—COOH} + HOC_2H_5 \xrightarrow[\text{catalyst}]{\text{Acid}} \text{R—}\underset{\substack{|\\ NH_2}}{\overset{\substack{H\\ |}}{\text{C}}}\text{—COOC}_2H_5 + H_2O$$

Ethyl ester of AA.

(c) *Reaction with amines.* Forms amides.

$$\text{R—}\underset{\substack{|\\ NH_2}}{\text{CH}}\text{—COOH} + \text{HHN - R} \rightarrow \text{R—}\underset{\substack{|\\ NH_2}}{\text{CH}}\text{—CO—NH—R} + H_2O$$

9. ***Reaction involving NH2 groups***

(a) *Reaction with mineral acids* (Salt formation). When AA or proteins are treated with HCl the acid salts are formed.

(b) *Reaction with formaldehyde.* With formaldehyde, he hydroxy methyl derivatives are formed which are insoluble in water and resistant to the attack of microorganisms.

(c) *Reaction with Nitrous acid* (*Van Slyke reaction*). The amino acids react with HNO_2 to liberate N_2 gas and to produce a-hydroxy acid.

(d) *Reaction with fluro-dinitrobenzene* (*FDNB*) or *Sanger's reagent.* In mildly alkaline solution, 1-fluro - 2, 4-dinitrobenzene reacts with α-amino acids to produce yellow coloured derivative, DNB-amino acid.

10. *Reaction involving both COOH and NH_2 groups* (a) Reaction with triketohydrindene hydrate (*Ninhydrin reaction*). Ninhydrin in a powerful oxidizing agent causes oxidative decarboxylation of α-amino acids producing CO_2, NH_3 and an aldehyde. The reduced ninhydrin then reacts with the liberated NH_3 forming blue-coloured Ruheman's complex.

11. ***Reactions involving—R group or side chain***

(a) *Biuret test.* Compounds containing peptide bonds produce a purple colour when treats with Biuret reagent (.2% alkaline $CuSO_4$). A substance Biuret is formed. Dipeptides do not respond to this reaction.

(b) *Xenthoproteic test.* Yellow colour develops when proteins are boiled with conc. HNO_3 due to presence of benzene ring. This reaction is due to nitration of phenyl rings. This is the test for tyrosine, tryptophan, phenylalanine.

(c) *Million's test.* When proteins are heated with $HgNO_3$ in HNO_3, a red colour develops. This reaction is specific for tyrosine. Tryptophan also responds to this reaction.

(d) *Hoplin's—Cole test* (or *Glyoxylic acid test*). Violet ring develops on addition of Conc. H_2SO_4 at the junction of protein and glyoxylic acid solution. This test is specific for tryptophan.

(e) *Folin's test.* Blue colour develops with phosphomolybdo-tungstic acid in alkaline soln-due to phenol group. Specific test for tyrosine.

Biological Importance of Proteins

Proteins constitute a large part of the cell-structure and are present in all the tissue. Many proteins have special physiological functions.

1. *Membrane proteins.* The integral proteins include translocases, the peripheral proteins include cytochrome—C and monamine oxidase.
2. *Enzymes.* The enzymes are biocatalysts to influence the rats of a chemical reaction. All the enzymes are proteins.

3. *Hormones.* Some of the messangers of our body, the hromones, are proteins.
4. *Blood proteins.* 6 major plasma components are albumen, α-1 globulin, α-2 globulin, β-globulin, γ-globilin and fibrinogen. All are proteins.

CARBOHYDRATES

The class of substances, known as carbohydrates, is comprises of a large number of relatively heterogenous compounds. These are synthesized form carbon dioxide and water in chlorophyll bearing cells during the process of photosynthesis. They are especial constituents of plants (cellulose, starch etc.) but also occur and serve important functions in animals. They serve as the chief source of energy in the food of many animals. Their energy value is 4 cal per gram and this energy is provided to the various synthetic needs of a cell. In carbohydrate carbon, hydrogen and oxygen are generally found in 1:2:1 ratio.

Structure

Structurally the carbohydrate are the polyhydric alcohols of carbon possessing active aldehyde or ketonic groups, which on hydrolysis yield to such products.

CLASSIFICATION

The carbohydrates may be classified according to their complexity. They are classified into following groups:

1. Monosaccharides
2. Oligosaccharides
3. Polysaccharides.

Monosaccharides

Monosaccharides are those sugars which cannot be hydrolysed into a simple form. Their general formula is $(CH_2O)n$. The value of n ranges from 3-7. If the monosaccharide has an aldehyde group—CHO it is called an aldose e.g. glucose and if a keto group $> C = O$ is present it is called a ketose e.g. fructose.

Monosacchrides include trioses, tetroses, pentoses, hexoses, heptoses. This classification is based on the basis of carbon atoms present in their molecules. The recent trend in the classification of monosaccharides is a combination of both the system. The aldeosugars and ketosesugars are classified as below. The suffix ('- *ore*) denotes that the sugar belongs to the aldosugar grop and the suffix (*-ulose*) denotes the ketosugas.

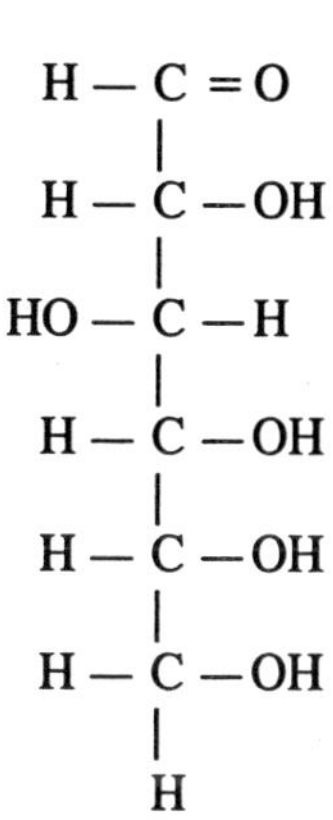

```
H — C = O
    |
H — C — OH
    |
HO — C — H
    |
H — C — OH
    |
H — C — OH
    |
H — C — OH
    |
    H
```

D-glucose

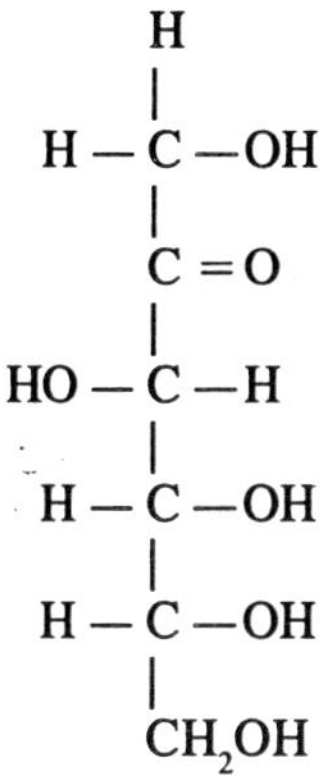

```
    H
    |
H — C — OH
    |
    C = O
    |
HO — C — H
    |
H — C — OH
    |
H — C — OH
    |
    CH2OH
```

D-fructose

```
CH2OH, C, O, HO—C—H, H, OH, C, H, H—C—OH, H, C, H
```

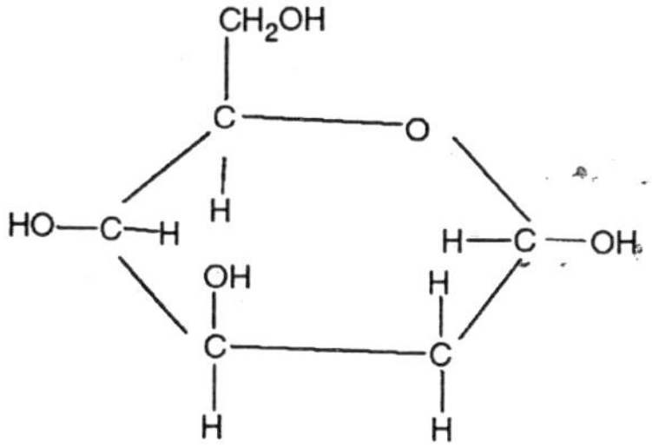

Ring structure of glucose

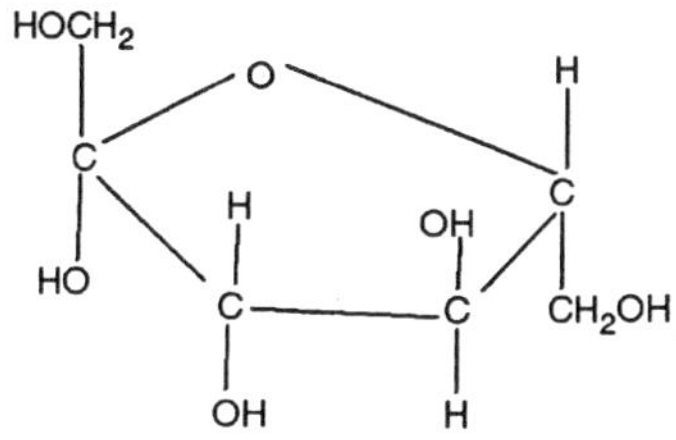

```
HOCH2, O, H, C, C, H, OH, HO, C, C, CH2OH, OH, H
```

Fructose

Glyceraldehyde occurs in two forms D-glyceraldehyde and L-glyceraldelyde. In D-glyceraldelyde the hydroxyl group (OH) on right side. In L-glyceraldelyde the position of the hydroxyl group is on the left on the asymmetric carbon atom.

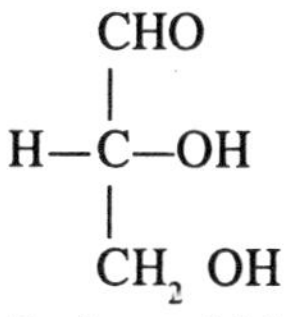

```
   CHO
    |
H—C—OH
    |
   CH2 OH
```

D-glyceraldehyde

```
    CHO
     |
OH—C—H
     |
    CH2 OH
```

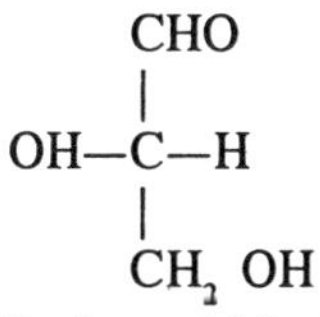

L-glyceraldehyde

It has now been well-established that in the crystalline form, the monosaccharides containing 5 or more carbon atoms exist in the *tautomeric* ring forms. Even in solutions, these sugars mostly occur in the ring forms. The free sugars mostly contain six membered ring in which five members are carbon atoms and the remaining one member is an atom of oxygen. The six membered ring is known as *pyranose ring*. In adition, there is evidence of the existence of five membered rign in the sugar in which four members are carbon atoms and the remaining one member is the atom of oxygen. The five membered rign is known as *furanose rang*. Trioses and tetroses do not possess ring structure. The free pentose sugars are largely found in pyranose forms but in glycosides and nucleic acids these exist in the pyranose form.

Monosaccharides		*Type*	*Name*
1. Triose	($C_3H_6O_3$)	Aldose	Glyceraldehyde
		ketose	Dihydroxy acetone
		Aldose	Erythrose
2. Tetrose	($C_4H_8O_4$)	ketose	Erythrulose
3. Pentose	($C_5H_{10}O_2$)	Aldose	Ribose
		Ketose	Ribulose
4. Hexoses	($C_6H_{12}O_6$)	Aldose	Glucose, glactose
		Ketose	Fructose
		Aldose	Persenlose
5. Heptose	($C_7H_{14}O_7$)	Ketose	Sedoheptulose

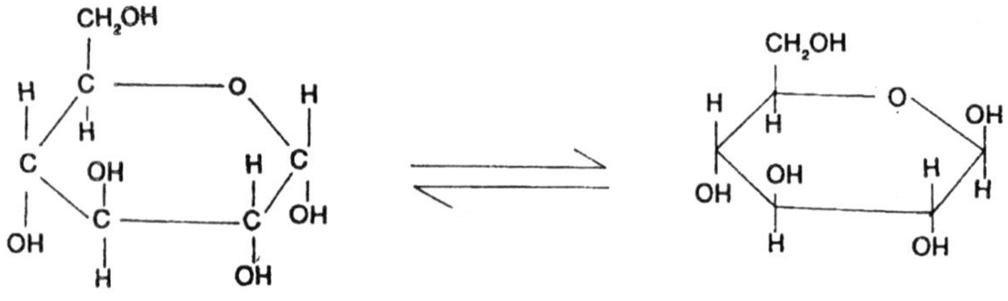

α-Form (glucose) β-Form (glucose)

In the pyranose type of hexoses, carbon at 'I' position is asymmetrical. If the hydroxyl group at position 'I' is *cis* to the hydroxyl group at position 2, it is known as α-form and if *trans* it is known as β-form. The α-form can readily pass into β-form when the sugar is brought into solution.

Properties of Monosaccharides

(a) Physical

The monosaccharides are sweet testing, colourless solids. They are soluble in water, partially in alcohols and insoluble in other. When a polarized light is passed through a solution of these carbohydrates, the plane of light is rotated to either right or left side. They contain asymmetric carbon atom hence exist in different isometric forms. The degree of optical rotation may change due to interconversion of isomeres. Fresh solution of glucose gives an optical rotation of +112° which change to + 52.7° on standing. The change in optical rotation is called *mutarotation.*

(b) Chemical

1. *Oxidation.* They can easily be oxidized by oxidizing agents. Glucose yields gluconic acid after oxidation with Tollen's reagent (ammonical Ag_2 O) or Fehlings solution (alkaline $CuSO_4$). The reduction of Tollen's reagent yields silver as polishing on the surface of tube whereas with the Fehling solution red ppt are obtained.

   When strong oxidizing agent is used like conc HNO_3, gluconic acid, is ultimately oxidizes to discarboxylic saccharic acid.

   Glucuronic acid is obtained in animal body on slow oxidation of glucose. Glucuronic acid combines with hormones. It is a major component of hyaluronic acid, heparin, mucoitin sulphate and chondriotine which are found in blood, skin and cartilage.
2. *Reduction.* Free aldehyde and ketone groups of mono-saccharides are reduced to alcoholic hydroxy groups by sodium—mercury amalgam and water. D-glucose after reduction yields a mixture of sorbitol and mannitol.
3. *Condensation.* Aldehyde groups of monosacharides condense with primary amines to form Schiff's base, when treated with hydroxylamine, glucose forms glucose oxime.
4. *Esterification.* The hydroxyl groups of alcohols in the carbohydrate may be converted to esters by treating with the appropriate acetylating agents. When D-glucose is treated with acetic anhydrine in the presence of pyridine, penta-acetyl glucose is formed.
5. *Methylation.* Methylating agents such as Ag_2O, CH_3OH react with monosaccharide to yield glycoside.
6. *Fermentation.* Monosaccharides such as glucose and fructose undergo alcholic fermentation by micro-organisms such as yeasts and produce ethanol and carbon dioxide.

Oligosaccharides

The oligosaccharides are those carbohydrates which on hydrolysis give two to five simple monosaccharide molecules. The oligosaccharides are composed of two to five monosaccharide units. During union of monosaccharde units water molecule is eleminated and the units are linked through an oxygen bridge. It is a glycosidic linkage. Their general formula is $(CH_2O)_{n-1}$.

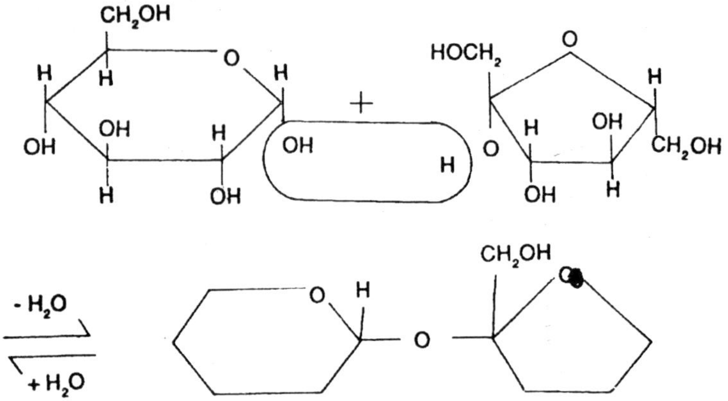

sucrose (diasaccharide)

The disaccharides have been classified into two groups namely, reducing and nonreducing. The reducing disaccharides are maltose, lactose, cellobiose, gentibiose and the non-reducing are sucrose and trehalose.

Cellobiose. Incomplete hydrolysis of cellulose given cellobiose. It is composed of two molecules of glucose linked by β-1, 4 glucosidic bond.

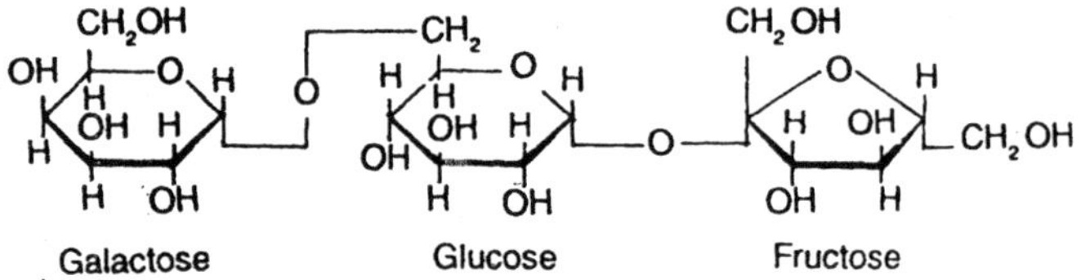

Galactose Glucose Fructose

Raftinose

Maltose. It is composed of two units of D-glucose joined together through their 1 and 4 carbon atoms. It is obtained as a hydrolytic product by the action of amylase on strach

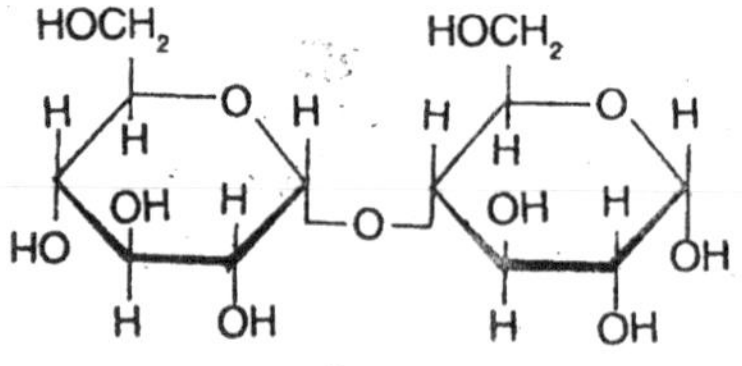

Lactose. Lactose is a disaccharide consisting of glucose and galactose which is synthesized in the mammary glands.

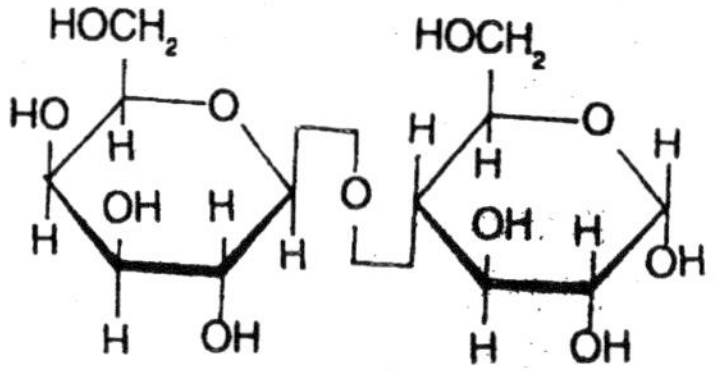

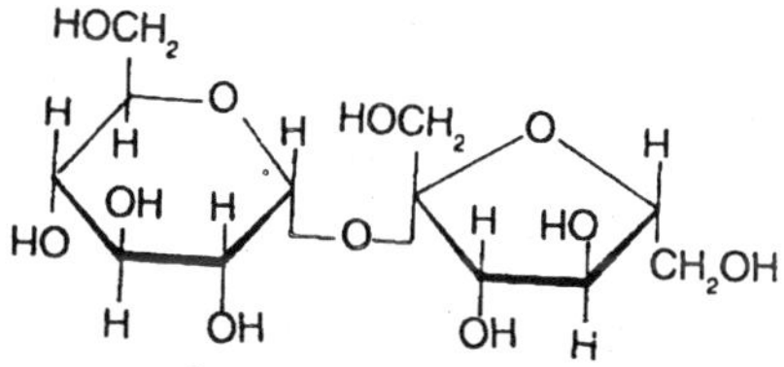

Raffinose. It is a trisaccharide consisting of fructose—glucose—galactose. On hydrolysis it yields *Melibiose* (glucose—galactose) and fructose.

Sucrose. It is formed by the union of one α-D-glucose and one β-D-fructose units with the elemination of one H_2O molecule. Hydrolysis of sucrose by dilute acid or sucrase produces a molecule of glucose and a molecule of fructose.

Polysaccharides

Polysaccharides may be regarded as carbohydrates formed by linking of a number of monosaccharides by glucosidic linkages. A carbohydrate having minimally 6 or more monosaccharide units may be regarded as polysaccharides. Their general formula is $(C_6H_{10}O_5)n$. They are tasteless, colourless amorphous powders which are insoluble in water. because of insolubility and large size, they form colloidal solutions and will not pass across natural animal membranes. They are chemically inert and do not ionize and for this reason very much suited as reserve food material such as glycogen in animals and starch in plants.

Polysaccharides consisting of only one type of monosaccharide units are called *homopolysaccharides* while those with different types of monosaccharde derivatives are *heteropolysaccharides*.

I. Homopolysacchardes

1. *Glycogen*. It forms the carbohydrate reserve of the animal tissues and it is mainly stored in the muscles and liver. Fungi and yeast do also contain glycogen. It is a branched chain polymer having 6000—30,000 glucose units.

2. *Starch.* It is the most important food source of carbohydrate and is found in potatoes, rice, cereals etc. It is hydrolysed in gut yielding dextrins and maltose and eventually glucose.

Treatment of starch with hot water dissolves amylose, while amylopectine remains as such:

Amylose. Contains about 200-500 glucose units which are arranged in the form of a straight chain. The molecular wt. is about 150,000. It gives intense blue colour with iodine.

Amylopectin. It has about 1000 glucose resideus and its molecular wt. is about 200,000-1,00,000. It has a branched structure.

3. *Agar.* It is a galactan consisting of both D and L glactose. It is used as a bacteriological culture medium.

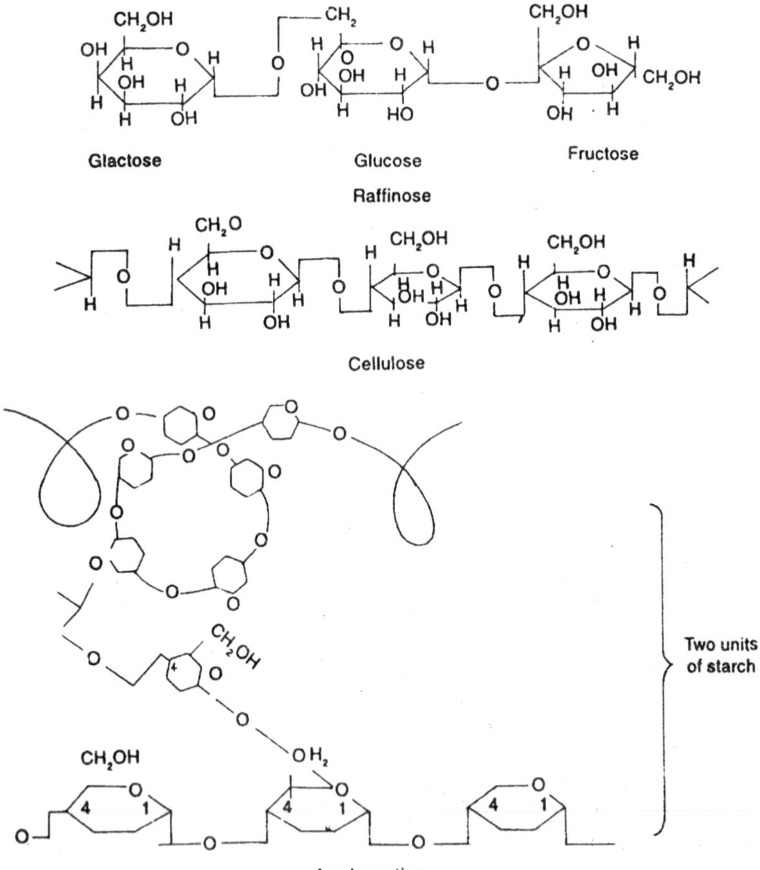

4. *Pectins*. These are abundant in fruits, particularly in the rim of citrus fruits like orange and lemons. They contain arabinose, glactose and galacturonic acid.
5. *Xylan*. In addition to cellulose all plants contain xylan. It is a hemicellulose and consists of D-xylose.

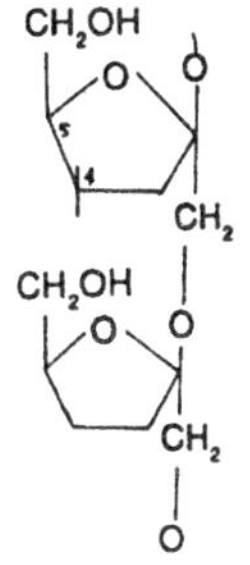

Inulin

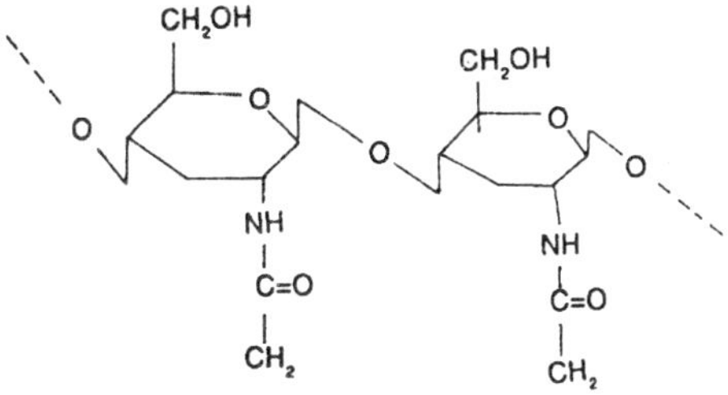

Chitiu

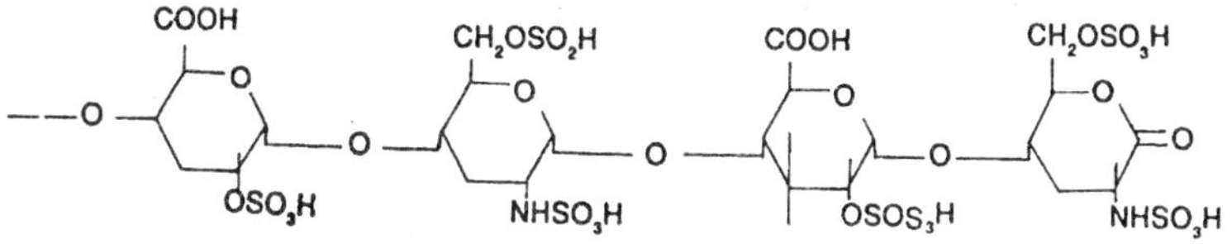

Heparin

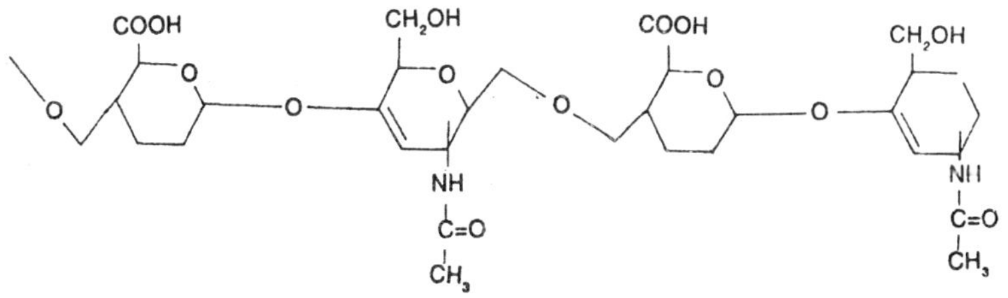

Hyaluronic acid

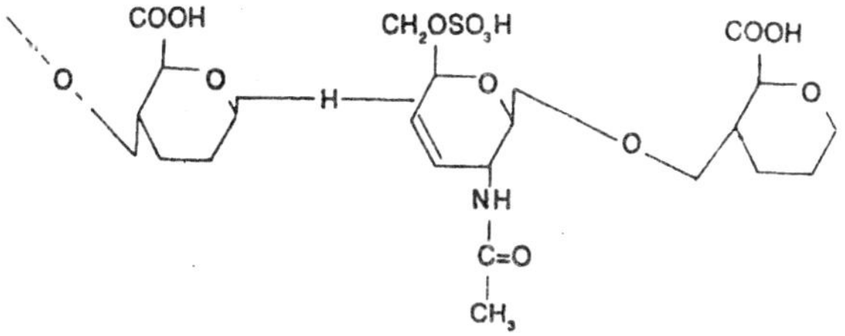

chondriotin sulfate

6. *Inulin.* It is a starch found in the tubers and roots of *Dahlia*, *Dandelions* etc. On hydrolysis it yields fructose. M. Wt. is about 5,000 and about 30-35 fructose units per mole are present.
7. *Dextrins.* They are the intermediate products formed during hydrolysis of starch to the glucose.
8. *Cellulose.* The cell wall of plants is formed by cellulose. The cellulose consists of a lenier chain of glucose units ranging 900-2000. It does not occur in the animal tissue and it cannot be utilized by man for energy production purposes. Herbivorous animals can, however, utilize cellulose with the help of microorganisms as they can digest cellulose.
9. *Chitin.* It is an important structural polysaccharide in invertebrates particularly in arthropods. Structurally, it consists of N-acetyl-D glucosamine units.

II. Heteropolysaccharides

A. *Glycoproteins.* These are protein-polysaccharide compounds occuring in tissue, particularly in mucus secretion. Examples are ovalbumin, fibrinogen, γ-globulin of serum, human chorionic gonadotropins, luteinizing hormones and the blood group substances of RBC (antigen).

B. *Mucopolysaccharides.* The most important mucopolysaccharides from biological point of view are:

1. *Heparin.* It is present in the liver, lungs and spleen having a molecular wt. about 20,000. The *exect* structure of heparin in unknown. It is found to be constituted by glucuronic acid, glucosamine and sulfuric acid. Sulfuric acid is linked to hydroxyl group of sugar derivatives as well as to amino group of glucosamine. Heparin prevents clotting of blood in the vessels.
2. *Hyaluronic acid.* It is a mucopolysaccharide present in connective tissue and acts as an intercellular connecting material. It is abundently present in the umbilical cord, vitreous fluid of eyes and in the synovial fluid present at the joints. This polysaccharide consists of N-acetyl glucosamine and glucuronic acid.
3. *Chondrotin sulfates.* They are found in the cartilage, adult bones, skin, cornea, tendons and heart valves. It consists of N-acetylgalactosamine and glucuronic acid.

Functions

The carbohydrates are very important biologically as a source of energy for the cell. The main source of energy is glucose. It the main form of crbohydrates which is **transported form cell** to cell by blood in animal and by sap in plants. **Carbohydrates also** help in the formation of cell wall in plants. Some **carbohydrates** may serve as the prosthetic group of certain proteins. **Glycogen** and starch **are** major storage materials in animals **and plants respectively.**

Lipids

Term lipid includes fats and fat-like substances. Strucrurally, the different substances of this group may not be similar to fats, but all are soluble in fat-solvents like alcohols, ether, chloroform, carbon tetrachloride, acetone etc. They are insoluble in water. Lipids, like carbohydrates also, contain carbon, oxygen and hydrogen. The carbon and hydrogen are present in larger quantity than oxygen. Some lipids have phosphorous and nitrogen. The lipids in the cell may serve as condensed reserve of energy as well as form the membranous structures.

Classification of Lipids

Lipids are classified into:

I. Simple Lipids

II. Compound Lipids

III. Derived Lipids

I. Simple Lipids

These are esters of fatty acids with various alcohols.

1. Natural Fats

These are the esters of fatty acids with glycerol. The chemical term for a natural fat is *triglycerides*. The triglycerides are formed by the combination of three molecules of fatty acids joined to one molecule of glycerol. As already stated triglycerides are neurtral fats, neutral because the acid ions are neutralized during their unification with glycerol; fats because the bulk of the molecule is devoid of electro-negative elements which can unite with hydrogen to form water molecule.

$$\begin{array}{lcccl} CH_2\ OH & & HOOC{-}R_1 & & CH_2OCOR_1 \\ | & & & & | \\ CHOH & + & HOOC{-}R_2 & \rightarrow & CHOCOR_2 \\ | & & & & | \\ CH_2OH & & HOOC{-}R_3 & & CH_2OCOR_3 \\ \text{Glycerol} & & \text{3 fatty acids} & & \text{Triglyceride} \\ \text{molecule} & & \text{molecules} & & + 3H_2O \end{array}$$

Triglycerides can exist in the solid or liquid form. It is based on the kind of fatty acid residues in its structure. The triglycerides which are blow 20°C called *oils* containing a large proportion of short-chained unsaturated fatty acids like *oleic, linoleic acid* etc. The triglycerides which are solid above 20°C are called *fats.* They contain long chained saturated fatty acids like *palmitic acid* and *stearic acid.*

2. Fatty acids

These are obtained by the hydrolysis of fats. These are monocarboxylic acids. The molecules of a fatty acid has a polar carboxyl group soluble in water and a non-polar hydrocarbon chain soluble only in fat solvents.

Table 2.3. Showing a few common fatty acids found in lipids.

Fatty acid		*Formula*
Saturated fatty acid	→	
Butyric acid	→	$CH_3(CH_2)_2$ COOH
Caproic acid	→	$CH_3(CH_2)_4$ COOH
Palmitic acid	→	CH_3 $(CH_2)_{14}$ COOH
Steraric acid	→	CH_3 $(CH_2)_{16}$ COOH
Unsaturated fatty acids		
Palmitoleic acid		CH_3 $(CH_2)_5$ (H=CH $(CH_2)_7$ COOH
Oleic acid		CH_3 $(CH_2)_7$ CH=CH $(CH_2)_7$ COOH
Linoleic acid		CH_3 $(CH_2)_4$ CH=CH CH_2 CH=CH $(CH_2)_7$ COOH
Linolenic acid		CH_3 CH_2 CH=CH CH_2 CH=CH CH_2 CH=CH $(CH_2)_7$ COOH

The fatty acids are classifed under three groups based on their degree of saturation and unsaturation.

(i) *Saturated fatty acids.* A saturated fatty acid contains as many hydrogen atoms as its carbon chain can hold. General formula for saturated fatty acid is R—COOH, where R is CH_3 (CH_2)n. n is varying from zero in acetic acid to 86 in mycolic acid. The most abunant saturated fatty acids in nature *palmitic* (C_{18}) and *Stearic* (C_{16}) *acids.*

(ii) *Unsaturated fatty acids.* They have one or more double bonds in their carbon chain. When there is a single double bond, results in the loss of 2 hydrogen atoms, such fatty acids are called *monous saturated fatty acids.* Their general formula is CnH_{2n}—1—COOH, examples are *palmitoletic acid* and *oleic acid.* When there ae 2,3,4 or more double bonds in the carbon chain with the consequent absence of 2,6,8 or more hydrogen atoms, such fatty acids are *polyunsaturated fatty acids*. The general formula is CnH_{2n}—2 COOH or CnH_{2n}—3 COOH. Examples are *linoleic acid* and *archidonic acids.*

Linoleic, linolenic and archidonic acid are often termed as *essential fatty acids.*

3. Waxes

Wexes are another class of simple lipis containing one molecule of fatty acid and one high molecular weight alcohol. The constituent acids and alcohols have usually 24-36 carbon atoms. The waxes has high melting points. They are chemically inert as they do not have double bonds in their hydrocarbon chains and are highly insoluble in water. They serve as protective converings on leaf surface (plants). *Bees wax* is an ester of palmitic acid with myricyl alcohol ($C_{30}H_{61}OH$) and *spermaceti* from the sperm whale is an ester of palmitic acid with cetyl alcohol ($C_{16}H_{33}OH$).

II. Compound Lipids

These are esters of fatty acids and alcohol with additional compounds, such as phosphoric acid, sugars, proteins etc. These are classified as follows:

(i) Phospholipids

Lipids containing phosphorous are phospholipids. They also have nitrogen containing bases and other substituents. The phospholipids are abundant in brain and nervous tissues. The different types of phospholipids are:

(a) *Phosphatidic acids.* These are compounds consisting of glycerol, two fatty acids and a phosphate group.

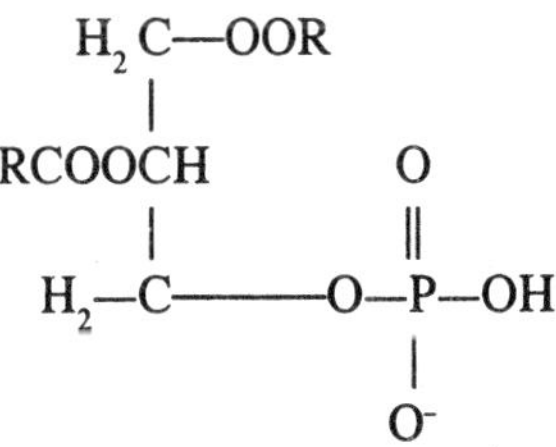

Here R_1 and R_2 represent the residues of the molecules of fatty acids. The phosphatidic acids do not found in any great quantity in tissues but these are important as in intermediate biosynthesis of triglycerides and other phospholipids.

(b) *Lecithins.* Lecithins are choline esters of phosphatidic acid. On hydrolysis they yield one molecule of glycerol, 2 molecules of fatty acids and one molecule of phosphoric acid to which a nitrogenous base choline is attached.

$CH_2.O.CO.R_1$
|
$CHO.CO.R_2$
|
O^-
|
CH_2O ——$OP—O—(CH_2)_2—N^{+\cdot}(CH_3)_3$
||
O

The fatty acids are palmitic, stearic, oleic, linolic and arachidonic acids. Lecithins are yellowish grey solids, soluble in ether and alcohols but insoluble in acetone. Lecithins get broken down by the enzyme lecithins to lysolecithin. This product (lysolecithin) has the ability to hemolyze the red blood corpuscles. Enzyme lecithinase occurs in the venom of snake cobra. and bee.

Lecithin is an important constituent of lipoproteins. Egg-yolk is a rich source of lecithin which also has an important role in fat metabolism in the liver.

(c) *Cephalins.* They resemble lecithins in most properties. The fundamental difference between the lecithins and cephalins is the nature of nitrogenous base. Cephalins contain ethanolamine, colamine and sometimes serine in place of choline.

$CH_2O.CO.\ R_1$
|
$CHO.CO.R_2$
|
| O
| |
$CH_2—O—P—O—(CH_2)_2\ N + H_3$
||
O

(d) *Plasmalogens.* These phospholipids are abundant in brian and muscle. They resemble lecithins and cephalins in structure but possess an aldehyde group in place of one of the fatty acids in typical phospholipid molecule.

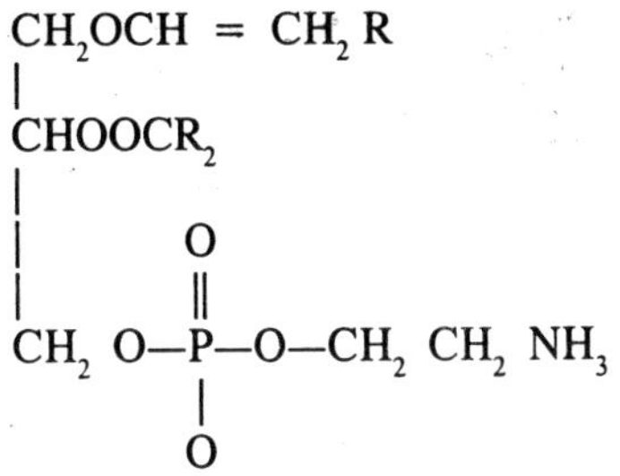

$$
\begin{array}{l}
CH_2OCH = CH_2\,R \\
| \\
CHOOCR_2 \\
| \qquad\quad O \\
| \qquad\quad \| \\
CH_2\;O{-}P{-}O{-}CH_2\;CH_2\;NH_3 \\
\qquad\quad\;\; | \\
\qquad\quad\;\; O
\end{array}
$$

(e) *Phosphoinositides.* Phosphoinositides contain hexahydric alcohol inositol. They can be either monophosphoinositides or diphosphoinositides. An another name lipoinositol was also proposed for these substances. They occur in animal and plants but diphosphoinositides have been reported from brain tissue only.

(f) *Phosphosphingosides.* Phosphosphingosides have been found to occur in high concentration in brain, nerves, lungs and spleen tissue. These contain a nitrogenous base sphingosine or its derivative which remains attached to long-chain fatty acid by its amino group. On hydrolysis they yield fatty acids, phosphoric acid, choline and sphingosine.

(ii) Glycolipids

The glycolipids occurs in brain tissue and in the myelin sheath of nerves, lungs, kidneys, spleen, liver, retina, egg-yolk etc. The glycolipids include two major catagories, cerebrosides and gangliosides.

(a) *Cerebrosides.* They occur in the brain and myelin sheath of nerves. they are based on sphinge mine and have in addition a fatty acid and a monosaccharide sugar but no phosphoric acid or glycerol. Individual cerebrosides are differentiated by the types of fatty acids in the molecule. the important types are:

Kerasin containing the saturated lignoceric acid, $CH_3\,(CH_2)_{22}\,COOH$.

Cerebron containing the cerebronic acid, $CH_3\,(CH_2)_{21}\,CHOH\,COOH$.

Nervon containing the nervonic acid $CH_3\,(CH_2)_7\,CH = CH\,(CH_2)_{13}\,COOH$.

Oxynervone containing hydroxy derivatives of nervonic acid $CH_3\,(CH_2)_7\,CH{=}CH\,(CH_2)_{12}\,CHOH\,COOH$.

(b) *Gangliosides.* These contain N-acetylneuraminic acid (sialic acid), fatty acids, sphingosine and 3 molecules of hexose.

III. Derived Lipids

These lipids include hydrolytic products of lipids as well as other lipid like compounds like sterols, carotenoids, hydrocarbous etc.

The *sterols* are solid wax-like substances chemically, they are alcohols and occur either as such or as esters of fatty acids. They are highly soluble in fat solvents. They all contain a cyclopentano-phenanthrene (sterane) nucleus (made up of three cyclohexane rings, in the phenanthrane type of arrangement and a terminal cyclopentane ring).

Cholesterol is animal origin occuring in bile, brain, spinal cord etc. It is obtained form human gall bladder stones which are deposited in the bile duct.

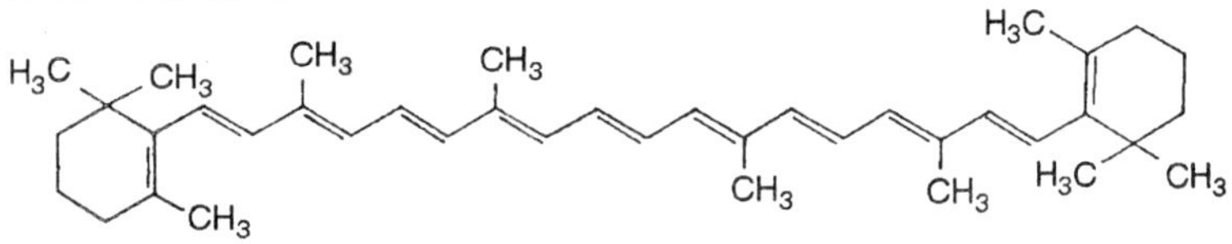

Ergosterol. It is similar to 7-dehydrocholesterol but differs in the side chain. It can be converted into vitamin D on exposure to the ultra violet light and, therefore, also called provitamin D.

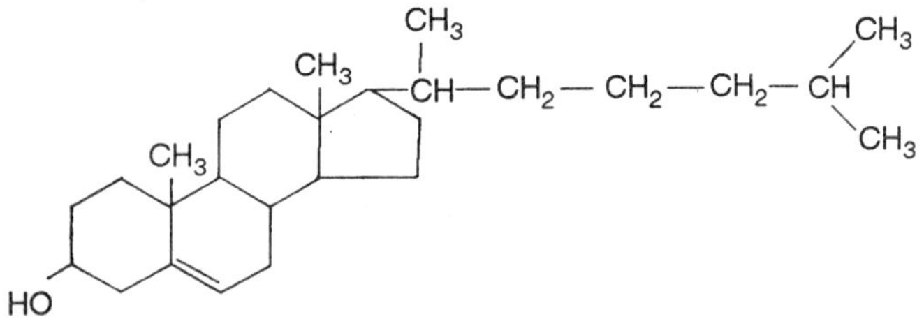

Carotenoids. These are also included in lipids because of their solubility in fat solvent. Carontenes consists of carbon and hydrogen only where as xanthophyll contain oxygen in addition. Vitamin A is derived from carotene. ***Estrogens, progesterone, testosterone*** and ***anderosterone*** are steroidal hormoens.

Prostaglandins

Prostaglandins are derivatives of fatty acids. They were first discovered in human seminal fluid secreted by prostate gland, hence the name. It has been shown now that prostaglandins are synthesized and released by many other tissues such as kidneys, testis, placenta, lungs, liver, uterus, gastrointestinal tract, brain and heart.

Table 2.4. Showing Elements that Occur in Protoplasm

S.No.	Name of elements	Approximate percentage	Function
Major Elements			
1.	Carbon	18	Forms backbone of all organic molecules.
2.	Hydrogen	10	Present in most organic com-pounds and major components of water.
3.	Oxygen	65	Cellular respiration; in organic compound and component of water.
4.	Nitrogen	03	Major components of all the amino acids, proteins and nucleic acids.
Tracer Elements			
5.	Sodium	0.2	For water balance, conduction of nerve impulse.
6.	Potssium	0.5	Conduction of nerve impulse, muscular contraction.
7.	Phosphorus	1.0	Nucleic acids formation; bones formation and in energy transfer.
8.	Magnesium	0.1	Constituent of certain enzymes (ATPase).
9.	Calcium	1.5	Blood clotting, muscle contraction, bones and teeth formation.
10.	Sulfur	0.3	Constituent of most proteins.
11.	Chloride	0.1	Negative ion of interstitial fluid.
12.	Iron	0.01	Component of haemoglobin and certain enzymes.

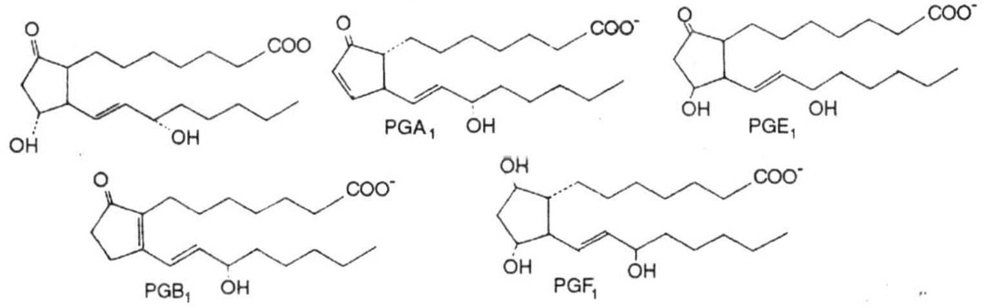

The prostaglandins are 20 carbon fatty acids including a five membered ring in their molecular structure. Different prostaglandins differ with one another in the number and position of double bonds and hydroxyl group substituents. Prostaglandins PGE, PGE_1, PGE_3, PGF_{1a}, PGF_{2a} and PGF_{3a} are considered as *primary prostaglandins.* Most of their action appear to be binding of hormones to membrane.

Recently, new type of prostaglandin has been isolated from human seminal fluid which has been designated as PGX^2.

Amino Acids

There is a common plan of construction for the thousands kinds of proteins in living systems. The 20 kinds of naturally occurring amino acid monomers are strung together in unbranched, linear polymer chains of proteins. These are the 20 amino acids specified in the genetic code that is universal to all organisms. Some other kins of amino acids are also found in cells, but they are either degradation products or residues that have been modified form oen of the 20 commonly occurring amino acids after this latter has been inserted into the polymer chain. Hydroxyproline is a major amino acid constituent of collagen in connective tissue, but proline residues are initially included in the protein and are converted to hydroxyproline after polymerization. Hydroxyproline is not one of the encoded acid, but proline is. Many proteins contain fewer than 20 kinds of amino acids. The relative proportions and the absolute number of the amino acid repertory vary from one protein to another, as a reflection of the specific in formation in genes, which are the blue prints for protein construction.

Table 2.5. Showing nomenclature of nucleic acids and their constituent units.

Base	*Nucleoside*	*Nucleotide*	*Nucleic Acid*
Purines			
Adenine (A)	Adenosine	Adenylic acid	RNA
	Deoxyadenosine	Deoxyadenylic acid	DNA
Guamine (G)	Guanosine	Guanylic acid	RNA
	Deoxyguanosine	Deoxyadenylic acid	DNA
Pyrimidines			
Cytosine (C)	Cytidine	Cytidylic acid	RNA
	Deoxycytidine	Deoxyadenylic acid	DNA
Thymine (T)	Thymidine	Thymidylic acid	DNA
Uracil (V)	Uridine	Uridylic acid	RNA

Nucleotides and Nucleic Acids

Nucleotides are involved in at least two major cellular functions: (1) they are monomeric units from which DNA and RNA polymers

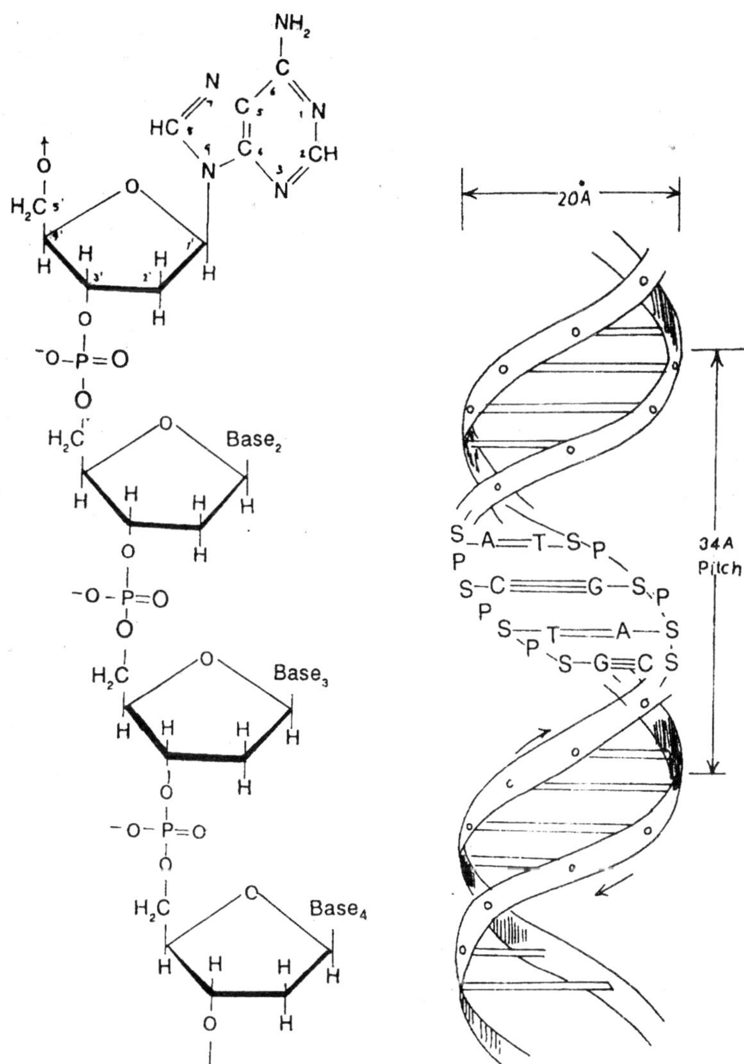

Fig. 2.6. The molecular organization of a backbone of DNA showing phosphodiester and glycosidic bonds.

Fig. 2.7. DNA and its paired bases.

are constructed, and (2) they act as agents in certain energy-transferring reactions during metabolism. A mononucleotide is made up of one nitrogen-containing organic base, one pentose sugar, and one phosphate residue derivative from phosphoric acid. When there is no phosphate group, the sugar-base combination is called a *nucleoside* (Table 2.5). For this reason, *nucleotides* (phosphate-sugar-base) are also called nucleoside phosphates. Nucleoside mono-, di-, and tri- phosphates contain one, two or three phosphate groups respectively.

The nitrogenous bases commonly found in nucleic acids and their nucleotide building blocks are derivatives of purine and pyrimidine. The commonly occuring purines *adenine* and *guanine* are found in both DNA and RNA, as in the pyrimidine compound *cytosine,* the second kind of pyrimidine in DNA is *thymine,* while its demethylated form, *uracil,* occurs in RNA.

Since each kind of nucleic acid contains one unique pyrimidine, it is convenient to study synthesis and activity of DNA or RNA using isotopically-labelled precursors containing one or the other of these bases. Usually the nucleosides uridine or thymidine, or other nucleotide forms, are added to the biological system under study.

The only difference in the pentose sugars of nucleotides is the presence of a hydroxyl group at carbon atom 2 of D-ribose in RNA, but a hydrogen at carbon-2 of 2-deoxy-D-ribose in DNA monomers and polymers. This seemingly simple difference is partly responsible for profound differences in stabilities, pairing potential, and functions of DNA and RNA.

Polynucleotides of both DNA and RNA varieties are built from mononucleotides that are linked convalently via phosphodiester bridges between the 3' position of one unit and the 5' position of hte next. Since there is no restriction on the ventrical sequence of adjacent mononucleotides in either DNA or RNA, a considerable variety of molecules is possible even though only 4 kinds of nucleotide monomers

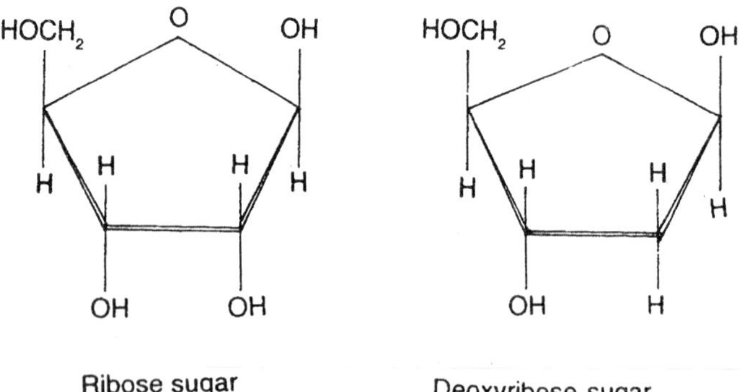

Fig. 2.8. Pentose sugar.

(one for each of the four kinds of bases in the combination with sugar and phosphate) are used in polymer construction. The theoretical variety is calcualted as 4", where 4 is the number of different kinds of nucleotides, and *n* is the number of monomers in the polymer. For a molecule made of only 75 monomeric units, as in some of the smallest RNAs, there may be 4^{75} different arrangements of the constituent units. Each arrangement theoretically constitutes a moleule of different specificity. Where the average gene may include about 500 nucleotides in a DNA sequence, 4^{500} different sequences are theoretically possible and, therefore, that many different and specific genes. Despite the apparently meager number of monomer types an astronomically high number of possible genes can be constructed.

Such variety can easily account for all past and present life forms.

The DNA Double Helix

DNA molecules usually have regular helical configurations because most DNA molecules consists of two *complementary polynucleotide strands*. The two strands are held together by *hydrogen bonds* between complementary pairs of purines and pyrimidines. Adenine always bind with thymine while guanine always binds with cytosine. This repeated

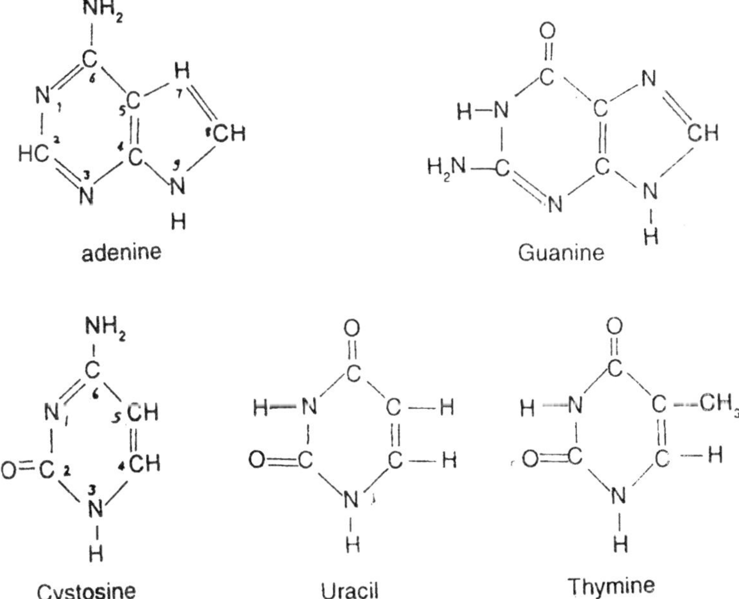

Fig. 2.9. Various heterogenous bases.

hydrogen bonding within the double helix structure and bonding between virtually all the surface atoms in the sugar and phosphate groups with water molecules serve to stabilize the structure.

Since the purine-pyrimidine pairs are found in the center of the molecule, their flat surface can stack on top of each other and thereby limit their contact with water. In double-helical molecules, a regular structure is possible because the comple-mentary base pairs are exactly the same size. Single polynucleotide chains could not have a regular backbone structure because pyrimidines are smaller than purines, which would cause the angle of helical rotation to vary with the sequence of bases.

DNA double helix molecules are very stable at physiological temperatures because: (1) disruption of the double helix breaks hydrogen bounds and brings hydrophobic purines and pyrimidines into contact with water, which is energetically unsatisfactory; and (2) there are many weak bonds within the DNA molecule, arranged so that most of them cannot break without many others breaking at the same time. Even though some hydrogen bonds may be broken by thermal motion, hydrogen bonds in the rest of the molecule remain intact and the molecule does not fall apart. In fact, when held together by more than ten nucleotide pairs the double helices are quite stable. At room temperature weak bonds is the stability of molecular shape, in proteins as well as in nucleic acids. At abnormally high temperatures there is more frequent breakage of weak bond, which become less stable as temperatures rise above physiological levels. Once a significant number of weak bonds have been broken, a protein or nucleic acid molecule usually loses its original form and changes to an inactive or denatured form.

3

ISOLATION OF CELL ORGANELLES

While cloning or selective culture conditions are the preferred methods for purifying a culture, there are occasions when cells do not grow with a high enough plating efficiency to make cloning possible or when appropriate selection conditions are not available. It may then be necessary to resort to a physical separation technique such as rate or density sedimentation. Physical separation techniques have the advantage that they give a high yield more quickly than cloning although not with the same purity.

The more successful separation techniques depend on differences in: (1) cell size; (2) cell density (specific gravity); (3) Cell surface charge; (4) cell surface chemistry (affinity for lectins, antibodies, or chromatographic media); (5) total light scatter per cell; and (6) fluorescence

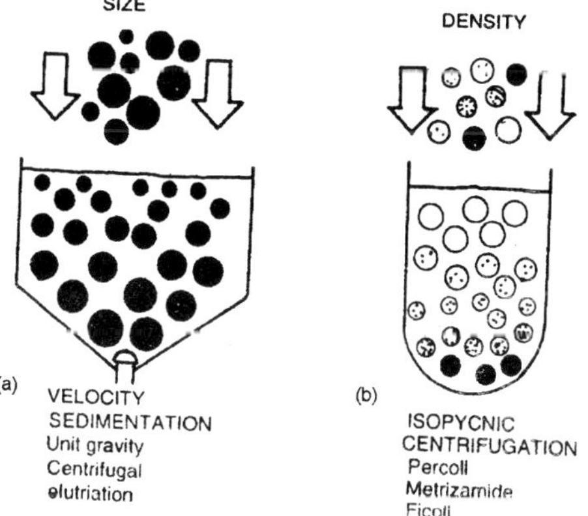

Fig. 3.1. Cell separation techniques. (a) Velocity sedimentation; (b) Isopycnic sedimentation.

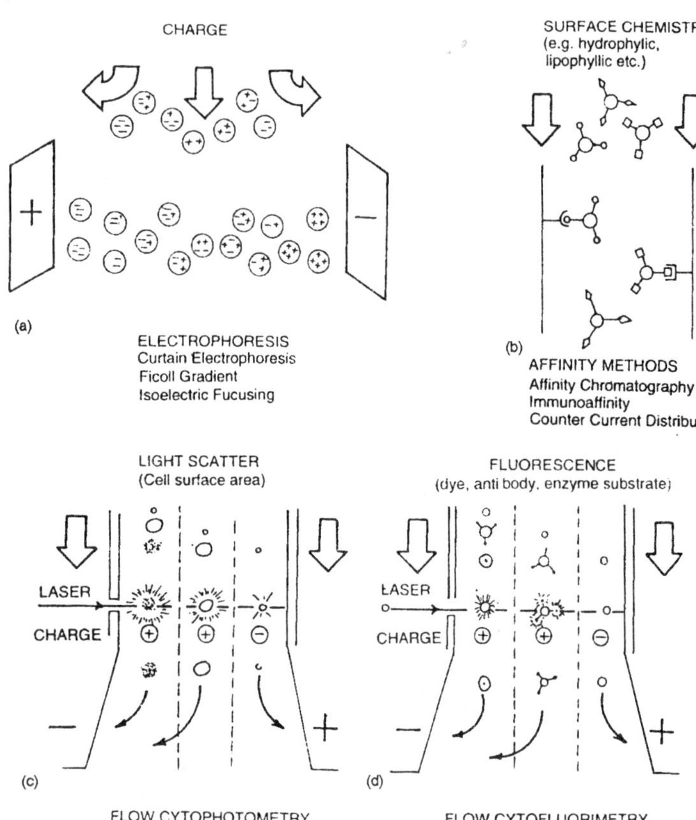

Fig. 3.2. Cell separation techniques.

emission of one or more cellular constituents or absorbed antibody. The apparatus required ranges from about $10-worth of glassware to $ 200,000-worth of complex laser and computer technology; the choice depends on the parameter that you are obliged to use and on your budget.

Cell Size and Sedimentation Velocity

The relationship between particle size and sedimentation rate at 1 g though complex for submicron particles is fairly simple for cells and can be expressed approximately as

$$v = \frac{r^2}{4} \quad ...(1)$$

where v=sedimentation rate in mm/hr and r=radius of the cell in μm.

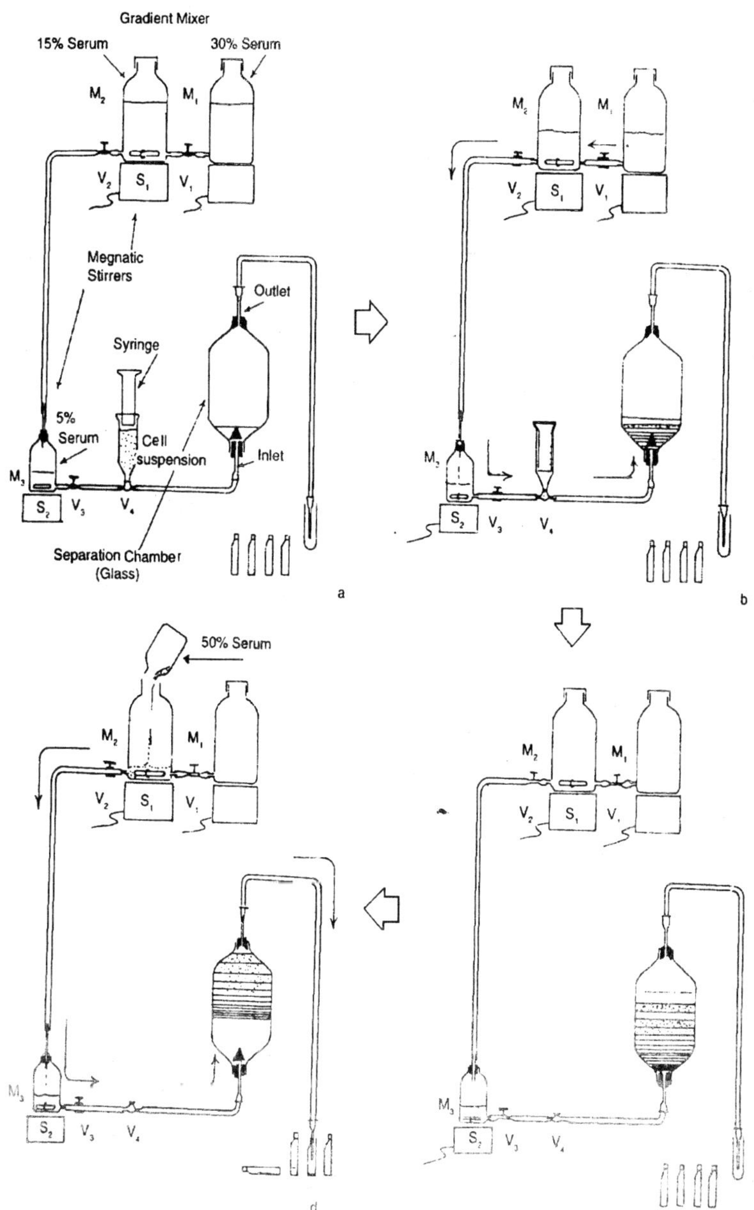

Fig. 3.3. Cell separation velocity sedimentation at unit gravity. Apparatus and position of valves at different stages of the procedure. (a) At start, loading cells. (b) Running in gradient. (c) After cell sedimentation. (d) Harvesting. V-valve; M—mixer vessel; S—stirrer.

Unit Gravity Sedimentation

The apparatus required can be assembled from routine laboratory glassware. To ensure stability of the column of liquid supporting the cells in the sedimentation chamber, it is formed from a serum, Ficoll, or bovine serum albumen gradient, and run into the chamber through a baffle to prevent turbulence.

The height of the separation chamber determines how long the sedimentation may run. Since this is usually 2-4 hr, in a low-viscosity

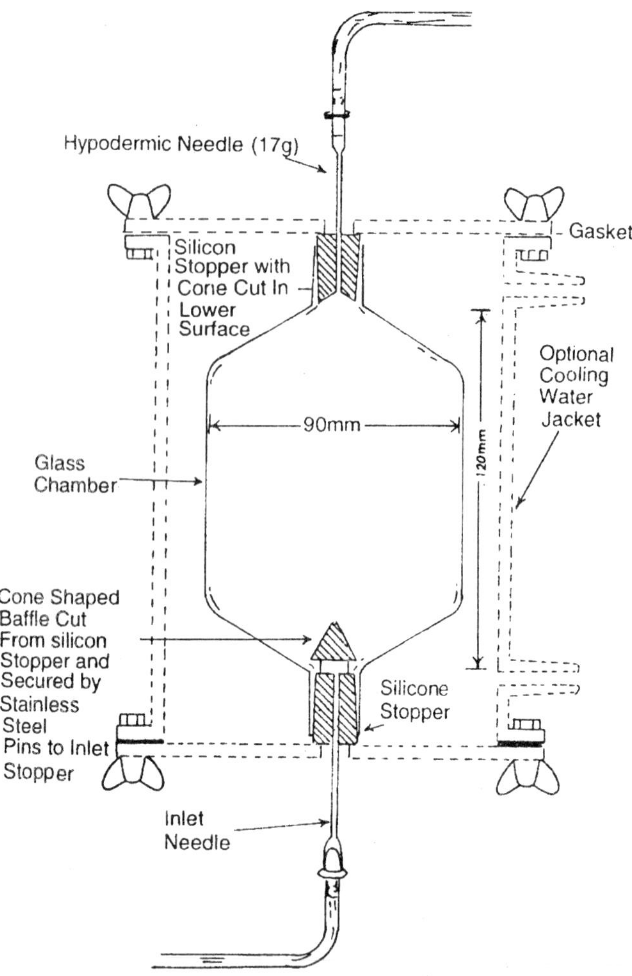

Fig. 3.4. Separation chamber for unit gravity sedimentation. The dotted outline is a cooling jacket for carrying out sedimentation at 4°C.

medium, 10 cm is approximately correct. A longer sedimentation time may give better resolution but may cause deterioration of the cells.

The width of the chamber controls the number of cells that may be loaded onto the gradient as the cell layer should be kept thin (~ 5 mm) and the cell concentration low (~ 106 ml).

The height and width (i.e., volume) also affect the filling rate. The chamber must not be filled too rapidly or turbulence will result, and it cannot be filled too slowly or the cells will sediment faster than the liquid level rises. The dimensions are optimal for separating about 2×10^7 cells of 15-18 μm diameter or up to 10^8 cells of 10-12 μm diameter.

The procedure for separating a typical cell suspension of average cell diameter 15μm is as follows.

Outline

Float cells on top of a gradient of serum in medium, allow cells to sediment through the gradient for about 3 hr, and run off gradient into culture vessels.

Materials

300 ml Eagle's MEMS (suspension salts) + 30% serum.

300 ml MEMS + 15% serum

20 ml MEMS + 5% serum

10 ml. 0.25% trypsin-citrate

30 ml PbS

20 ml MEMS + 3% serum

hemocytometer or cell counter flotation medium (1M sucrose or 20% Ficoll)

25-cm^2 flsks

growth medium

Protocol

1. Prepare apparatus. Incorporate Luer connections to allow for disassembly for sterilization. Package and autoclave.
2. Assemble and check that valves V_1, V_2, V_3 and V_4 are closed.
3. Add 300 ml 30% serum is medium to mixer vessel M_1 and 300 ml 15% serum in medium to mixer vessel M_2.
4. Check that stirrer S_1 is functioning.
5. Add 20 ml 5% serum in medium to mixer M_3 and check that stirrer S_2 is functioning.

6. Open V_4 to connect syringe to separation chamber and insert 20 ml PBS into separation chamber.
7. Opern V_4 to M_3 line, open V_3, and dray a little 5% serum into the syringe (just enough to fill line). Close V_3 and V_4.
8. Prepare cell suspension, e.g., by trypsinizing primary culture for 15 min in 0.25% trypsincitrate. Disperse cells carefully in 3% serum in medium and check that a single cell suspension is formed.
9. Take up 20 ml at 106 /ml (maximum) into syringe and connect to V4 inlet.
10. With syringe held vertically, open V_4 to M_3 line, open V_3, and draw a littler 5% serum into syringe to clear any bubbles from M_3 line and V_4.
11. Turn valve V_4 to separation chamber line and draw a little PBS into syringe to clear any bubbles from this line.
12. Insert cell suspension slowly into chamber; avoid mixing cell suspension with the overlaying PBS layer. Take care to stop while a little fluid is left in the syringe to avoid injecting any air bubbles back into the line. If difficulty is encountered injecting cells smoothly, without turbulence, remove piston from syringe and allow cells to run in under gravity alone by raising V_4.
13. Start stirrers S_1 and S_2.
14. Open V_4 to connect M_3 line to separation chamber.
15. Open V_1 and adjust flow rate by opening V_2 to give 15 ml./min (~ 5 drops/s) at M_3. Cell suspension will now float up into separation chamber on gradient of serum. Check for turbulence at baffle as suspension and gradient run it. If there is any, reduce flow rate at M_3 by closing V_2.
16. When gradient mixers M_1 and M_2 are empty, but before M_3 empties, close V_3 and V_2.
17. It should be possible to see the cell layer in the sedimentation chamber and to follow the cells as they sediments. As they do, the cell band will become wider and more diffuse. Check for signs of "streaming" in the early stages of sedimentation (tails of cells which sediment ahead of the main band). This occurs when the cell concentration is too high or the step between the cells and the gradient is too steep.
18. After about 20 min, close V_1 and add 90 ml 50% serum to M_2. Open V_3 and adjust flow rate at M_3 to 15 ml/min. Stop when M_2 is empty but before M_3 empties by closing V_3 and V_2.

19. Add 500 ml. flotation medium (1 M sucrose or 20% Ficoll) to M_1 and M_2, open V_1 and V_2, and let some of the flotation medium run into M_3. Close V_2.
20. When sedimentation is complete, i.e., cell band midway down separation chamber, open V_3, and adjust V_2 to give a flow rate of 15 ml/ min in M_3.
21. Collect eluate from top of chamber via elution line and run into graduated culture vessels, e.g., 25-cm^2 flasks, 10 ml per flask. Mix the contents of each flask and take sample for cell counting.
22. Seal and incubate flasks for 24 hr, replace medium with fresh medium at standard serum concentration and volume.

Variations

Gradient medium. If serum and regular culture medium are used, then it is possible to culture cells directly from the eluate. Fetal bovine serum causes less reaggregation than calf or horse serum. If serum is found to be unsuitable, gradients can be formed from bovine serum albumen or Ficoll (Pharmacia).

Aggregation. Aggregation can be reduced by enclosing the separation chamber in a cooling jacket and running the whole process at 4°C. Mixers M_1, M_2 and M_3 must all be kept cold also. Water-driven

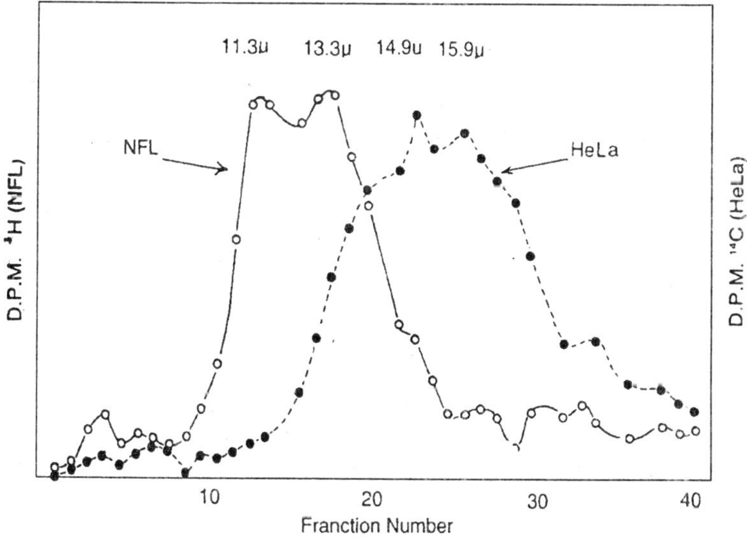

Fig. 3.5. Elution profiles of artificial mixture of HeLa and NFL (normal lumen lung fibroblasts) after sedimentation at 1 g for 3 hr.

magnetic stirrers may be used at S_1 and S_2 to minimize overheating of gradient.

Pump. Gravity is used in this example as the cheapest and simplest method for generating the flow of gradient medium, but if desired, a peristatlic pump may be inserted at V_3.

Sedimentation of cells at unit gravity is a simple low-technology method of separating cells. It works well for many cell types, e.g., brain hemopoietic cells and HeLA/fibroblast mixtures and can be performed in regular physiological media. The cells must be singly suspended, however and there is a practical limit of about 10^8 cells that may be separated.

Pretlow and others have used specially formed gradients of Ficoll to separate cells by sedimentation velocity at higher g forces on a zonal rotor. The gradients are shallow and of relatively low density to minimize the effect of cell density on sedimentation rate. Cells of may different types have been separated by this method, and it appears to have a wide application.

Centrifugal Elutriation

The centrifugal elutriator is a device for increasing the sedimentation rate and improving the yield and resolution by performing the separation in a specially designed centrifuge and rotor. Cells in the suspending medium are pumped into the separation chamber in the rotor while the rotor is turning. While the cells are in the chamber, centrifugal force will tend to force the cells to the outer edge of the rotor. Meanwhile the suspending medium is pumped through the chamber

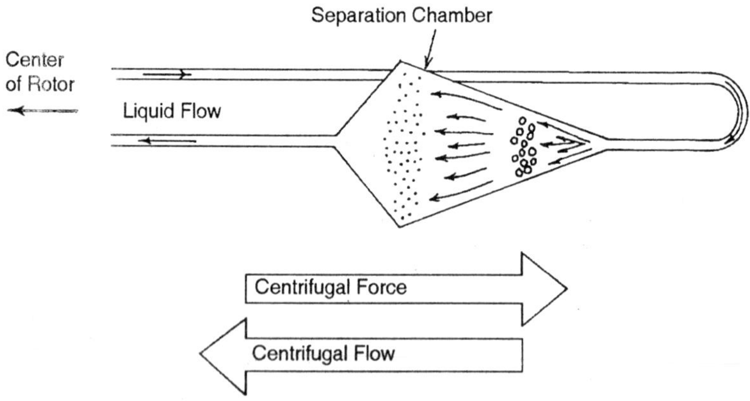

Fig. 3.6. Separation chamber of elutriator rotor.

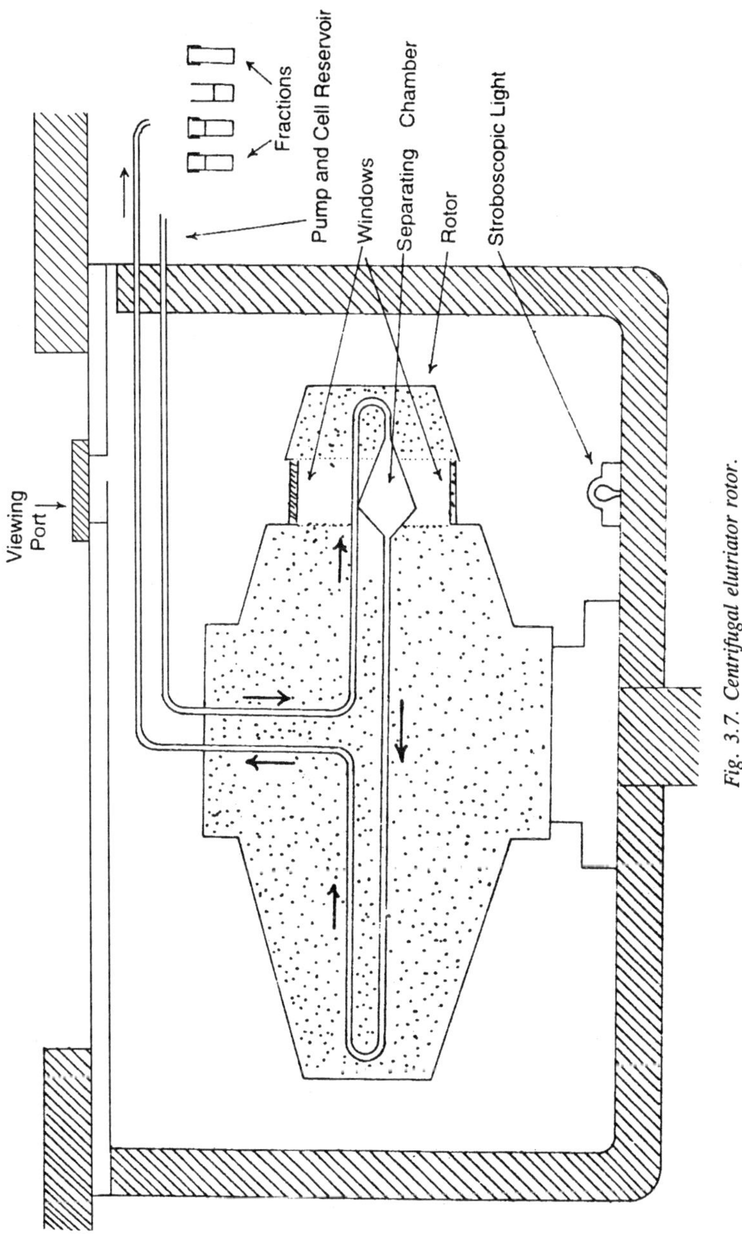

Fig. 3.7. Centrifugal elutriator rotor.

such that the centripetal flow rate of the cells. If the cells were uniform, they would remain stationary, but since they vary in size, density and cell surface configuration, they tend to sediment at different rates.

As the sedimentation chamber is tapered, the flow rate is increases toward the edge of the rotor and a continuous range of flow rates is generated. Cells of differing sedimentation rates will, therefore, reach equilibrium at different positions in the chamber. The sedimentation chamber is illuminated by *stroboscopic light* and can be observed through

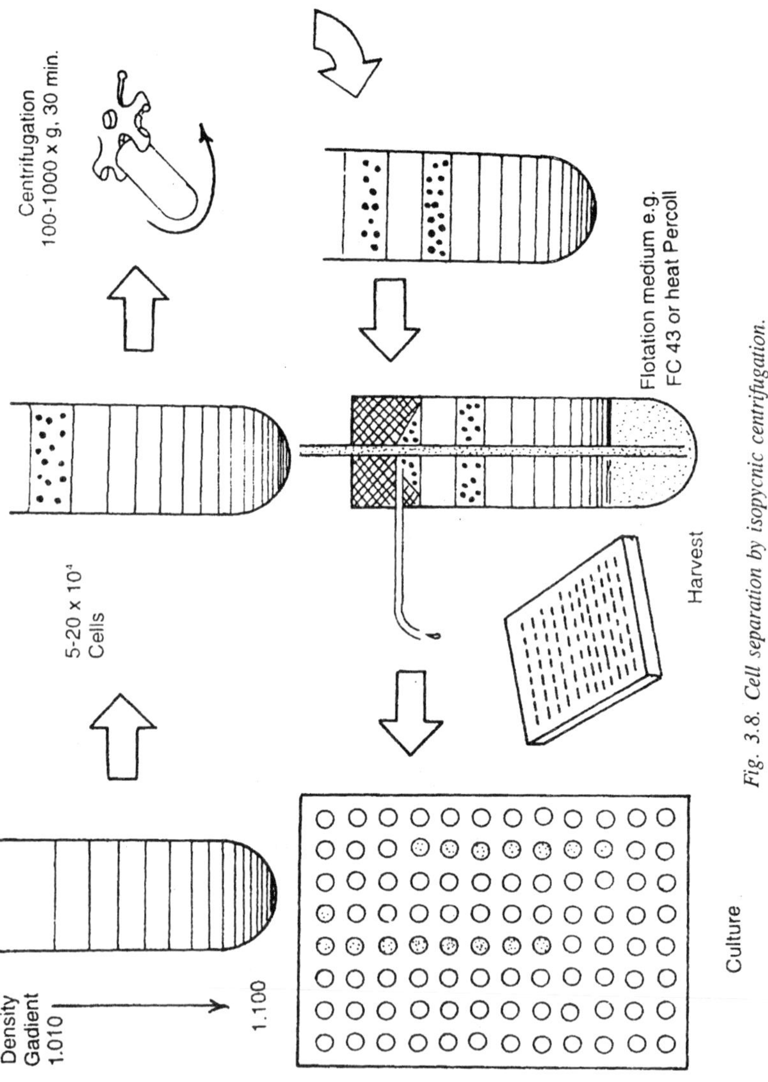

Fig. 3.8. Cell separation by isopycnic centrifugation.

a viewing port. When the cells are seen to reach equilibrium, the flow rate is increased and the cells are pumped out into receiving vessels. The separation can be performed in complete medium and the cells cultured directly afterward.

Equilibrium is reached in a few minutes and the whole run may take 30 min. On each run 10^8 cells may be separated and the run may be repeated as often as necessary. The apparatus is, however, fairly expensive and a considerable amount of experience is required before effective separations may be made. A number of cell types have been separated by this method as have cells of different phase of the cells cycle.

Cell Density and Isophycnic Sedimentation

Separation of cells by density can be performed at low or high *g* using conventional equipment. The cells sediment in a density gradient to an equilibrium position equivalent to their own density (*isopycnic sedimentation*). Physiological media must be used and the osmotic strength carefully monitored. The density medium should be nontoxic, nonviscous at high densities (1.10 g/ ml) and exert little osmotic pressure in solution. Serum albumen, dextran, Ficoll metrizamide (Nygaard) and Percoll (Pharmacia) have all been used successfully; Percoll (colloidal silica) is one of the more effective media currently available.

Outline

Form gradient; (1) by layering different densities of Percoll; (2) by high-speed spin; or (3) with special gradient former. Centrifuge cells through Percoll gradient (or allow to sediment at unit gravity), collect fractions, and culture directly.

Materials

Culture medium (sterile)
medium + 20% Percoll (sterile)
25-ml centrifuge tubes (sterile)
PBSA (sterile)
0.25% trypsin (sterile)
syringe or gradient harvester (sterile)
24-well plates or microtitration plates (sterile)
refractometer or density meter
hemocytometer
cell counter

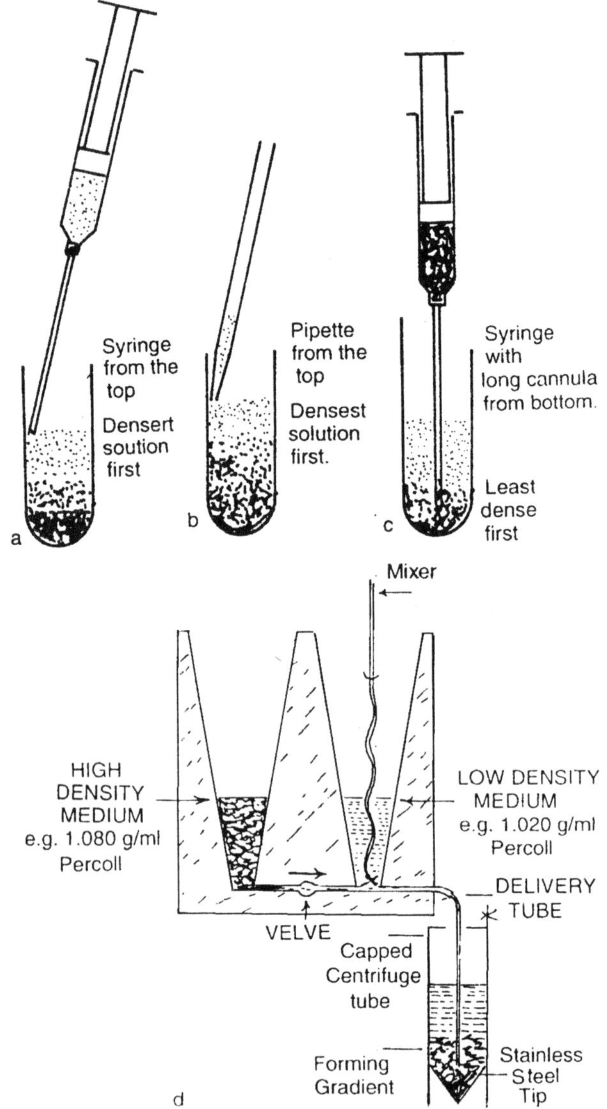

Fig. 3.9. Layering density gradients (a) by syringe from the top, (b) by pipette from the top, (c) by syringe from the bottom, (d) by gradient mixing device.

Protocol

1. *Prepare gradient*: (1) Prepare two media, one regular culture medium and one with 20% Percoll; (1) adjust the density of the

Percoll solution to 1.10 g/ml and its osmotic strength to 290 mOsm kg; (3) mix the two media in varying proportions to give the desired density range (e.g., 1.020-1.100 g/ml) in ten or 20 steps; and (4) layering one step over another, build up a stepwise density gradient in a 25-ml centrifuge tube. Gradients may be used immediately or left overnight.

Alternatively, place medium containing Percoll of density 1.085 g/ml in a tube and centrifuge at 20,000 g for 1 hr. This generates a sigmoid gradient, the shape of which is determined by the starting concentration of Percoll, the duration and centrifugal force of the centrifugation, the shape of the tube, and the type of rotor. A continuous linear gradient may be produced by mixing, for example, 1.020 g/ml with 1.08 g/ml Percoll in a gradient-forming device.

2. Trypsinize cells and resuspend in medium plus serum. Check that they are singly suspended.
3. Layer up to 2×10^7 cells in 2-ml medium on top of the gradient.
4. The tube may be allowed to stand on the bench for 4 hr or centrifuged for 20 min at between 100 and 1,000 g.
5. Collect fractions using a syringe, or a gradient harvester (MSE/Fisons). Fractions of 1 ml may be collected into a 24-well plate or 0.1 ml into microtitration plates. Samples should be taken at

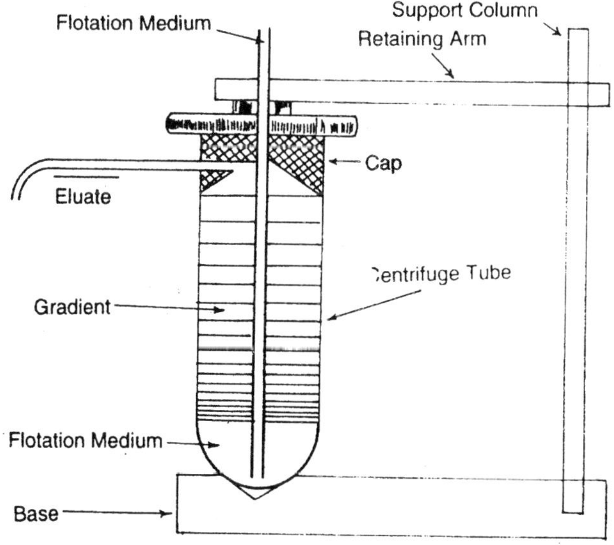

Fig. 3.10. Gradient harvester (Fisons/M.S.E.).

intervals for cell counting and determination of the density (r) of the gradient medium. Density may be measured on a *refractometer* (Hilger) or density meter (Paar).

6. Add equal volume of medium to each well and mix (to ensure cells settle to bottom of well). Change the medium to remove the Percoll after 24-28 hr incubation.

Variations

Cell may be incorporated into the gradient during formation by centrifugation. Only one spin is required although spinning the cells at such a high *g* force may damage them.

Other media

Ficoll is one of the most popular media as it, like Percoll, can be autoclaved. It is a littler more viscous at high densities and may cause agglutination of some cells. Metrizamide (Nygaard), a nonionic

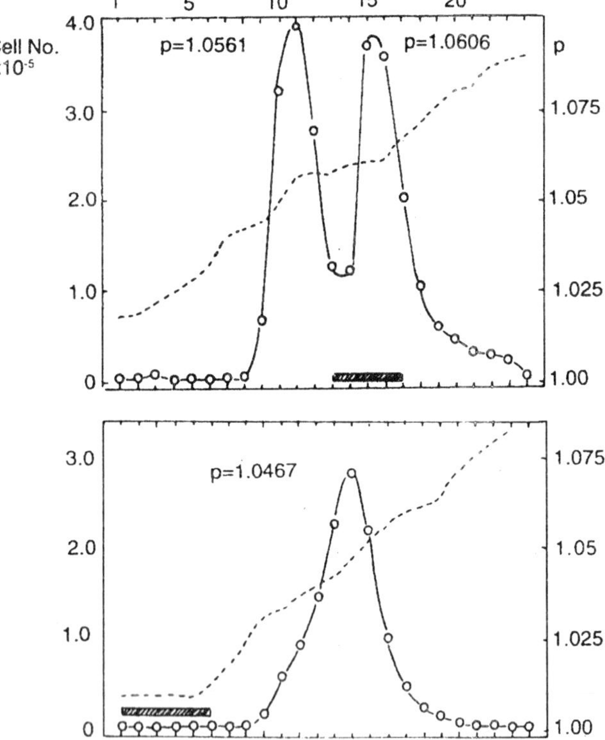

Fig. 3.11. Incorporation of metrizamide (Nygaard) into cells during isopycnic centrifugation.

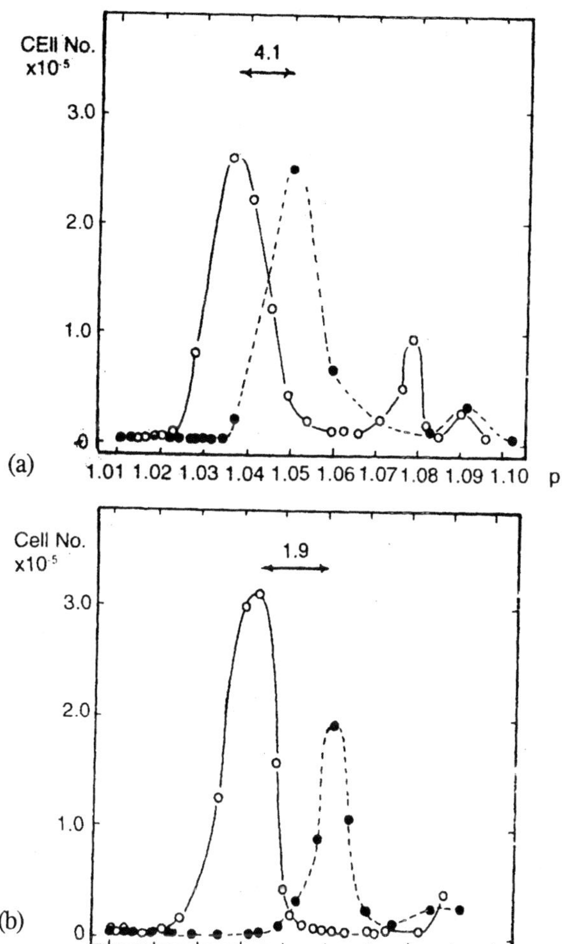

Fig. 3.12. Sedimentation profiles of HeLa and MRC-5 cells, centrifuged to equilibrium in gradients of metrizamide in culture medium, a, b.

derivative of metrizoate, which is a radio-opaque-iodinated substance used in radiography (Isopaque, Hypaque, Renografin) and in lymphocyte purification (e.g., Lymphoprep) is less viscous at high densities but may be incorporated into some cells as is Isopaque. Where such media are used, cells should always be layered on top of the gradient and not mixed in during formation.

Marker beads

Pharmacia manufacture coloured marker beads of standard densities which may be used to determine the density of regions of the gradient.

Isopycnic sedimentation is quicker than velocity sedimentation at unit gravity and gives a higher yield of cells for a given gradient volume. It is ideal where clear differences in density exist between cells. Cell density may be affected by the gradient medium (e.g., metrizamide, by the position of the cells in the growth cycle, and by serum.

This type of separation can be done on any centrifuge, as high *g* forces are not required, and can even be performed at 1 g.

Fluorescence-Activated Cell Sorting

This technique operates by projecting a single cell stream through a laser beam in such a way that the light scattered from the cells is detected by a photomultiplier and recorded. If the cells are pretreated with fluorescent stain (e.g., propidium iodide or Chromomycin A_3 for DNA) of fluorescent antibody, the fluorescence emission excited by the laser is detected by a second photomultiplier tube. This information is processed and displayed as a two or three-dimensional graph on an oscilloscope. If specific coordinates are then set to delineate sections of the display, the cell sorter will divert cells with the properties that would place them within these coordinates (e.g., high or low light scatter, high or low fluorescence) into a receiver tube placed below the cell stream. The cell stream is deflected by applying a charge to it as it passes between two oppositely charged plates. The charges is applied briefly and at a set time after the cell has cut the laser beam such that only one cell is deflected into the receiver. A low cell concentration in the cell stream is required such that the gap between cells is sufficient to prevent two cells being deflected together.

All cells having similar properties will be collected into the same tube. A second set of coordinates may be set and a second group of cells collected simultaneously into a second tube by changing the polarity of the cell stream and deflecting the cells in the opposite direction. All remaining cells will be collected in a central reservoir.

This method may be used to separate cells with any differences that may be detected by light scatter (e.g., cell size) or fluorescence (e.g., DNA, RNA, protein, enzyme activity, specific antigens.) It is an extremely powerful tool but limited by cell yield (about 107 cells is a reasonable maximum) and the very high cost of the instrument (approximately $100,000). It also requires a full-time, skilled operator.

Other Techniques

The many other techniques which have been used successfully to separate cells are too numerous to describe in detail

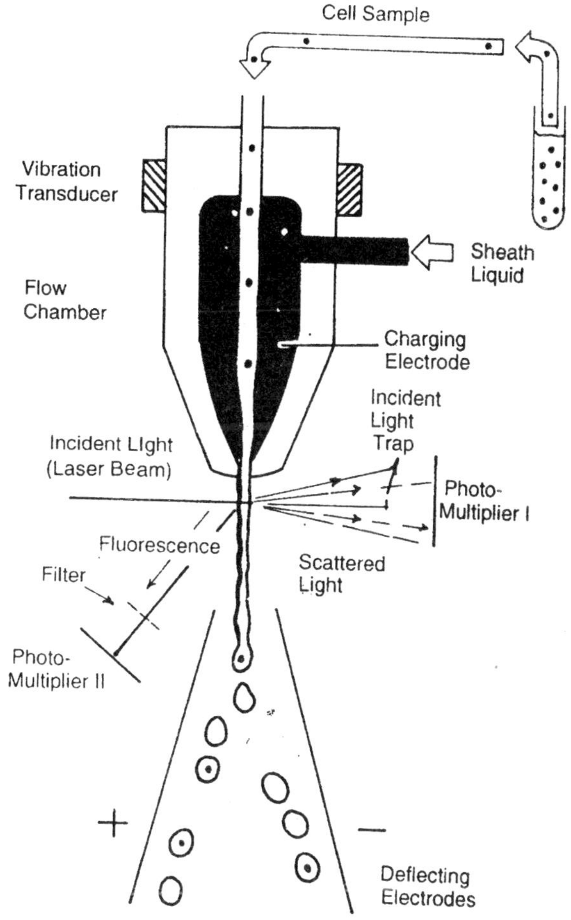

Fig. 3.13. Principle of operation of flow cytophotometer.

Electrophoresis either in Ficoll gradient or by curtain electrophoresis; the second technique is probably more effective and has been used to separate kidney tubular epithelium.

Affinity chromatography on antibody or plant lectins bound to nylon fiber or Sephadex (Pharmacia). These techniques appear to be useful for fresh blood cells but less so for cultured cells.

Counter current distribution has been used to purify murine ascites tumor cells, but the viability may be too low for subsequent culture.

As so many techniques exist, it is difficult for the novice to know where to start. Like so many other areas of investigation, it is best to

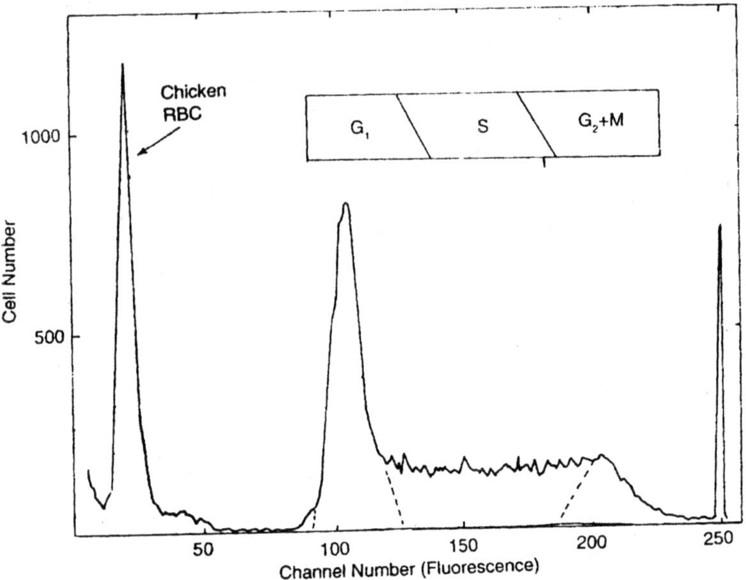

Fig. 3.14. Printout from FACS II. Friend (murine erythroleukemia) cells were fixed in methanol as a single cell suspension and stained with Chromomycin A_3.

start with a simple technique such as velocity sedimentation at unit gravity or isopycnic centrifugation. Density gradient analysis may also be used in conjunction with velocity sedimentation in a two-stage fractionation. If there are still problems of resolution or yield, then it may be necessary to employ high-technology methods such as centrifugal elutriation, curtain electrophoresis, or fluorescence-activated cell sorting.

4

OUTER COVERING OF CELL

The outer most limit of a cell is composed of living or non-living materials or both. Whatever their chemical constitution and structural organization, their function includes regulation of the flow of materials into and out of the cell and they provide some degree of support and maintenance of cell shape and cell size. Plasma membrane is variously called as *cell membrane*, *plasmalemma*, *plasma membrane* etc. The term plasma membrane was given by *Nageli* in 1855. On account of the technical difficulties it is not possible to investigate the structure of plasma membrane in every kind of cell. Most of the information on the subject has accumulated through the study of mammalian R.B.C. and the myelin sheath of the nerve fibres. This membrane is so thin that is cannot be resolved with the light microscope, but in some cells it is covered by thicker protective layers that are within the limits of microscopic resolution. For example, most plant cells have a thick cellulose wall that covers and protects the true plasma membrane.

Some animal cells are surrounded by cement-like substances that constitute visible cell walls. Such layers, also called extraneous coats, generally play no role in permeability, but do have other important functions. For the study of their structure, chemical composition and for knowing the physiological and biochemical nature of the plasma membrane or any other cytoplasmic organelle the first thing which we face is their isolation is pure state.

METHODS FOR ISOLATION

The ideal isolated membrane component is that which does not have any non-membrane contamination. The isolation of the membrane can be regarded as the removal of other cell components from the cell. Their operation is somewhat less difficult in the non-nucleate red blood cells. During hemolysis the membrane structure loosen sufficiently to allow the cell contents to escape without rupturing completely. After this hemolysis the isolation of erythrocyte plasma membrane is easy. However, the product obtained depends upon the method of lysis and the pH of the liquid. The other procedure of getting the plasma membrane is introduced by *Wolport* and *O'Neill* in 1962 by treating the *Amoeba* with buffered : 45% glycerol or 2.4 M sucrose solution, caused the cell contents to shrink away from the cell membrane, which retained its characteristic shape. The membrane were fused from the cell contents by gently homogenization and were subsequently collected in bulk by centrifuging density.

Chemical Composition

The plasma membrane is composed mainly of protein, lipid, and a small percentage (1 to 5 percent) of oligosaccharides that may be attached to either the lipids (glycolipids) or the proteins (glycoproteins). There is a wide variation in the lipid protein ratio between different cell membranes. Myelin is an exception, in the sense that the lipid predominates; in the other cell membranes there is higher protein/lipid ratio. In myelin the area occupied by the protein is insufficient to cover that of the lipids, whereas in a red cell ghost the opposite situation is found.

Lipids

The main lipid components of the plasma membrane are the phospholipids, cholesterol and galactolipids; their proportion varies in different cell membranes. Myelin differs, with regard to lipid composition, from other cell membranes found in the brain. The major proportion of membrane phospholipids is represented by phosphatidylcholine, phosphatidylethanolamine, and sphingomyelin, all of which have no net charge at neutral pH (i.e., neutral phospholipids) and tend to pack tightly in the bilayer. This property is also shared by cholesterol. Five to 20 per cent of the phospholipids are acidic, including : phosphatidylinositol, phosphatidylserine, cardiolipin phosphatidylglycerol, and sufolipids. Acid phospholipids are negatively charged and in the membrane are associated principal with proteins by way of lipid-protein interactions. Recent studies demonstrate that there is an asymmetry in the erythrocyte membrane regarding not only the protein, but also the phospholipids.

There are more choline phospholipids and glycolipids in the external half of the bilayer and more amino phospholipids in the inner, or

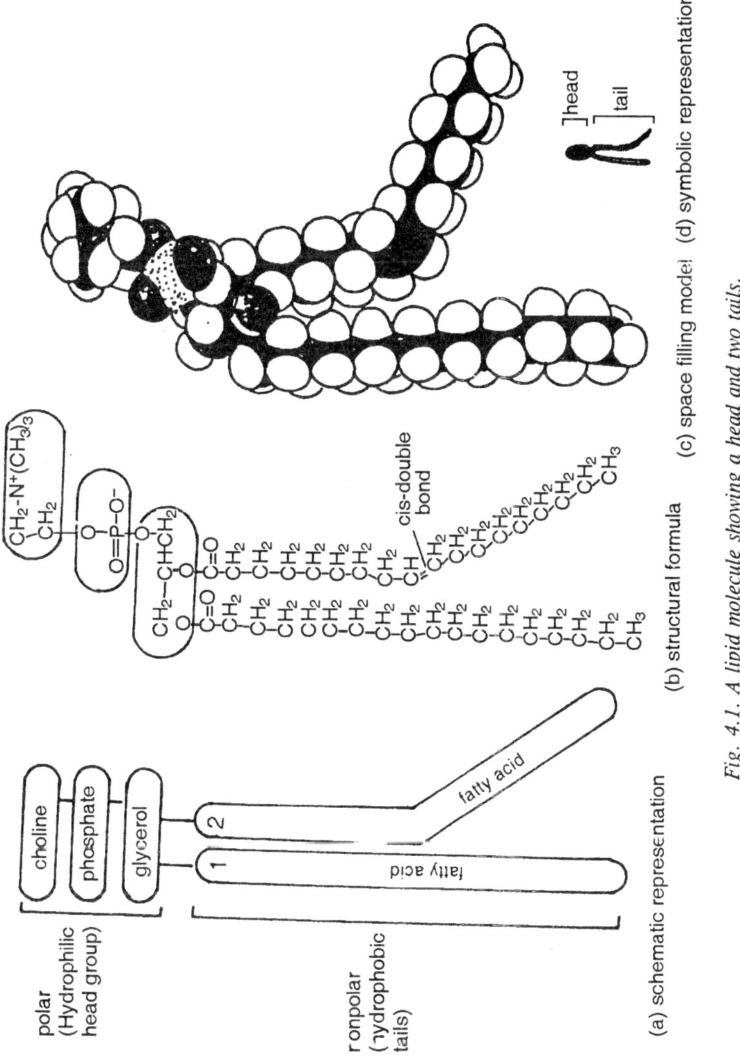

Fig. 4.1. A lipid molecule showing a head and two tails.

cytoplasmic, half of the bilayer. It is assumed that this asymmetry is rather stable and that there is no exchange of lipids across the bilayer.

Carbohydrates

In red cell ghosts hexose, hexosamine fucose, and sialic acid are bound mainly to proteins; the same in true of carbohydrates in liver membrane. Sialic acid is sensitive to neuraminidase and is attached to proteins by N-acetylgalactosamine on the outer surface of the membrane.

Because of the presence of sialic acid residues, as well as carboxyl and phosphate groups, the outer surface of the membrane is negatively charges; consequently, positively charged proteins may be bound by electrostatic interactions to the plasm membrane. Only a small amount of sialic acid exists in the form of gangliosides (i.e., glycolipids) in the plasma membrane of liver. However, gangliosides are important constituents of the neuronal surface and are probably involved in ion transfers. The preferential localization of gangliosides in the acetyl-cholinesterase rich nerve-ending membranes has been demonstrates.

Proteins

Proteins represent the main component of most biological membranes. They pay an important role, not in the mechanical structure of the membrane, but also as carriers or channels, serving for transport; they may also be involved in regulatory or ligand-recognition properties. In addition, numerous enzymes, antigens and various kinds of receptor molecules are present in plasma membranes. Membranes contain three different classes of proteins, structural proteins, enzymes and carrier proteins. *Structural proteins* form the 'backbone' of the cell membrane. They have little catalytic activity and are extremely lipophilic. Their amino acid composition is nearly the same.

The plasma membrane consists largely of structural proteins. The average molecules weight of structural proteins is 3 × 104. Enzymes from the major component of many membranes and are catalytic proteins. The endoplasmic reticulum, mitochondria, and plasma membrane contain many enzymes. The structure of the enzymes varies from membrane to membrane. Some 30 enzymes have been detected in isolated plasma membranes. Those most constantly found are 5' nucleotidase, Mg^+ATPase, Na^+—K^+ activated—Mg^{2+} ATPase, alkaline phosphatase, adenyl cyclase, acid phosphomonoesterase, and RNAs. Some enzymes have a preferential localization; for example, alkaline phosphates and ATPase more abundant at the bile capillaries, while disaccharidases are present in microvillae of the intestine.

A specific localization with a mosaic arrangement has been postulated for some of these enzymes. Disaccharidase forms 5 to 6 nm globular units coating the membrane of the microvillae. The plasma membrane lacks the respiratory chain and glycolytic activity. Of all the enzymes mentioned, Na^+—K^+ activated—Mg^{2+} ATPase is one of the most important because of its role in ion transfer across the plasma membrane. This enzyme is dependent on the presence of lipids and is inactivated when all lipids are extracted.

Carrier proteins or permeases transport substances cross the membrane against the concentration gradient. The molecular weight of structural and carrier proteins are rather similar. The amount of protein varies in different cell membranes. Myelin contains only 20% protein, plasma membranes about 50% and the inner mitochondrial membrane 75%. The plasma membrane proteins fall in two main categories, *intrinsic* or *integral proteins* and *extrinsic* or *peripheral proteins*. The former are firmly associated with the membrane, while the latter have a weaker association and are bound by electrostatic interaction.

Human erythrocyte glycoproteins consist of three chemically distinct regions. (1) N-terminal part external to the membrane and containing all the carbohydrates, (2) a middle hydrophobic region located within the membrane and (3) a hydrophilic C-terminal portion, rich in proline but lacking carbohydrate, on the internal side of the membrane. The middle intramembranous part appears to be intimately associated with the membrane phospholipids. The glycoprotein of human erythrocyte membrane has a polypeptide backbone to which are attached two types of oligosaccharide chains, straight chain and a longer breached one at about 10 sites.

Molecular Structure of Plasma Membrane

All biological membranes, including the plasma membrane and the internal membranes of eukaryotic cells, have a common overall structure; they are assemblies of lipid and protein molecules held together by noncovalent interactions. The lipid molecules are arranged as a continuous double layer 4 to 5 nm thick. This lipid bilayer provides the basic structure of the membrane and serves as a relatively impermeable barrier to the flow of most water-soluble molecules. The protein molecules are "dissolved" in the lipid bilayer and mediate the various functions of the membrane; some serve to transport specific molecules into or out of the cell; others are enzymes that catalyze membrane-associated reactions; and still others serve as structural links between the cell's cytoskeleton and the extracellular matrix, or as receptors for receiving and transducing chemicals signals from the cell's environment.

All cell membranes are dynamic, fluid structures; most of their lipid are protein molecules are able to move about rapidly in the plane of the membrane. Membranes are also asymmetrical structures: the lipid and protein compositions of the two faces differ from one another in ways that reflect the different functions performed at the two surfaces. Although the specific lipid and protein components vary greatly from one type of membrane to another, most of the basic structural and functional concepts discussed in this chapter are applicable to intracellular membranes as well as to plasma membranes.

Lipid Bilayer

The first indication that the lipid molecules in biological membranes are organized in a bilayer came from an experiment performed in 1925. Lipids from red blood cell membranes were extracted with acetone and floated on the surface of water. The area they occupied was then decreased by means of a movable barrier until a monomolecular film (a monolayer) was formed. This monolayer occupied a final area about twice the surface area of the original red blood cells. Because the only membrane in a red blood cell is the plasma membrane, the experimenters concluded that the lipid molecules in this membrane must be arranged as a continuous bilayer.

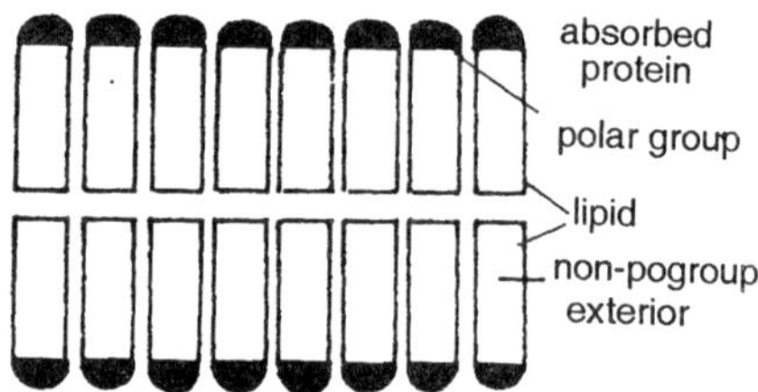

Fig. 4.2. The lipid membrane of Gorter and Grendel (1925).

The conclusion was right, but it turned out to be based on two wrong assumptions that fortuitously compensated for each other. On the one hand, the acetone did not extract all of the lipid. On the other, the surface area calculated for the red blood cells was based on dried preparations and was substantially less than the true value seen in wet preparations. Nonetheless, the conclusions drawn from this experiment had a profound influence on cell biology; as a result, the lipid bilayer became an accepted part of most models of membrane structure, long its existence was actually established.

Daniel-Davson Model or Protein-lipid-protein or Sandwich Model

Harvey and *cole* (1931) indicated the existence of protein by studying the surface tension of cells. This led them to propose a lipoprotein model of the cell membrane. According to this model the plasma membrane consists of two layers of lipid molecules as shown in the lipid bilayer model. The lipid molecules have their polar regions on the outer side. Globulin proteins are thought to be associated with the polar groups of the lipids. The non-polar hydrophobic ends of the two

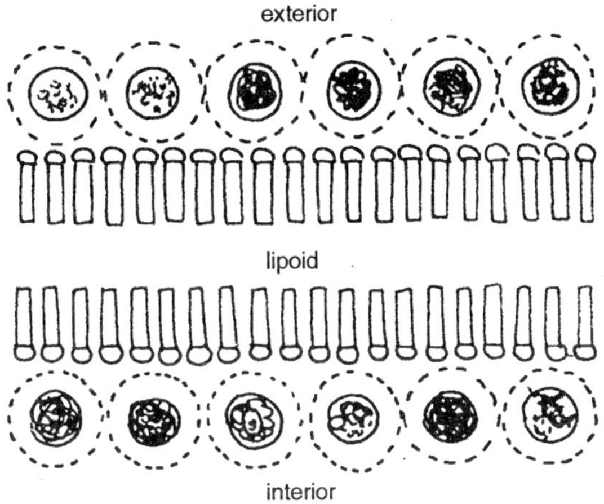

Fig. 4.3. The original Danielli-Davson model.

layers of lipids face each other, whereas their polar hydrophilic ends are associated with protein molecules by electrostatic interaction. Protein-linked polar pores are present in the membrane. These pores are formed by periodic continuity of outer and inner layers of proteins plasma membrane.

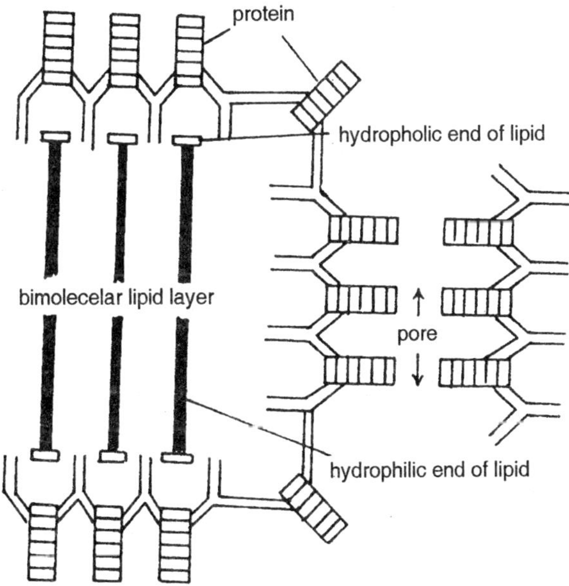

Fig. 4.4. The cell membrane with protein lined pores.

Modifications of Danielli-Davson membrane model

Several modifications of the above arrangement have been described:

(a) With folded proteins on both the surfaces and helical proteins extending into the pores.

(b) With folded β-chain protein on one side and globular protein on the other side.

(c) Coiled α-chains of helical protein on the surfaces of lipid bilayer.

(d) Some plasma membrane have folded β-chains of proteins on both the surfaces of lipid bilayer.

(e) With globular proteins on both the surfaces.

Robertson's Unit Membrane Model

Unit membrane model was put forward in the year 1953 while studying cell under electron microscope. The basic unit membrane structure was considered to be general for a wide variety of plant and animal cells. All cell organelles such as Golgi body, mitochondria, endoplasmic reticulum, nuclear membrane etc., have the unit membrane structure. The unit membrane is considered to be trilaminar with a bimolecular lipid layer between two protein layers. Two parallel outer dense osmiophilic layers of 20Å which correspond to the two protein layers. The middle light coloured osmiophobic layer is about 35Å in thickness corresponding to the hydrocarbon chains of the lipids. Thus the unit membrane is about 7Å in thickness.

In this respect it resembles the Danielli-Davson model it, however differs from the Daneilli-Davson model in that the protein is asymmetrical. On the outer surface is mucoprotein, while on the inner surface is non-mucoid protein. Objections to unit membrane theory.

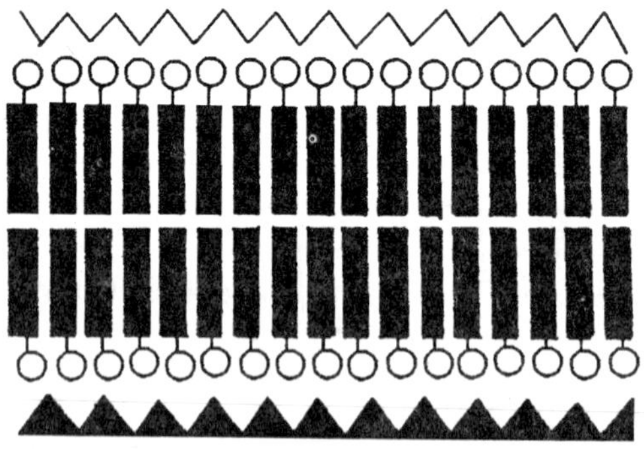

Fig. 4.5. Robertson's unit membrane model.

Objection to the unit membrane model increased during the 1960 and this led to reexaminations of lipid-protein interactions and to new models. Studies of *F.S. Sjostrand* (1963), of smooth endoplasmic reticular, mitochondrial and chloroplast membranes underscored the differences between observed features of membranes and the uniformity that was required by the unit membrane concept. Mitochondrial and chloroplast membranes contain displays of particulate units in or on the membrane. The plasma membrane did not present the same appearance as mitochondrial or chloroplast membranes. It seemed that different models might be needed to described different functional types. This unsuitable approach became unnecessary when a mosaic membrane model proposed.

Greater Membrane Model

Like the trilaminar model here too the lipid layer is sandwiched between two layers of structural proteins. *Robertson* described the different nature of outer and inner surfaces of the membrane. The inner surface was thought to be covered with unconjugated protein, and the outer surface with glycoprotein, which is super imposed on the structural protein oligosaccharide chains with negatively charged sialic acid terminals are attached to the glycoprotein.

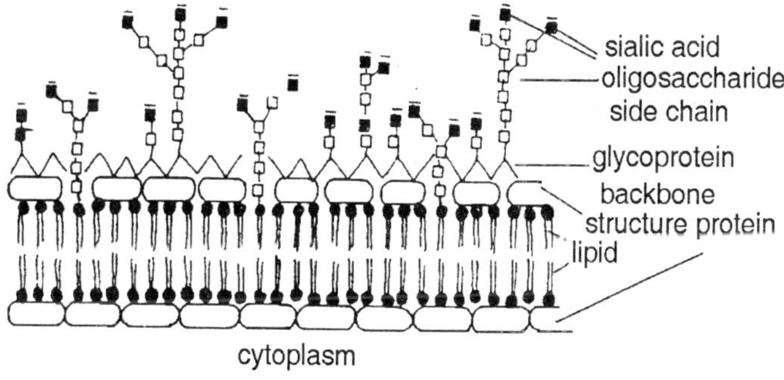

Fig. 4.6. The greater membrane model of plasma membrane.

Micellar Model

An alternative interpretation of molecular structure of plasma membrane has been postulated by *Hilleir* and *Hoffman* (1953). They have suggested that biological membranes may have a non-lamellar pattern, consisting instead of a mosaic of globular subunits know as *micelles,* which have a lipid core and a hydrophilic shell of polar groups. Lipid micelles are possible building-blocks for membranes since they tend towards spontaneous association.

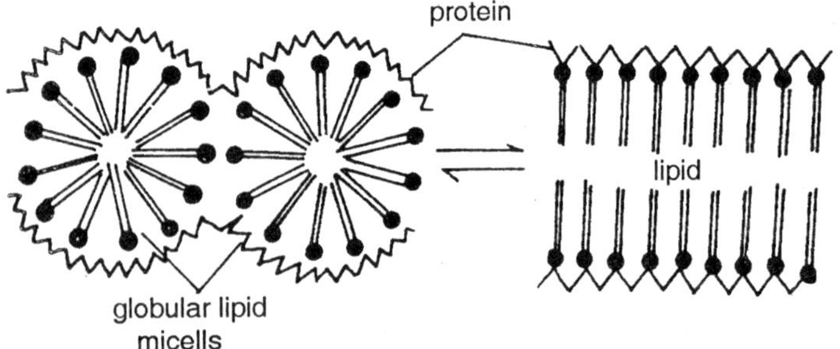

Fig. 4.7. Transformation between micellar and lamellar states of plasma membrane.

In this model of membrane structure the protein components of the membrane may form a monolayer on either side of the plane of lipid micelles. Individual units of the micellar mosaic might be replaced by individual enzymes molecules or by arrays of enzymes with a precise-three dimensional organization, enabling specific functions to be 'built in' to the membrane structure. The spaces between the globular micelles are thought to form water-filled pores 0.4 nm (4Å) in diameter, line partly by the polar group of the micelles and partly by the polar groups of associate protein molecules.

Fluid Mosaic Model

This model was proposed by *Singer* and *Nicolson* (1972). According to this concept, the lipid molecules are arranged to form a rather continuous bilayer that forms the structural frame work of plasma membrane. The protein molecules are arranged in two different manners. Some proteins are located exclusively adjacent to the outer and inner surfaces of lipid bilayer and are called *extrinsic proteins*. Other protein penetrate lipid bilayer partially or wholly and form *integral* or *intrinsic proteins*. The lipids and integral proteins of plasma membrane are *amphipatic* in nature. The term amphipaty was coined by *Hartley,* 1936 for those molecules which have both hydrophobic and hydrophilic groups.

The amphipatic molecules tend to constitute liquid crystalline aggregates in which hydrophobic or non-polar groups are situated inside the bilayer, and hydrophilic groups are directed towards the water phase. Therefore, the lipid molecules form a rather continuous bilayer. The integral proteins are intercalated in the lipid bilayer, with their polar regions protruding from the surface and non-polar embedded in the lipid bilayer. This arrangement explains why the active sites of enzymes and antigenic glycoproteins are exposed to the outer surface

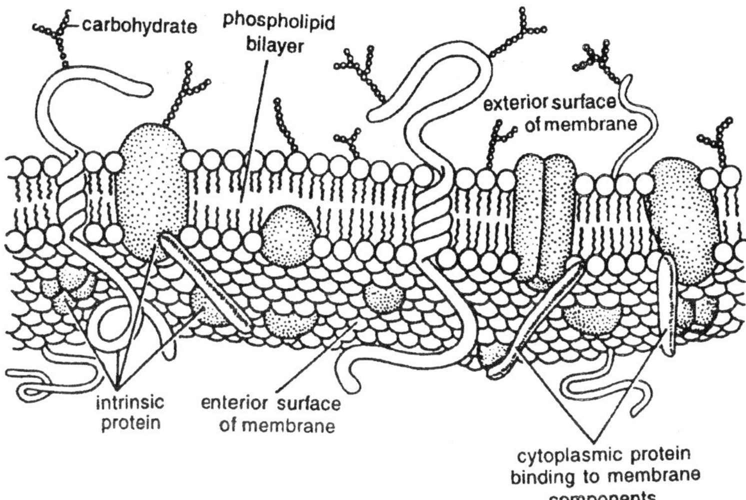

Fig. 4.8. Fluid mosaic model of cell membrane.

of the membranes. The quasifluid structure of plasma membrane explains the movement of cluster of protein molecules of considerable size across the membrane.

Pores in Plasma Membrane

Plasma membrane is perforated by pores. These have a diameter of about 0.35 nm (nanometer), slightly larger than the sodium ions. Less than 0.1 percent of the plasma membrane is perforated by pores while 99.9 percent of the cell surface is impenetrable for ions. Several models of structures of pores have been proposed. Some of them are :

1. *Paving block pores.* According to this concept the pores are regarded to be the corners of the closely filled nearly hexagonal paving blocks of lipid and protein subunits.
2. *Ionophore.* The ionophores are small polypeptides whose one end is hydrophobic and other hydrophilic. The hydrophobic (outer) end dissolves in the membrane while the hydrophilic end (inner side) pick up ions or water-soluble materials and dumps them on the other side. The ionophores help in exchange of substances from or into the cell.
3. *Structural pores.* These are permanent cylindrical holes that interrupt the otherwise continuous bilayer sheet.
4. *Protein channel pores.* These pores are considered to be parts of the lipid-globular protein mosaic model. These form small channels

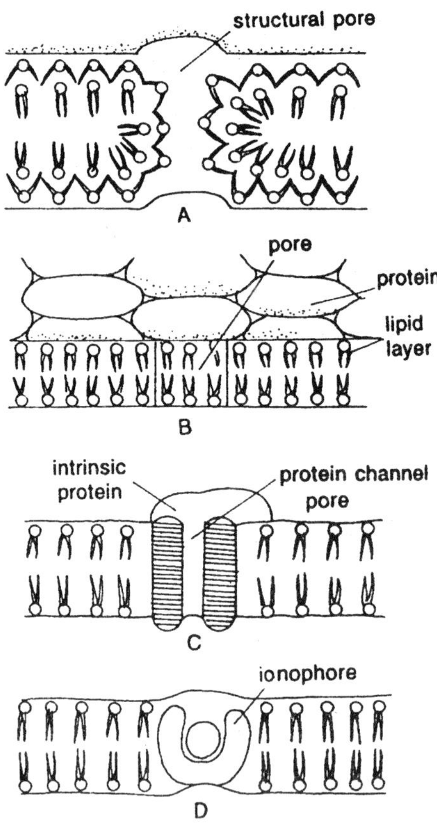

Fig. 4.9. Different models of structure of pores. A—Structural pore; B—Paving block pore; C—Protein channel pore; D—Ionophore.

of specific proteins embedded in the membrane through which ions and small molecules can diffuse.

5. *Dynamic pores.* These pores are transient cylindrical holes rather than being permanent. These appear only at the time of intake.

Specialization or Modifications

With the increased resolution of the electron microscope numerous specialization of cell surface have been recognized. Following description of *Fawceett* (1958) deals with the various specializations of plasma membrane studies topographically.

Microvilli

In the intestinal epithelium microvilli are very prominent and form a compact structure that appears under the light microscope as a striated border. These microvilli, which are 0.6 to 0.8 μm long and 0.1 μm in diameter, represent cytoplasmic process covered by the plasma membrane. Within the cytoplasm core fine microfilaments are observed which in the subjacent cytoplasm form a terminal web. The outer surface of the microvilli a covered by a coat of filamentous material (fuzzy coat) composed of glycoprotein macromolecules.

Microvilli increase the effective surface of absorption. For example, a single cell may have as many as 300 microvilli, and in a square millimeter of intestine there may be 200,000,000. The narrow spaces between the microvilli form a kind of sieve through which substances must pass during absorption. Numerous other cells, in addition to intestinal epithelium, have microvilli, although fewer in number. They have been found in mesothelial cells of the gallbladder, uterus, and yolk sac, in hepatic cells, and so forth.

The brush border of the kidney tubule is similar to the strained border, although it is of larger dimensions. An amorphous substance between the microvilli gives a periodic acid-Schiff reaction for polysaccharides. Between the microvilli, at the base, the cell membrane invaginates into the apical cytoplasm. These invaginations are apparently pathways by which large quantities of flow enter by a process similar to pinocytosis.

Desmosomes or Macula Adherens

Desmosomes are cell junctions found mainly in the cells of simple columnar epithelium. These occur as specialized areas along the contact surfaces. Under light microscope the desmosomes are seen as darkly stained bodies. Under electron microscope these appear as button-like thickenings on the inner surface of plasma membranes of adjacent cells at the point of contract. The thickenings are traversed by fine cytoplasmic fibrils called *tonofibrils*, which form a kind of loop in a wide arc. These filaments stabilize the junction and act as anchoring sites for the cytoplasmic structures.

The plasma membranes of adjoining cells in the regions of desmosomes are separated by an intercellular space about 30-35 nm. It is filled with intervening dense coating material that forms a dark line in the middle. It is formed of mucopolysaccharides and proteins. The desmosomes are primarily concerned with cell adhesion, but also help in maintaining cell-shape, providing it rigidity and cellular support. The former is brought about by the intercellular coating substance and latter by the tonofibrils.

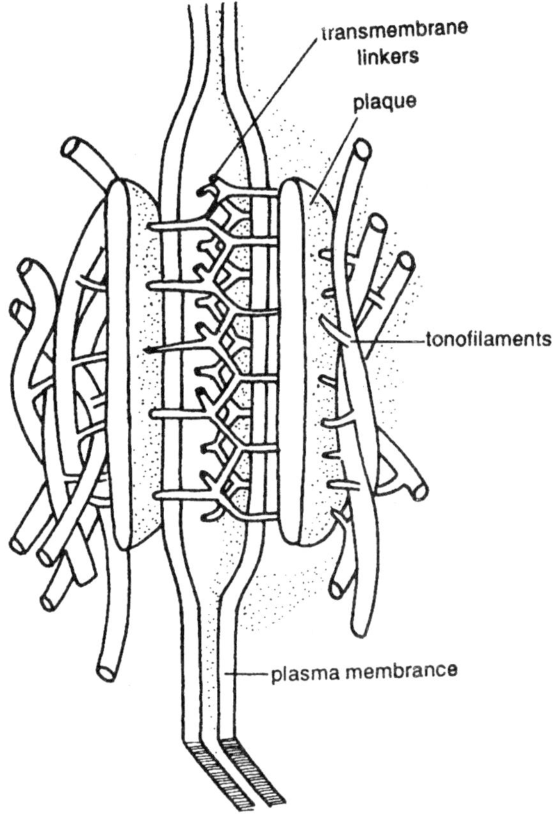

Fig. 4.10. Spot desmosome.

Plasmodesmata

Sometimes, the cells are joined by bridges of cytoplasm passing between pores of cell wall or plasma membrane between the adjacent cells, such connections care called plasmodesmata. They are usually simple but anastomosing plasmodesmata may also found. Their distribution and number may also very considerably. They were discovered by *Tangl* (1879) and were named as such by *Strasburger* (1882). Endoplasmic reticulum often is closely associated with the cell surface, at the points where plasmodesmata are present.

Through them cytoplasmic continuity is often maintained among the adjacent cells. They provide a mean for interaction between adjacent cells which are separated in other regions. Through them the material can pass from cell to cell. It is not known whether all plasmodesmata

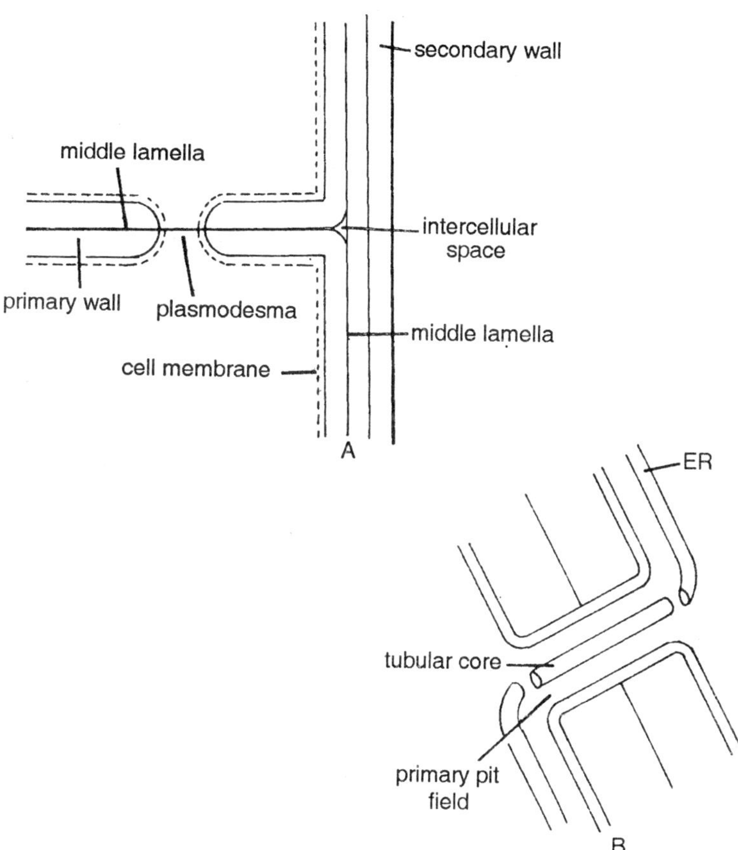

Fig. 4.11. A-B. A part of cell wall showing primary pit field and details of plasmodesma.

are similar to each other. There exist some difference because they are not only produced at the time when cell divides but also formed spontaneously between cells that have grown into contacts with one another, e.g. tyloses in xylem vessel elements. They may occur singly or they can be aggregated into groups. In many primary walls, the plasmodesmata are usually associated with a reduced disposition of wall material, and he area then is known as primary pit or field.

Hemidesmosomes

These are found in the basal surface of some epithelial cells. Their structure is similar to desmosomes but these but these are represented by one half; their counterpart usually represented by collagen fibrils.

Terminal Bars

The terminal bars are also known as intermediary junctions or *zonula adhaerens*. The terminal bars are similar to desmosomes except they lack in the tonofibrils. In terminal bar the plasma membrane is thickened and the cytoplasm of thickened area is dense. The terminal occur in the intermediary portion of the plasma membrane of columnar cells just below the surface. The correct identity of zonula adhaerens is still questionable.

Membrane Interactions

Another aspect of cell membranes that deserve discussion is the interaction between membranes of different cells. Intercellular communication is important in many cell functions and especially during development of the organism, when cells are constantly interacting with other cells. The nature of membrane interactions may vary from complete cytoplasmic bridges between cells to localized areas of membrane junctions that may involve an area of contact as small as a few angstroms or as large as several micrometers. The structural nature of the actual contact generally falls into one of three categories; gap junctions, tight junctions, and septate junctions. *Gap junctions* appear as multilayered structures when observed with the electron microscope. They appear to be two unit membranes closely apposed to each other with a 20 to 40Å gap between. The total thickness of the entire gap

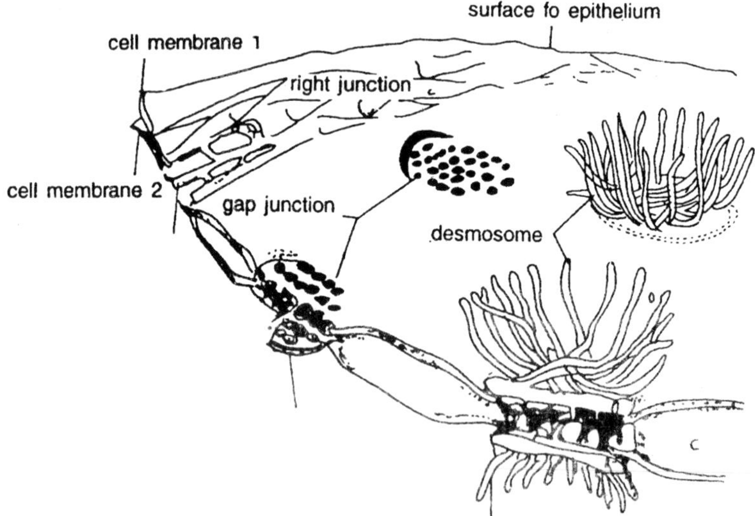

Fig. 4.12. Diagram showing tight junction, gap junction and desmosome.

junction is 170 to 190 Å, and they are found in both vertebrates and invertebrates. They are not found in skeletal muscle fibers or red blood cells. *Tight junctions* are found only in vertebrates and occur in cells such as epithelial cells. These junctions appear to be true fusions between the two membranes, and they are 100 to 140Å thick. *Septate junctions* have been found only in invertebrates. They are much larger than the other types of junctions and are characterized by electron-dense cross bridges that extend between the two cell membranes.

Permeability of Membranes

The membranes of a cell pass small ions and molecules through them. The passage of ions or molecules may occur as passive diffusion, or active transport evolving the expenditure of energy. In passive diffusion, membranes may be classed according to their degree of permeability.

1. *Selectively permeable.* Most membranes of the cell belong to this category. Such membranes allow water and certain selected ions and small molecules to pass through, but prohibit other ions as well as small and large molecules.
2. *Impermeable.* A membrane of this kind allows nothing to pass through it. Certain unfertilized fish eggs, such as trout, are permeable only to gases, water labelled with deuterium does not penetrate the egg.
3. *Dialyzing membranes* The endothelial cells and heir basement membranes of the capillaries and nephron can act as a dialyzer. In this way hydrostatic pressure forces water molecules and crystalloids across the membrane down their concentration gradients while restricting the passage of colloids.
4. *Semipermeable.* No cell membranes are in this category. A model membrane may be constructed to allow passage of water molecules, but no solute particles.

Membrane Function

In order to survive, the cell must exchange with its environment. Metabolic essentials, such as oxygen, salts, and nutrients, must get into the cell, and waste products, such as carbon dioxide and other metabolites, must pass out of the cell. All of these exchanges take place across the cell membrane by a variety of processes. Although it is really not possible to present one unifying concept of membrane transport, it is reasonable to group the membrane transport phenomena by the type of molecule being regulated.

Passive Diffusion

Passive diffusion is straight diffusion of water, O_2, or CO_2 through the cell membrane from an area of greater concentration to an area of lower concentration. The rate and speed of the diffusion is generally proportional to the difference concentration of the substance between the two regions. When the concentration in both regions becomes equal, net diffusion eases.

Free Diffusion

According to a large number of evidences, many substances move though membranes at rates of free diffusion that are directly proportional to their solubility in lipid. Water molecules are a notable exception to this rule, since they freely diffuse through membranes regularly and rapidly. It has been suggested that membranes contain 1 nm-wide pores that are lined by hydrophilic residues. Such openings would be large enough for water molecules but would hardly accommodate other water-soluble substances to pass through the narrow passageway.

The suggestion is quite logical to explain diffusion of water through membranes, but there is little direct evidence to support the concept. Free diffusion along a concentration gradient could be maintained for entry and exit of metabolites and waste products as long as substances were changed or washed away to keep one end of the gradient lower in concentration. If metabolites are chemically changed on entering the cell, then the concentration of the metabolite remains high outside the cell and is kept low inside the cell if it is not retained in its original form. Similarly, wastes leaving the cell could continue to move from the higher concentration inside as long as these substances were washed away or removed somehow from the immediate vicinity of the cell.

Facilitated Diffusion

Certain substances, such as glucose and amino acids, also move across the membrane as a function of a concentration differential. However, these substances do so only up to a certain concentration level. When the concentration of glucose outside the cell surpasses a certain level, the rate of diffusion no longer increases. It has been suggested that this is because certain specific reactive sites on the cell surface are saturated with the glucose molecules. This theory proposes that there are specific membrane associated carrier molecules that complex with the glucose and "facilitate" its diffusion into the cell.

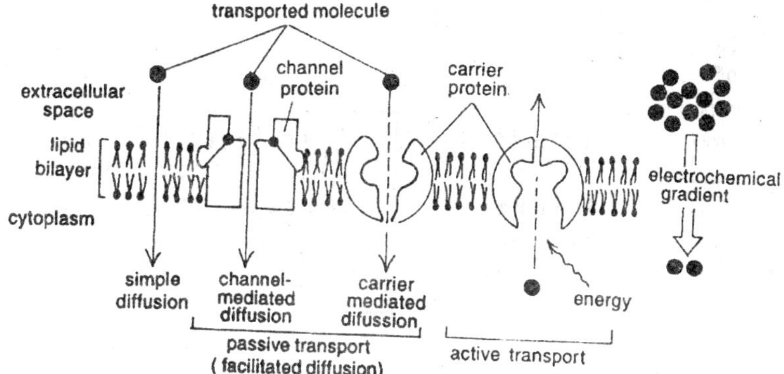

Fig. 4.13. Schematic diagram showing various types of transports across the membrane: simple diffusion, passive transport (down on electrochemical gradient) and active transport (against an electrochemical gradient).

Active Transport

Active transport often involves charged ions, such as Na^+ and K^+, and electrolytes. These substances do not necessarily move across the cell membrane in response to a concentration differential. In fact, active transport is a mechanism that promotes the movement against a concentration gradient and results in the buildup of a marked concentration differential. Because active transport is process that work against a concentration gradient, it is not surprising to learn that it requires the expenditure of energy. The process involves the use of carrier molecules within the cell membrane proper. These molecules apparently shuttle back and forth between the inner and outer cell membrane surfaces and either pick up or release the particular molecule bcing regulated. This entire process involves the expenditure of energy according to the equation ATP $\rightarrow$ ADP^+ P_1 + energy.

Ion Pump

Potassium ions, often, suggest that there must be energy available for such a "pumping" mechanism. *Hepel* observed in 1939 that in animals fed with potassium—deficient diet, the muscle cells exchange almost 50% of their K^+ by sodium (Na) even though under normal circumstances, these cell are practically impermeable to sodium ion. The passage of Na^+ could be carried out exclusively by an active process, which is sometimes called the "Sodium pump". Because there is a good evidence that other ions may be transported by a similar mechanism. We can speak in general of an "ion pump". Such a mechanism was postulated by *Hober* in 1911 under the name of "Physiological permeability". There is a carrier molecule 'X'. What

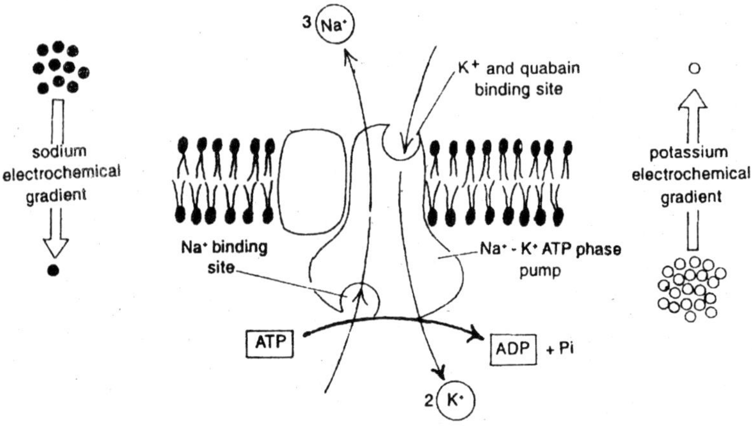

Fig. 4.14. Diagram of the Na^+-K^+ ATPase in the cell membrane.

this carrier X might be is unknown, but in the case of Na^+ and K^+ transport, it is now thought possibly to be ATP itself or an ATPX compound.

The entire mechanism could itself or an ATPX compound. The entire mechanism could work as shown in the figure given above. K^+ combines with X to form K^+-X, which then moves across the membrane and unloads the K^+ to the inside cell, with the X still remaining in the membrane. It then combines with ATP to form ATPX. The later hypothetical substance is then attached by an adenosine, triphosphate giving ADP and inorganic phosphate and free X once again. The free X can then take up another K^+ and the ADP must be rephosphorylated by a mechanism inside the membrane to give ATP once again.

Translocation across the Membrane

The carrier proteins assist hydrophilic molecules across a membrane thickness of 6 to 10 nm. The metabolites are considerably smaller than 6 nm, so it is important to know how these molecules are translocated across this relatively large distance by the carriers. Several alternatives have been proposed, but two have been studied more intensively than the other possibilities. One alternative hypothesis postulates that the carrier binds with the hydrophilic molecule and that then the entire transport protein rotates across the membrane and delivers its bound metabolite to the other side.

The second alternative proposes that the carrier is fixed in place within the membrane, and that the carrier molecule undergoes a conformational change that translocates the binding site across the

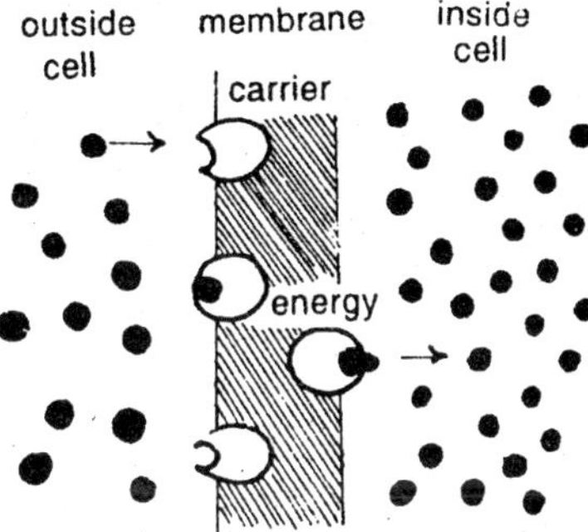

Fig. 4.15. Showing translocation across the membrane by the carrier mechanism.

membrane and the bound metabolite along with it at the same time. Once the metabolite has been translocated the binding site is freed and restored to its original conformation, ready to bind another hydrophilic molecule in another transport event. This second alternative has been referred to as the *fixed-pore mechanism*. The first alternative is known as the *carrier mechanism*.

Transport by Vesicle Formation

Most cell membranes can enclose materials in vesicles and bring the substances into the cell in this way, or package materials for discharge from the cell in a reverse process. The process is called *endocytosis* when materials are brought in, and *exocytosis* when vesicle discharge takes place. Endocytosis has features that are analogous to active transport. For example, substances enter along an "uphill" concentration gradient, and energy is required to support the process.

Endocytosis will stop if poisons that stops energy production in the cell are added, and the process can be stimulated by the addition

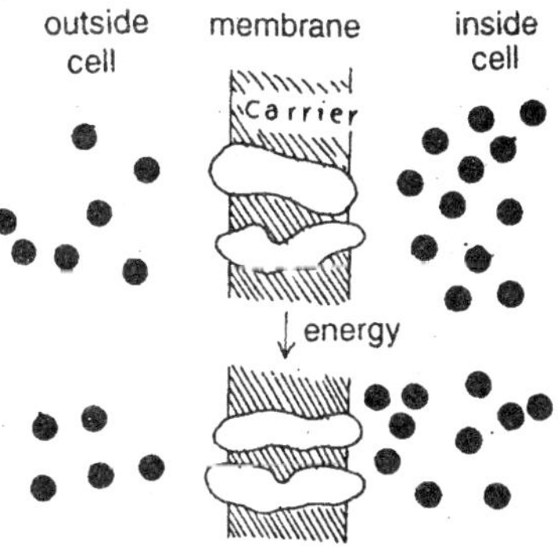

Fig. 4.16. Showing the fixed pore mechanism for selective transport.

of ATP to cells in suspension. Various cell secretions are discharged from the cell by exocytosis. The mucus droplets of intestinal goblet cells, digestive enzyme precursors in granule packages from pancreatic cells, and other cell secretions leave the cells in which they are produced by this general pathway. Although more difficult to see by light microscopy, numerous endocytotic infolded regions can be seen along the plasma membrane in suitable electron micrographs. According to the nature of intake of food or foreign substances, the endocytosis may be classified into types :

Phagocytosis

In some cases, cells may ingest rather larger, solid particles through plasma membrane. This activity is called *phagocytosis* (Gr. *Phagein* = to eat; *kytos* = cell). It is found in large number of protozoans and among certain cells of the metazoans. Among protozoans, phagocytosis is intimately associated with amoeboid movement and is the only means for obtaining nutrition. Among metazoans it is generally a means of defense than serving the cell nutrition. This permits the ingestion of bodies which are foreign to the organisms, like bacteria, dust particles and various colloids. Among mammals this property is found very highly developed in the granular leucocytes.

The particles become absorbed at the surface of membrane and later on they are taken into the cytoplasm by infolding of the plasma membrane which soon piched off forming vesicles consisting of the particle envelope by a membrane. The vesicle so formed may then fuse and assume various sizes, or they may fragment. Is the contact of transportant enough to stimulate the sequence of events culminating in the formation of vesicle? Certainly not. Whatever information available clearly indicate that the organism or substance to be phagocytized must be *cationic* in nature. There are, however, cases when the transportant is not cationic in nature (for instance eating of bacterium by W.B.C.). In such cases it has been observed that the transportant first become coated by a phagocytosis-promoting substance. The substance is called *opsonin*, which is cationic in charge.

Kinds of phagocytosis

According to the physical and chemical nature of foreign substance following types of phagocytosis have been recognized.

(a) *Ultraphagocytosis or colloidopexy.* The process in which plasma membrane ingests smaller colloidal particles is known as colloidopexy or ultraphagocytosis e.g. leucocytes and the macrophagic cells of mammals.

(b) *Chromopexy* When the cell ingests colloidal chromogen particles phagocytotically the process is known as *chromopexy*, e.g. some mesoblastic cells.

Piocytosis

When the ingestion of fluid material in bulk takes place by the cell through the plasma membrane, the process is known as *pinocytosis* (*Gr. pinein*=to drink). The process of pinocytosis was first observed by Edward in Amoeba and by Lewis (1931) in the cultured cells. In the process of pinocytosis, the particle free globules of fluid are surrounded and ultimately engulfed by the clasping folds of the cytoplasm. The plasma membrane forms membranous vacuoles around the fluid globules. Such membrane bound vacuoles are called *pinosomes*. The pinosomes, later on, are transported to the interior of the cell where they are fused with the secretory granules or lysosomes. In the food vacuoles the digestion of food substances takes place and the digested food is diffused to the surrounding cytoplasm. The pinocytosis can be observed ordinarily in the cells by light microscopy.

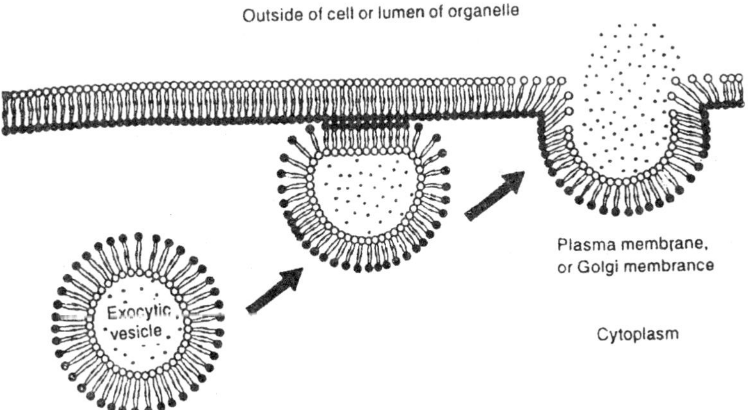

Fig. 4.17. A model of exocytosis.

Micropinocytosis

Electron microscopic observation have been made on the pinocytotic process at sub-cellular or sub-microscopic level ;in he cells. The pinocytosis which occurs at sub-microscopic level is known as micropinocytosis. In the process of micropinocytosis, the plasma membrane invaginates to form small vesicles of 650Å diameter. These vesicles have openings on both outer and inner surfaces which suggest the possible transportation of fluid through these vesicles to the cell.

The micropinocytosis have been observed in endothelial cells, Schawn and satellite cells of nerve ganglion, macrophages, muscle cells and reticular cells, etc.

Emeiocytosis or Exocytosis or Cell Vomiting

The process of exudating the secretory products to outside the cell cytoplasm is known as an *emeiocytosis*. In cells of pancreas, the vacuoles containing enzymes move from the interior of the cytoplasm towards the surface. Here they fuse with plasma membrane and discharge their contents to the exterior.

Origin of Plasma Membrane

There are two interpretation to explain the nature and origin of plasma membrane :

1. Cytoplasm may be passive and plasma membrane may be formed due to accumulation of surface active substances at the phase boundary. Such an explanation gets support from the observation that a new plasma membrane is formed wherever, it is destroyed, resulting into new plasma surface. However, requisite quantities of lipoproteins must be present in the ground plasm, for the formation of plasma membrane.
2. Plasma membrane may be an independent organelle which autonomously enlarges with growth.

A relationship between plasma membrane and other cell organelles has been postulated. In many cases, connections between plasmalemma and endoplasmic reticulum (ER) and also between plasmalemma and nuclear envelope have been shown. It has also been suggested that plasmalemma could give rise to endoplasmic reticulum. However, according to *Frey-Wyssling* and *Muhlethaler* (1955), published micrographs do not clearly settle this issue. Therefore, it is doubtful whether or not there is a direct connection between plasmalemma and ER, but such a connection with Golgi membranes has been shown.

5

CHEMISTRY OF LIFE IN CELL

The life in a cell is due to nucleic acid and the most interesting thing is that the nucleic acid itself is non-living. *Friedrich Miescher* in (1868) isolated a material from pus cells by digesting them for weeks with dilute HCl and called this material as *nuclein*. *Hoppe Segler* and his co-workers confirmed the work of *Miescher* and also proved the presence of nuclein in yeast and the erythrocytes of the birds and reptiles and various other tissues. The term *nucleic acid* was introduced by *Altmann*. *Albrecht Kossel*, *P.A. Levine* and *Walter Jones* described the chemical nature of nucleic acid. According to them the nucleic acid is composed of phosphoric acid, a sugar and nitrogenous bases. *Franklin W. Stahl* presented first evidence that nucleic acid forms the genetic material. *Chargaff* (1951) described the occurrence of nitrogenous bases in equal proportions. *Dotty* (1961) has emphasized much on the physical properties of DNA. In 1962 *Willkins*, *Klatson* and *Crick* proposed a model to explain the double helicular structure of DNA. They also shared the Nobel Prize for the same.

Biological Role

The functions of DNA may be summarized below:

1. It contains the genetic information that is transmitted from generation to generation, which is achieved by self-replication of DNA during cell growth and division so that two daughter double helical molecules of DNA are obtained, each identical to parent DNA.
2. It expresses its encoded genetic information for the synthesis of RNA and proteins for metabolic function and control of all cellular

activities. The genetic information is carried in the form of genes and expressed at appropriate times.

A gene is defined as the sequence of bases in DNA which specifies the complete amino acid sequence of a polypeptide chain or the base sequence of an RNA molecule (rRNA, tRNA). The sequence that specifies a polypeptide chain is commonly called a structural gene.

Most genes of eukaryotic organisms do not consist of a single continuous sequence which is transcribed into mRNA. Rather, they are interrupted by regions called introns which do not specify the protein product. The regions which are transcribed and specify the final protein product are called as *exons*.

Characteristics and Properties

1. *Genetic material.* DNA is the molecule of heredity and is responsible for the progeny to have the same characteristics as their parents.
2. *DNA content.* The DNA content of a cell is remarkably constant for each species (except in germ cells and when chromosomal variations occurs) and cannot be altered by environmental circumstances, with change in age or nutritional status.
3. *Base composition.* DNA isolated from different tissues of the same organisms has the same base composition. The base composition of DNA varies from one species to the other; while the DNA from closely related species has more or less similar base composition.

   In nearly all DNAs, the number of adenine residues is equal to the number of thymine residues i.e., A=T, and the number of guanine residues is equal to the number of cytosine residues, i.e., G=C or A+G = T+C or

$$\frac{A+G}{T+C}=1$$

4. *Effect of pH.* DNA is a polybasic acid due to the presence of phosphate groups which are fully ionized at physiological pH. Because of negative charges present DNA binds strongly to histones and cations like Na^+ and Mg^{2+}. pH also affects the stability of the double helical structure of DNA. The hydrogen bonded base pairs are stable between pH 4.0 and pH 10.0. Outside these limits, their hydrogen bonds break and the complementary strands separate from each other, a process known as *denaturation*.

5. *Effect of temperature.* When highly polymerized double-stranded DNA is slowly heated, the double helix 'melts', as a result the double-stranded structure is converted to a random coil over a range of a few degrees of temperature. This transition from a helix to a coil results in increase in absorbance. The midpoint temperature (T_m) is the melting temperature of the helix of a specific DNA polymer. The T_m's of different DNA's increase linearly as a function of the percentage of G-C base pairs.
6. *Absorbance.* The purine and pyramidine bases found in the DNA and also RNA, strongly absorb ultraviolet radiation of wavelength at 260 nm. This property is used to identify and estimate nucleic acids. The high molecular weight DNA typically has an optical density at 260 nm which is about 35-40 percent less than the optical density expected from adding up the individual absorbances of bases in the DNA. This phenomenon is called the hypochromic effect which is explained by the fact that in a helical structure, the bases are stacked one above the other. Interaction of π electrons between the bases then results in a decrease in absorbancy.
7. *Hydrolysis.* Gentle acid hydrolysis of DNA at pH 3.0 causes selective hydrolytic removal of all its purine bases without affecting the pyrimidine-deoxyribose bonds or the phosphodiester bonds of the backbone. The resulting DNA derivative devoid of the purine bases is called an apurine acid. Selective removal of the pyrimidine bases by hydrazine produces apyrimidinic acid. DNA is not hydrolyzed by dilute alkali unlike RNA because of no 2′-hydroxyl groups.

Enzymes that hydrolyze the phosphodiester bonds of nucleic acids are collectively known as nucleases. Nucleases can be classified by their point of attack upon the polynucleotide chain. Those that attack the polymer at either its 3′ or 5′ terminus and sequentially remove nucleotide residues one at a time or as small oligonucleotides are known as *exonucleases*; those that attack within the chain are called *endonucleases*.

Chemistry of Nucleic Acids

Having identified the genetic material as the nucleic acid DNA (or RNA), we need to examine the chemical structure of these molecules. Their structure will tell us a good deal about how they function.

Nucleic acids are made by joining *nucleotides* in a repetitive way into long, chainlike polymers. Nucleotides are made of three components: phosphate, sugar, and a nitrogenous base. When incorporated

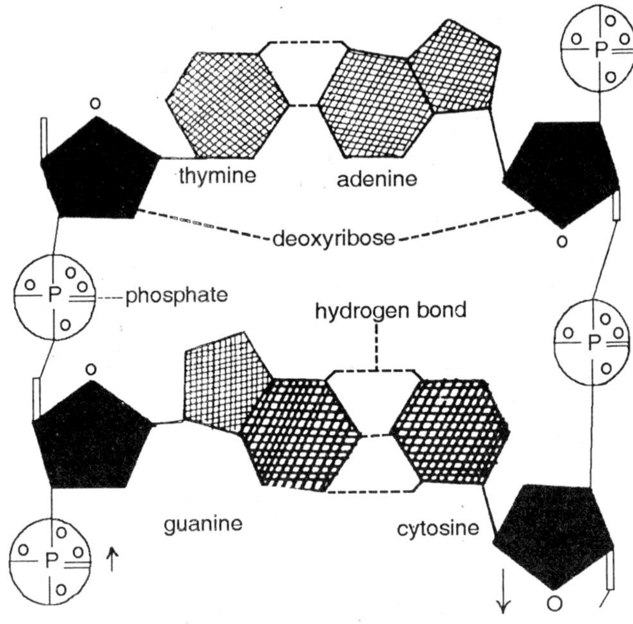

Fig. 5.1. Showing antiparallel nature of backbones of DNA.

into a nucleic acid, a nucleotide contains one each of the three components. But, when free in the cell pool, nucleotides usually occur as triphosphates. The energy held in the extra phosphates is used, among other purposes, to synthesize the polymer. A *nucleoside* is a sugar-base compound. Nucleotides are therefore nucleoside phosphates. The sugars differ only in the presence (ribose in RNA) or absence (deoxyribose in DNA) of an oxygen in the 2′ position. The carbons of the sugars are numbered 1′ to 5′. The primes are used to avoid confusion with the numbering system of the bases. DNA and RNA both have four types of bases (two *purines* and *pyrimidines*) in their nucleotide chains. Both molecules have the purines *adenine* and *guanine* and the pyrimidine *cytosine*. DNA has the pyrimidine *thymine*; RNA has the pyrimidine *uracil*. Thus three of the nitrogenous bases are found in both DNA and RNA, whereas thymine is unique to DNA and uracil is unique to RNA.

A nucleotide is formed in the cell by attachment of a base to the 1′ carbon of the sugar and attachment of a phosphate to the 5′ carbon of the same sugar, the nucleotide takes its name from the base. Nucleotides are linked together (*polymerized*) by the formation of a bond between the phosphate of one nucleotide and the hydroxyl (OH) group at the 3′ carbon of an adjacent molecule. Very long strings of nucleotides can be polymerized by this *phosphodiester bonding*.

Table 5.1. Components of Nucleic Acids

			Base	
	Phosphate	*Sugar*	*Purines*	*Pyrimidines*
DNA	Present	Deoxyribose	Guanine	Cytosine
			Adenine	Thymine
RNA	Present	Ribose	Guanine	Cytosine
			Adenine	Uracil

Functional Structure

Although the identity of the nucleotides that polymerized to form a strand of DNA or RNA was known, the actual structure of these nucleic acids when they function as the genetic material remained unknown until 1953. The general feeling was that the biologically active structure of DNA was more complex than a single string of nucleotides linked together by phosphodiester bonds and that several interacting strands were involved.

In 1953, Linus Pauling, a Nobel laureate who had discovered the a-helical structure of proteins, was investigating a three-stranded structure for the genetic material, whereas Watson and Crick decided that a two-stranded structure was more consistent with available evidence. Three lines of evidence directed Watson and Crick: the chemical nature of the components of DNA, X-ray crystallography, and Chargaff's ratios.

DNA X-Ray Crystallography

Maurice Wilkins, Rosalind Franklin, and their colleagues were using *X-ray crystallography* to analyze the structure of DNA. The molecules in a crystal are arranged in an orderly fashion, such that when a beam of X rays is passed through the crystal, the beam will be scattered. The pattern of the scatter can be recorded on photographic film. The nature of this pattern depends on the structure of the crystal. The cross in the center of the photograph indicates that the molecule is a helix; the dark areas at the top and bottom come from the bases, stacked perpendicularly to the main axis of the molecule.

Chargaff's Rule

Until Erwin Chargaff's work, scientists had laboured under the erroneous *tetranucleotide hypothesis* in which it was believed that DNA was made up of equal quantities of the four bases; therefore, a subunit of this DNA consisted of one copy of each base. Chargaff carefully analyzed the base composition of DNA in various species. He found that although the relative amount of a given nucleotide differs among species, the amount of adenine equaled that of thymine and the amount of guanine equaled that of cytosine. That is, in the DNA of all the organisms studied, there is a 1:1 correspondence between the purine and pyrimidine bases. This is known as *Chargaff's rule*. Chargaff's observations disproved the tetranucleotide hypothesis; the four bases of DNA were not in a 1:1:1:1 ratio. His results were extremely important to Watson and Crick in the development of their model.

Table 5.2. Nucleotide Nomenclature

Base	Nucleotide (Nucleoside monophosphate)	*Abbreviation*					
		Mono-phosphate		Dipho-sphate		Tripho-sphate	
		Ribose	*Deoxy-ribose*	*Ribose*	*Deoxy-ribose*	*Ribose*	*Deoxy-ribose*
Guanine	Guanosine monophosphate	GMP		GDP		GTP	
	Deoxyguanosine monophosphate		dGMP		dGDP		dGTP
Adenine	Adenosine monophosphate	AMP		ADP		ATP	
	Deoxyadenosine monophosphate		dAMP		dADP		dATP
Cytosine	Cytidine monophosphate	CMP		CDP		CTP	
	Deoxycytidine monophosphate		dCMP		dCDP		dCTP
Thymine	Deoxythymidine monophosphate		dTMP		dTDP		dTTP
Uracil	Uridine monophosphate	UMP		UDP		UTP	

Table 5.3. Percentage Base Composition of Some DNAs

Species	*Adenine*	*Thymine*	*Guanine*	*Cytosine*
Human Being (Liver)	30.3	30.3	19.5	19.9
Mycobacterium tuberculosis	15.1	14.6	34.9	35.4
Sea Urchin	32.8	32.1	17.7	18.4

The Watson-Crick Model

With the information available, Watson and Crick began making molecular models. They found that a possible structure was one in which two helices coiled around one another (a *double helix*) with the sugar-phosphate back-bones on the outside and the bases on the inside. This structure would fit the dimension established for DNA by X-ray crystallography if the bases from the two strands were opposite each other and formed rungs in a helical ladder.

The diameter of the helix could only be kept constant (about 20Å—angstrom units) if there were one purine and one pyrimidine base per rung. Two purines per rung would be too big and two pyrimidines would be too small. After further experimentation with models of the bases, Watson and Crick found that the hydrogen bonding necessary to form the rungs of their helical ladder could occur readily between certain base pairs, the pairs that Chargaff found in equal frequencies. Thermodynamically stable hydrogen bonding occurs between thymine

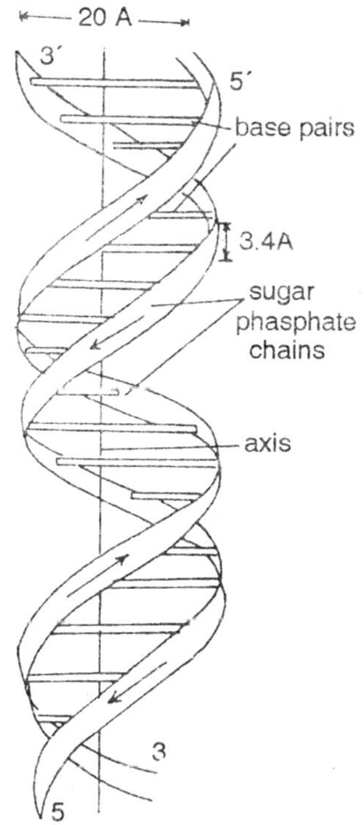

Fig. 5.2. Watson and Crick's model of DNA showing double helical structure.

and adenine and between cytosine and guanine. The relation is called *complementarity*. There are two hydrogen bonds between adenine and thymine and three between cytosine and guanine.

Another point about DNA structure relates to the fact that *polarity* exists in each strand. That is, one end of a DNA strand will have a 5′ phosphate and the other end will have a 3′ hydroxyl group. Watson and Crick found that hydrogen bonding could only occur if the polarity of the two strands ran in opposite directions; that is, the two strands were *antiparallel*.

Molecular Structure of DNA

The DNA molecule is a polymer consisting of several thousand pairs of nucleotide monomers. Each nucleotide consists of the pentose sugar—*deoxyribose*, a *phosphate* group, and a *nitrogenous base*, which may be either a *purine* or a *pyrimidine*.

Pentose Sugar

Levine (1909) identified ribose sugar as a main constituent of nucleic acid structure. *Mori* (1929) isolated sugar from the guanine nucleoside and showed that it is deoxyribose sugar. It is pentose type which in DNA molecule shows the absence of one oxygen molecule from carbon-2 position of ribose sugar. Both deoxyribose and ribose (pentose sugars of nucleic acids) have a pentagonal ring with five carbons, among which two (i.e., 3′ and 5′) are attached to phosphoric acid and three (1) to the base This sugar is called *deoxyribose* and it simply acts as a support column to which bases are attached.

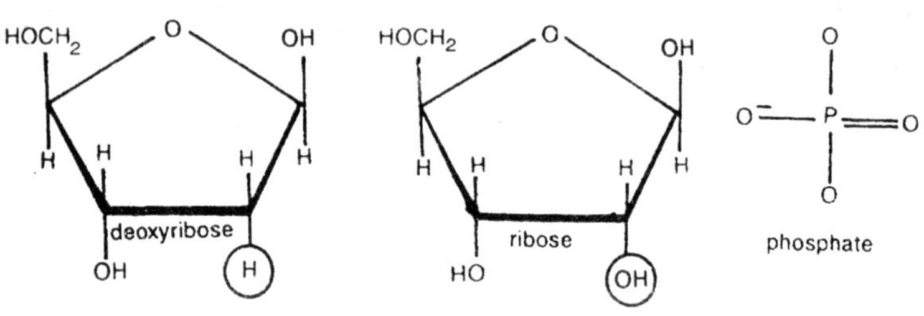

deoxyribose ribose phosphate

Fig. 5.3. Pentose sugars and phosphate.

Phosphate

In the DNA strand the phosphate groups alternate with deoxyribose. Each phosphate group is joined to carbon atom 3′ of one deoxyribose and to carbon atom 5′ of another. Thus each strnd has a 3′ end and a 5′ end. The two strands are oriented in opposite directions. The 3′

end of one strand corresponds to the 5′ end of the other. Consequently the oxygen atoms of deoxyribose point in opposite directions in the two strands. *Phosphodiester bonds* are formed between the sugars of two different nucleotides and a phosphate group.

Nitrogenous Bases

The nitrogenous bases of nucleic acid are of two types: *Purine* and *Pyrimidine*. Purine bases comprise mainly adenine (A) and guanine (G) which are common to both DNA and RNA while pyrimidine bases comprise cytosine (C) and thymine (T) in DNA and in the cases of RNA, thymine (T) is replaced uracil (U). These bases are arranged linearly as the back bones of chains which (back bones) are composed of alternating sugar and phosphate. The base have specific way of combining, if C is found in one chain G will be opposite to it and in other if A is on one T must be on the other. Or in other words adenine (A) is always paired with thymine (T) and guanine (G) with cytosine (C).

Among bases A-T and G-C, two hydrogen bonds are formed between A and three hydrogen bonds are formed between C and G. This hydrogen bond formation precludes A-C or G-T pairs. Only these arrangements A-T and G-C are possible, for two purines would occupy too much space to allow a regular helix and correspondingly, two pyrimidines would occupy too little. The stickness of these pairing rules result in a complementary relation between the sequences of bases on the two interwined chains. For example, if we have a sequence ATGTC on one chain, the opposite chain must have a sequence TACAG.

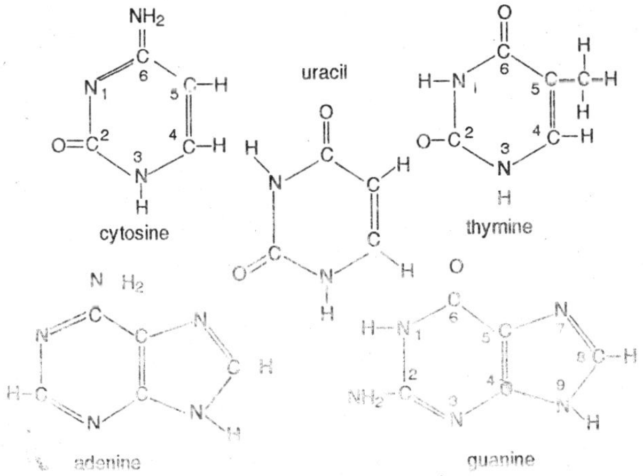

Fig. 5.4. Common nitrogenous bases of nucleic acids.

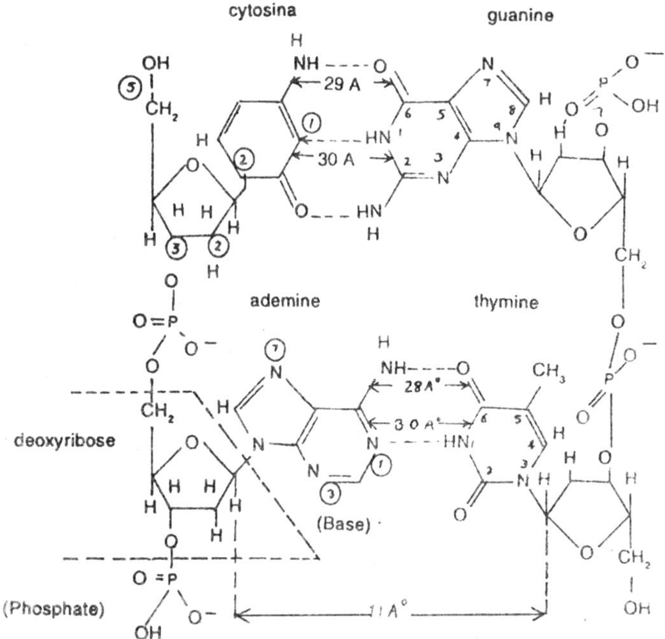

Fig. 5.5. Segment of a DNA molecule.

The hydrogen atom with its positive charge is shared between an oxygen atom and a nitrogen atom, both with slight negative charges. Although hydrogen bonds are weak, the fact that there are so many gives stability to the DNA molecule. The weak hydrogen bonding enables the two strands of the DNA to separate during replication.

The bases are joined to the pentoses by N-C *glycosidic bonds*. For the purine, the glycosidic bond is between the C_1 position of the pentose sugar and the N_9 position of the bases. For the pyrimidines the linkage joins the C_1 and N_2 positions.

Nucleosides and Nucleotides

A sugar molecule and a nitrogenous base form a *nucleoside*, and a nucleoside plus a phosphate group form a *nucleotide*. In other words a nucleoside is a base-sugar combination and a nucleotide is a nucleoside phosphate. The nucleotides of RNA are called ribonucleotides, and those of DNA deoxyribonucleotides. Ribonucleotides contain the sugar ribose, and deoxyribonucleotides the sugar deoxyribose. The nucleosides are usually abbreviated as A, T, G or C, with *d*-as a prefix for deoxynucleosides (e.g., dG-is the abbreviation for deoxy guanosine).

Table 5.4. Four Nitrogen Bases, Nucleosides and Nucleotides of DNA Molecule.

Nitrogen base	*Base deoxyribose =deoxyribo-nucleoside*	*Deoxyribonucleoside + Phosphoric acid = Deoxyribonucleotide*	*Abbreviation for nucleotide*
1. Adenine (A)	Deoxyadenosine	Deoxyadenylic acid (Deoxyadenosine monophosphate)	3´-dAMP
2. Guanine (G)	Deoxyguanosine	Deoxyguanylic acid (Deoxyguanosine monophosphate)	3´-dGMP
3. Cytosine (C)	Deoxycytidine	Deoxycytidylic acid (Deoxycytidine monophosphate)	5´-dCMP
4. Thymine (T)	Deoxythymidine	Thymidylic acid (Deoxythymidine monophosphate)	5´-dTMP

Nucleosides

The nucleosides are compounds formed by linking purine and pyrimidine bases to either D-ribose or 2-deoxy-D-ribose in a N-β-glycosidic bond. The point of attachment of the base to the sugar is N-9 of the purines or N-1 of the pyrimidines to C-1 of D-ribose or 2-deoxy-D-ribose. The carbon atoms of the sugar are designated by prime numbers (i.e., C-1´, C-5´), while the atoms in the bases lack the prime sign.

Table. 5.5. Lists the trivial names of the purine and pyrimidine nucleosides which are related to the bases that occur in RNA and DNA.

Table 5.5. Names of nucleosides.

Base	*Ribonucleoside*	*Deoxyribonucleoside*
Adenine	Adenosine	2´-Deoxyadenosine
Guanine	Guanosine	2´-Deoxyguanosine
Uracil	Uridine	2´-Deoxyuridine
Cytosine	Cytidine	2´-Deoxycytidine
Thymine	Thymine ribonucleoside	2´-Deoxythymidine

Nucleotides

These are phosphoric acid esters of nucleosides in which phosphoric acid is esterified with one of the hydroxyl groups of D-ribose (2´, 3´ and 5´ hydroxyl group) or 2´-deoxy-D-ribose (3´ and 5´ hydroxyl group).

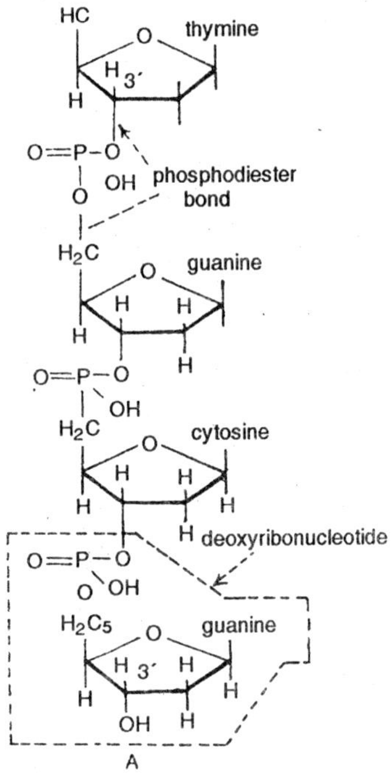

Therefore, 2´, 3´ or 5´ ribonucleoside monophosphate and 3´ or 5´ deoxyribonucleoside monophosphates can be formed. However, the 5´ position is most commonly phosphorylated.

Table 5.6. Biologicaly important nucleotides* and their nomenclature.

Ribonucleotides	*Deoxyribonucleotides*
Adenosine-5´-monophosphate (adenylic acid; AMP)	Deoxyadenosine-5´-monophosphate (deoxyadenylic acid; dAMP)
Guanosine-5´-monophosphate (guanylic acid; GMP)	Deoxyguanosine-5´-monophosphate (deoxyguanylic acid; dGMP)
Cytidine-5´-monophosphate (cytidylic acid; CMP)	Deoxycytidine-5´-monophosphate (deoxycytidylic acid; dCMP)
Uridine-5´-monophosphate (uridylic acid; UMP)	Deoxythymidine-5´-monophosphate (deoxythymidylic acid; dTMP)

* Each of the 5´-monophosphates exists as the 5´-diphosphate and 5´-triphosphate. Thus, as an example, there occurs GMP, GDP, GTP, dGMP, dGDP and dGTP.

Nucleoside monophosphates can be linked to a phosphate or a pyrophosphate group through anhydride bonds to give nucleoside di- and triphosphate, respectively. The compounds are called acids or mono-, di- or triphosphate accordingly. The structure of the mono-, di- and triphosphates of adenosine are shown in figure as examples.

In the absence of oxygen atom at C-2′ of the above sugar ring, the structures are correspondingl known as deoxyadenosine-5′-monophosphate (dAMP), deoxyadenosine-5′-diphosphate (dADP) and deoxyadenosine-5′-triphosphate (dATP), respectively. A list of biologically important nucleotides is present in table.

An important discovery has been the identification of cyclic nucleotides. An important cyclic nucleotide is 3′5′-cyclic adenosine monophosphate (3′,5′-cyclic AMP or cAMP) which is called a second messenger plays a key role in the biochemical action of a number of hormones.

Metabolic Function of Nucleotides

All types of cells contain a wide variety of nucleotides and their derivatives. Nucleotides serve many functions some of which are as follows:

(i) Role in energy metabolism

ATP is the main form of chemical energy available to the cells. It is generated in cells by oxidative phosphorylation and substrate-level phosphorylation. ATP is utilized to drive metabolic reactions, as a phosphorylating agent, and is involved in such processes as muscle contraction, active transport and maintenance of cell membrane integrity. As a phosphorylating agent, ATP serves as the phosphate donor for the generation of the other nucleoside-5′-triphosphates (e.g. GTP, UTP, CTP).

(ii) Monomeric units of nucleic acids

The nucleic acids, DNA and RNA are composed of monomeric units of the nucleotides as building-blocks.

(iii) Physiological mediators

cAMP plays an important role as a 'second messenger' in epinephrinc- and glucagon-mediated control of glycogenolysis and glycogenesis. cGMP acts as a mediator of cellular events. ADP is important for normal platelet aggregation and hence blood coagulation.

(iv) Components of coenzymes

Coenzymes such as NAD^+, FAD and coenzyme A are important metabolic constituents of cells and are involved in many metabolic pathways.

(v) Activated intermediates

The nucleotides also serve as carriers of activated intermediates required for a variety of reactions. UDP-glucose is a key intermediate in the synthesis of glycogen and glycoproteins. CTP is utilized to generate CDP-choline, CDP-ethanolamine which are involved in phospholipid metabolism.

(vi) Allosteric effectors

Many of the regulated steps of the metabolic pathways are controlled by the intracellular concentrations of nucleotides.

Table 5.7. Showing Amount of Various Bases in Different Tissues.

S.No.	*Source*	*Adenine*	*Guanine*	*Cytosine*	*Thymine*	*A+T / G+C*
1.	Human liver	30.3	19.5	19.9	30.3	1.53
2.	Human sperm	30.7	19.3	18.8	31.2	1.62
3.	Hen red cells	28.8	20.5	21.5	29.2	1.38
4.	Rat bone marrow	28.6	26.4	21.5	28.4	1.33
5.	Herring sperm	27.8	22.2	22.6	27.5	1.23
6.	*Paracentrotus lividus* (sea urchin) sperm	32.8	17.7	18.4	32.1	1.85
7.	Salmon	29.7	20.8	20.4	29.1	1.43
8.	Wheat germ	26.5	23.5	23.0	27.0	1.19
9.	Yeast	31.3	18.7	17.1	32.9	1.79
10.	*Diplococcus pneumoniae*	29.8	20.5	18.0	31.6	1.59
11.	K-12 *Escherchia coli*	26.0	24.9	25.2	23.9	1.00
12.	*Mycobacterium tuberculosis*	15.1	34.9	35.4	14.6	0.42
13.	Bacteriophage T_2	32.5	18.2	16.7	32.6	1.86

Structural Variation in DNA

Following three types of DNA have been recognized.

1. Double stranded DNA
2. Single Stranded DNA
3. Circular DNA

Double Stranded DNA

This is the common DNA present in all the living organisms. These contain two polynucleotide chain running antiparallel and twisted around each other in the form of regular double helix. The detailed structure of this type of DNA has already been explained.

Single Stranded DNA

At first it was thought that all DNA molecules are double stranded except during replication, when a small region around the replicating fork is temporarily in a non-hydrogen-bonded, single-stranded form. It therefore came as quite a surprise when experiments revealed that the DNA of several groups of small bacterial viruses exists as single-stranded molecules in which the amount of A is not equal to the amount of T and the amount of G does not equal the amount of C. Among these single-stranded phages are the spherically shaped ϕX174 and S13 viruses and the rod-shaped f1 and M13 viruses.

The chromosomes of the parvoviruses, minute viruses that infect many vertebrate organisms, are also single stranded DNA molecules. When these single-stranded viral chromosomes enter their host cells, they serve as templates for the formation of complementary strands. The resulting double helices in turn serve as templates for new single strands that then become incorporated into new virus particles. Thus, the fundamental mechanism for orderning nucleotides during the synthesis of single-stranded DNA is basically the same as that used for double-helical DNA. Nucleotide selection always occurs by attaction of the complementary base. Single-stranded DNA replication usually differs from double-helical replication in that it uses only one of the two complementary strans (the—strand) as a template for the progeny (+) strand.

Although single-stranded DNA can serve as the chromosome of a small virus, it would not be very effective in storing genetic information within the chromosomes of cells. In bacteria and in many eukaryotic cells (e.g., the haploid phase of yeast cells), there usually is only one copy of a given gene. If interphase chromosomes contained single-stranded DNA, with the double helix existing only briefly during mitosis, then the daughter cells would contain two completely different sets of genetic informations. This follows from the fact that the two complementary chains do not have identical base sequences and hence would code for entirely different amino acid sequences.

The double-strand ensures that each daughter cell will contain the same genetic information. The double-stranded form also permits effective DNA repair mechanisms to exist. For example, when one strand is damaged by exposure to X-rays, the remaining strand can provide the genetic information to rebuild the damaged section. It is probably no accident that only very small viral chromosomes are single-stranded. If they were to become, say, the size of T2, they would present too large a target for chain-damaging events.

Structure of Single-stranded DNA

Single-stranded DNA molecule have a strong tendency to fold back on themselves to form irregular double-helical hairpin loops whenever their sequences permit significant numbers of nucleotides to base-pair. Imperfect as these loops are, they nonetheless are energetically favoured under physiological salt conditions, since they allow much more effective stacking of the flat hydrophobic surfaces of the bases than is possible in any fully extended single-stranded structure.

Often, as many as half the bases of single-stranded DNA are so hydrogen-bonded, and their molecules are highly compacted. If, however, there are only minimal numbers of, neutralizing cations (e.g., less than or equal to 0.01 M Na^+) then the electrostatic repulsion between the partially unneutralized phosphates will keep the single-stranded chains highly extended, and there will be fewer hairpin loops. Single-stranded DNA is always denser than double-helical DNA. Much more complete hydrogen bonding to water is possible for the atoms of the highly regular double helix than for the atoms of the inherently irregularly shaped single-stranded DNA. In the absence of base-pairing hydrogen bonds, Van der Waal's interactions take over and bring the atoms of DNA closer together than would be the case if they formed regular hydrogen bonds with each other. An analogy can be made with behaviour of water, which becomes less dense as it forms the regular, hydrogen-bonded lattice of crystalline ice.

Rigorous Crystallography

X-ray diffraction patterns from parallel-oriented fibers of DNA provided the first clues that the polynucleotide chains of DNA have helical conformations. They also told us that DNA was a multichained molecule composed of two or three polynucleotide chains. However, the double-helical nature of DNA did not directly emerge from X-ray diffraction analysis alone. Equally important was the use of model building in which the question was asked. Given the chemical features of a single DNA chain, into what three-dimensional helical conformations could it fold? The simplest models were those in which the sugar-phosphate backbones were on the outside with the bases stacking in the center.

The double helix emerged when it was realised that thymine and guanine had keto, not enol, configurations and that by base-pairing adenine to thymine and guanine to cytosine, a stereochemically pleasing, regular helical molecule resulted. They were originally discovered through their antimicrobial and anticancer attributes. Each time these intercalating agents become inserted into a DNA molecule, they necessarily *increase* the spacing of successive base pairs along the helical axes to roughly 7Å, almost the distance between phosphate atoms in a fully extended polynucleotide chain. In this situation, very little rotation is possible around the helical axis, and so intercalating agents not only extend double helices, but extensively unwind them. For example, when a molecule of either ethidium bromide (an inhibitor of DNA synthesis) or actinomycin D (a powerful inhibitor of RNA synthesis) intercalates, the rotation angle between the two adjacent base pairs is reduced from 36° to 10°. The fact that intercalation occurs of readily indictes that it must be energetically favoured, with the van der Waals bonds holding the inserted molecules to the base pairs being stronger than those found between conventionally stacked base pairs. Intercalation is additional evidence for the *metastability* of the double-helical structure—its ability to temporarily assume many inherently unstable configurations that normally quickly revert back to the standard B conformation. One such metastable variant must be short stretches of extended chains with gaps separating adjacent base pairs, into which an intercalating agent may bind.

The Chromosomes of Viruses, E.coli, and Yeast are Single DNA Molecules

The first estimates of the average molecular weights of DNA centered at about a million, the size needed to encompass an average-size bacterial gene coding for some 300 to 400 amino acid. Therefore, it seemed natural to equate single DNA molecules with single genes. However, these early reports were inaccurate owing to DNA breakage during its isolation and study. Now it is clear that virtually all undegraded DNA molecules contain the information of at least several genes.

The most certain molecular weight values come from DNA-containing viruses. Regardless of whether the DNA content is relatively small or large, each virus particle contains a single DNA molecule. For example, all the DNA of the small monkey (simian) virus SV40 is present within a single molecule of molecular weight $\sim 3 \times 10^6$ daltons (5×10^3 has pairs, or 5 kbp), while the DNA molecule of the large bacterial virus T2 has a molecular weight of 1.2×10^8 daltons (2×10^3 kbp). In these cases, the entire viral chromosome, rather than separate genes, corresponds to a single DNA molecules. Likewise, the chromosome of an *E. coli* cells is a single DNA molecule whose molecular weight is about 2.5×10^9 daltons (about 4×10^3 kbp) and whose extended length is, roughly 1 mm. DNA molecules of the yeast *Saccharomyces cerevistiae* range in size between the T2 and *E. coli* DNAs, with their average size being that expected if each of the yeast's 17 chromosomes contain one DNA molecule.

The centromeres of yeast chromosomes (if not those of all eukaryotic chromosomes) do not represent discontinuities between separate DNA molecules, but instead are specialized regions of DNA evolved to interact with the spindle bodies upon which chromosomal segreation occurs during cells division. As of yet, there is no direct proof that the very much larger chromosomes of higher plants and animals (often 50 times larger than the *E. coli* chromosomes) also contain only one DNA molecule. However, we now expect that the one chromosome—one DNA molecule rule will hold for the chromosomes of all organisms. In any case, some DNA molecules are larger than any other biological molecules by several powers of ten.

Circular Versus Linear DNA Molecules

Autoradiography and electron microscopy, initially suggested that all DNA molecules are linear and have two free ends. But when it became possible to take a better look at undergraded DNA, many DNA molecules were found to be circular. For instance, the small monkey DNA virus SV40 has a 5000-base pair circular double-helical chromosome; the similarly short chromosomes of single-stranded phages are likewise circular, as are almost all autonomously replicating plasmid DNAs.

Most, if not all, bacterial chromosomes are also circular We suspect that the DNA found in the rare circular chromosomes of higher cells are likewise circular molecules. Circular shapes were initially puzzling, since they seemed to present obstacles to the untwisting of double helices during DNA replication. Only when specific enzymes that first snip and then join DNA chains were discovered did the untwisting dilemma disappear. Equall important is the realization that linear DNA molecules do not have the uncomplicated structures first envisioned for them. As we see in the next chapter, replicating the ends of DNA molecules is not a straightforward process.

All linear DNA molecules have evolved special tricks to replicate their ends, as well as to prevent their free ends from either being nibbled back by cellular enzymes or being enzymatically ligated together to form even larger chromosomes. For example, the ends of the linear adenovirus chromosomes have specialized proteins covalently attached to the 5′ ends of strands; and poxvirus chromosomes have closed hairpin loops at their ends, with their basic structures being that of largely self-complementary circular single strands. Still other linear viral chromosomes (e.g., T2 and T7) have the same sequence at both ends, allowing the ends of the chromosome to recombine together during DNA replication to form very long, end-to-end aggregates (concatamers). Moreover, some DNA molecules that are linear when isolated from a virus particle (e.g., phage λ) are found as circles inside the host cell. This tells us that the linear and circular forms of such DNA molecules are interconvertible. Starting with a closed circle, a specific enzyme introduces two breaks, one in the + strand and one in the – strand. As these breaks are very close to each other, the intervening hydrogen bonds occasionally are broken by thermal agitation, and then the circle unfolds. Most importantly, the resulting linear form contains single-stranded ends that have complementary nucleotide sequences ("*stickly ends*").

As a later time the linear form can base-pair and resume a circular configuration. If the mission phosphodiester bonds are then reformed, the covalent circle is regenerated. There is solid evidence that the phage λ DNA interconverts between its circular and linear forms using precisely this mechanism. Later, we shall see that the duplication of such "sticky" DNAs involves circular replicative intermediates. Thus, the linear form is most likely an adaptation for injection of the viral chromosome through the narrow phase tail.

Supercoiling of Circular DNA

DNA is a very flexible structure, its exact molecular parameters are a function of both the surrounding ionic environment and the nature of the DNA-binding proteins with which it is complexed. Because their ends are free, linear DNA molecules can freely rotate to accommodate changes in the number of times the two chains of the double helix twist about each other. But once the two ends become covalently linked to form circular DNA molecules, the absolute number of times the chains twist about each other (the *linkage number*) cannot change. For the most part, changes in the average number of base pairs per turn of the double helix will necessarily be accommodated by the formation of the appropriate number of supercoils in the opposite direction.

Supercoiling refers to the further twisting of double-helical DNA molecules. Untwisting of the double helix usually leads to supercoiling in the negative (left-handed) direction while overtwisting leads to positive (right-handed) supercoiling. The supercoiled state is inherently less stable than uncoiled DNA, and the cutting, or *nicking*, of a single strand instantly converts a supercoiled molecule into its simple (*relaxed*) circular state. Because circular DNA molecules become increasingly compacted as they become more supercoiled, relaxed DNA is easily distinguished from supercoiled DNA by its slower sedimentation in a centrifugal field and by the longer time it takes to move through an agarose gel. At the present time gel electrophoresis affords the most direct way to measure supercoiling, since it can separate molecules that differ by only single turns.

Just because isolated DNA molecules would energetically prefer to be in the relaxed state does not mean that the "natural state" of DNA is relaxed. In fact, virtually all DNA within both prokaryotic and eukaryotic cells exists in the negative supercoiled state. As such it seldom, if ever, occurs as free DNA, but is complexed with specific DNA-binding proteins to form compacted molecules called *chromatin*. How this compaction occurs is best understood for eucaryotic chromatin, whose most prominent DNA-binding components are the histones. *Histones* are relatively small, positively charged, arginine- and lysine rich proteins that aggregate together to form discrete ellipsoid-shaped packets (histone cores) around which the DNA supercoils. The resulting *nucleosomes* give to chromatin its beaded appearance.

Since the same collection of histones binds to nearly all sections of DNA, histones are thought to play essentially structural roles, as opposed to enzymatic or regulatory roles. Only about half the mass of chromatin proteins is histone. The remaining proteins are not nearly as well characterized with their exact functions yet to be determined. Viral DNA chromosomes are also complexed with proteins, both when multiplying within cells and when packaged into virus particles. The SV 40 viral chromosome is at all time compacted into 24 histone-containing nucleosomes identical it structure to those existing in the chromosomes of their host cells. When freed from its protein components, SV 40 DNA is found as a negative supercoil. In contrast, no histones are complexed with the DNA found in adenovirus particles.

The vertebrate viruses encode a unique DNA binding protein to help package their DNA within their protein capsules. When, however, an adenovirus DNA functions within a cell, its own DNA-binding protein is released and replaced with the same histone components that bind to all other cellular DNA.

DNA Supercoiling Around Nucleosome

In forming the nucleosomes of eucaryotic cells, 200-base-pair-long segments of DNA negatively (left-handedly) supercoil twice around the histone cores. The energy lost by supercoiling may be partially compensated by the energy gained from the ionic and hydrogen bonds formed between the histones and the DNA. The number of supercoils in solution need not be the same as found in chromatin. In chromatin, the double helix is slightly more twisted than in solution, with 10 base pairs per helical turn in chromatin versus 10.5 base pairs per helical turn in naked DNA in solution. As a result, there are fewer superhelices found in solution than found in chromatin.

Histone-like Proteins in Prokaryotes

For many decades, it was believed that bacterial DNA, unlike eukaryotic DNA, occurs naked and does not have a compacted chromatin-like arrangement. But recently, using more genetle preparative procedures, condensed *E. coli* chromosomal sections have been seen that are organized into bead-like packets from which small, basic proteins analogous to the histones can be extracted. That bacterial DNA is complexed with proteins that have histone-like properties undoubtedly reflects its need to be regularly compacted in order to function.

Crystallization of these proteins, DNA-binding protein II, reveals that its 9500-dalton chains associate in pairs as dimers containing extended arginine containing arms able to interact with the phosphates of one turn of the DNA backbone. So it is likely that dimers sited adjacently along prokaryotic DNA are oriented into a helical arrangement with the DNA bound on the outside. Interestingly, the average *degree of supercoiling* (i.e., the number of super-helicle twists per ten base pairs) is about 0.05 for all naturally occuring DNA supercoils, regardless of their source.

Topoisomerases of Supercoiled DNAs

That supercoiling not only occurs but is biologically very important is affirmed by the existence of the enzyme topoisomerase II, which specifically generates the negative supercoils that characterize so much of chromosomal DNA. *Topoisomerases* are a group of enzymes that convert (isomerize) one topological version of DNA into another. They do so by changing the linkage number, which is the number of times two DNA chains twist around each other.

Prokaryotic topoisomerase II (sometimes called *gyrase*) uses the energy of ATP to generate negative supercoils by untwisting DNA in the left handed direction. Its eukaryotic counterpart, however, may be capable of using ATP to generate negative supercoils only in the presence of other, yet to be described proteins. The supercoiling action of topoisomerase II is counterbalanced by a second enzyme, topoisomerase I, which converts supercoiled DNA to the unstrained, energetically more favourable relaxed state. The relative amounts of topoisomerase I and topoisomerase II in cells are finely tuned, tending to create just the right amount of negative supercoiling. Thus, mutations that lower the number of topoisomerase I molecules are viable only if the number of topoisomerase II molecules also decrease.

Both topoisomerase I and II work by catalyzing the breakage and rejoining of DNA phosphodiester bonds. Unlike virtually all other enzymes, their action does not lead to new patterns of covalent bonds. Rather, their role is to create temporary gaps in polynucleotide chains.

When acting topoisomerase do not create free ends but instead become themselves covalently attached to one of the two broken ends (depending on the specific enzymes, either the 3´ and 5´ end). Through such catalysis, a tyrosine group on the topoisomerase becomes linked to the terminal phosphate group of the cut polynucleotide chain. The free energy present in the original phosphodiester bond is thus preserved so that it can be used to rejoin the broken chain. When a DNA chain is broken by a topoisomerase, its broken ends do not fall apart but are held together by the topoisomerase. At no time do the broken ends have the capacity to rotate freely. If that happened, topoisomerase would be limited to only completely relaxing double helices. Instead, individual topoisomerases function to make discrete changes of either one positive turn (topoisomerase I) or two negative turns (topo-isomerase II) in the linkage number. Such discrete steps result from DNA chains passing through either transient single-stranded breaks (topoisomerase I) or transient double-stranded breaks (topoisomerase II). Topoisomerases are constructed in such a way that they can undergo reversible conformational changes that create cavities through which DNA chains can pass.

The ATP requirement for bacterial topoisomerase II (gyrase)-induced supercoiling most likely reflects the use of ATP in mediating the necessary conformational changes that lead to chain passage. Topoisomerase I, however, relaxes supercoiled DNA without requiring a cyclical input of energy. Complete understanding of how topoisomerase

I and II work can occur only when their precise structures are determined through X-ray crystallographic procedures. Even now, however, the prediction can be made that double helices wrap themselves around topoisomerase II in positive supercoils prior to the start of the cutting-rejoining cycle. Without this restraint on the orientation of the DNA, topoisomerase II would break as well as make negative supercoils, and the net result of its action would be the eventual relaxation of the double helical substrate to the uncoiled state.

Looped and Supercoiled Structure

The fact that linear DNA molecules have free ends would seem to preclude their possession of supercoiled segments. Yet, examination of gently isolated linear eukaryotic chromosomes shows that their chromatin is organized into a large number of successive looped domains organized along a scaffold containing two major DNA-binding proteins. Somehow, attachment to the scaffold prevents the rotation of one domain from being transmitted to adjacent sections, since the DNA within each of these loops independently supercoils and may be under different torsional strain.

There is much evidence both from *Drosophila's* giant salivary chromosomes and from the looped lamp brush chromosomes of the salamander that the individual loops represent functional units of chromatin, with given loops usually being transcribed into one or more very long RNA molecules. How the protein scaffold might maintain independently supercoiled loops was a complete mystery until recently. Now it is less so, following the discovery that a major component of the scaffold is none other than topoisomere II.

The data presented illustrate several points:

1. The sixteen possible nearest-neighbour frequencies occur with a large number of frequencies.
2. The sums of the vertical columns show that the amount of A is equal to the amount of T and that G equals C, thus indicating the DNA was probably replicated correctly.
3. The two DNA strands are of opposite polarity. This is borne out by the frequency equivalence of the pairs of sequences: CpT and ApG, GpT and ApC, GpA and TpC, and CpA and TpG, as predicted by antiparallel DNA strands. Were the two strands of the same polarity, different matching sequences would have been predicted, for example, TpA and ApT, GpA and CpT, CpA and GpT, etc.

To show that newly synthesized DNA is made using a DNA template requires two rounds of nearest neighbour analysis. In the first round the originally isolated DNA is used in the reaction and a set of 16 nearest neighbour frequencies are obtained as described. In the second round the enzymatically synthesized DNA is used in the reaction and a second set of frequencies is produced.

The results show good agreement between the two sets of frequencies, thus indicating that DNA plays a template role in DNA replications in vitro. Since the early, comparatively, crude in vitro DNA synthesis experiments, a large number of refinements have been made. For example, the reaction mixtures now duplicate the conditions that are present in growing cells such that it is possible to synthesize DNA in vitro that is identical in all respects with DNA produced in vivo. The reaction mixtures required for efficient DNA synthesis vary, depending on the DNA used as the template. In general, there is a basic set of enzymes and proteins required for the synthesis of all DNA sources. Beyond that, each DNA requires a number of specific proteins for new synthesis to occur, and the actual set of proteins needed depends on the DNA in question.

Types of DNA's

Prokaryotic DNA

Also called the *circular a superhelicular DNA*. The DNA molecules of prokaryotes and most viruses are circular. A circular molecule may be a covelently closed circle, which consists of two unbroken complementary, single strands, or it may be a *nicked circle*, which has one or more interruption (nicks) in one or both strands. With few exceptions, covalently closed circles are twisted. Such a circle is said to be a *superhelix* or a *supercoil*. It has also been discussed already.

Eukaryotic DNA

It is the filamentous type of DNA found in all eukaryotic cells of animals and plants and has already been discussed.

Extranuclear DNA

Also known as non-chromosomal or cytoplasmic DNA. In cytoplasm this DNA is associated with some of cell organelles as given belows:

(a) *Mitochondrial DNA*

Mitochondrial DNA is usually found in cyclic double stranded, supercoiled molecules, the exceptions being the linear mitochondrial DNA molecules from *Tetrahymena* and *Parameciui*. Marmialian mitochondrial DNA molecules are not packaged into nucleosomes. They are about 15 kbp long and can therefore code for 15 to 20 proteins. However, some yeast ones are considerably larger and *Saccharomyces* mitochondrial DNA is 75 kbp long.

Plant mitochondrial DNA is much longer still. Yeast mitochondrial DNA molecules have been widely studied since they are readily amenable to genetic analysis. Mitochondrial DNA can only codes for a small proportion of mitochondrial proteins. Mitochondrial DNA from several mammals, *Xenopus* and *Drosophila*, has been sequenced and the sequence analysed. There are genes for two ribosomal RNAs, 22 tRNA's and for 13 protein most or all of which are involved in electron transport. The only region of mammalian mitochondrial DNA which is non-coding is the *D-loop region* involved in the initiation of DNA replication. This is also the region at which transcription of both strands is initiated.

Transcription continues uninterrupted around the cyclic molecule and the transcripts are the processed to give individual messenger, ribosomal and tRNAs. The tRNA forms the puncturation between the various protein coding regions and provides the signals for the processing enzymes. Plant mitochondrial DNA is apparently much more complex than animal mitochondrial DNA. It consists of per mutation of basic structure related to each other by recombination.

(b) Chloroplast DNA

Chloroplast DNA is in general much larger than mitochondrial DNA, being in the molecular weight range 100 million (150 kbp). In contrast to mitochondria which have from one to ten molecules of DNA per organelle, chloroplasts tend to have a very large number of copies of the DNA molecules in each organelle, in some cases greater than one hundred. Like mitochondrial DNA, the DNA in chloroplasts carries the coding information for essential membrane components, tRNA and rRNA. All known chloroplast DNA molecules are cyclic and supercoiled.

(c) Kinetoplasts DNA

The kinetoplast is part of highly specialized mitochondrion found in certain groups of flagellated protozoa such as trypanosome. Its DNA (kDNA) consists of an interlinked series of many thousands of cyclic DNA molecules which vary in size from 0.6 kbp to 2.4 kbp depending from the type of trypanosomes from which they are obtained. These components, which are known as *minicircles*, are further interlinked with a much smaller number of larger circular DNA molecules of above 30 kbp in size known as *maxicircles* in the majority of system analyzed. While maxicircles appear to perform the connectional functions of mitochondrial DNA in trypanosomes, minicircles are microheterogenous in sequence and size and there is no evidence to suggest that they are ever transcribed so that it is possible that they may fulfil some structural rather than coding role.

Satellite DNA

At the other extreme DNA with a $Cot_{1/2}$ value as low as 10^{-3} moles of nucleotide seconds $litre^{-1}$ consists largely of *satellite DNA*. This represents highly repeated sequences of which there may be a million or more copies per haploid genome, which are usually quite short and are arranged in tandem arrays. The origin of the name satellite relates to the method of its isolation on caesium chloride buoyant density gradients of sheared DNA where it will sometimes form a satellite band separate from main DNA band, due to its differing content of adenine and thymine residues.

The simplest known DNA is poly [d(A-T)], which occurs in certain crabs. Other satellites can have any number upto several hundred base pair which are repeated in tandem fashion along the genome. The distribution of satellite DNA among chromosomes varies. Some chromosomes have virtually no satellite sequences while others are largely composed of satellite sequences. In general, satellite DNA appears to be concentrated near the centromere of the chromosomes in the heterochromatin fraction. DNA sequence analysis has shown that the basic repeat unit of satellite DNA is itself made up of sub repeats. For example, the major momse satellite has a repeating structure of 234 base pairs made up of four related 58 and 60 bp segments each in turn made up of 28 and 30 bp sequences. The satellite between and within the related species are themselves related in an evolutionary sense by cyclic rounds of multiplication and divergence of an initial short sequence.

Fold-back DNA

Also known as *palindromic DNA*. It is a special class of DNA sequences comprising 3-6% eukaryotic DNA. The size range is from 300 to 1200 base pairs and the molecules have a $Cot_{1/2}$ value of less than 10^{-5} moles of nucleotide second $litre^{-1}$. This palindromic DNA is represented in all frequency classes and is widely distributed throughout the metaphase chromosomes. Some palindromic DNA arises when two copies of the *Alu* sequences are present close to one another in opposite orientations and it was a result of the ability of such DNA to renative instantaneously.

Tautomeric form of DNA

An important chemical feature of DNA is the position of the hydrogen atoms in the purine and pyrimidine bases. Before 1953, many chemists thought that some of these hydrogen atoms randomly moved from one ring nitrogen or oxygen atoms to another and so could not be assigned a fixed location. Now we realize that although such movements, called *tautomeric shifts* do occur, these hydrogens have preferred atomic locations.

The nitrogen atoms attached to the purine and pyrimidine rings are usually in the *amino* (NH_2) form and only rarely assume the *imino* (NH) configuration. Likewise, the oxygen atoms attached to the C6 atoms of guanine and thymine normally have the *keto* (C-O) from and only rarly take up to *enol* (COH) configuration. It is essential to the biological functioning of DNA that the hydrogen atoms have relatively stable locations. If the hydrogen atoms had no fixed positions, adenine could often pair with cytosine and guanine with thymine, and sequence of the bases on the two intertwined chains would not necessarily be complementary. If that were the case, the DNA could not function as a genetic molecule, for it is the complementary relationship between the opposing chain sequences that gives DNA its capacity for self-replication.

Replication of the double helix involves strand separation followed by formation of complementary DNA chains using the now free single strands as templates to attract the appropriate partner bases dictated by AT and GC base-pairing rules. The amino forms adenine and cytosine and the enol forms of guanine and thymine must indeed occur only very rarely compared to their amino and keto alternatives. Otherwise, the many errors (mutations) incurred during DNA replication would be incompatible with orderly cell growth and division.

Unique DNA

In human cells it is generally classified as that DNA which has a $Cot_{1/2}$ value of about 1000 moles of nucleotide seconds $litre^{-1}$. It comprises about half of the total haploid DNA content and is thought to consist of the sequences coding for most enzyme functions for which there is only one or a small number of genes per haploid genome. The genes coding for the various chains of globin or the enzyme glucose 6-phosphates fall into this category.

Repetitive DNA

In this type of DNA certain bases or nucleotides are repeated many times. Among the repetitive DNA is a fraction which reanneals with a Cot value of between 100 and 1000 moles of nucleotides seconds litre^{-1}. The sequences represented in this group are generally thought to be those coding for proteins which form major structural components of the cell such as the histones. The genes for rRNA and tRNA also fall into this category.

Z-DNA or Left Handed DNA

On the basis of the arrangement of pentose sugar forming chains of DNA two forms of DNA have been reported. Usually the sugar chain has the pentose sugar with ascending sequence of carbon atoms. This is right handed DNA or B-DNA. Recently in 1979, another form of DNA have pentose sugar with ascending arrangement of carbon atom has been reported and named Z-DNA or left handed DNA.

(a) Resemblances between Z-DNA and B-DNA

(i) Both are double helical.

(ii) The two strands of double helix are antiparallel in both DNAs.

(iii) Both forms exhibit G≡C pairing.

(b) Differences between Z-DNA and B-DNA

(i) Z-DNA has left handed helical sense as against right handed helical sense of B-DNA.

(ii) Due to a different arrangement of molecules within the Z-DNA polymer, the phosphate backbone follows a zig-zag course, while in B-DNA it is regular.

(iii) In Z-DNA, the sugar residues have alternating orientation so that repeating unit is a dinucleotide as against the B-DNA where repeating unit is a mononucleotide and the orientation of sugar molecules is not alternating.

(iv) In Z-DNA, one complete helix i.e. a twist through 360°, has twelve base pairs or six repeating dinucleotide units (12 base pairs) while in B-DNA, one complete helix has only ten base pairs or ten repeating units.

(v) Because twelve base pairs are accommodated in one helix in Z-DNA, as against ten in B-DNA, the angle of twist per repeating unit (dinucleotide) is 60° as against 36° in B-DNA.

(vi) One complete helix is 45Å in Z-DNA it is 34Å in B-DNA.

(vii) Since bases get more length spread out in Z-DNA and since the angle of tilt is 60°, they are more closer to the axis and hence the diameter of the Z-DNA molecule is 18Å, whereas it is 20Å in B-DNA.

DENATURATION AND RENATURATION OF DNA

Single-stranded DNA

Single-stranded DNA molecules rarely occur naturally. The best known example is the DNA molecule from the small spherical bacteriophage ϕX174 first isolated by *Sinsheimer* in 1959 but it is also found in the filamentous bacteriophages such as fd. Among the animal viruses single-stranded DNA is found in the parvo viruses. Some of these naturally occurring single-stranded DNA's are circular and other linear. The former can be distinguished by their insensitivity to exonucleases. In general they are comparatively small molecules with less than 10,000 nucleotides.

The molar proportions of the bases do not show the usual equivalence of A and T, and G and C, required for double helix formation and the bases react readily with formaldehyde since the amino groups are not protected by hydrogen bondings as they are in double stranded DNA. Single-stranded DNA molecules are very much more flexible than double-stranded molecules of the same size since they lack the rigid double helical structure. In general they behave in solution in a manner similar to RNA molecules.

Hypochromic Effect

When double stranded DNA molecules are subjected to extremes of temperature of pH, the hydrogen bonds in the double helix are ruptured and the DNA collapses into two single-stranded molecules. If heat is used as the denaturant, the temperature at which this collapse occurs is known as the T_m or transition temperature. The absorption at 260 nm of any polynucleotide is due to that of its component bases. However, this absorption tends to be suppressed in the double-stranded DNA molecule where the bases are stacked above one another and inhibited from swinging out freely in solution in hydrogen bonds, and consequently it is very much lower than that of equimolar amounts of the component bases or nucleotides free in solution. This inhibition of absorption is to some extent relieved when the DNA molecule goes through the helix-coil transition and the bases are no longer so rigidly stacked although they still interact to some extent.

As a consequence of this absorption of DNA solutions rises by about 20-30 percent as the DNA undergoes the melting process, and the transition process is usually measured by ultraviolet spectroscopy.

The increase in absorbance on melting is known as the *hyperchromic effect*.

Such a transition can be characterized by several factors:

1. *The nature of the DNA*. Homogenous DNA, such a viral DNA, melts over a short temperature range but heterogeneous DNA melts over a longer range.
2. *The (G + C) content of the DNA*. The melting temperature of any DNA can be related to its (G+C) content since this base pair confer extra stability on the molecule. In DNA molecules such as those from bacteriophage l, in which some regions are richer in (G+C) than others, the transitions of both regions can be observed.
3. *The nature of the solvent.* In low concentrations of counterion the transition temperature is low and its width broad. At high concentrations of counterion the T_m is raised and with width of the transition becomes sharp. However, if 'denaturing' salts such as sodium perchlorate are present, addition of more salt will lower the T_m since the rupture of apolar bonds caused by the anion will overcome the ionic stabilization of the cation.

The helix-coil transition is also associated with a change in density of the DNA molecule, the single-stranded DNA being more dense than the equivalent double stranded form with the same (G+C) content.

The Renaturation of DNA

When two DNA strands are returned from the extreme conditions which caused them to melt to their original state they may reassociate to form a double helix again. However, whether or not they do so depends on a variety of factors. In principle the process should follow simple second-order kinetics but, because of the high probability of two sequences which were not previously matched forming an imperfect union which is then difficult to dissociate, the degree of renaturation can vary from less than 1 percent according to the nature of the sample and the conditions of renaturation.

1. *The nature of the sample*. Simple sequence DNA molecules such as $d(G)_a$ $d(C)_n$ have no difficulty finding the appropriate sequence with which the reanneal and do so without difficulty. However, if a eukaryotic DNA sample from a large genome is reannealed, clearly some of the sequences will have to encounter many other non-complementary sequences in solution before they find the correct partner. Thus if most of the DNA from eukaryotic cells

is quickly cooled to a low temperature, so that the diffusion of the DNA in solution is inhibited, few of the single strands will reassociate.

2. *The temperature of the reassociation process.* At very low temperatures (4°C) not only a diffusion limited but, for a DNA molecule which has become mismatched with a strand having only a few complementary bases, the opportunities to break away and continue its search for the correct complementary strands are reduced. Consequently DNA which is heated beyond the T_m and then quickly cooled to a low temperature will be denatured whereas solutions maintained at high temperatures below the T_m may renature.
3. *The size of the DNA fragments.* Large string-like fragments of single-stranded DNA encounter diffusion problems and frequently cannot reanneal correctly since this effectively reduces their opportunities for finding complementary strands. For this reason DNA is often sheared for reannealing experiments.
4. *The ionic strength of the solution.* Two highly charged DNA molecules are likely to repel one another, and the presence of salt is necessary to mask this repulsion in renaturation.
5. *The concentration of the DNA.* Clearly, at higher concentrations the probability of two complementary strands encountering each other is raised.
6. *The time allowed for reannealing experiments.* If renaturation is allowed under ideal conditions, two DNA samples of identical concentration should take different times to reanneal according to the genome size. For this reason the term *Cot value* has been defined for the study of reannealing of DNA and also for the study of the formations of DNA-RNA hybrids. *Co* represents the DNA concentration and *t* represents time in seconds. This is again monitored by ultraviolet spectroscopy or, more frequently, by hydroxyapatite chromatography since this can be used to separate double- and single-stranded DNA molecules and can be used at higher concentrations and hence for shorter times.

6

Mediator Nucleic Acid

Ribonucleic acid usually occurs in nature as long unbranched polymeric molecule formed of single chain. RNA is generally present in the cytoplasm as well as in nucleolus. *Casperson* 1950 and *Brachet* in 1955 suggested that there is an association between RNA and protein synthesis. A large number of studies have been undertaken to characterise physically the nature and structure of RNA and their biochemical properties and by now we have acquired a lot of knowledge about the various types of RNA and their molecular structures but still there are various gaps to be filled to make a complete picture. Some plant viruses (e.g., TMV, turnip yellow mosaic viruses, wound tumour viruses, etc.), animal viruses (e.g., influenza viruses, foot and mouth viruses; rous sarcoma viruses, poliomyelitis viruses reoviruses, etc.) and bacteriophages (e.g., MS2, etc.) contain ribonucleoic acid (RNA) as their genetic material. That is why in these cases it is called the *Genetic RNA*.

Table 6.1. Genetic RNA in Different Viruses

Types of Viruses	*Name of Viruses*	*Type of RNA*
1. Plant viruses	1. TMV	1. Single stranded
	2. Wounded tumour	2. Double stranded
2. Animal viruses	3. Influenza virus	3. Single stranded
	4. Poliomyelitis	4. Single stranded
	5. Reo virus	5. Double stranded
3. Bacteriophages	6. MS_2	6. Single stranded
	7. F_2	7. Single stranded
	8. r_{17}	8. Single stranded

Molecular Weight of RNA

The molecular weight of RNA may be determined by light scattering measurements, by sedimation velocity measurements, by viscosity measurements, by equilibrium ultracentrifugation or by polyacrylamide gel electrophoresis in formawide.

Bacteria, *Actinomycetes,* blue green algae and higher plant chloroplasts all have rRNA's of molecular weight 1.1×10^6 (23S) and 0.55×10^6 (16S) whereas the corresponding values for higher plants, ferns, algae, fungi and some protozoa are 1.3×10^6 (26S) and 0.7×10^6 (18S). The 18S components is common to all animals, but the large 28S component has evolved from 1.4×10^6 daltons in sea urchins to 1.75×10^6 daltons is mammals. In mitochondria (mammalian), the rRNA's are somewhat smaller's the 21S species is 0.56×10^6 daltons and the 12S species 0.36×10^6 daltons. Whlst the ribosomal RNAs form most organisms possess broadly similar base compositions with G plus C content between 50 and 60 percent, there are some exceptions to this, e.g. *Drosophila* (40%) and *Tetrahymena* (43%).

Primary Structure of RNA

RNA usually occur in nature as long unbranched polymeric molecule made up of single chain or helix of polynucleotide strand: Ribnucleic acid is composed of pentose sugars, phosphoric acid and nitrogenous bases. The pentose sugar of RNA is ribose sugar. The sugar forms the back bone along with the phosphoric acid just in a manner studied in DNA.

Phosphoric acid is also one of the constituent of the RNA which along with the pentose sugar forms the back bone, on which the nitrogenous bases are linearly arranged, as shown in the Fig. On the bases of phosphate or phosphoric acid, the chemical constituents of RNA can be written in two ways:

Nitrogenous Base + Ribose Sugar + Phosphate = Nucleotides

Nitrogenous Base + Ribose Sugar = Nucleoside

The nitrogenous bases of ribonucleic acid are of two types:

(i) Purine

(ii) Pyrimidine.

Purine bases comprise mainly adenine (A) and guanine (G) while Pyrimidine bases comprise cytosine (C) and Uracil (U).

These bases are joined to the pentoses by N-C *glycosidic bonds.* For the purine bases the glyclosidic bond is between the C_1 position of the pentose sugar and the N_9 position of the base. For the pyrimidines, the linkage joins the C_1 and N_3 positions in figure given below:

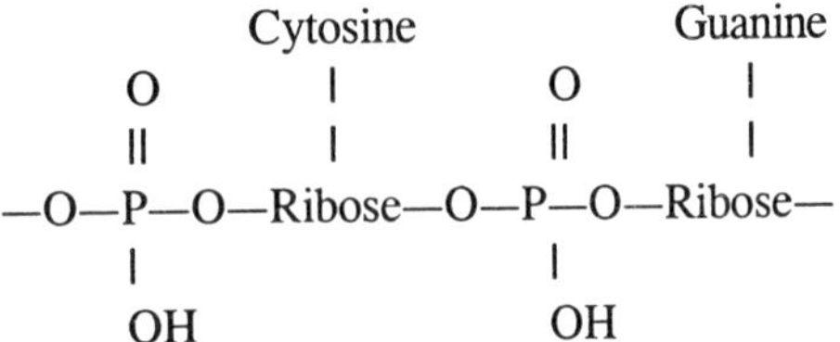

The bases are arranged on the back bone of the chain which is composed of alternating sugar and phosphate. The bases are attached to the ribose sugar in the same way, the bases in DNA are attached.

Secondary Structure of Ribonucleic Acid

Generalization as to the secondary structure of RNA is probably less justified than in the case of DNA, as the available information is much less extensive. The available information does permit the following conclusions:

1. There is no evidence for the existence of more than one polyribonucleotide strand in the natural RNAs.

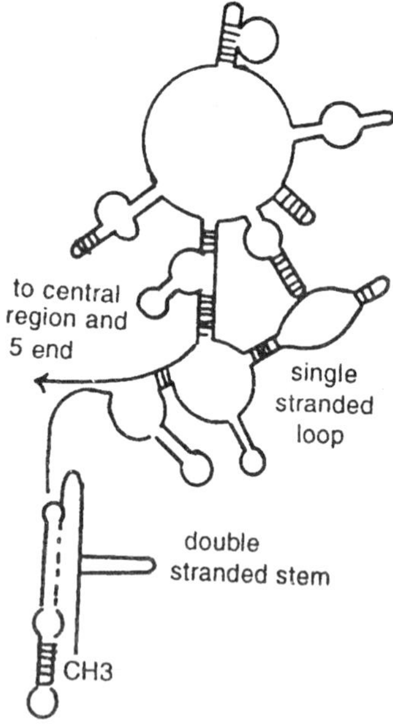

Fig. 6.1. Showing the secondary structure of RNA.

2. Hence the helical regions of natural RNA arise from the hair pin like bending of the single strand back upon itself.
3. The helical regions are stabilized by A—U and C—G interactions similar to those which stabilize the confirmation of DNA. However, the irregular base composition of RNA does not allow the incorporation of the entire molecule into double perfect helix of this type, and the helical zone co-exist with the random segments.
4. Two alternative models for the structure of RNA may be postulated:

(a) The non-helical fraction of RNA may take the form of extended amorphous zones separating segments of nearly perfect helical organization. This model pre-suppose that extensive complementary sequences exist within the single strand. These tend to seek each other out to form perfect or nearly perfect, helical regions.

(b) Alternatively, nucleotides which do not participate in the helical organization may occur largely as numerous small loops external to the helically paired structure.

Types of Ribonucleic Acid

Four types of ribonucleic acids have been studied and they are as follows:

1. mRNA
2. tRNA
3. rRNA
4. vRNA

1. Messenger RNA (mRNA)

Studies by *Huxley* and later by *Volkin* and *Astrachan* with T_2 bacteriophage infected (bacterial virus, *E.coli*) in 1956 led to the first existence for the unique kind of the RNA, later called messenger RNA. *Jacob* and *Monod* (1961) who first proposed this name, believed messenger to be necessary to convey the message of the genetic code from the DNA of the nucleus to the cytoplasm. This messenger is known as mRNA and it acts as a template for the translation of the DNA code into a specific protein. Thus it helps in determining the structure of protein.

mRNA molecules exist in a large variety of lengths, depending on the length of the polypeptide chain for which they code. Its molecular weight and sedimention value vary considerably. Generally the life span of mRNA is relatively short, although in some eukaryotic cells there is evidence of some degree of stability.

Further mRNA is always complementary to a portion of strand of DNA, with the exception that uracil replaces thymine. It should therefore hybridize with the DNA from which it was transcribed.

It is now an established fact that when the code has been transcribed from DNA on to mRNA, the later leaves the nucleus passes through the nucleus membrane into the cytoplasm. Here it moves to the ribosomes, the site of protein synthesis. mRNA molecules attaches reversibly to the surface of ribosome always binding to the smaller sub-units. The magnesium cation, Mg^{++} is involved in the formation of a complex between mRNA and ribosomes.

Types of mRNA

On the basis of size and the coding two types of mRNA has been described:

(a) *Monocistronic mRNA*. Mostly the mRNA carries the codons of single cistron (i.e., codes for one complete protein molecule) of the DNA. Such mRNA molecule is called monocistronic mRNA. For example, for the synthesis of a polypeptide chain of 300 to 500 amino acid residues, a monocistronic mRNA of *E.coli* contains 900 to 1500 nucleotides in its molecule.

(b) *Polygenic or polycistronic mRNA*. Sometimes a mRNA molecule carries the codes from several adjacent DNA cistrons and become much longer in size. This type of mRNA is called polygenic or polycistronic mRNA. For example, for the metabolism of the histidine protein the cell synthesizes about 10 specific enzymatic proteins and a mRNA in this case may carry codons for all the 10 enzymes.

Informosomes

In eukaryons mRNA is associated with protein forming ribonucleoprotein complexes. Some of these complexes remain free in the cytoplasm without being attached to the polyribosomes. These are named as informosomes by *Spirin*. These are very stable and can remain in the cell cytoplasm for several days. The stability is attributed by the presence of protein sheath around mRNA molecule. In informosomes proteins and mRNA are found in the ratio of 4:1. These occur in the form of particles of 80S or less.

Since informosomes are very stable, these are used by the cell is protein synthesis only when the is delay in translation. In embryonic cells, genetic apapratus starts functioning only late during organogenesis. Therefore, in early stages of cleavage when there is no rRNA, informosomes govern the process of protein synthesis.

Stability

The cell does not contain quantities of mRNA. This is because mRNA, unlike other RNAs is constantly undergoing breakdown. It is broken down to its constituent ribonucleotides by ribonucleases. In bacteria, mRNA may be so short-lived that while one end is translating protein the other end may be undergoing breakdown. In *E.coli* the average half-life of some mRNA is about two minutes.

Eukaryotic cells, on the other hand, contain metabolically stable mRNA. Mammalian reticulocytes are immature RBC which have lost their nuclei but have retained ribosomes. These cells can synthesize haemòglobin for many hours and even days by utilizing the mRNA transcribed by the nuclei when they were present.

2. Transfer Ribonucleic Acid

In the literature, t-RNA molecule have been variously termed tRNA, sRNA for soluble RNA, or adaptor RNA. It forms about 10-15% of the total RNA in most of the existence. Each tRNA contains approximate 80 nucleotides. The soluble or t-RNA forms large varieties of different cells, is homogenous in its molecular size having a molecular weight of about 25000. The nucleotide sequence of tRNA was first worked out by *Holley et.al.* (1965) for yeast alanine tRNA.

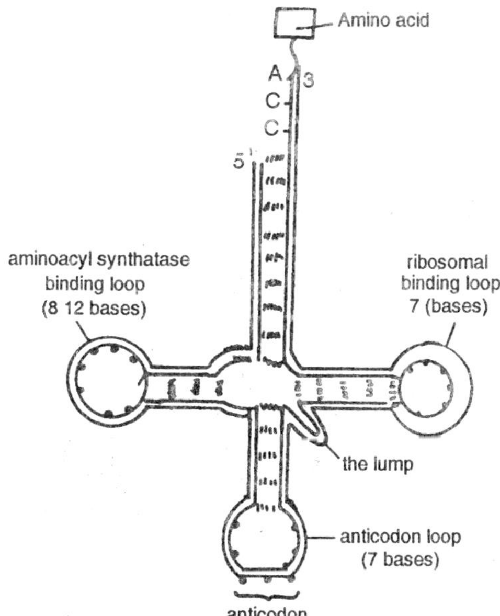

Fig. 6.2. Clover leaf model of tRNA.

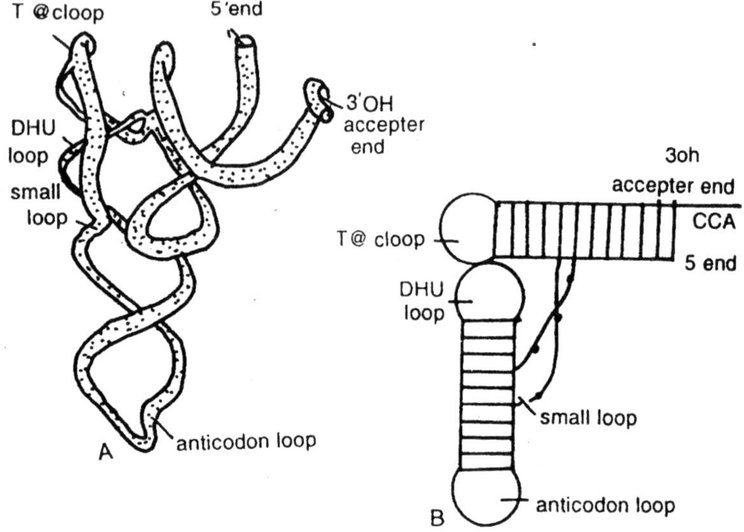

Fig. 6.3. Three dimensional structure of yeast phenylalanine tRNA.

Since then the sequence of about 75 different tRNAs have been established.

According to the Holley's leaf model the tRNA is a polynucleotide chain which is folded upon itself to form 5 arms. As a result of the folding the 3' and 5' ends of the chain come near each other. An arm consists of a stem and a loop. Bases are arranged in pairs in arms. There is no base pairing in the loops. The 3'end of the polynucleotide chain ends in CCA base sequence. This represents site for the attachment of activated amino acid. The end of the chain terminates with guanine base. The bent in the chain of each tRNA molecule contains a definite sequence of three nitrogenous bases which constitute the anticodon. It recognizes the codon on mRNA. Four different regions or special sites can be recognized in the molecule of tRNA. These are:

(i) *Amino acid attachment site.* It occurs at the 3'end of the tRNA chain and has -OH group of ribose molecule free to pair. This -OH group combines with the specific amino acid in the presence of ATP forming amino-acyl tRNA. It is common to all the tRNA molecules.

(ii) *Recognition site.* It contains a specific base sequence which dictates the attachment of correct amino acid to the tRNA molecule. It matches with the amino acid activating enzyme through which attachment of amino acid to tRNA takes place.

(iii) *Anticodon or codon recognition site.* This site has three unpaired based (triplet of base) whose sequence is complementary with a codon (triplet) in mRNA. Therefore, it determines the pairing of tRNA with the specific codon (triplet) of mRNA. It is therefore, the most specific region of tRNA molecule.

(iv) *Ribosome recognition site.* This helps in the attachment of tRNA to the ribosome. This site is common to all the molecules of tRNA.

Three dimensional structure of tRNA. In order to understand the structure-function relationship of tRNA, its three dimensional structure (TDS) should be known. With the availability of tRNA in crystalline form in 1968, TDS of tRNA could be studied through X-ray crystallography as was done for DNA double helix. About a dozen models for TDS were proposed, but the latest and most acceptable model was proposed in 1973 by *S.H. Kim.* He suggested that TDS of tRNA takes the shape of letter L with a thickness 20Å. This can be easily derived from two dimensional clover leaf model. The extra arm which varies in different tRNA molecules can be extended without distoring TDS conformation. The CCA stem projects out and can take different orientations.

Unusual bases

In addition to the usual basses, A, U, G and C, tRNA contain a number of unusual bases, and in this respect differs from mRNA and rRNA. The unusual bases of tRNA account for 5-20% of the total

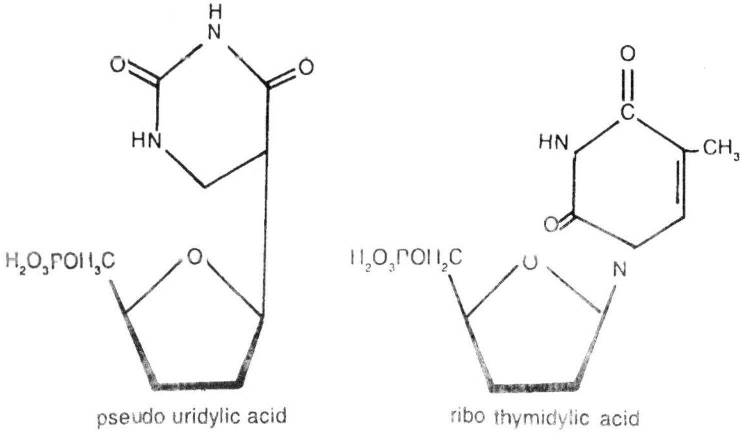

Fig. 6.4. Showing the structural formula of Pseudo-Uridylic acid and Ribothymidylic acid.

RNA of cell. Most of the unusual bases are formed by methylation (addition of $-CH_3$ or methyl group to the usual bases) e.g., cytosine and guanine on methylation yield methylcytosine and methylguanine, respectively. Precursor tRNA molecules transcribed on the DNA template contain the usual bases. These are then modified to unusual bases. The unusual bases are important because they protect the tRNA molecule against degradation by RNAse. This protection is necessary because RNA is found floating freely in the cell.

Some of the unusual bases of tRNA are methylguanine (GMe), dimethylguanine (GMe_2), methylcytosine (Me), ribothymine (T) pseudouridine (ψ), dihydrour-idine (DHU_2, H_2U, $\dot{U}H_2$), inosine (I) and methylinosine (IMe, MeI).

3. Ribosomal Ribonucleic Acid rRNA

Ribosomes are small particles of about 200Å to 250Å in diameter, and are generally present in the cytoplasm either lying free in the cytoplasm or attached to the outer membrane of endoplasmic reticulum or nuclear membrane. These particles are ribosomes containing about 60% ribonucleic acid or RNA which is ribosomal RNA ro rRNA and 40% protein. It is generally agreed that cytoplasmic ribosomes or their subunits are made in the nucleus and are subsequently transferred to the cytoplasm.

However, the mode of their passages across the nuclear membrane is still a matter of controversy. Even from the morphological evidence, it would appear that the reticular or microvesicular spheres of the nucleus could be engaged in either the synthesis of rRNA, or its assembly, or both. The finding that hybridization of rRNA takes place with the chromatin associated with the nucleolar region suggests that rRNA is synthesized on the part of the chromosome traversing the nucleolus (the nucleolar organizer) or, in some cases, on DNA detached from the chromosome and associated with the nucleolus.

7

Biosynthesis of DNA

During cell division the chromosomes which are made up of DNA molecules undergo spletting and the sister chromatids move apart to maintain the usual number of chromosomes. Each chromatid has a single chain of DNA. To make it double and to convert chromatid upto chromosome the duplication of DNA becomes essential.

Replication of the DNA Molecule

Kornberg showed that DNA can replicate in a test tube with no cells present. All that is required is a mixture containing DNA, a specific enzyme (which he called DNA-polymerase), and a mixture of the four precursors: the nucleoside triphosphates deoxy-ATP, deoxy-CTP, deoxy-GTP, and deoxy-TTP. If any one of the four nucleoside triphosphates is omitted from the reaction mixture, DNA does not replicate itself. The intact DNA serves as a template for the reaction—a guide to the exact placement of nucleotides in the new strand. Where there is a T in the template, there must be an A in the new strand, and so forth.

Two other models of how the double helix might replicate were suggested after the original paper by Watson and Crick. In the model of conservative replication, the original double helix would serve somehow as a template but would either be reconstituted or, perhaps, would never unwind at all. Thus the new molecule would contain none of the atoms of the original. According to the model of dispersive replication, fragments of the original molecule would serve as templates, assembling two molecules, each containing old and new parts, perhaps at random. In *semiconservative replication* (the model proposed by *Watson* and *Crick*), the original two strands would separate, and each would function as the template for a new partner. Each molecule produced by semiconservative replication would therefore consist of one old and one new strand. After a short time, experimental work confirmed the model of semiconservative replication.

Synthesis of DNA from monomeric units of deoxyribonucleotides using a pre-existing DNA molecule as a template is DNA replication. Three mechanistic models have been proposed regarding DNA replication. These are:

(i) Dispersive
(ii) Conservative
(iii) Semi-conservative.

(i) Dispersive

According to this model, it was proposed that the original DNA is broken into many fragments, which are more or less uniformly distributed among the progenies. Inside the progeny, these fragments grow to form complete DNA segment. However, according to this model one would expect unequal distribution of genes among progenies leading to great variations among them. It would lead to irregular arrangement of nucleotides. However, these expectations are not

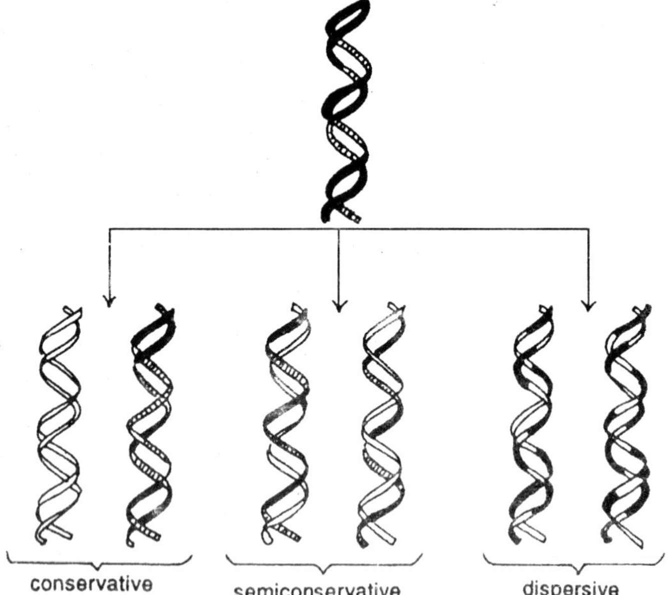

Fig. 7.1. A diagram illustrating three possible modes of DNA replication.

realized and hence the dispersive mechanism of DNA replication does not find support.

(ii) Conservative

According to this model, the original DNA is copied as such and then one copy of the complete DNA is transmitted to one of the progenies. Thus, according to this model, both primary and secondary structures of the DNA are conserved. There is neither breakage nor unwinding of the parental DNA during replication. The experimental evidence however, do not support this model as well, although such a mechanism of DNA replication is possible structurally and chemically.

(iii) Semi-conservative

This mechanism is based on Watson-Crick's model of DNA structure and is now accepted mechanism of DNA replication. The replication of DNA involves the unwinding of double delical DNA molecule but no breakage of the separated strands. Thus, the primary but not the secondary structures of parental DNA are conserved in progenies.

The idea of semiconservative mechanism of DNA replication came from the careful studies of the double helical model of DNA structure. The complimentary strand structure is an indication of the possible strand separation and formation of complimentary strands on each of the free single strands. During semiconservative replication, the hydrogen bonds between the complimentary base pairs are broken and the two separated strands start replicating as soon as a few bonds are broken. The two strands do not separate completely before the new strands are formed. That is why during the process of DNA replication some 'Y' shaped regions in the DNA molecule are observed. Each strand can act as a template or mould for the formation of new complimentary chains. The nucleotides are put together into short pieces of DNA by one of the DNA polymerases. The short segments of the newly synthesized DNA are known as *Okazaki fragments*. The complimentarity of the strands is maintained because of the selective pairing between A and T and G and C. The small Okazaki fragments are joined together to form complete DNA strands by the enzyme polynucleotide ligase. In experiments, where ligase is selectively inhabited, the accumulation of Okazaki fragments take place.

Experimental Proof

A clever experiment by Matthew Meselson and Franklin Stahl convinced the scientific community that semiconservative replication is the correct model. Working at the California Institute of Technology

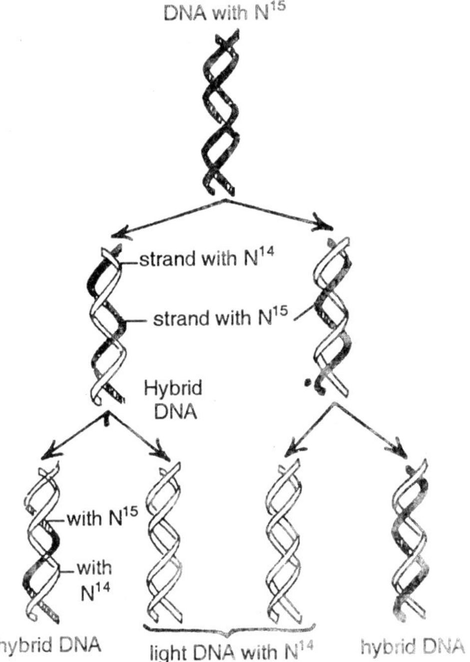

Fig. 7.2. Meselson and Stahl's experiment.

in 1957, they devised a simple way to distinguish old strands of DNA from new ones. The key was to use a "heavy" isotope of nitrogen. Heavy nitrogen (^{15}N) is a rare, nonradioactive isotope that makes molecules more dense than chemically identical molecules containing the common isotope ^{14}N. To study DNA of different densities (that is, DNA containing ^{15}N versus DNA containing ^{14}N), Meselson, Stahl, and Jerry Vinograd invented a new centrifugation procedure that allowed them to determine the density of DNA from a specific sample. At a certain molarity, a solution of cesium chloride (CsCl) has a density very close to that of DNA; at high gravitational forces produced in an ultracentrifuge, cesium ions sediment to some extent, thus establishing a density gradient. When a DNA sample is dissolved in CsCl and centrifuged at about 100,000 times the force of gravity, the DNA gathers in a layer in the centrifuge tube at a position where the density of the CsCl solution equals that of the DNA. To cluster in this way, DNA that is initially lower in the tube, where the density is greater than its own, must rise; DNA that is in a region of lower density must sink.

After developing this method of measuring DNA densities, Meselson and Stahl could begin experimenting. They grew a culture of the bacterium *Escherichia coli* for 17 generations on a medium in which the nitrogen source (ammonium chloride, NH_4Cl) was made with ^{15}N instead of ^{14}N. As a result, all the DNA in the bacteria was "heavy." Another culture was grown on medium with ^{14}N. They extracted DNA from both cultures. When these extracts were combined and centrifuged with CsCl, two separate DNA bands formed, showing that this method would work for separating DNA samples of slightly different densities.

Meselson and Stahl then conducted their main experiment. They grew another culture on ^{15}N medium and *transferred* it to normal ^{14}N medium. *E. coli* reproduces every 20 minutes, and Meselson and Stahl collected some of the bacteria from each generation after the transfer. They extracted DNA from the samples. After DNA was duplicated and the cells divided to produce each new generation, the DNA banding in the density gradient was different from the original banding. Initially, the DNA was uniformly labeled with ^{15}N and hence was relatively dense. After one generation, when the DNA had been duplicated once, all the DNA was of an intermediate density. After two generations, there were two equally large DNA bands: one of low density and one of intermediate density. In samples from subsequent generations, the proportion of low-density DNA increased steadily.

These data can be explained by the semiconservative model of DNA replication. The high-density DNA had two ^{15}N strands, the intermediate-density DNA had one ^{15}N and one ^{14}N strand, and the low-density DNA had two ^{14}N strands. In the first round of DNA replication, the strands of the double helix, both heavy with ^{15}N, separated; during the process of separation, each acted as the template for a second strand, which contained only ^{14}N and hence was less dense. Each double helix then consisted of one ^{15}N and one ^{14}N strand and was of intermediate density. In the second replication, the ^{14}N-containing strands directed the synthesis of partners with ^{14}N, creating low-density DNA, and the ^{15}N strands got new ^{14}N partners.

If the DNA had replicated in accord with either of the other models, the results would have been quite different. Under the conservative model, after one generation there would have been two bands—one for heavy DNA (^{15}N–^{15}N) and the other for light (^{14}N–^{14}N); no DNA of intermediate density would have formed at any time. If dispersive replication had taken place, the first round of replication would have produced DNA of intermediate density, but the density of all the DNA would have decreased with each subsequent replication. The crucial observation proving the semiconservative model was that intermediate-density DNA ($^{15}N-^{14}N$) appeared in the first generation and continued to appear in subsequent generations.

Cairn's Autoradiography Experiment

J. Cairns demonstrated the semiconservative type of replication by using a technique of autoradiography as given in the following lines:

In autoradiography technique, the material is first supplied with a suitable radioactive material like tritiated thymidine (H^3-TdR; H^3 is heavy isotope of hydrogen and it replaces normal hydrogen in thymidine to give rise to tritiated thymidine). Tritiated thymidine is used since this will selectively label only DNA and will not label RNA, since thymine base is absent in RNA. The tritiated thymidine gets incorporated into DNA and replaces ordinary thymidine. The material is then sectioned or else the cells may be broken down to release the intact bacterial chromosome on slides. These slides are then covered by photographic emulsion and stored in the dark. During this storage the particles emitted by tritiated thymidine will expose the film, which can be developed. This photograph will then show the regions of the presence of tritium and thus indirectly the presence of labelled DNA.

Using this above technique, the replication of DNA could be easily followed by *J. Cairns* and the results were reported in 1963. During incorporation of tritiated thymidine, autoradiographs could be prepared

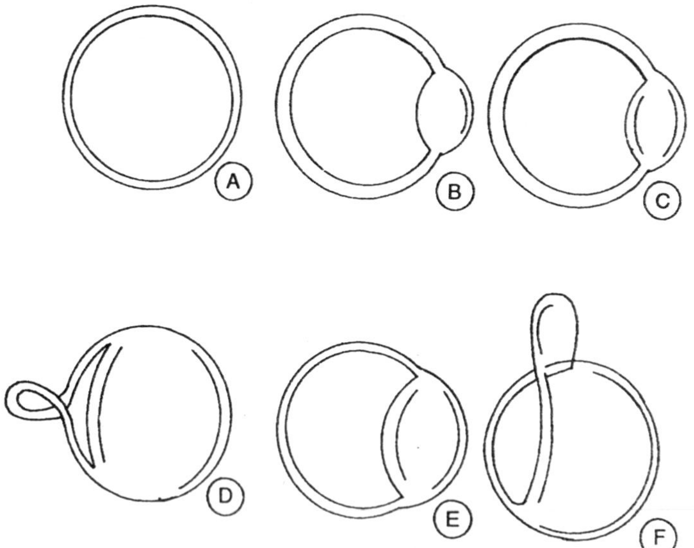

Fig. 7.3. Cairn's model for circular DNA replication.

at regular known intervals. Autoradiographs from this replicating material prepared at regular known intervals demonstrated semi-conservative mode of replication. It would be expected that in regions, where one cycle of replication of DNA has been completed, the density of dots will be higher than in the region where the replication has not taken place. The lighter density of dots is considered to indicate that only one of the two strands is labelled, while a heavier density of dots will indicate that only one of the two strands is labelled, while a heavier density of dots will indicate that both strands are labelled. Such a situation was actually observed. The rate at which the replication proceeds could also be worked out by measuring the length of DNA undergoing replication in a known interval of time. The generation time was worked out by *Cairns* as 30 minutes in *E. coli*. The length of the chromosome was worked out to be about 1 mm. The rate of replication as obvious would be approximately 30μ to 40μ per minute (1 mm = 1000μ).

That after replication, one of the two strands in the daughter DNA molecules is derived from the parent molecule and the other is synthesized afresh. In θ shaped figure, which is obtained in the second cycle of replication is presence of label, the two areas in the split region would never be equally labelled. For instance, one arc would be twice as heavily labelled as the other arc. This is what was actually observed by *Cairns*. Thus the observation support the semiconservative type of replication of DNA.

Taylor's Experiment on Vicia faba Root Tips

J.H. Taylor (1957) and his coworkers also demonstrated the semiconservative method of DNA duplication in the root tip cells of *Vicia faba* by autoradiography. The roots were grown in a medium containing radioactive thymidine, so that the radioactivity is incorporated in the DNA of these cells. The outline of this labelled chromosome on a photographic film appears in the form of scattered black dots of silver grains. When these root tips with labelled chromosomes were transferred to the unlabelled medium containing colchicine and studied for radioactivity, the following observtions were made:

1. In the chromosomes of first generation the radioactivity was found to be uniformly distributed in both the chromatids, because in them the original strand of DNA double helix was labelled with radioactivity and the new onc was non-labelled.
2. In the chromosomes of second generation only one of the two chromatids in each chromosome was radioactive.

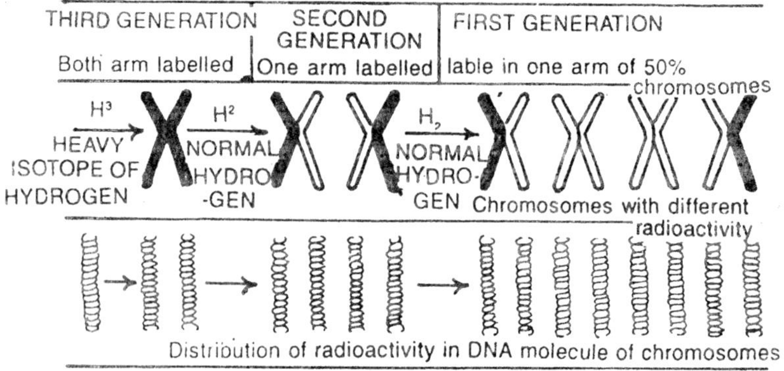

Fig. 7.4. Taylor's experiment on Vicia faba.

This experiment demonstrates the semiconservative method of chromosome replication. But as it is known that each chromatid is composed of only one double helical molecule of DNA, it is the replication of DNA.

ROLE OF ENZYMES AND PROTEINS REPLICATION

The complicated process of DNA replication in *E. coli* requires many different proteins and enzymes, some of which also function in other cellular process such as the repair of DNA damage and genetic recombination. The key enzyme in the synthesis of new DNA is DNA polymerase.

In *E. coli* there are three DNA polymerases. Each catalyzes the DNA template-directed condensation of deoxyribonucleoside 5′-triphosphates. There are significant differences in their activity in DNA synthesis and in the nuclease (DNA or RNA break-down) activities associated with them. All three polymerases catalyze new DNA synthesis in the 5′-3′ direction. The rate of DNA synthesis catalyzed by the three enzymes varies circular prokaryotic DNA molecules replicate bidirectionally (in both directions away from the origin of replication). In these cases there are two replication forks that are mirror images of one another; picture two Ys joined head-to-head by the two pairs of arms. The area of a double-stranded DNA molecule that has denatured for replication is called a *replication bubble*.

In *E. coli* the unwinding of the DNA is catalyzed by an enzyme called helicase, the product of a gene called *rep*. For each 10 base pairs of DNA unwound, one turn of the helix becomes untwisted. As a result, as the helix unwinds a torsional strain is imposed on the DNA. That is, since the DNA molecule is circular, the pulling apart of the helix at one location will cause increased tightening of the molecule elsewhere, much like what happens when the strands of a piece of rope that is fixed at each end are pulled apart. This torsional strain is relieved by the action of enzymes called topoisomerases, which cause single-stranded breaks in DNA away from the replication forks and then allow one strand to rotate relative to the other strand. The unwinding of the DNA produces single-stranded regions, which are stabilized by DNA *single-stranded binding* (SSB) *proteins*. Each SSB protein is a tetramer of a 74,000 dalton subunit, and this tetramer binds to eight bases of single stranded DNA. Over 250 tetramers bind to each replication fork. Once the strands have started to unwind, the internal bases become available for the formation of bonds with bases in the new chain. Initiation of DNA replication next takes place. In *E. coli*, primases bind to the single-stranded DNA of both arms of the replication fork and synthesize short primers. The primers are lengthened by the action of DNA polymerase III, which synthesizes the complementary DNA chains to the template strands. Note that, because of the opposite polarities of the two DNA template strands and the requirement for a 5′- to -3′ direction of new DNA synthesis, the primers are located at different relative positions on the two template strands.

The DNA helix continues to unwind. On the template on the left the new strand continues to be synthesized continuously (in the same

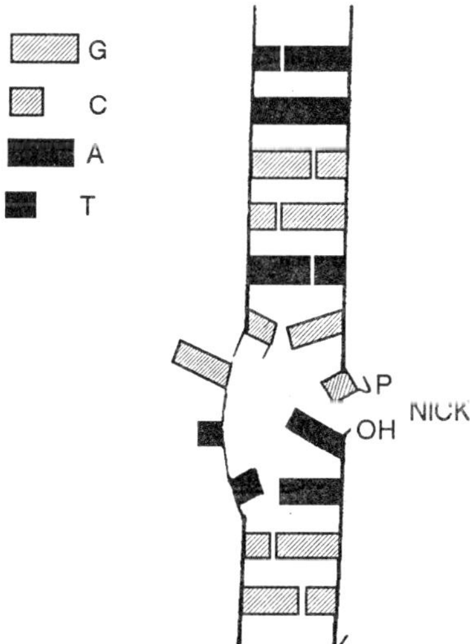

Fig. 7.5. A nicked duplex DNA molecule such as is formed by an endonuclease enzyme.

direction as the direction of unwinding). However, because DNA polymerases can only synthesize DNA in the 5′-to-3′ direction, the new synthesis on the template on the right has gone as far as it can. Thus, a new initiation of DNA synthesis occurs on the right-hand template on the newly exposed single-stranded template close to the site of helicase activity. As before, a primer is made, which is lengthened by DNA polymerase III action. The overall result is that the new DNA strand being made on the left-hand template is synthesized continuously while the new DNA being made on the right-hand template is synthesizd discontinuously so that Okazaki fragments are produced. Eventually the Okazaki fragments are joined together into a continuous DNA strand. This process requires the activities of the enzymes DNA polymerase I and DNA ligase. If we consider two adjacent Okazaki fragments, the 3′ end of the newer DNA fragment is adjacent to but not joined to the primer 5′ end of the previously synthesized fragment. The DNA polymerase III that has just completed the synthesis of the newer fragment now dissociates from the DNA and DNA polymerase I takes its place. This enzyme continuous the 5′-to-3′ synthesis of the newer DNA fragment, at the same time removing the primer of the older fragment through the action of the 5′-to-3′ exonuclease function of DNA polymerase I. When DNA polymerase I is finished, there is a gap between the two new DNA fragments, and this gap is sealed in a reaction catalyzed by DNA ligase, thereby producing a longer DNA strand. The whole process is completed until all the DNA is replicated.

Replication Fork

How is semiconservative DNA replication accomplished? That is depends upon enzymes should not surprise you. We now know that there are different types of DNA polymerases, with different functions, and that the replication process is intricate. Kornberg's basic observations, including the need for a DNA template and for a mixture of nucleoside triphosphates, still hold. He also showed that nucleotides are always added to the growing chain at the same end: the 3′ end, the end at which the DNA strand has a free hydroxyl groups on the 3′ carbon of its terminal deoxyribose. This hydroxyl groups reacts with a phosphate group on the 5′ carbon of the deoxyribose of a deoxyribonucleoside triphosphate, and thus the chain grows. Bonds linking the phosphate groups of the deoxyribonucleoside triphosphate break and thereby release the energy for this reaction. Two of the phosphate groups diffuse away, and one becomes part of the sugar-phosphate backbone of the growing DNA molecule.

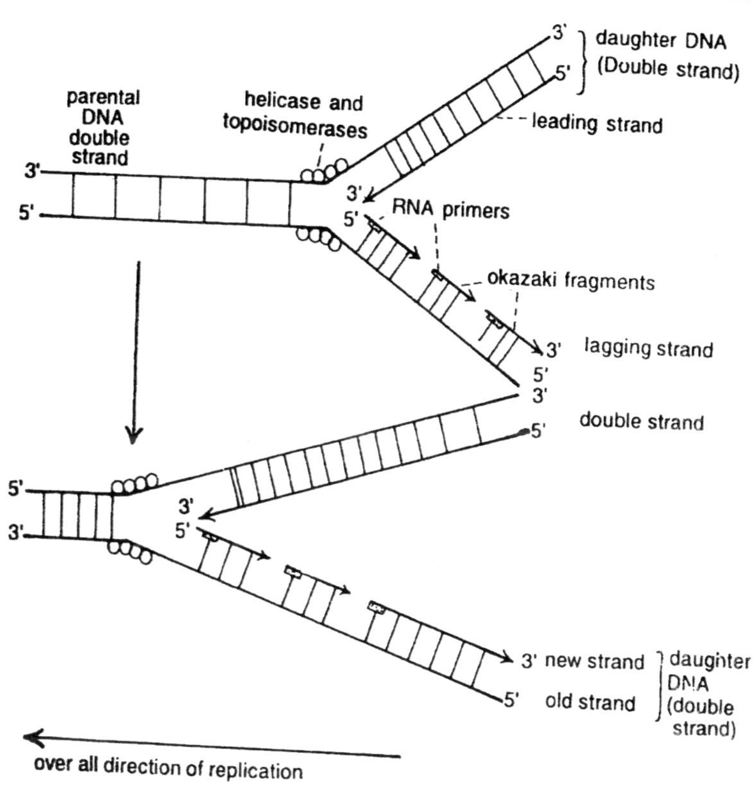

Fig. 7.6. Diagrammatic representation of discontinuous synthesis of DNA.

For double-stranded DNA to replicate, the strands must unwind and separate from each other. Only then can they function as templates for the synthesis of new, complementary strands. The unwinding results in a *replication fork*—a moving, Y-shaped structure that is the region where new DNA strands are being synthesized. Recall that the two original strands are antiparallel, with the 3′end of one strand paired with the 5′ end of the other. As the replication fork moves along the parent DNA molecule, an enzyme, DNA polymerase III, catalyzes the replication of both strands. How can this be accomplished, given that new nucleotides are added only at the 3′ end of a polynucleotide chain?

One parent strand is being exposed beginning at its 3′ end, which presents no problem—its complementary strand is synthesized continuously as the replication fork proceeds. This daughter strand is called the *leading strand*. The other daughter strand, the *lagging strand*, is produced in discontinuous spurts (100 to 200 nucleotides at a time in eukaryotes; 1,000 to 2,000 at a time in prokaryotes). The discontinuous stretches are synthesized just as the leading strand is, by adding the 5′ end of a nucleotide to the 3′ end of the daughter strand, but the stretches are synthesized in the opposite direction with respect to the replication fork. These stretches of new DNA for the lagging strand are called *Okazaki fragments* after their discoverer, the Japanese biochemist Reiji Okazaki. While the leading strand grows continuously "forward," the lagging strand grows in shorter, "backward," stretches with gaps between them. The gaps between the Okazaki fragments are then filled in by DNA polymerase I, and another enzyme, *DNA ligase*, links the fragments.

Working together, two DNA polymerases, DNA ligase, and several other proteins do the complex job of DNA synthesis with a speed and accuracy that are almost unimaginable. In *E. coli*, the complex makes new DNA at a rate in excess of 1,000 base pairs per second and makes mistakes in fewer than one base in 10^8–10^{12}.

On a bacterial chromosome, DNA synthesis begins at just one point, the *origin of replication*. Each chromosome of a eukaryote, on the other hand, has many origins of replication. DNA synthesis may thus proceed simultaneously in many areas of a single eukaryotic chromosome. Synthesis proceeds in both directions from an origin of replication as two replication forks move away from it.

Enzymes used in Replication

The enzymatic synthesis of DNA is a complex process, primarily because of the need for high fidelity in copying the base sequence and for physical separation of the parental strands. The number of steps that must be completed is far too great to be accomplished by a single enzyme and, in fact, about twenty proteins are known at present to be necessary. Thus, in an effort to provide some understanding with a minimum of confusion, each step in the process will be treated separately. We will consider the basic chemistry of polymerization, the source of the precursors, the problems raised by the chemistry of polymerization, the means of initiating and terminating synthesis, and the mechanisms for eliminating replication errors.

Polymerases

In 1957, Arthur Kornberg showed that in extracts of *E. coli* there exists a DNA polymerase (now called *polymerase I* or *pol I*). This enzyme was able to synthesize DNA from four precursor molecules—

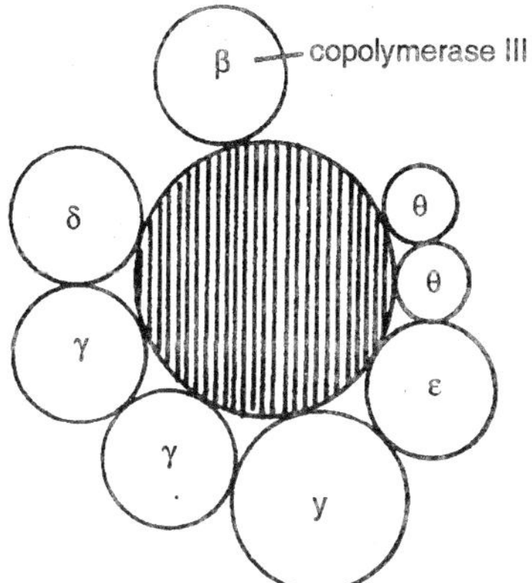

Fig. 7.7. DNA polymerase-III holoenzyme. It consists of subunit α, β, γ, ε θ, δ *and* ε.

namely, the four deoxynucleoside 5´-triphosphates (dNTP), dATP, dGTP, dCTP, and dTTP—as long as a DNA molecule to be copied (a *template* DNA) was provided. Neither 5´-monophosphates nor 5´-diphosphates, nor 3´-(mono-, di-, or tri-) phosphates can be polymerized—only the 5´-triphosphates are substrates for the polymerization reaction; soon we will see why this is the case. Some years later, it was found that pol I, though playing an essential role in the replication process, is not the major polymerase in *E. coli*; instead, the enzyme responsible for advance of the replication fork is polymerase III or pol III. Pol III also exclusively uses 5´-triphosphates as precursors and requires a DNA template before polymerization can occur. Pol I and pol III have many features in common and, in fact, a few types of DNA molecules replicate by using only pol I. The overall chemical reaction catalyzed by both DNA polymerases is:

$$\text{Poly(nucleotide)}_n\text{-3}'\text{-OH} + \text{dNTP} \rightarrow \text{Poly(nucleotide)}_{n+1}\text{-3}'\text{-OH} + \text{PP}$$

in which PP represents pyrophosphate cleaved from the dNTP.

Pol I and pol III have many features in common. Both enzymes only polymerase deoxynucleoside 5´-triphosphates and can do so only while copying a template DNA. Furthermore, polymerization can only occur by addition to a *primer*—that is, an oligonucleotide hydrogen-bonded to the template strand and whose terminal 3´-OH group is available for reaction (that is, a "free" 3´-OH group). The meaning of a primer is already made clear, which depicts six potential template molecules; of these, only three can be said to be active—(c), (e), and (f)—each of which has a free 3´-OH group. The lack of activity with (d) and the direction of synthesis with (e) and (f) indicate that nucleotides do not add to a free 5′-P group. The lack of any synthesis with (a) or (b) indicates that addition to a 3′-OH group cannot occur if there is nothing to copy. Thus we draw two conclusions:

1. Both a primer with a free 3′-OH group and a template are needed.
2. Polymerization consists of a reaction between a 3′-OH group at the end of the growing strand and an incoming nucleoside 5′-triphosphate. When the nucleotide is added, it supplies another free 3′-OH group. Since each DNA strand has a 5′-P terminus and a 3′-OH terminus, strand growth is said to proceed in the 5′→3′ (5′-to-3′) direction.

Occasionally polymerases add a nucleotide terminus that cannot hydrogen-bond to the corresponding base in the template strand. This may be purely a mistake or may result from the tautomerization of adenine and thymine. In any case, it is important that the unpaired base be removable while its incorrectness is recognizable—namely, as an unpaired base at the 3′-OH terminus of a growing strand.

Pol I responds to an unpaired terminal base by terminating polymerizing activity, because the enzyme requires a primer that is correctly hydrogen-bonded. When such an impasse is encountered, a 3′→5′ exonuclease activity, which may be thought of simply as pol I running backwards or in the 3′→5′ direction, is stimulated, and the unpaired base is removed. After removal of this base, the exonuclease activity stops, polymerizing activity is restored, and chain growth begins again. This exonuclease activity is called the *proofreading* or *editing function* of pol I.

Another function of polymerase I is that of a 5′→3′ exonuclease. This activity has the following features:

1. Nucleotides are removed from the 5′-P terminus only, one by one.
2. More than one nucleotide can be removed by successive cutting.
3. The nucleotide removed must have been base-paired.
4. The nucleotide removed can be either or the deoxy-or the ribo-type.
5. Activity can be at a nick as long as there is a 5′-P groups.

The main function of the 5′→3′ exonuclease activity is to remove ribonucleotide primers. The 5′→3′ exonuclease activity at a single-strand break (nick) can occur simultaneously with polymerization. That is, as a 5′-P nucleotide is removed, a replacement can be made by the polymerizing activity. Since pol I cannot form a bond between a

3′-OH group and a 5′-monophosphate, the nick moves along the DNA molecule in the direction of synthesis. This movement is called *nick translation*.

Experimental conditions can be chosen so that polymerization will occur at a single-strand break without concomitant 5′→3′ exonuclease activity. The growing strand then displaces the parental strand. This is thought to be an important step in the mechanism of genetic recombination. Of all *E. coli* polymerases known to date, polymerase I is the only one capable of carrying out an unaided displacement reaction. In other strand displacement reactions, auxilary proteins are required and ATP is cleaved to fuel the unwinding of the helix; this will be discussed when the events at a replication fork are described.

Pol III is a very complex enzyme. In its most active form it is associated with eight other proteins to form the *pol III holoenzyme*, occasionally termed pol III. The term holoenzyme refers to an enzyme that contains several different subunits and retains some activity even when one or more subunits is missing. The smallest aggregate having enzymatic activity is called the *core enzyme*. The activities of the core enzyme and the holoenzyme are usually very different. Genes encoding five of the subunits have been identified; these are called *dnaE*, *dnaN*, *dnaQ*, *dnaX*, and *dnaz*. The *dnaE* protein possesses the major polymerizing activity but each of the subunits, except for the *dnaQ* protein is essential for replication. Pol III shares wtih pol I a requirement for a template and a primer but its substrate specificity is much more limited. For instance, pol III cannot act at a nick nor is it active with single-stranded DNA primed by either a DNA or RNA nucleotide fragment. The principal activity *in vitro* is on gapped DNA in which the gap is less than 100 nucleotides long. Such a gap is akin to the state of the DNA at a replication fork—that is, the parental strands are separated and bear short single-stranded regions ahead of the growing daughter chain.

Pol III cannot carry out strand displacement either, and another system is needed to unwind the helix in order that a replication fork will be able to proceed. The enzyme, like pol I, possesses a 3′→5′ exonuclease activity which performs the major editing function in DNA replication. This function is carried out by the *dnaE* subunit, which is also the major polymerizing subunit, as we have just mentioned. The *dnaQ* subunit plays an important role in editing, also, but the biochemical basis of the role is not yet known; it probably interacts with the *dnaE* subunit. The principal evidence supporting the view that it is involved in providing fidelity to the replication process is that bacteria containing a mutation in the *dnaQ* gene have a somewhat higher mutation frequency. Pol III also possesses a 5′→3 exonuclease activity; however, the enzyme acts only on single-stranded DNA so that it cannot carry out nick translation. The biological role of the 5′→3′ exonuclease activity of pol III is unknown at present. Although pol III holoenzyme is the major replicating enzyme in *E. coli*, much less is known about it than about pol I, because it is a more complex enzyme. Study of pol III is currently an active field of research.

All known polymerases (for both DNA and RNA) are capable of chain growth in only the 5′→3′ direction; that is, the growing end of the polymer must have a free 3′-OH group. It is possible for the following reasons that the enzymes evolved in this way to facilitate editing. If 3′→5′ growth were to occur, the growing strand would also be terminated with a 5′-triphosphate and the 3′-OH group of the incoming nucleotide would react with it. Chemically this is certainly acceptable but since the bonds formed contain only a single phosphate, an editing function would leave a free 5′-monophosphate. In order for chain growth to proceed, an enzymatic system would be needed to enter the replication fork and convert the monophosphate to a triphosphate. There is already a great deal going on in the replication fork, so that it would seem more economical for the cell to require 5′→3′ growth exclusively. However, the observation that chain growth proceeds in only one direction introduces what is probably the greatest complication in the entire replication process; this will be described shortly.

DNA Ligase

Neither replication from a primed circular single strand nor gap filling results in a continuous daughter strand. Discontinuity results because no known polymerase can join a 3′-OH and a 5′-monophosphate group. The joining of these groups is accomplished by the enzyme *DNA ligase*, which functions in replication and other important processes. *E. coli* DNA ligase can join a 3′-OH group as long as both are termini of adjacent base-paired deoxynucleotides—the enzyme cannot bridge a gap.

In the usual polymerization reaction, the activation energy for phosphodiester bond formation comes from cleaving the triphosphate. Since DNA ligase has only a monophosphate to work with, it needs another source of energy. It obtains this energy by hydrolyzing either

ATP or nicotine adenine dinucleotide (NAD); the energy source depends upon the organism from which the DNA ligase is obtained. The *E. coli* DNA ligase uses NAD.

Continuous and Discontinuous DNA Replication

Autoradiographic evidence leads us to believe that replication is occurring simultaneously on both strands. *Continuous* replication is, of course, possible on the 3′→5′ template strand, which begins with the necessary 3′-OH *primer*. (Primer is double-stranded DNA—or, as we shall see, a DNA-RNA hybrid—continuing as single-stranded DNA template. The strand being synthesized has a 3′-OH available). A *discontinuous* form of replication takes place on the complementary strand, where it occurs in short segments, backward, away from the Y-junction. These short segments, called *Okazaki fragments* after *R. Okazaki* who first saw them, average about 1,500 nucleotides in prokaryotes and 150 in eukaroytes. The strand synthesized continuously

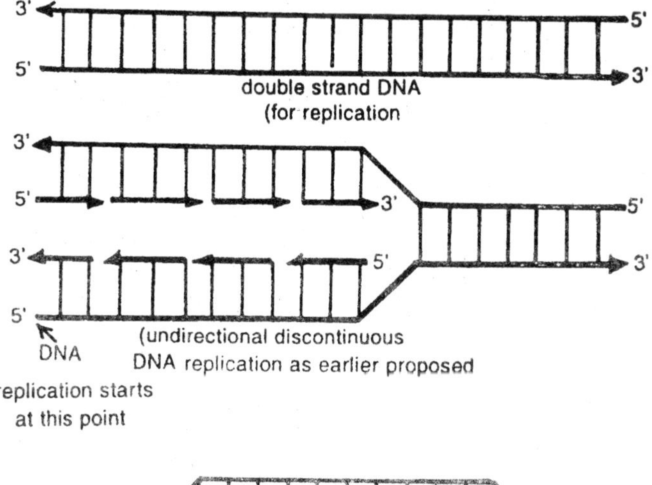

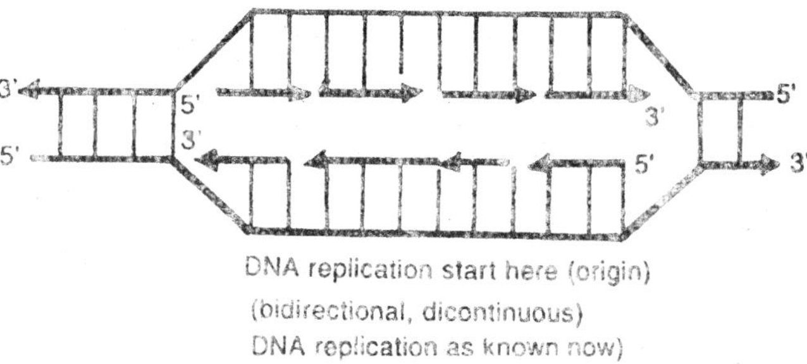

Fig. 7.8. Discontinuous DNA replication.

is referred to as the *leading strand*, and the strand synthesized discontinuously is referred to as the *lagging strand*.

Once initiated, continuous DNA repliction can proceed indefinitely. DNA polymerase III on the leading strand template has what is called high *processivity*: once it attaches, it does not release until the entire strand is replicated. Discontinuous replication, however, requires the repetition of four steps primer synthesis, elongation, primer removal with gap filling, and ligation.

Primer synthesis and elongation

In order for Okazaki fragments to be synthesizd, a primer must be created de novo (Latin, from the beginning). None of the DNA polymerases can create that primer. Instead, one of two enzymes, either *RNA polymerase*, the transcribing enzyme or, more commonly, *primase*, an RNA polymerase coded for by the *dnaG* gene, creates the primer. It is from two to sixty nucleotides, depending on the species, at the site of Okazaki fragment initiation. The result is a short RNA primer that provides the free 3′-OH group that DNA polymerase III needs in order to synthesize the Okazaki fragment. DNA polymerase III continues until it reaches the primer RNA of the previously synthesized Okazaki fragment. At that point it stops and releases from the DNA.

All three prokaryotic polymerases not only can add new nucleotides to a growing strand in the 5′→3′ direction but also can remove nucleotides in the opposite 3′→5′ direction. This property is referred to as *3′→5′ exonuclease activity*. Enzymes that degrade nucleic acids are classified as *exonucleases* if they remove nucleotides from the end of a nucleotide strand or as *endonuclease* if they can break the sugar-phosphate backbone in the middle of a nucleotide strand. At first glance, exonuclease activity seems like an extremely curious property for a polymerase to have—curious unless we think about its ability to check complementarity. If the complementarity is improper, which is to say that the wrong nucleotide has been inserted, the polymerase can remove the incorrect nucleotide, put in the proper one, and continue on its way. This is known as the *proofreading* function of the DNA polymerase. In addition, the RNA primers of Okazaki fragments can be removed by exonuclease activity.

Role of primer

DNA polymerase I is a polymerase when it adds nucleotides, one at a time, and an exonuclease when it removes nucleotide one at a time. To complete the Okazaki fragment, DNA polymerase I acts in both capacities. (Mutants of DNA polymerase I cannot properly connect Okazaki fragments.) DNA polymerase I completes the Okazaki fragment by removing the previous RNA primer and replacing it with DNA nucleotides. When DNA polymerase I has completed its nuclease and polymerase activity, the two previous Okazaki fragments are almost complete. All that remains is a single phosphodiester bond to be made.

Ligation

DNA polymerase I cannot make the final bond to join the Okazaki fragment to the previously synthesized DNA. An enzyme, *DNA ligase*, completes the task by making the final phosphodiester bond in an energy-requiring reaction.

A question of evolutionary interest is why RNA is used for priming of DNA synthesis. Why not use DNA directly and avoid the exonuclease and resynthesis activity? One possible answer is that because priming is inherently more error-prone then regular DNA synthesis it is best for the cell to have the primer nucleotides removed and replaced by DNA synthesized in a less error-prone fashion before DNA synthesis is completed. If the priming nucleotides are RNA, then DNA polymerase I can recognize and remove them in the final stage of Okazaki fragment synthesis, at which time it replaces them with DNA nucleotides inserted with a low error rate.

Another question of evolutionary interest is why DNA synthesis cannot take place in the 3′→5′ direction. Perhaps the answer has to do with proofreading and the exonuclease removal of incorrect nucleotides. When an incorrect nucleotide is found and removed, the next nucleotide brought in, in the 5′→3′ direction, will have a triphosphate end available to provide the energy for its own incorporation. Consider what would happen if the polymerase were capable of adding nucleotides in the opposite direction. The energy for the diester bond would be coming from the triphosphate already attached in the growing 3′→5′ strand. Then, if an error in complementary were detected and the most recently added nucleotide were removed from the 3′→5′ strand by the polymerase, the last nucleotide in the double helix would no longer have a triphosphate available to provide energy for the diester bond with the next nucleotide brought in. Continued polymerization would thus require additional enzymatic steps to provide the energy for the process to continue. This could slow the process down considerably. As it is, the process works at a speed of about four hundred nucleotides incorporated per second with an error rate of about one incorrect pairing per one hundred thousand bases, improved to a rate of only one mistake in ten million by exonuclease proofreading. (Other repair system can improve this error rate another thousandfold, to about one error every 10^{10} times an average base is replicated.

The Initiation of DNA Replication

Each replicon (e.g., the *E. coli* chromosome or a segment of eukaryote chromosome) must have a region in which DNA replication is initiated. In *E. coli* this region is referred to as the genetic locus *oriC*. In order for DNA replication to begin, several steps must occur. First, the specific origin site must be recognized by the appropriate protein. Then the site must be opened and stabilized. And, finally, a replication fork must be initiated in both directions, involving continuous and discontinuous DNA replication. Although many of the proteins involved are known, all the steps at the enzymatic level are not, and hence our understanding is a bit sketchy. Following is a description, most of whose steps are known.

OriC, the origin of replication in *E. coli*, is about 245 base pairs long and is recognized by proteins called *initiator proteins* that open up the double helix. The initiator proteins then take part in the attachment of *primosomes*, a complex of two proteins: a primase, which creates RNA primers, and DNA *helicase*, which unwinds DNA at the Y-junction. As the primosomes move along, they create RNA primers used by DNA polymerase III to initiate Okazaki fragments. At some point, leading-strand synthesis begins and Y-junction activity then proceeds as outlined earlier.

In some phages and plasmids, the initiation of replication is not with an RNA primer but with a protein. This protein provides the primer configuration with an OH group from an amino acid. The generality of this type of priming has not been established. Another interesting protein interaction at the origin of replication involves the reverse of initiation of DNA synthesis, the prevention of the initiation of DNA synthesis. This is accomplished by a newly discovered protein, called an "off switch." That is, this protein binds to the DNA at *oriC* and apparently prevents DNA replication from beginning. It does this by its binding activity that prevents the initiator proteins from opening the DNA. Thus this protein may be a very important component in control of the cell cycle stopping the cell cycle from beginning. Presumably, when the appropriate time comes for the cell cycle to begin, the protein is removed.

Events at the Y-Junction

We now have the image of DNA replication proceeding by a primosome, moving along the lagging strand template, opening up the DNA (helicase activity), and creating RNA primers (primase activity). One DNA polymerase III moves along the leading-strand template generating the leading strand by continuous DNA replication, whereas a second DNA polymerase III moves backward, away from the Y-junction, creating Okazaki fragments. *Single-strand binding proteins* (ssb proteins) keep single-stranded DNA stabilized (open) during this process, and DNA polymerase I and ligase are connecting Okazaki fragments.

This simple picture is slightly complicated by the fact that a single DNA polymerase seems to do the entire lagging strand, rather than dropping off the DNA at the completion of an Okazaki fragment and being replaced by a new one at the newest primer near the Y-junction. In addition, there is evidence that the lagging and leading-strand synthesis is coordinated. The *replisome* model has arisen in which both copies of DNA polymerase III are attached to each other and work in concert with the primosome at the Y-junction. According to this model, a single replisome consisting of two copies of the DNA polymerase III *holoenzyme* (each actually made of seven subunits), a helicase, and a primase, move along the DNA. The leading-strand template is immediately fed to a polymerase, whereas the lagging - strand template is not acted on by the polymerase unit an RNA primer has been placed on the strand, meaning that a long (fifteen hundred base) single strand has been opened up.

As the replisome moves along, another single-stranded length of the lagging-strand template is formed. At about the time that the Okazaki fragment is completed, a new RNA primer has been created. The Okazaki fragment is released and a new Okazaki fragment is begun, starting with the latest primer taking the replisome back to the same configuration, but one Okazaki fragment farther along.

Supercoiling

The simplicity and elegance of the DNA molecule masks an inevitable problem of coiling. Since the DNA molecule is made from two strands that wrap about each other, certain operation, such as DNA replication and its termination, meet topological difficulties. Up to this point, we have seen the circular *E. coli* chromosome in its "relaxed" state. However, there are enzymes in the cell that cause DNA to become overcoiled (positively *supercoiled*) or undercoiled (negatively supercoiled). Positive supercoiling comes about either from too many turns of the DNA in a given length or from the molecule wrapping around itself.

Positive supercoiling comes from having the circular duplex wind about itself in the same direction as the helix twists (right handed), whereas negative supercoiling comes about by having the duplex wind about itself in the opposite direction as the helix twists (left handed). The former state increases the number of turns of one helix around the other side (the *linkage number*, L), whereas the latter decreases it. The three forms of DNA, all have the same sequence yet differ in their linkage number. They are referred to as topological isomers (*topoisomers*). The enzymes that create or alleviate these states are called *topoisomerases*.

Topoisomerases affect supercoiling by either of two methods. Type I topoisomerases break one strand of a double helix and, while binding the broken ends, pass the other strand through the break. The break is then sealed. Type II topoisomerases (e.g., *DNA gyrase* in *E. coli*) do the same sort of thing only instead of breaking one strand of a double helix, they break both and pass another double helix through the temporary gap.

As DNA replication proceeds, positive supercoiling builds up ahead of the Y-junction. This is eliminated by the action of topoisomerases that either create negative supercoiling ahead of the Y-junction in preparation for replication or alleviate positive supercoiling after it has been created. The major components of DNA replication in *E. coli* are summarized in table 7.1.

Termination of Replication

The termination of the replication of a circular chromosome presents no major topological problems. The theta-structure replication finishes with both Y-junctions having proceeded around the molecule. The leading strand on one template closes in on the lagging strand begun in the other direction with the same happening on the other template. The process stops with about twenty-five twists remaining at no particular spot on the chromosome (there is no "termination" locus). A topoisomerase then release the two circles and DNA polymerase I and ligase close them up.

Several different mechanisms have been explored for the termination of the linear chromosomes of some viruses and all eukaryotic genomes. Linear molecules have the problem of completing the last Okazaki fragment. An RNA primer on the very tip of the

Table 7.1. Summary of the Enzymes Involved in DNA Replication in E.coli.

Enzyme (Protein)	*Genetic Locus*	*Function*
DNA polymerase I	*pol A*	Gap filling and primer removal
DNA polymerase II	*pol B*	?
DNA polymerase III		
α subunit	*dnaE* (*polC*)	DNA replication
β subunit	*dnaN*	DNA replication
γ subunit	*dnaX*	DNA replication
δ subunit	?	DNA replication
ε subunit	*dnaQ*	3′→5′ exonuclease
θ subunit	?	DNA replication
τ subunit	*dnaX*	DNA replication
Initiator protein	*dnaA*	Binds to origin of replication
RNA polymerase subunit	*rpoA, B, C, D*	RNA primer in some system
Primase	*dnaG*	RNA primer in some system
DNA ligase	*lig*	Closes nicked DNA strands
Helicase	*rep*	Unwinds DNA for replication
Ssb proteins	*ssb*	Single-strand stability
DNA topoisomerase I	*topA*	Supercoiling of DNA
DNA topoisomerase II		
α subunit	*gyrA* (*nalA*)	ATPase
β subunit	*gyrB* (*cou*)	Cutting, closing of DNA

3′→5′ template cannot be replaced by DNA polymerase I, assuming even that a final primer can be put on the very tip of the molecule. In eukaryotes, an enzyme, telomerase, attaches repeats of a short sequence at each chromosome tip.

Replication Models

The model of DNA replication that we have presented here comes primarily from evidence gathered in *E. coli*, which replicates by way of the *theta*-structure intermediate. However, two other modes of replication occur in circular chromosomes: rolling-circle and D-loop.

Rolling-Circle Model

In the *rolling-circle* mode of replication, a nick (a break in one of the phosphodiester bonds) is made in one of the strands of the circular DNA, resulting in replication of a circle and a tail. This form of replication occurs in the Hfr *E. coli* chromosome, or the F plasmid, during conjugation. The F^+ or Hfr cell retains the circular daughter while passing the linear tail into the F^- cell. This method is also used in several phages, which fill their heads (protein coats) with linear DNA replicated from a circular parent molecule.

In the model for rolling-circle replication, the nick made in one strand creates a free 3′-OH end and a free 5′-PO_4 end. Synthesis of a new circular strand occurs by addition of nucleotides to the 3′ end using the complementary intact strand as a template. No primer is needed because the original break produces a primer configuration (3′-OH). As nucleotides are added to one end of the broken strand in a continuous fashion, the other end is displaced as a 5′-PO_4 tail. As replication of the circular templates occurs, the 5′-PO_4 tail is replicated in a discontinuous manner, and the resulting double helix can be severed from the double-helical circle by a nuclease. DNA ligase closes the replicated circular strand and can join the ends of the replicated tail into a circle in the F^- cell, or can package the linear molecule in a phage head, depending upon which type of circular DNA has been replicated.

D-Loop Model

Chloroplasts and mitochondria have their own circular DNA molecules that appear to replicate by a slightly different mechanism than those described. The origin of replication is at different point on each of the two parental template strands. Replication begins on one strand, displacing the other while forming a displacement loop or *D-loop* structure. Replication continues until the process passes the origin of replication on the other strand. Replication is then initiated on the second strand, in the opposite direction. The result is two circles. Some species have chloroplasts and mitochondria with circular DNAs that have multiple D-loops formed.

Eukaryotic DNA Replication

As we saw earlier, linear eukaryotic chromosome usually have multiple origins of replication resulting in figures referred to as "bubbles" or "eyes." Multiple origins allow eukaryotes to replicate their larger quantities of DNA in a relatively short time, even though eukaryotic DNA replication is considerably showed by the presence of histone proteins associated with the DNA to form chromatin. For example, the *E. coli* replication fork moves about twenty-five thousand base pairs per minute, whereas the eukaryotic Y-junction moves only about two thousand base pairs per minute. The number of replications in eukaryotes varies from about five hundred in yeast to as many as sixty thousand in a diploid mammalian cell.

Much less is understood about eukaryotic DNA replication because of the complexity of eukaryotes and the relatively shorter time during which they have been studied effectively. We presume that eukaryotes have solved the same problems faced by prokaryotes in a similar, but not identical, fashion. For example, eukaryotes have five types of DNA polymerases, named DNA polymerase α, β, γ, δ, and ε. DNA polymerases γ, δ, and ε have exonuclease activity. DNA polymerases α and δ are the major replicating enzymes, with polymerase α replicating the lagging strand and polymerase δ replicating the leading strand. The role of polymerase ε is unclear; it seems capable of regular leading- or lagging-strand replication. DNA polymerase β is the major repair polymerase (like polymerase I in prokaryotes). DNA polymerase γ appears to be concerned primarily with mitochondrial DNA replication.

Table 7.2. Eukaryotic DNA Polymerases

Enzyme	*Function*
DNA polymerase α	Replication of nuclear chromosomes (lagging strand)
DNA polymerase β	Repair of nuclear chromosomes
DNA polymerase γ	Replication of mitochondrial chromosomes
DNA polymerase δ	Replication of nuclear chromosomes (leading strand)
DNA polymerase ε	Probably replication of nuclear chromosomes

8

BIOSYNTHESIS OF PROTEIN

Proteins are the molecules responsible for catalyzing most intracellular chemical reactions (enzymes), for regulating gene expression (regulatory proteins), and for determining many features of the structues of cells, tissues, and viruses (structural proteins). A protein is composed of one or more chains of amino acids that are covalently joined. The chains of amion acids are called *polypeptides*. The 20 different amino acids commonly found in natural polypeptides can be in any number and any order. Because the number of amino acids in a polypeptide molecule usually ranges from 100 to 1000, the number of different protein molecules that is possible is enormous.

Each amino acid contains a carbon atom (the α carbon) to which is attached one carboxyl group (—COOH), one amino group (—NH_2), and a side chain commonly called an R group. The R group are generally chains or rings of carbon atoms bearing various chemical groups. The simplest side chains are those of glycine (—H) and of alanine (CH_3). Polypeptide chains are formed when the carboxyl group of one amino acid joins with the amion grioup of a second amino acid; the resulting chemical bond is an ordinary covalent bond called a *peptide bond*. Thus, the basic unit of a protein is a polypeptide chain in which α-carbon atoms alternate with peptide units to for a backbone having an ordered array of side chains.

The two ends of every polypeptide molecule are distinct. One end has a free —NH_2 group and is called the *amino terminus*; the other end has a free -COOH group and is the *carboxyl terminus*. Polypeptides are synthesized by adding individual amion acids to the carboxyl end of the growing chain. Conventionally the amion acids of a polypeptide chain are numbered starting with the amino acid at the amion end.

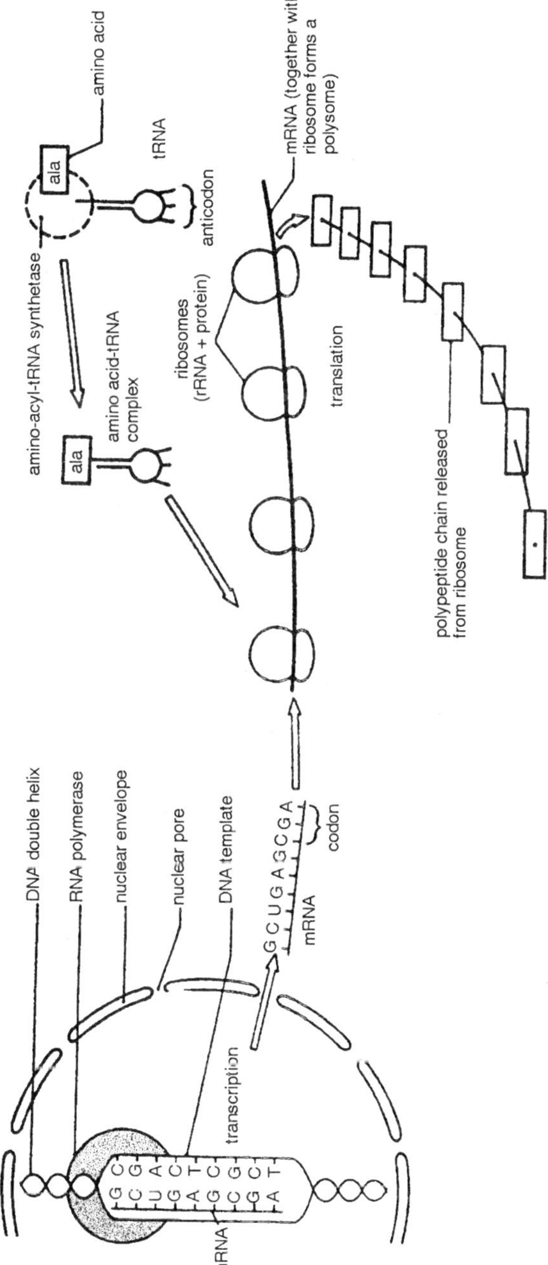

Fig. 8.1. Simplified summary diagram of the major structures and processes involved in protein synthesis in the cell.

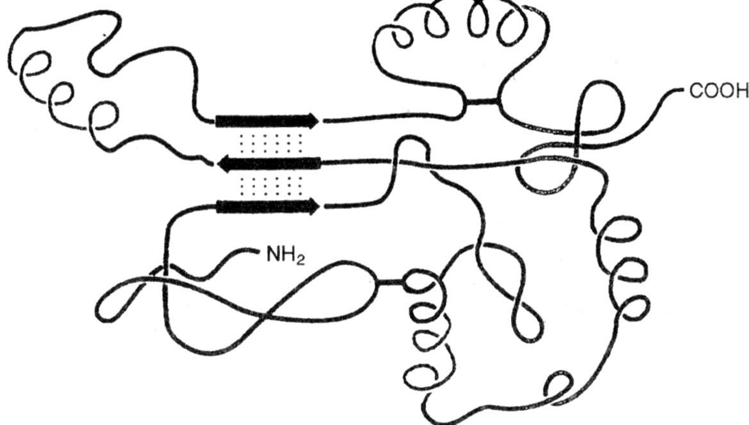

Fig. 8.2. A schematic diagram of the path of the backbone of a polypeptide, showing possible ways in which the polypeptide may be folded. Heavy black arrows represent β sheets; the dots joining the arrows represent hydrogen bonds.

Most polypeptide chains are highly folded, and a variety of three-dimensional shapes have been observed. The manner of folding is determined primarily by the sequence of amino acids —in particular, by noncovalent interactions between the side chains—and so each polypeptide chain tends to fold into a unique three-dimensional shape as it is being synthesized. In some cases, protein folding is interactions with other proteins in the cell. The rules of folding are complex and shape cannot usually be predicted from the amino acid sequence except for the simplest proteins. On the average. the molecules fold so that amino acids with charged side chains tend to be on the surface of the protein (in contact with water) and those with uncharged side chains tend to be internal. Specific folded configurations also result from hydrogen-bonding between prepaid groups. Two fundamental polypeptide structures are the α helix and the β sheet. Covalent bonds may also form between the sulfur atoms of some pairs of cysteines.

Many protein molecules consist of more than one polypeptide chain. When this is the case, the protein is said to contain *subunits*. The subunits may be identical or different. For example, hemoglobin, the oxygen carrier of blood, consists of four subunits, two each of two different types.

Relations Between Genes and Polypeptides

Most genes contain the information for the synthesis of only one polypeptide chain, Furthermore. the *sequence* of nucleotides in a gene determines the *sequence* of amino acids in polypeptide. This point was first proved by studies of the tryptophan synthetase gene *trpA* in *E. coli*, a gene in which many mutations had been obtained and accurately mapped. The effects of numerous mutations on the amino acid sequence of the enzyme were determined by directly analyzing the amino acid sequences of the wildtype and mutant enzymes. Each mutation was found to result in a single amino acid substituting for the wildtype amino acid in the enzyme; more importantly, *the order of the mutations in the genetic map was the same as the order of the affected amino acids in the polypeptide chain.* This attribute of genes and polypeptdes is called *colinearity*, which means that the sequnce of base pairs in DNA determines the sequence of amino in the polypeptide in a colinear or point-to-point manner. Colinearity is universally found in prokaryotes. However, we will see later that in eukaryotes noninformational DNA sequences interrupt the continuity of most genes, the order but not the spacing between the mutations correlates with amino acid substitution.

TRANSCRIPTION

The first step in gene expression is the synthesis of an RNA molecule copied from the segment of DNA that constitutes the gene. The basic features of the production of RNA are described in this section.

General Features of RNA Synthesis

The essential chemical characteristics of the enzymatic synthesis of RNA resemble those of DNA synthesis.

1. The precursors is the synthesis of RNA are the four ribonucleoside 5'-triphosphates— namely, adenosine triphosphate (ATP), guanosine triphosphate (GTP), cytidine triphosphate (CTP. and uridine triphosphate (UTP). They differ from the DNA precursors only in that the sugar is ribose rather than deoxyribose and the base uracil (U) replaces thymine(T).
2. In the formation of RNA, a sugar-phosphate bond is formed between the 3'-hydroxyl group of one nucleo-tide and the 5'-triphosphate of a second nucleotide. This is the same chemical reaction as that which occurs in the synthesis of DNA, but the enzyme is different.

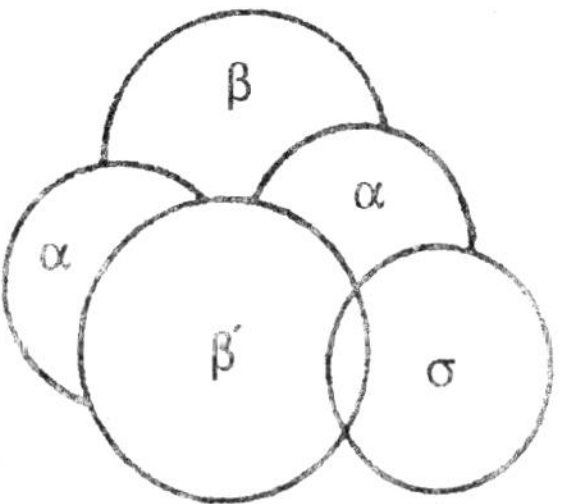

Fig. 8.3. A model of the structure of prokaryotic RNA polymerase showing association of five polypeptides (α,ββ σ)

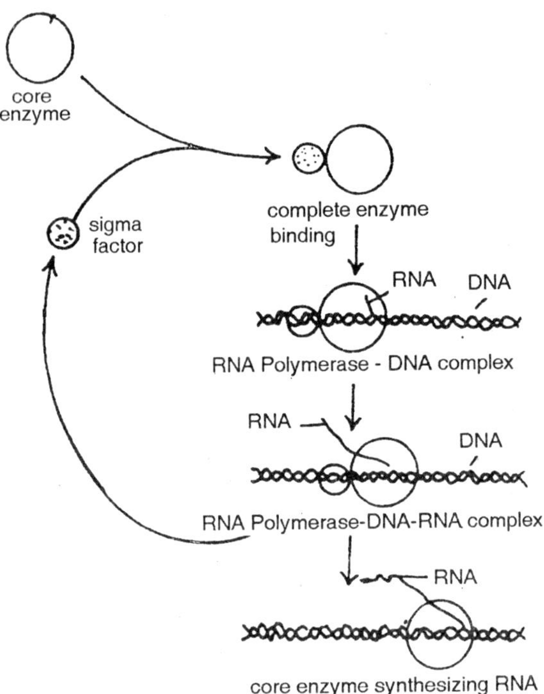

Fig. 8.4. Role of sigma factor and core enzyme of RNA polymerase during transcription.

3. The sequence of bases in an RNA molecule is determined by the base sequence of the DNA template. Each base added to the growing end of the RNA chain is chosen for its ability to base-pair with the DNA template strand: thus, the bases C, T, G, and A in a DNA strand cause G, A, C, and U, respectively, to be added to the growing end of an RNA molecule.
4. Nucleotides are added only to the 3'-OH end of the growing chain: as a result, the 5' end of a growing RNA molecule bears a triphosphate group. (The 5' → 3' direction of chain growth is the same as that in DNA synthesis.)

A significant difference between DNA polymerase and RNA polymerase is that *RNA polymerase is able to initiate chain growth without a primer.*

An important feature of RNA synthesis is the following:

Introns and Exons

In 1977 biologists were surprised to discover that the DNA of a eukaryotic gene is longer than its corresponding mRNA. It should be the same length because the mRNA is a direct copy. It was discovered that immediately after the mRNA is made, certain sections of the molecule are cut out, before it is used in translation. The sections of the gene that code for these unused pieces of RNA are called *introns*. The remaining sections of the gene are the code for the protein and are called *exons*. The size and arrangement of introns is very variable and characteristic for a particular gene. In prokaryotes there are no introns.

One possible function for introns has come with the discovery that the same mRNA may have different introns removed in different cells. The gene therefore has alternative introns and can code for different, though similar, proteins. This increases its potential use.

An example is the calcitonin gene. Two different forms of mRNA can be produced by this gene, depending on which introns are removed. One is produced in the thyroid gland and codes for the protein calcitonin, which had 32 amino acids. Calcitonin is a hormone which acts to lower calcium levels in the blood. The other is produced in the hypothalamus and codes for a protein with 37 amino acids which is similar to calcitonin and is called CGRP (calcitonin gene-related peptide). This is a powerful vasodilator agent. It is also released from nerve endings in some parts of the peripheral nervous system.

Protein Synthesis in Prokaryotes

There are three major steps in protein synthesis: initiaion, elongation, and termination. These will be discussed in turn.

Initiation

Initiator tRNA. The first amino acid in the syntheis of all bacterial polypeptides is N-formyl-methionine (fmet), which is a modified methionine amino acid in which the α-amino group is "blocked" and therefore cannot participate in peptide bond formation. The formyl group is added to the methionine after the amino acid has become attached to a specific tRNA, called tRNA. fmet. This reaciton is catalyzed by the enzyme *transformylase*. In many cases the fmet that starts a polypeptide chain is subsequently removed by enzymatic action.

Biochemical analysis has shown that at least two species of tRNA that can be charged with methionine are present in all prokaryotic organisms: one is that tRNA involved with initiaton, and the other species is responsible for the insertion of methionine elsewhere in the polypeptide chain. The latter rRNA is designed rRNA.met. Both of these tRNAs in bacteria are aminoacylated by the same enzyme, but only tRNA, fmet is a substrate for the transformylase-catalyzed reaction.

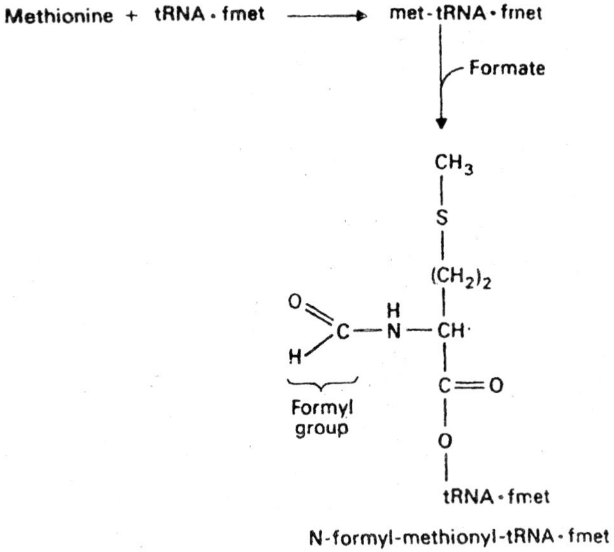

Methionine + tRNA · fmet ——→ met-tRNA · frnet

Formate

CH_3 — S — $(CH_2)_2$ — CH(—N(H)—C(=O)H) — C=O — O — tRNA · fmet

Formyl group

N-formyl-methionyl-tRNA · fmet

Fig. 8.5. Synthesis of N-formylmethionyl-tRNA.

Both tRNAs read AUG (the only methionine codon), but in addition tRNA.fmet can recognize GUG and UUG codons. RNA-sequencing studies have shown that both molecules havae an anticodon that is complementary to AUG. The two tRNA molecules do differ in some other properties. For example, the binding of fmet-TRNA.fmet to ribosomes is catalyzed by an initiator factor whereas the binding of met-tRNA.met is catalyzed by elongation factors. The two tRNAs apparantly bind to the ribosome at different sites. Thus it is clear that fmet.tRNA.fmet must have a strucutre that is specific for its role in initiation.

Ribosome binding sites

In bacteria, the first step in initiation is the formation of a complex between the 30S ribosomal subunit, fmet-TrNA, and an mRNA molecule. The 50S subunit is added later to form the active 70S ribosome (monosome). The mRNA may contain information for one to several distinct polypeptide chains. For each of the segments coding for a polypeptide, there is a specific nucleotide sequence for orienting the mRNA correctly and in the right reading frame on the ribosome. These sequences are called the *ribosome binding sites*.

Most of the ribosome binding sites have apurine-rich sequence about 8 to 12 bases upstream from the AUG start codon. This equence

Message origin	Ribosome binding site sequence
E. coli lac Z	UUC ACA CAG GAA ACA GCU AUG ACC AUG AUU
E. coli trp B	AUA UUA AGG AAA GGA ACA AUG ACA ACA UUA
E. coli RNA polymerase β	AGC GAG CUG AGG AAC CCU AUG GUU UAC UCC
Phage λ cro	AUG UAC UAA GGA GGU UGU AUG GAA CAA CGC

Fig. 8.6. Some prokaryotic ribosome binding sites. The initiation codon, AUG, is boxed. The larger boxed regions indicate the regions of contiguous complementarity (including allowable G-U base pairs) to the 3' end of 16S rRNA.

and other bases in this region are complementary to a pyrimidine-rich region, including at least CCUCC at the 3' end of 16S rRNA. The mRNA region that binds in this way is called the *Shine-Dalgarno sequence* after the discoverers of this relationship. Thus it appears that the formation of complementary base pairs between mRNA and 15 S rRNA in the 30S ribosomal subunit allows the ribosomes to locate and bind to the initator regions in the mRNA.

Initiation factors and initiation

In addition to mRNa, fmet-tRNA, and ribosomal subunits, three protein initiaion factors (IF-1, IF-2, and IF-3) and GTP are required for the initiation process to occur. First the properties of the initiation factors are discussed and then the scheme proposed for the initiation processes in protein synthesis is presented.

1. *IF-3.* The IF-3 factor weighs 23,000 daltons and functions in binding mRNA to the 30S subunit. It also acts as a dissociation factor for separating the 30S and 50S subunits after polypeptide synthesis is complete. Like all the IFs, IF-3 is found bound to free 30S subunits and can be released by washing the subunits in 0.5 M ammonium chloride.

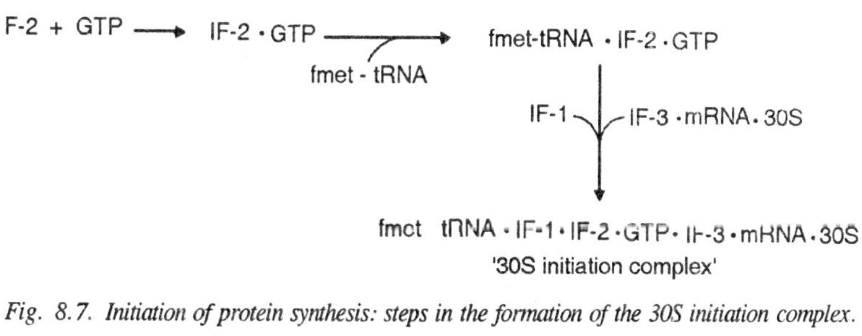

F-2 + GTP ⟶ IF-2 · GTP ⟶ (fmet - tRNA) fmet-tRNA · IF-2 · GTP

↓ IF-1, IF-3 · mRNA . 30S

fmet tRNA · IF-1 · IF-2 · GTP · IF-3 · mRNA · 30S
'30S initiation complex'

Fig. 8.7. Initiation of protein synthesis: steps in the formation of the 30S initiation complex.

Experiments with radioacative If-3 have shown that it is capable of binding to both 30S subunits and to mRNA molecules. In an in vitro protein-synthesizing system, IF-3 enhances the binding of fmet-tRNA to mRNA.30S subunit complexes. It is attractive to suppose that IF-3 recognizes mRNAs by the AUG or GUG initiation codons, but there is no solid evidence on this point.

In summary, the initiation reaction in which IF-3 is involved is:

IF-3 + mRNA + 30S subunit → (IF-3.mRNA.30S) complex

2. *IF-2*. The 80,000 dalton IF-2 protein in involved with the binding of the initiator tRNA to the IF-3.mRNA.30S complex. The high-energy molecule GTP is used in this reaction. In vitro experiments have shown that IF-2 and GTP will bind to form a complex that is stabilized when it is turn forms a complex with fmet-tRNA This latter complex then binds with the IF-3.mRNA.30S complex and the IF-1 protein factor (9000 daltons) to forms the 30S initiation complex.

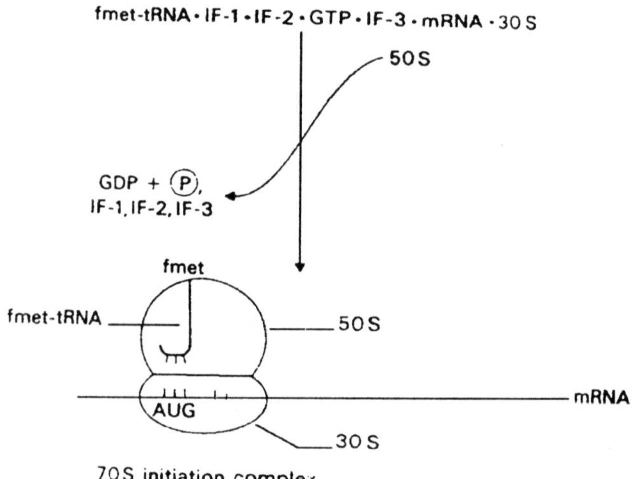

Fig. 8.8. Initiation of protein synthesis: addition of 50S ribosomal subunit to 30S initiation complex leads to formation of 70S ribosome in frame on the mRNA.

3. *Dissociation of initiation factors from the initiation complex*. The initiation factors function to bring fmet-tRNA, mRNA and 30S subunits into a stable association. The next step is the addition of a 50S subunit to form a 70S initiation complex. This leads to the hydrolysis of GTP to GDP + P and the release of three intiation factors. The factors can then be used for further initiaton reactions on the same or different mRNA.

Elongation

The 70S ribosome has two sites for binding aminoacyl-tRNA. In protein synthesis, charged tRNA binds first to a site called the A (aminoacyl) site. Then the amino acid it carries becomes joined to the growing polypeptide chain carried by the tRNA at the site called the P (peptidyl) site by the formation of a peptide bond.

It is not known whether the fmet-tRNA enters the A site and then moves to the P site or whether it enters the P site directly. Before

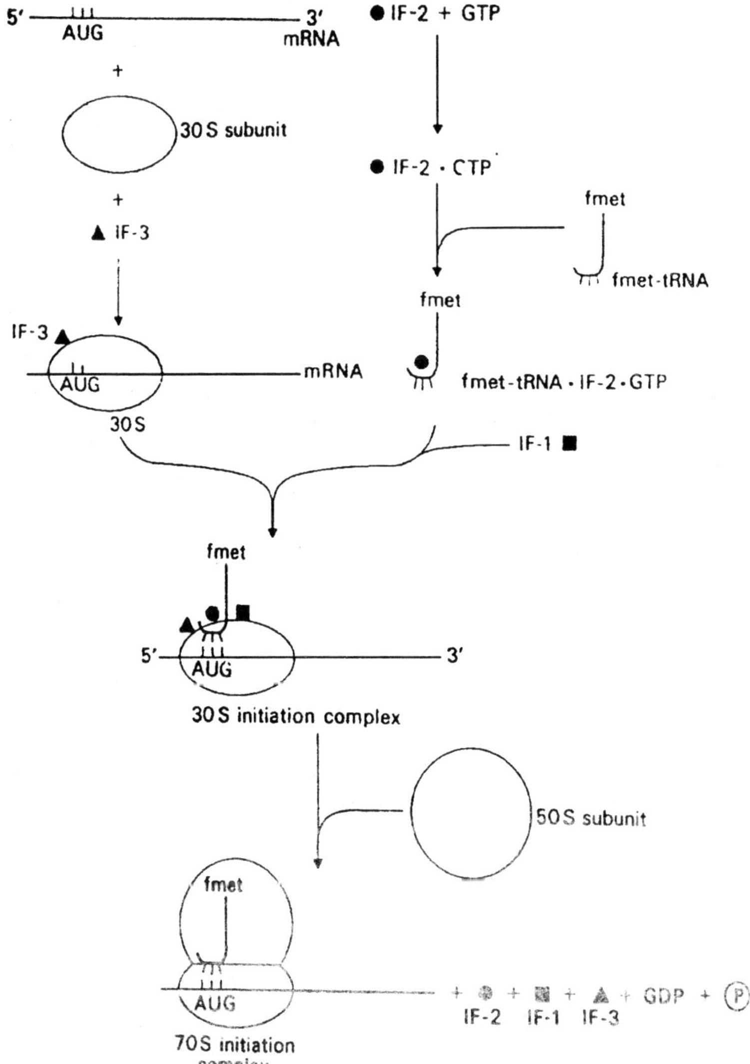

Fig. 8.9. Summary of the steps in the initiation of protein synthesis in prokaryotes.

further protein synthesis can occur, however, the fmet-tRNA must become located in the P site hydrogen-bonded to the start codon on the mRNA. Once this has occurred a cyclic sequence of events commences in which one amino acid at a time is added to the growing polypeptide chain. This is called *elongation.*

Binding of aminoacyl-tRNA

The charged tRNA with the complementary anticodon to the codon in the reading frame of the A site becomes bound to that site of the ribosome in a reaction requiring *elongation factor* T (EE-T) and GTP. This factor can be isolated from the soluble proteins of *E. coli*, and by column chromatography it can be separated into two polypeptides: Ts, which is stable and weighs about 30,000 daltons, and Tu, which is unstable and weights 42,000 daltons.

EF-T has been shown to bind with GTP and this is postulated to bring about the dissociation of the factor into the two polypeptides, resulting in the formation of an EF-Tu.GTP complex and releasing free EF-Ts. The next step in the elongation process is the binding of aminoacyl-tRNA to the complex to produce an aminoacyl-tRNA.Tu.GTP complex. There is evidence that this complex is an intermediate in aminoacyl-tRNA binding to ribosomes. Once the charged tRNA is bound in the A site, GTP is hydrolyzed as a result of the enzymatic action of one or more 50S ribosomal proteins. This hydrolysis cause the release of EF-Tu in a complex with GTP. the latter is released and the elongation factor can reassociate with EF-Ts. The process can then be repeated with another aminoacyl-tRNA.

(a) Tu + Ts (Elongation factor T) + GTP → Tu + GTP + Ts

(b) Tu + GTP + aa-tRNA (amino acyl-tRNA) → aa-tRNA · Tu · GTP complex

(c) aa-tRNA · Tu · GTP + active 70S ribosome → aa-tRNA·70S (charged tRNA) enters A site) + Tu·GDP + P_i (released from ribosome)

(d) Tu · GDP + Ts → Tu · Ts

Experiments with an analog of GTP that cannot be hydrolyzed have shown that GTP hydrolysis is required for release of EF-Tu from the ribosome but it is not needed for aminoacyl-tRNA binding to the ribosome. Other experiments have shown that binding of fmet-tRNA to the ribosome does not require EF-Tu.

Peptide bond formation

At the beginning of the this stage, a tRNA carrying the growing polypeptide chain is located in the P site, and an aminoacyl-tRNA is

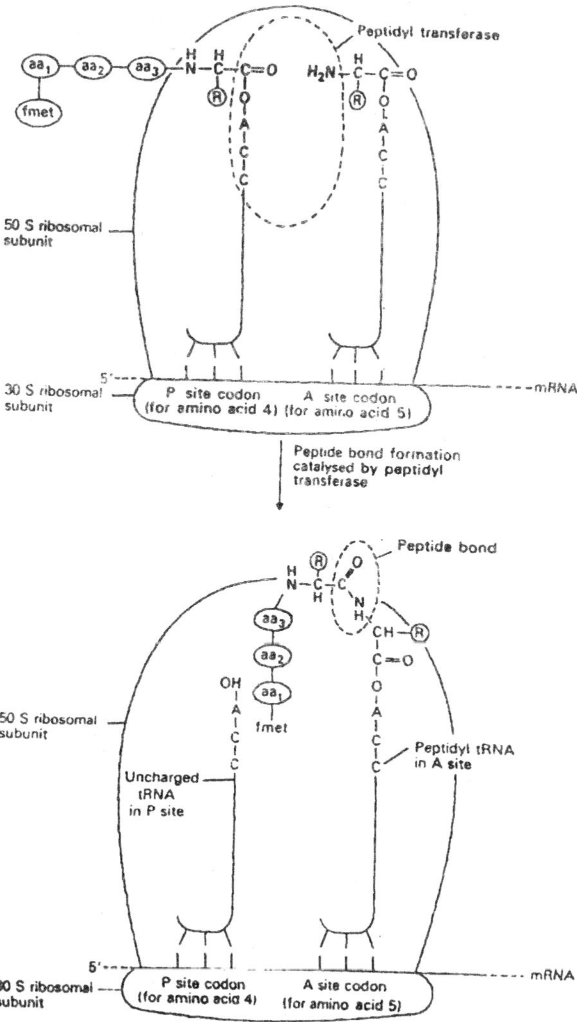

Fig. 8.10. Diagrammatic representation of peptide bond formation on ribosomes catalyzed by peptidyl transferase.

located in the A site. Thee tRNAs are maintained in positions conducive for peptide bond formation of the hydrogen bonds between the respective codons and anticodons and by the tertiary structure of the ribosome. The peptide bond is formed with the aid of the enzyme, *peptidyl transferase*, which is a ribosomal protein of the 50S subunit. The end result of the reaction is that the polypeptide chain is one amino acid longer, and the growing polypeptide chain has been transferred from the tRNA in the P site to the tRNA in the A site. The tRNA in the P site, which now has no amino acid bound to it, is called an *uncharged tRNA*.

Translocation

Once the peptide bond has been formed and the polypeptide chain is on the tRNA in the A site, the next step is advancement of the ribosome precisely one codon (three nucleotides) down the mRNA, a process called *translocation*. During this translocation event, the peptidyl-tRNA remains attached to the mRNA by codon-anticodon–pairing properties and thus becomes located in the P site. The A site is then vacant, and the aminoacyl-tRNA specified by the new codon there becomes bound by the process already described. The uncharged tRNA left in the P site after peptide bond formation is also released from the ribosome during translocation.

Elongation factor G (EF-F), a 72,000–84,000 dalton protein, and GTP hydrolysis are needed for translocation to occur, but it is not yet known how the translocation mechanism works. One GTP molecule is hydrolyzed for each translocation event. It appears that EF-G molecule is hydrolyzed for each translocation event. It appears that EF-G leaves the ribosome after translocation, since EF-Tu and EF-G cannot interact with the ribosome at the same time.

Termination

The end of the polypeptide chain is indicated on a mRNA molecule by a specific *chain-terminationg* (stop) *codon*. Three such codons are known: UAA, UAG, and UGA. No naturally occurring tRNA has an anticodon for any of these stop codons, and therefore no amino acid can be put into the polypeptide. Three specific termination factors have been shown to be involved in regarding the stop codon. they differ in their codon specificity and GTP requirement (Table 8.1).

RF1 and RF2 have overlapping specificities for the stop codons. They have been shown to interact with the termination codons by interaction at the A site. The RF3 factor apparently plays a stimulatory role in RF1 and RF2 activity. There is some evidence for a GTP requirement in the RF3 factor's activty. In any event, chain termination, as mediated by these factors, involves the cleavage of the carboxyl group of the C-terminal end of the polypeptide chain from the tRNa in the P site. This results in the release of the polypeptide and the now uncharged tRNA. The ribosome will then move along the mRNA until a new initiation sequence is encountered (as it may be in polycistronic mRNAs), or it will dissociate from the mRNA. If none is found, when the ribosome is released from the mRNA, IF-3 functions to keep the two subunits apart. Thus, when a new 70S initiation complex is formed, the two subunits are drawn randomly from the free pools of 30S and 50S subunits.

Table 8.1. Properties of prokaryotic termination factors.

Termination factor	*Molecular weight (daltons)*	*Stop codons recognized*	*GTP requirement*
RF1	44,000	UAA and UAG	No
RF2	47,000	UAA and UGA	No
RF3	46,000	None	Yes

While the polypeptide chain is being synthesized, the primary sequence of amino acids directs the three-dimensional shape. In other words, the elongating chain begins to assume its final shape as it is being made. Indeed, some enzyme activity can be detected on ribosomes that have not yet completed the synthesis of an enzymatic polypeptide.

Polysomes

Efficient translation of an mRNA molecule cannot be achieved by a single ribosome moving along it. The amount of space a ribosome

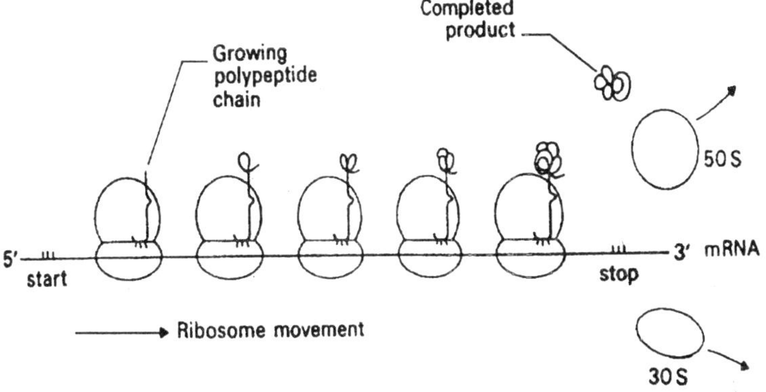

Fig. 8.11. Diagrammatic representation of a polysome engaged in protein synthesis.

takes up on a mRNA is relatively small, and thus several ribosomes can work on the mRNA at once. The association of a number of ribosomes on a single mRNA chain is called a *polyribosome* or *polysome*, and this allows several polypeptide chains to be made from each mRNA. The length of the polypeptide chain on a given ribosome will be directly proportional to how far the ribosome has moved along the mRNA from the 5' end of the molecule. The existence of polysomes explains why a cell needs so little mRNA, while at the same time it contains so much more protein.

Relationship of Transcription and Translation

In bacteria the mRNA typically becomes associated wth ribosomes while synthesis of the mRNA molecule is continuing. This is possible owing to the lack of a nuclear membranes so that as the 5' end of the growing mRNA molecule is displaced form the DNA as the double helix reforms, the ribosome binding site becomes available. Ribosomes then load on to the mRNA in rapid sequence, the first being close behind the RNA polymerase.

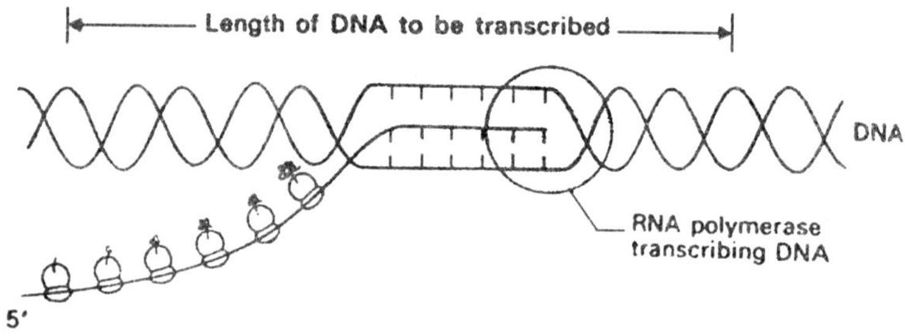

Fig. 8.12. Schematic of the possible translation of an mRNA while it is still being transcribed in prokaryotes.

To give some idea of the rates of these processes, the mRNA for the tryptophan biosynthetic operon is transcribed at a rate of about 1000 nucleotides per minute and the translation process proceeds at about the same rate. Thus approximately 350 amino acids can be polymerized into polypeptide chains each minute.

Another important aspect of translation is the lability of the mRNA. As mentioned in an earlier chapter, prokaryotic mRNAs are considered to be short-lived in that degradation of the molecule by 5'–exonuclease action competes wth the ribosome-mediated initiation of protein synthesis. Continued mRNA synthesis, then, is necessary for continued polypeptide synthesis.

Protein Synthesis in Eukaryotes

The steps and mechanisms of protein synthesis are similar in both eukaryotes and prokaryotes. As previously discussed, the ribosomes are different, and this is also the case with the soluble protein factors.

Initiation

Initiation of protein synthesis involves the binding of mRNA to the ribosomes. In eukaryotes it has now been established that the 5'-cap structure is necessary to get efficient binding but the 3' poly(A) sequence apparently is not needed. There is good evidence, however, that the poly(A) sequence stablizes the mRNA during the translation process. The precise mechanism whereby the eukaryotic message binds to the ribosome is not known, although it is most likely that RNA–RNA and RNA–protein interactions are involved. To date the nucleotide sequence has been determined to the 5'-side of the AUG start codon for a number of eukaryotic mRNAs and there are very few common features. Strikingly, while the last 50 nucleotides of *E.. coli* 16S rRNA and eukaryotic 18S rRNA are highly homologous and similiar secondary structure models can be built, the eukaryotic rRNA does *not* have the CCUCC sequence characteristic of prokaryotic rRNA. Also, there is no Shine-Dalgarno sequence in the eukaryotic mRNa. Thus it appears that, unlike the case in prokaryotes, there is not a fixed nucleotide sequence that plays a role in ribosome binding to the message.

As in prokaryotes the initiation codon is AUG, and a special initiator methionyl-tRNa recognizes that signal in the message. Unlike its prokaryotic counterpart the methonine carried by the tRNA does not become formylated, since the appropriate enzyme system does not exist in eukaryotic cells. The initiator tRNAcan be distinguished from the met-tRNA that reads AUG codons elsewhere in the message, however, by the fact that it can be formylated in vitro in the presence of an *E. coli* extract. Hence in eukaryotes it is also appropriate to define the two methionine-accepting tRNAs as tRNA.fmet and tRNA.met.

At least in mammals, there are many more initiation factors (labeled eIFs for eukaryotic initiation factors) than in prokaryotes. In many cases the proteins have not been purified to homogeneity, and thus their absolute roles in protein synthesis are uncertain. Between them all, they carry out the initiation events performed by the three prokaryotic IFs. It remains to be seen to what extent the situation in mammals is generalizable throughout the eukaryotes.

Elongation

As in prokaryotes, there are two elongation factors: eEF-1 (equivalent to prokaryotic EF-T) and eEF-2 (equivalent to prokaryotic EF-G). eEF-1 has been studied in a number of systems, and in general it exists in multiple forms. Purified eEF-1 from rabbit reticulocytes, for example, has a molecular weight of 186,000 and consists of three subunits weighing 62,000 daltons each. In some systems the subunits aggregate to produce molecules of greater than 1 million daltons. Regardng the function of eEF-1, much less is known than in the prokaryotes. The eEF-1 from rabbit reticulocytes, for example, has been shown to bind to aminoacyl-tRNA and to GTP, and thus to facilitate bindng of the aminoactyl-tRNA to the A site in ribosomes. During this step, GTP is hydrolyzed to DGP as a result of GTPase activity of the elongation factor, and an eEF-1.DGP complex is released from the ribosome.

The eukaryotic eEF-2 is similar to prokaryotic EE-G, although the two are not interchangeable in *in vitro* systems. The factor from rabbit reticulocytes has a molecular weight of 96,500–110,000 daltons and, after binding with GTP, binds to the ribosome. This event results in hydrolysis of GTP to GDP, translocation of the ribosome one codon down the message, and release of an eFF-2.GDP complex. All these steps are similar to the events that take place in prokaryotes, one exception being that the eukaryotic factor forms a stable complex with GTP whereas the prokarotic factor does not.

Termination

The same chain termination codons are functional in eukaryotes as in prokaryotes. One release factor has been identified in rabbit reticulocytes, and this has a molecular weight of 115,000 daltons and may be a dimer. This factor recognizes all three chain termination codons and it requires GTP to carry out its function. No stimulatory factor analogous to the porkaryotic RF-3 has been found in eukaryotes.

Protein Synthesis and Cellular Compartmentation in Eukaryotes

In prokaryotes there is no nuclear membrane to separate the transcription process from the translation process. The process of a nuclear membrane and the various modification process peculiar to mRNAs in eukaryotes present many levels at which the regulation of gene expression can be affected. These include transcription itself, the processing of the primary transcript to produce mature mRNA,

RNA-RNA splicing, and the movement of mRNA from the nucleus to the cytoplasm.

In eukaryotic cells, the cytoplasm contains a network of interconnecting channels bounded by membranes called the *endoplasmic reticulum* (ER). The membranes involved are continuous and may in fact connect to the nuclear membrane and the cell membrane. Close examination of the ER reveals that it is differentiated into two types, *smooth* (SER) and *rough* (RER), which are distinguished by the fact that the latter has ribosomes bound to it (hence the rough appearance) whereas the former does not. Thus, ribosomes in the cytoplasm are either membrane bound or free. The membrane-bound ribosomes synthesize proteins that are either secreted from the cell or that are packaged in lysosomes (where the proteins degrade other proteins). Thus, for example, pancreatic cells that secrete enzymes into the intestine are extremely rich in RER. The free ribosomes synthesize all other proteins found in the cell, that is, those in the cytoplasm, nucleus, mitochondria and chloroplasts (if present).

The proteins is to be secreted are made on the ribosomes of the RER and then transferred across the membrane into the channel system. The mRNAs for the secreted proteins must somewhow become associated specifically with the ribosomes of the RER. In 1975, G. Blobel and B. Dobberstein proposed a *signal hypothesis* to explain this. They suggested that there is a unique sequence of codons located to the 3' side of the initiator AUG codon which is present only in mRNAs for proteins that must be transferred across membranes. Translation of these codons results in a specific amino acid sequence at the N-terminal end of the protein. Then they postulated that the special end of the protein facilitates the attachment of the ribosome to the membrane so that the protein can be transferred across it. Once the protein has been completed, they proposed that the ribosome dissociates from the ER.

9

TRANSCRIPTIONAL CONTROL

Jacob and Monod proposed the operon model in 1961 for the co-ordinate regulation of transcription of genes involved in specific metabolic pathways. The operon is a unit of gene expression and regulation which typically includes.

- The *structural genes* (any gene other than a regulator) for enzymes involved in a specific biosynthetic pathway whose expression is co-ordinately controlled.
- Control elements such as an *operator sequence*, which is a DNA sequence that regulates transcription of the structural genes.
- *Regulator gene(s)* whose products recognize the control elements, for example a repressor which binds to and regulates an operator sequence.

The Lactose Operon

Escherichia coli can use lactose as a source of carbon. The enzymes required for the use of lactose as a carbon source are only synthesized when lactose is available as the sole carbon source. The lactose operon (or lac operon) consists of three structural genes: lacZ, which codes for b-balactosidase, an enzyme responsible for hydrolysis of lactose to balactose and glucose; lacY which encodes a galactoside permease which is responsible for lactose transport across the bacterial cell wall; and lacA, which encodes a thiogalactoside transacetylase. The three structural genes are encoded in a single transcription unit, lacZYA, which has a single promoter P_{lac}. This organization means that the three lactose operon structural proteins are expressed together as a polycistronic mRNA containing more than one coding region under

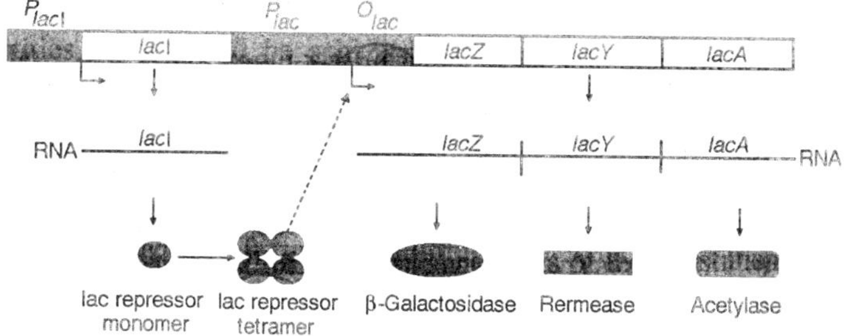

Fig. 9.1. Structure of the lactose operon.

the same regulatory control The lacZYA transcription unit contains an operator site o_{lac} which is positioned between bases —5 and +21 and the 5'-end of the P_{lac} promoter region. This site binds a protein called the lac repressor which is a potent inhibitor of transcription when it is bound to the operator. The lac repressor is encoded by a separate regulatory gene lacI which is also a part of the lactose operon lacI is situated just upstream from P_{lac}.

The Lac Repressor

The lacI gene encodes the lac repressor which is active as a tetramer of identical subunits. It has a very strong affinity for the lac operator-binding site, O_{lac}, and also has a generally high affinity for DNA. The lac operator site consists of 28 bp which is palindromic. (A palindrome has the same DNA sequence when one strand is read left to right in a 5' to 3' direction and the complementary strand is

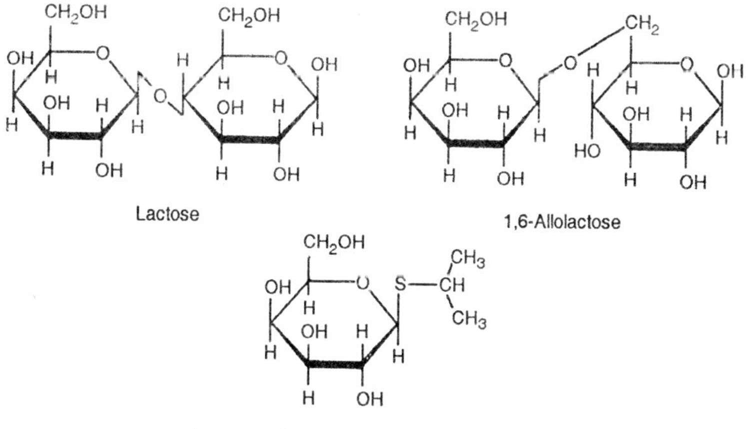

Lactose

1,6-Allolactose

Isopropylthiogalactopyranoside (IPTG)

Fig. 9.2. Structure of lactose, allolactose and IPTG.

read right to left in a 5' to 3' direction. This inverted repeat symmetry of the operator matches the inherent symmetry of the lac repressor which is made up of four identical subunits. In the absence of lactose, the repressor occupies the operator-binding site. It seems that both the lac repressor and the RNA polymerase can bind simultaneously to the lac promoter and operator sites. The lac repressor actually increases the binding of the polymerase to the lac promoter by two orders of magnitude. This means that when lac repressor is bound to the O_{lac} operator DNA sequence, polymerase is also likely to be bound to the adjacent P_{lac} promoter sequence.

Induction

In the absence of an inducer, the lac repressor blocks all but a very low level of transcription of lacZYA. When lactose is added to cells, the low basal level of the permease allows its uptake, and b-galactosidase catalyzes the conversion of some lactose to allolactose.

Allolactose acts as an inducer and binds to the lac repressor This causes a change in the conformation of the repressor tetramer, reducing its affinity for the lac operator. The removal of the lac repressor from the operator site allows the polymerase (which is already sited at the adjacent promoter) to rapidly begin transcription of the lazZYA genes. Thus, the addition of lactose, or a synthetic inducer such as isopropyl-β-D-thiogalactopyranoside (IPTG) very rapidly stimulates transcription of the lactose operon structural genes. The subsequent removal

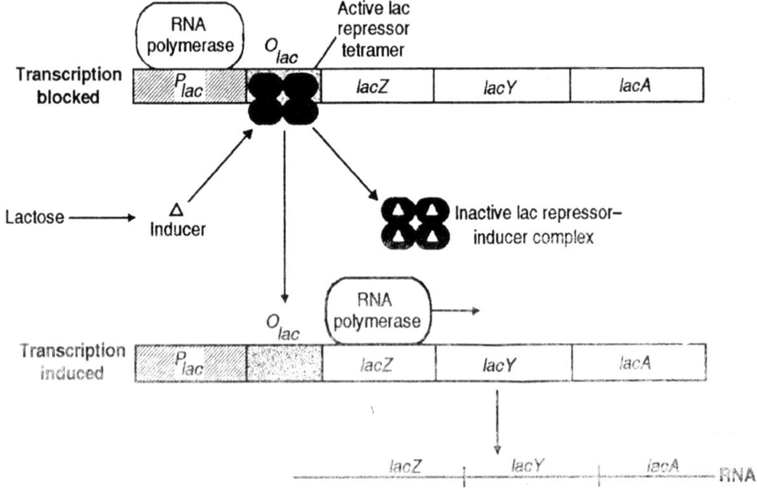

Fig. 9.3. Binding of inducer inactivates the lac repressor.

of the inducer leads to an almost immediate inhibition of this induced transcription, since the free lac repressor rapidly re-occupies the operator site and the lacZYA RNA transcript is extremely unstable.

cAMP Receptor Protein

The P_{lac} promoter is not a strong promoter. P_{lac} and related promoters do not have strong-35 sequences and some even have weak–10 consensus sequences. For high level transcription, they require the activity of a specific activator protein called cAMP receptor protein (CRP). CRP may also be called catabolite activator protein or CAP. When glucose is present, *E. coli* does not require alternative carbon sources such as lactose. Therefore, catabolic operons, such as the lactose operon, are not normally activated. This regulation is mediated by CRP which exists as a dimer which can not bind to DNA on its own, nor regulate transcription. Glucose reduces the level of cAMP in the cell. When glucose is absent, the levels of cAMP in E. coli increase and CRP binds to cAMP. The CARP-cAMP complex binds to the lactose operon promoter P_{lac} just upstream from the site for RNA polymerase. CRP binding induces a 90° bend in DNA, and this is believed to enhance RNA polymerase binding to the promoter, enhancing transcription by 50-fold. The CRP-binding site is an inverted repeat and may be adjacent to the promoter (As in the lactose operon), may lie within the promoter itself, or may be much further upstream from the promoter. Differences in the he CRP-binding sites of the promoters of different catabolic operons may mediate different levels of response of these operons to cAMP *in vivo*.

The TRP Operon

The Trypotophan Operon

The trp operon encodes five structural genes whose activity is required for trypotophan synthesis. The operon encodes a single transcription unit which produces a 7 kb transcript which is synthesized downstream from the trp promoter and trp operator sites P_{trp} and O_{trp} Like many of the operons involved in amino acid biosynthesis, the trp operon has evolved systems for co-ordinated expression of these genes when the product of the biosynthetic pathway, trytophan, is in short supply in the cell. As with the lac operon, the RNA product of this transcription unit is very unstable, enabling bacteria to respond to changing needs for tryptophan.

The Trp Repressor

A gene product of the separate trpR operon, the trp repressor, specifically interacts with the operator site of the trp operon. The

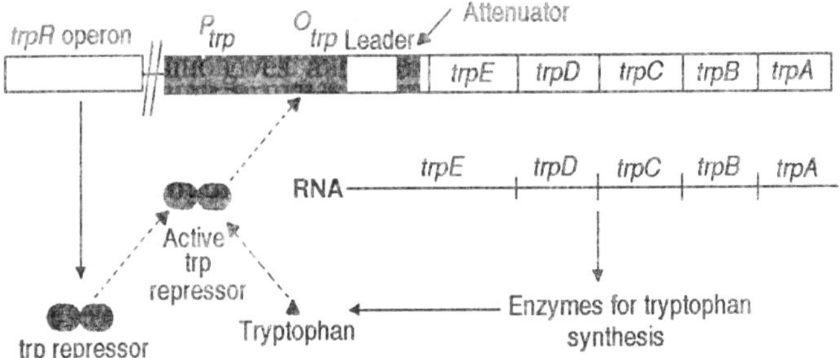

Fig. 9.4. Structure of the trp operon and function of the trp repressor.

symmetrical operator sequence, which forms the trp repressor-binding site, overlaps with the trp promoter sequence between bases -21 and +3 and +3. The core binding site is a palindrome of 18 bp. The trp repressor binds tryptophan and can only bind to the operator when it is complexed with tryptophan. The repressor is a dimer of two subunits which have structural similarity to the CRP protein and lac repressor. The repressor dimer has a structural with a central core and two flexible DNA-reading heads each formed from the carboxyl-terminal half of one subunit. Only when tryptophan is bound to the repressor are the reading heads the correct distance apart, and the side chains in the correct conformation, to interact with successive major grooves of the DNA at the trp operator sequence. Tryptophan, the end-product of the enzymes encoded by the trp operon, therefore acts as a co-repressor and inhibits its own synthesis through end-product inhibition. The repressor reduces transcription initiation by around 70-fold. This is a much smaller transcriptional effect than that mediated by the binding of the lac repressor.

The Attenuator

At first, it was thought that the repressor was responsible for all of the transcriptional regulation of the trp operon. However, it was observed that the deletion of a sequence between the operator and the trpE gene coding region resulted in an increase in both the basal and the activated (depressed) levels of transcription. This site is termed the attenuator and it lies towards the end of the transcribed leader sequence of 162 not that precedes the trpE initiator codon. The attenuator is a rho-independent terminator site which has a short GC-rich palindrome followed by eight successive U residues. If this sequence is able to form a hairpin structure in the RNA transcript, then it acts as a highly efficient transcription terminator and only a 140 bp transcript is synthesized.

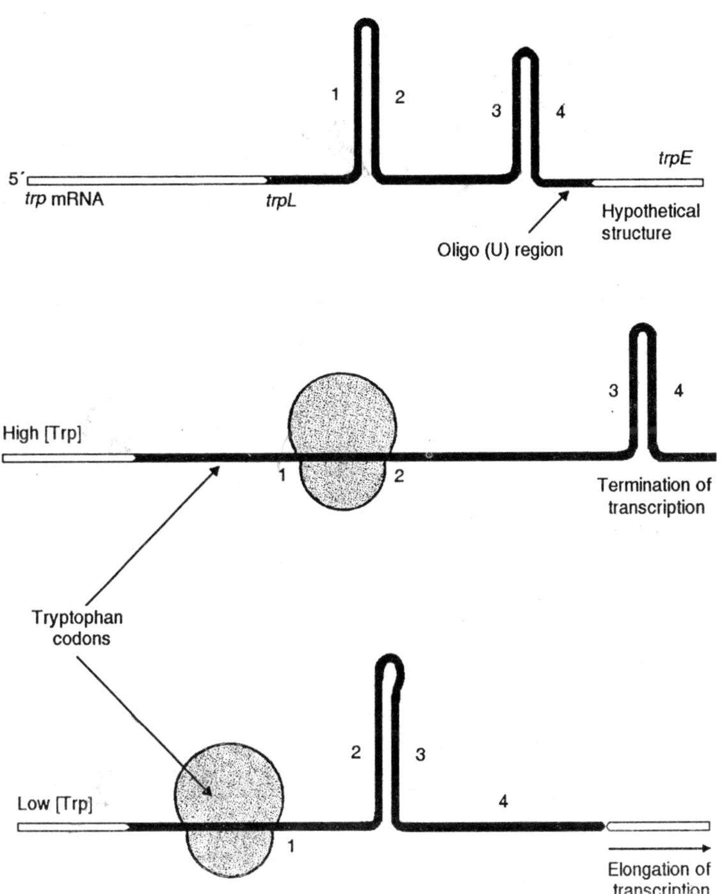

Fig. 9.5. Transcriptional attenuation in the trp operon.

Leader RNA Structure

The leader sequence of trp operon RNA contains for regions of complementary sequence which can form different base-paired RNA structures. These are termed sequences 1, 2, 3, and 4. The attenuator hairpin is the product of the base pairing of sequences 3 and 4. The attenuator hairpin is the product of the base pairing of sequences 3 and 4 (3:4 structure). Sequences 1 and 2 are also complementary and can form a second 1:2 hairpin. However, sequence 2 is also complementary and can form a second 1:2 hairpin. However, sequence 2 is also complementary to sequence 3. If sequences 2 and 3 form a 2:3 hairpin structure, the 3:$ attenuator hairpin cannot be formed and transcription termination will not occur. Under normal conditions, the formation of the 1:2 and 3:4 hairpins is energetically favourable.

The Leader Peptide

The leader RNA sequence contains an efficient ribosome-binding site and can form a 14-amino-acid leader peptide encoded by bases 27–68 of the leader RNA. The 10th and 11th codons of this leader peptide encode successive tryptophan residues, the end-product of the synthetic enzymes of the trp operon. This leader has no obvious function as a polypeptide, and tryptophan is a rare amino acid; therefore, the chances of two tryptophan codons is succession is low and, under conditions of low tryptophan availability, the ribosome would be expected to pause at this site. The function of this leader peptide is to determine tryptophan availability and to regulate transcription termination.

Attenuation

Attenuation depends on the fact that transcription and translation are tightly coupled in E. coli; translation can occur as an mRNA is being transcribed. The 3'-end of the trp leader peptide coding sequence overlaps complementary sequence the two trp codons are within sequence overlaps complementary sequences the two trp codons are within sequence 1 and the stop codon is between sequences 1 and 2. The availability of tryptophan (the ultimate product of the enzymes synthesized by the trp operon) is sensed through its being required in translation, and determines whether or not the terminator (3:4) hairpin forms in the mRNA.

As transcription of the trp operon proceeds, the RNA polymerase pauses at the end of sequence 2 until a ribosome begins to translate the leader peptide. Under conditions of high tryptophan availability, the ribosome rapidly incorporates tryptophan at the two trp codons and thus translates to the end of the leader message. The ribosome is then occluding sequence 2 and, as the RNA polymerase reaches the terminator sequence, the 3:4 hairpin can form, and transcription may be terminated. This is the process of attenuation.

Alternatively, if tryptophan is in scarce supply, it will not be available as an aminoacyl tRNA for translation, and the ribosome will tend to pause at the two trp codons, occluding sequence 1. This leaves sequence 2 free to form a hairpin with sequence 3, known as the anti-terminator. The terminator (3:4) hairpin cannot form, and transcription continues into trpE and beyond. Thus the level of the end product, tryptophan, determines the probability that transcription will terminate early (attenuation), rather than proceeding through the whole operon.

Importance of Attenuation

The presence of tryptophan gives rise to a 10-fold repression of trp operon transcription through the process of attenuation alone. Combined with control by the trp repressor (70fold), this means that tryptophan levels exert a 700-fold regulatory effect on expression from the trp operon. Attenuation occurs in at least six operons that encode enzymes concerned with amino acid biosynthesis. For example, the His operon has a leader which encodes a peptide with seven successive histidine codons. Not all of these other operons have the same combination of regulatory controls that are found in the trp operon. The His operon has no repressor-operator regulation, and attenuation forms the only mechanism of feedback control.

The Arabinose Operon of E. coli

The arabinose operon is another example of glucose-sensitive operon. As with lactose, when arabinose is absent, only a few molecules of the enzymes needed for arabinose catabolism are present in the cell. When arabinose is added (provided glucose is absent), there is a vary rapid increase in the number of arabinose catabolic enzymes. This is controlled by a different mechanism from that described for the lactose operon.

The gene governing the metabolism of arabinose comprise what is called a regulation, which is composed of at least three operons. The *araBAD* operon contains the gene for the enzymes involved with the conversion of L-arabinose to D-xylulose 5-phosphate. The controlling sites for this operon are located adjacent to it. Two operons control the transport of arabinose into the cell: *areE*, which is the structural gene for the L-arabinose binding protein, and *araF*. The regulator gene for the system, *araC*, is located between the *araBAD* controlling site region and the leu operon. The *araC* gene controls the expression of *araBAD* by its positive and negative action in the controlling site region. Since *araBAD*, *araE*, and *araF* are inducible by L-arabinose and controlled coordinately by *araC*, it is assumed that the structures of the three controlling site regions are similar. The following discussion will focus on the *araBAD* operon.

The operon is thought to be controlled as follows. The *araC* gene codes for a P1 protein, which has repressor function and exerts its effect by binding to that adjacent *araO* (operator) controlling site and

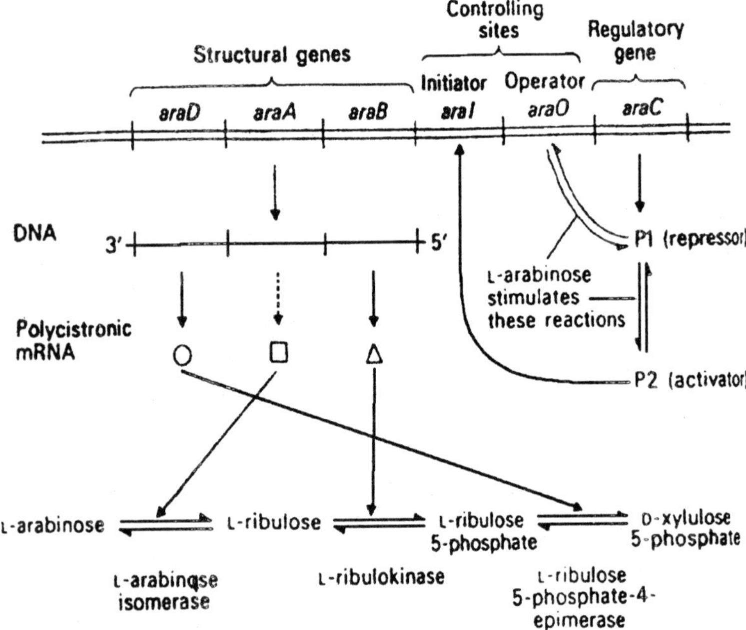

Fig. 9.6. The araBAD (arabinose) operon E. coli and the associated controlling sites and regulatory gene.

preventing the RNA polymerase from binding. Thus the operon is under negative control by P1. When L-arabinose is present, it stimulates the release of P1 from the DNA and the conversion of P1 to P2, which is an activator of the operon. The P2 binds to the *araI* (initiator) site, facilitating RNA polymerase binding and the initiation of transcription. (All this, of course, requires the prior binding of cAMP-CGA complex, and this is thought to occur in the same vicinity.) The three structural genes are transcribed on a single polycistronic mRNA. The operon, then, is under positive control by P2.

Much of this is hypothesis, but there is good evidence for some parts of it. There is genetic evidence for the existence of the araI site, and it is thought that part of this has promoter activity and another part is involved with cAMP-CGA binding. The function of the *araC* gene has been demonstrated by the study of genetic mutants. Mapping experiments with these mutants have shown that *araC* consists of only one cistron. Moreover, *araC* nonsense mutants have been shown to have no cis effect on the *araBAD* operon, thus indicating that *araC* is not in the BAD operon.

Three classes of *araC* alleles are known:

1. *araC*$^+$. The wild type allele renders the operon inducible; the three enzymes are induced by L-arabinose.
2. *araD*$^+$. These occur with high frequency and result in a pleiotropoically L-arabinose-negative phenotype. In other words, the enzymes are not inducible by L-arabinose.
3. *araC*^{c}. These are quite rare and give a pleiotropically constitutive phenotype in that the enzymes are produced even in the absence of the inducer.

.As with the regulatory mutants of the lactose operon, diploid studies have been used to obtain an understanding of the function of the *araC* gene. From these studies it was sown there *araC*$^-$ is recessive to C$^+$ in either the cis or trans arrangement. The C$^-$ alleles are complemented by A$^-$, B$^-$, and D$^-$ alleles, and thus the pleiotropic negative phenotype is not the result of a polarity effect on the araBAD operon. The conclusion from studies of C$^-$ and C$^+$C$^-$ strains was the C$^+$ produces a protein that, in the presence of L-arabinose, is necessary for the expression of the region. This suggested some positive control in the system and contrasts with the lactose operon C$^-$ mutants, which are constitutive because of the loss of negative control

The Cc alleles are cis- and trans-dominant to C$^-$, suggesting that they produce the activator P2 in the absence of L-arabinose; this activator is able to turn on an operon that is either cis or trans to the Cc allele. On the other hand, *C*$^+$ is dominant to *C*^{c}. This suggests that there is some negative control of the operon. Based on the model for regulation of the operon that was presented (which was, of course, proposed on the basis of the data now being discussed), in the absence of arabinose, P1 acts as a repressor, preventing expression of the operon by araCc activator. That is, when P1 is on the operator, transcription ceases even if P2 is present.

There is some biochemical evidence to support the regulatory model. Studies of heat-sensitive *araC*– mutants have shown that both the repressor and activator functions are heat-labile, thereby indicating that arac produces a protein that can serve both functions. The *araC* protein has been purified and it has been shown to have both repressor and activator activity. Indeed there is some evidence that the P2 form of the protein is a dimer of the P1 form. There is also evidence that L-arabinose interacts directly with the *araC* protein to bring about the necessary conversion. Also, there is direct evidence that the activator form of *araC* protein, P2, is required for transcription of the operon. In an *in vitro* system, synthesis of ara mRNA shows an absolute requirement for *araC* protein.

In conclusion, the L-arabinose regulation is under both positive and negative control, with the *araC* protein playing a pivotal role in the regulatory process. The exact nature of the controlling sites remains to be worked out. In contrast to the lactose operon where inhibition must be removed for the genes to be expressed, the arabinose operon requires activation for transcription to begin.

10

Cloning of Cells

There are two types of organisms-acellular and multicellular. The growth and development of an individual depends exclusively on the growth and multiplication of the cells. It was *Virchow* who first of all adequately stated the cell division. In animal cell the cell division was studied in the form of segmentation division or cleavage by *Prevost* and *Dumas* in 1824. The mechanism of cell division was not precisely investigated until long afterward but *Remak* and *Kolliker* showed that the process involves a division of both the nucleus and the cytoplasm. The term *karyokinesis* was introduced by *Schleicher* (1878) to designate the changes of nucleus during division, and the term *cytokinesis* was introduced by *Whiterman* (1887) to designate the associated changes taking place in the cytoplasm.

Cell division is necessarily the avoidance of ageing, and secondly for the segregation of an individual into semi-independent units which leads to efficiency. Thus, we see that cell division is a widespread phenomenon that is essential not only for the maintenance of life but also for the development of the organism itself.

Cell division can be conveniently described as:

(i) *Direct division.* Where the nucleus and cell body undergo a simple mass division into two parts. It is also called *amitosis*.

(ii) *Indirect division.* Here the nucleus undergoes complicated changes before it is divided into two daughter nuclei.

Having seen how the DNA in the nucleus is replicated and repaired, we turn now to the process whereby the two copies of each chromosome that have been generated during the prior S phase are separated from each other and partitioned into daughter cells. These processes are mitosis and cytokinesis.

The Stages of Mitosis

Mitosis has been known and studied for a century, but only in the past 25 years has significant progress been made toward understanding the mitotic process at the molecular level. We will begin by surveying the morphological changes that occur in a cell as it undergoes mitosis; later we will examine the underlying molecular mechanisms.

Morphologically, mitosis can be described as a series of five phases, based primarily on the appearance and behaviour of the chromosomes. As with any dynamic process, we must remember that the division into phase is somewhat arbitrary and that the phase are primarily a convenience for studying and describing the process.

The five phases of mitosis are prophase, prometaphase, metaphase, anaphase, and telophase. (An alternative term for prometaphase is simply "late prophase").

Interphase

The period of metabolic activity during which cell division is not in a process, has been called the 'intèrphase.' This is frequently referred to as the 'resting phase' but this term is not appropriate because the cell is metabolically most active at this stage that is why *Berril* and *Huskins* (1936) referred it as the *energy phases.* The interphase is the period between the telophase of one division and the prophase of the new cell division. During this phase the cell does everything except division. It is during interphase that the genes self-duplicate and carry on their function of supervising synthesis.

The chromatin granules in the nucleus are not readily distinguishable in the living cell, but may be brought out by treatment with chemicals which kill, fix and stain them. They appear at first glance to be scattered throughout the nucleus, but careful study has produced evidence that they are arranged in a definite pattern as long coiled strands and appear as a thread like net work in ordinary stained preparation.

"Nuclear sap" or, "Karyoplasm" fills the interstics between the chromosomes. One of more rounded bodies, the *nucleoli* are usually present. Between the nucleus and the surrounding cytoplasm, is the *nuclear membrane.* In the cytoplasm adjacent to the nucleus, there is a body, the *central body,* which consists of two granules or, after each granule has replicated, of two pairs of granules, the *centrioles.*

A typical cell cycle, including interphase lasts from 20-24 hrs. Interphase in the longest period in the cell cycle, and may last for several days in cells.

Interphase can be further divided into form sub-phases:

1. G_1-phase
2. S-phase
3. G_2-phase
4. M-phase.

G_1-phase includes the synthesis and organization of the substrate and enzyme necessary for DNA synthesis. Therefore, G_1, is marked by the synthesis of RNA and protein. G_1-phase is followed by the S-phase where the synthesis of DNA occurs.

During G_2-phase, all the metabolic activities are performed. M-phase is the period of chromosomal division.

The relative lengths of these phases differ in different organisms. A human cell in culture at 37°C, completes the mitotic cycle in about 20 hours and the M-phase lasts for only one hour. Temperature and cell environment plays an important role in determining the rate of cell division. Even the non-meristematic cells can sometimes be made to divide by changing the environmental conditions. Those cells which are not going to divide any more, have the mitotic cycle at the G_1 phase and start differentiating.

The cells shows following changes:

1. The cell, as a whole, attains the maximum growth and possesses synthesized proteins for energy for various divisions and processes.
2. The nuclear membrane is intact and the chromosomes are found in the form of more or less loosely coiled threads, somewhat closely appressed to the membrane. In this condition of chromosomes, most of the cytologists regard them to be duplicated, while some workers are of the opinion that they are multipartite.
3. The two centrioles, which are found at right angles to each other replicate into two each. *Mazia* (1961) has described that, if the replication is checked, then division will not take place.
4. For the future spindle condensation of protoplasm into a coherent area of jelly-like consistency also takes place. The spindle also starts growing and pushes the centrioles apart.
5. DNA synthesis occurs during autosynthetic interphase, when the chromosomes and dispersed.
6. Chromocentre are also conspicuous during the interphase.

Duration of Cell Division

The time required for completion of mitosis varies from cell type to cell type and is related to the length of the G_1 phase. Temperature, within certain limits, also affects the duration of the process. In general the metaphase and anaphase stages are of short duration; most of the time of cell division is spent in prophase and telophase stages. It must be remembered that the period between cell division, interphase, is usually long. For instance, in some mammalian cell cultures 16 to 20 hours between cell divisions is a common occurrence.

Many cells of both plants and animals studied in tissue culture show the following durations in the cell cycle.

G_1	10–20 hours (usually less than 50 percent of the total)
S	6–8 hours
G_2	1–4 or more hours (usually less than 20 percent of the total)
M	1 hour
Total	18–33 hours

Formation of Mitotic Apparatus: Prophase

Toward the end of G_2, the chromosomes start to condense from the extended, highly diffuse form of interphase chromatin to the dense, coiled structures characteristic of mitosis. Although the transition from interphase to mitotic prophase is not sharply defined, a cell is considered to be in *prophase* when the chromosomes have condensed to the point of being visible as threads in the light microscope. Each chromosome has duplicated during the preceding S phase and now consists of two sister chromatids. Sister chromatids are tightly attached to each other at a constricted region, the *centromere*, which corresponds to a particular stretch of the chromosome's DNA. As the chromosomes condense, the nucleolus (or nucleoli) gradually disappears.

Meanwhile, outside the nucleus, another important organelle has sprung into action. This is the *centrosome*, an amorphous cloud of material that, in most animal cells, surrounds a pair of *centrioles*. Because they are lacking in some mitotic cells, including all plant cells and fungal cells, centrioles cannot be essential for mitosis, and their function in the centrosome remains a mystery. However, the centriole structure—a cylinder made of microtubules—is related to the centrosome's role in the cell. The centrosome is a cellular organizing center for microtubules. During interphase, the microtubules of the cytoskeleton originate there. During prophase, the cytoskeletal

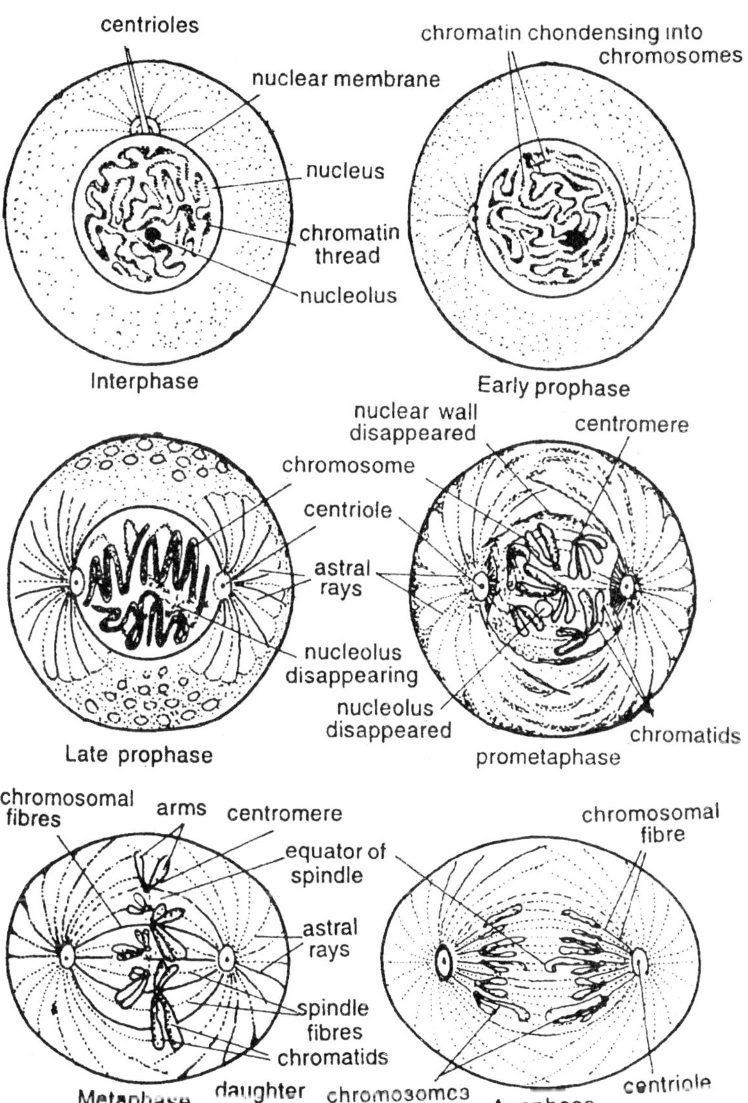

Fig. 10.1. Mitotic cell division in animal cells.

microtubules disassemble, and their tubulin subunits start to reassemble to form the *mitotic spindle*, the apparatus that will distribute chromosomes to the daughter cells. The centrosome, including its two centrioles, has duplicated during interphase, and in prophase the two centrosomes are seen to be moving apart from each other. Radiating from them are microtubules that are growing to form the mitotic spindle. The starburst of microtubules in the immediate vicinity of a centrosome is called an aster. The terms centrosome and aster were first used for animal cells but are now used more broadly.

Prometaphase

The start of *prometaphase* is marked by the fragmentation of the nuclear envelope into membranous vesicles, allowing the mitotic spindle to enter the nuclear area. Eventually the two centrosomes are at opposite poles of the cell. On each chromosomal centromere, proteins assemble to form a protein-DNA complex called a *kinetochore*; thus there are two kinetochores on each chromosome, one on each chromatid. The two kinetochores face in opposite directions, as the diagram shows. Some of the spindle microtubules "capture" (attach to) kinetochores; others interact with microtubules coming from the other centrosome. Forces exerted within the assembly of microtubules throw the chromosomes into agitated motion and gradually move them toward the center of the cell.

Division of the Centromeres: Metaphase

The second stage of mitosis, *metaphase*, begins when the pairs of sister chromatids align in the center of the cell. When viewed with a light microscope, the chromosomes appear to be lined up in a circle along the inter circumference of the cell, as the equator girdles the earth. An imaginary plane perpendicular to the axis of the spindle that passes through this circle is called the *metaphase plate*. The metaphase plate is not an actual structures but rather an indication of where the future axis of cell division will occur. Positioned by the microtubules attached to the kinetochores of their centromeres, all of the

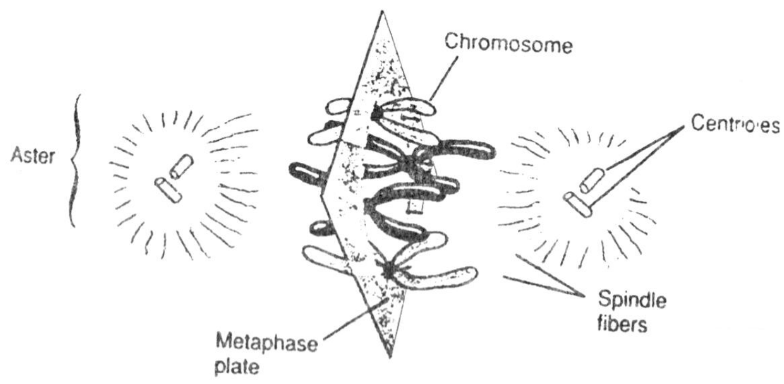

Fig. 10.2. The metaphasic plate.

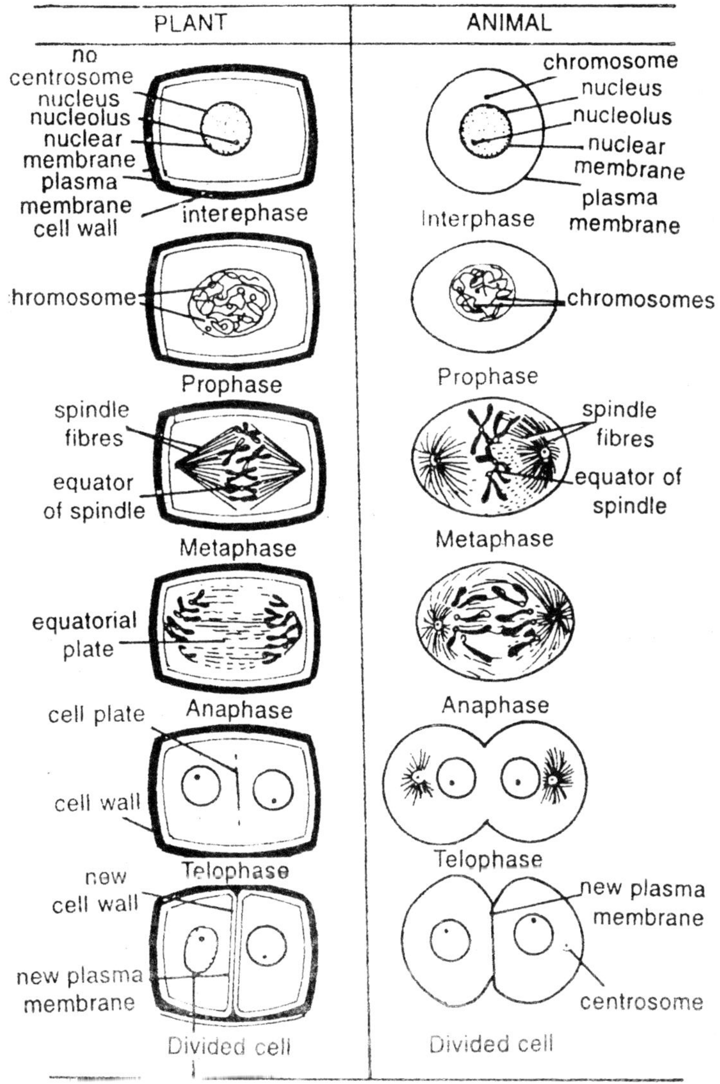

Fig. 10.3. Differences in mitosis in plants and animal cells.

chromosomes line up on the metaphase plate, their centromeres neatly arrayed in a circle, each equidistant from the two poles of the cell.

At the end of metaphase, the centromeres divide. Each centromere splits in two, freeing the two sister chromatids from their attachment to one another. Centromere separation is synchronous for all the chromosomes, but the mechanism that achieves this synchrony is not known.

Separation of the Chromatids : Anaphase

Of all the stages of mitosis, anaphase is the shortest and the most beautiful to watch. Freed from each other, the sister chromatids are pulled rapidly toward the poles to which their kinetochores are attached. In the process, two forms of movement take place simultaneously, each driven by microbutules.

First, *the poles move apart*, as microtubular spindle fibers that are physically anchored to opposite poles slide past each other, away from the center of the cell. Because the chromosomes are attached to the poles by another group of microtubules, they move apart, too. If the cell is bounded by a flexible membrane, is becomes visibly elongated. This part of the anaphase is called *Anaphase B*.

Second, *the centromeres move toward the poles*, as the microtubules that connect them to the poles shorten. This shortening process is not a contraction, since the microtubules do not get any thicker. Instead, tubulin subunits are removed from the kinetochore ends of the microtubules by the organizing center. As more subunits are removed, the chromatid-bearing microtubules are progressively disassembled, and the chromatids are pulled ever closer to the poles of the cell at the rate of about 1 μm/min. This part of anaphase is called *Anaphase A*.

Reformation of Nuclei: Telophase

The separation of sister chromatids achieved in anaphase completes the accurate partitioning of the replicated genome, the essential element of mitosis. In *telophase*, the spindle apparatus is disassembled, as the microtubules are broken down into tubulin monomers that can be used to construct the cytoskeleton of the daughter cells. A nuclear envelope forms around each set of sister chromatids, which can now be called chromosomes, since each has its own centromere. The chromosomes soon begin to uncoil into the more extended form that permits gene expression. An early group of genes to be expressed are the rRNA genes, resulting in the reappearance of the nucleolus.

Cytokinesis

Mitosis is complete at the end of telophase. The eukaryotic cell has partitioned its replicated genome into two nuclei, which are positioned at opposite ends of the cell. While mitosis has been going on, the cytoplasmic organelles, including mitochondria and chloroplasts (if they are present), have also been reassorted to the areas that will

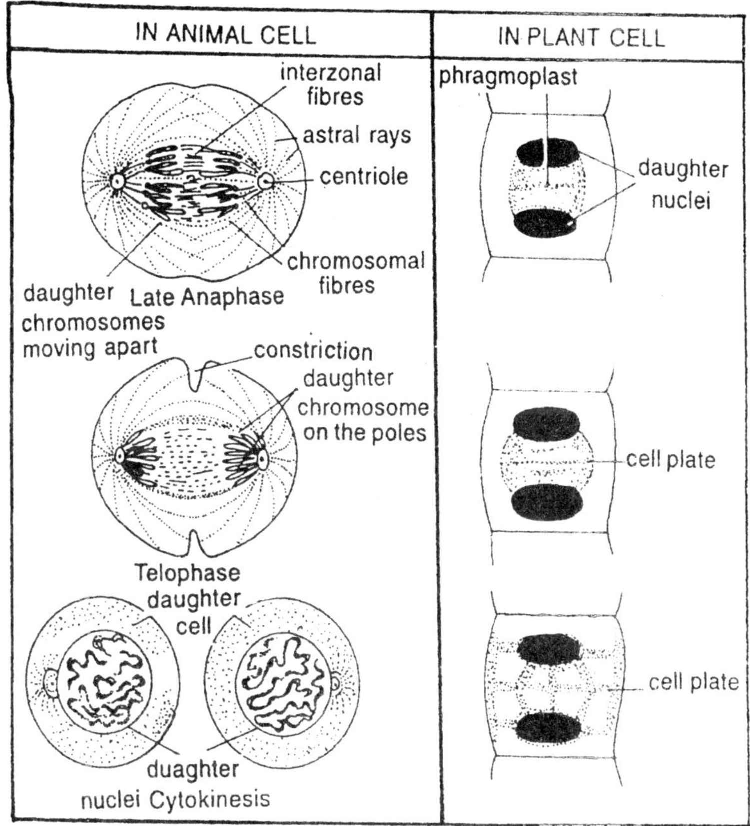

Fig. 10.4. Division of cell cytoplasm in animal and plant cell.

separate and become the daughter cells. The replication of organelles takes place before cytokinesis, often in the S or G_2 phase. The process of cell division is still not complete at the end of mitosis, however, because the division of the cell proper has not yet begun. The phase of the cell cycle at which cell division occurs is called *cytokinesis*. It generally involves the cleavage of the cell into roughly equal halves.

In the cells of animals and all other eukaryotes that lack cell walls, cytokinesis is achieved by means of a constricting belt of actin filaments. The sliding of these filaments past one another decreases the diameter of the belt and pinches the cell, creating a *cleavage furrow* around the circumference of the cell. As constriction proceeds, the furrow deepens until it eventually extends all the way into the center of the cell, at which point the cell is divided in two.

Plant cells possess a cell wall that is far too rigid to be deformed by actin filament sliding. Instead, they assemble membrane components in their interior, at right angles to the spindle apparatus. This expanding membrane partition is called a *cell plate*. It continues to grow outward until it reaches the interior surface of the plasma membrane and fuses with it, effectively dividing the cell in the two. Cellulose is then laid down on the new membranes, creating two new cell walls. The space between the daughter cells becomes impregnated with pectins and is called a *middle lamella*.

In fungi and some groups of protists, the nuclear membrane does not dissolve and mitosis is confined to the nucleus. When mitosis is complete in these organisms, the nucleus divides into two daughter nuclei, one of which goes to each daughter cell during cytokinesis. This separate nuclear division phase of the cell cycle does not occur in plants, animals, or in most protists.

Control of the Cell Cycle

Research of the cell cycle has tended to focus traditionally on the events of mitosis, at least in part because the segregating chromosomes are readily visible in the light microscope. This attention to the movements of the chromosomes led biologists to conclude that the cell cycle was dissimilar in different organisms, and even in different tissues, because the chromosomes they were studying often seemed dissimilar in appearance and arrangement. The advent of sophisticated immunological and genetic engineering techniques over the last decade has led to a radical change in that conclusion. It now seems clear that the events of the cell cycle are coordinated in much the same way in all eukaryotes. The control system that human cells utilize first evolved among the protists over a billion years ago, and today it operates in essentially the same way in fungi as it does in humans. The proteins that regulate the cell cycle have been conserved so carefully that many of them function just as well when transferred from a human cell into a yeast cell.

General Strategy of Cell Cycle Control

The goal of controlling any cyclic process is to adjust the duration of the cycle so that there is sufficient time for all events to occur, without expending any more time than is necessary. In principle, there are a variety of ways to achieve this goal. An internal clock can be employed to allow adequate time for each phase of the cycle to be completed. That is how many organisms control their daily activity cycles. The disadvantage of using such a clock as a control strategy for the cell cycle is that it is not very flexible. The time required for growth or DNA replication can vary greatly, depending upon changes in the local environment of a cell. One way to achieve a more flexible and sensitive regulation of a cycle is simply to let the completion of each phase of the cycle trigger the beginning of the next phase, like a runner passing a baton to start the next leg in a relay race. Until recently, this is how biologists thought the cell division cycle was controlled. However, we now know that eukaryotic cells employ a separate centralized controller to regulate the process: at critical points in the cell cycle, further progress is dependent upon a central set of "go/no-go" switches that are regulated by feedback from the cell.

This mechanism is the same one that engineers use to control many processes. The furnace that heats a home in the winter typically goes through a daily heating cycle, as the thermostat is turned to a lower setting at night to conserve energy while we are sleeping, and then to a higher setting during the day to warm the house while we are active. When the daily cycle reaches the morning "turn on" check point, sensors report whether the house temperature is below the set point (e.g., 70°F). If it is, the thermostat triggers the furnace, which warms the house. If the house is already at least that warm, the thermostat does not start up the furnace, as no added heat is necessary. Similarly in the cell cycle, there are key check points where feedback signals from the cell about how big it is and the condition of its chromosomes can either trigger subsequent phases of the cycle or delay them to allow more time for completion of the current phase.

The cell cycle is eukaryotes is controlled at three principal check points:

Cell growth is assessed at the G_1 check point

Located near the end of G_1, just before entry into S phase, this check point makes the key decision of whether the cell will divide or not. In yeasts, where it was first studied, it is called START. If conditions are favourable for division, the cell begins to copy its DNA, initiating S phase. The G_1 check point is where more complex eukaryotes typically arrest the cell cycle if environmental conditions make cell division impossible, or if the cell passes into G_0 for an extended period.

DNA replication is assessed at the G_2 check point

The second check point occurs at the G_2 and triggers the start of M phase. If this check point is passed, the cell initiates the many molecular processes that are involved in mitosis.

Mitosis is assessed at the M check point

Occurring at metaphase, the third check point triggers the exit from mitosis and the beginning of G_1, the major growth period of the cell cycle.

Molecular Mechanism of Cell Cycle Control

How does central control of the cell cycle work? The basic mechanism is quite simple and is similar to gene control mechanisms. A set of proteins interact at the check point to trigger the next events in the cycle, and their activity is sensitive to the condition of the cell. There are two key types of proteins that participate in this interaction: cyclin-dependent protein kinases and cyclins.

Cyclin-dependent protein kinases (*Cdk's*) are enzymes that phosphorylate (that is, add phosphate groups to) the serine and threonine amino acids of important cellular enzymes and other proteins. At the G_2 check point, for example, Cdk's phosphorylate histones, nuclear

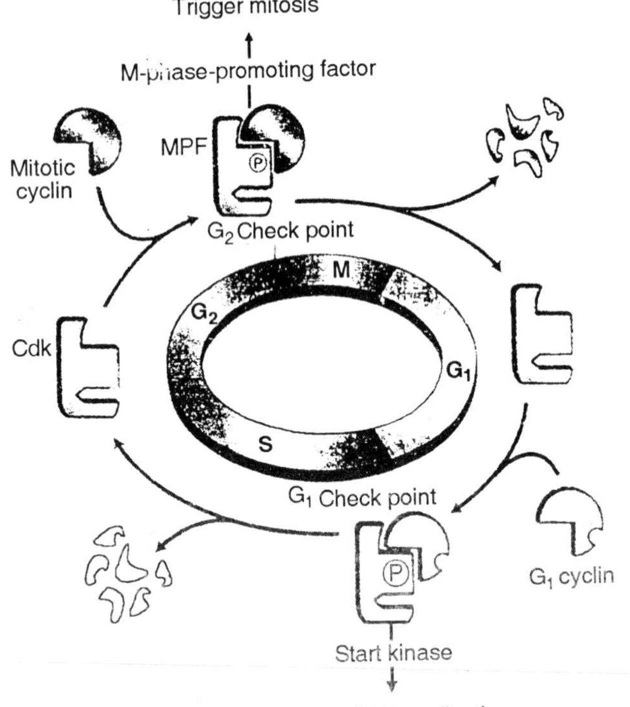

Fig. 10.5. Control of cell cycle.

membrane filaments, and the microtubule-associated proteins that form mitotic spindle. Phosphorylation of these components of the cell division machinery causes them to initiate activities that carry the cycle past the check point and into mitosis. All three check points appear to use the same Cdk molecules in yeasts; in mammals, there is a unique Cdk for each check point.

Cyclins are proteins that bind to Cdk's enabling the Cdk's to function as enzymes. Cyclins are so named because they are destroyed and resynthesized during each turn of the cell cycle. Different cyclins regulate the three check points.

Let us take a closer look at how cyclins and Cdk's interact to control the G_2 and G_1 check points of the cell cycle.

The G_2 Check Point

During G_2, the cell gradually accumulates G_2 cyclin (also called mitotic cyclin), which binds to Cdk to form a complex called MPF (mitosis promoting factor). At first, MPF is not active in carrying the cycle past the G_2 check point, but eventually a few molecules of MPF are phosphorylated and activated by other cellular enzymes. These activated MPF's in turn increase the activity of the enzymes that phosphorylate. MPF, setting up a positive feedback that leads to a very rapid increase in the cellular concentration of activated MPF. When the level of activated MPF exceeds the threshold necessary to trigger mitosis, G_2 phase ends.

MPF sows the seeds of its own destruction. The length of time the cell spends in M Phase is determined by the activity of MPF, for one of its many functions is to activate proteins that destroy cyclin. As mitosis proceeds to the end of metaphase, levels of Cdk stay relatively constant, but increasing amounts of G_2 cyclin are degraded, causing progressively more MPF to lose its activity and initiating the events that end mitosis. After mitosis, the gradual accumulation of new cyclin starts the next turn of the cell cycle.

The G_1 Check Point

The G_1 check point is thought to be regulated in a similar fashion. In unicellular eukaryotes like yeasts, the main factor controlling the start of DNA replication is cell size. Yeast cells grow and divide as rapidly as possible, and they make the START decision by comparing the volume of the cytoplasm to the size of the genome. As the cells grow their cytoplasm increases in size while their amount of DNA remains constant. Eventually a threshold ratio is reached that promotes the production of cyclins and thus triggers the next round of DNA replication and cell division.

Controlling the Cell Cycle in Multicellular Eukaryotes

The cells of multicellular eukaryotes are not free to make individual decisions about cell division in the way yeast cells are. The organization of the body cannot be maintained without severely limiting cell proliferation, so that only certain cells divide, and only at appropriate times. The inhibition of individual cell growth by other cells can be seen readily in mammalian cells growing in tissue culture: a single layer of cell expands over a culture plate until the growing border of cells comes into contact with neighbouring cells, and then the cells stop dividing. If a sector of cells is cleared away, neighbouring cells rapidly refill it and then stop dividing again. How are the cells able to sense the density of the cell culture around them? Each growing cell apparently takes up minute amounts of positive regulatory signals called growth factors (such as MPF;) that stimulate cell division. When neighbouring cells have taken up what little of the growth factor is present, there is not enough left to trigger celi division in any one cell.

Growth Factors and the Cell Cycle

It has already been observed a cell-cell interactions, growth factors work by triggering intracellular signaling systems. Fibroblasts, for example, possess numerous receptors on their plasma membranes for one of the first growth factors to be identified, platelet-derived growth factor (PDGF). Binding of PDGF to a membrane receptor initiates an amplifying chain of internal cell signals that stimulates cell division. PDGF was discovered when investigators found that fibroblasts would grow and divide in tissue culture only if the growth medium was provided with blood serum (the liquid that remains after blood clots); blood plasma (blood from which the cells have been removed without clotting) would not work. The researchers hypothesized that platelets in the blood clot were releasing into the serum one or more factors required for growth. Eventually, they isolated such a factoı and named if PDGF. Growth factors like PDGF act to override cellular controls that otherwise inhibit cell division. When a tissue is injured, release of PDGF by platelets triggers neighbouring cells to divide, helping to heal the wound. Only a tiny amount of PDGF (approximately 10^{-10} M) is required to stimulate cell division.

Over 50 different proteins that function as growth factors have been isolated and more undoubtedly exist. Each is recognized by a

Table 10.1. Growth Factors of Mammalian Cells

Factor	*Range of Specificity*	*Effects*
Epidermal growth factor (EGF)	Broad	Stimulates cell proliferation in many tissues; plays a key role in regulating embryonic development.
Erythropoietin	Narrow	Required for proliferation of 'red blood cell precursors and their maturation into erythrocytes
Fibroblast growth factor (FGF)	Broad	Initiates the proliferation of many types of stem cells; acts as a signal in embryonic development
Insulin-like growth factor	Broad	Stimulates metabolism of many cell types; potentiates the effects of other growth factors in promoting cell proliferation
Interleukin-2	Narrow	Triggers the division of activated T lymphocytes during the immune response
Mitosis-promoting factor (MPF)	Broad	Regulates entrance of the cell cycle into the M phase.
Nerve growth factor (NGF)	Narrow	Stimulates the growth of neuron processes during neural development
Platelet-derived growth factor (PDGF)	Broad	Promotes the proliferation of many connective tissues and some neuro-logical cells
Transforming growth factor b (TGF-b)	Broad	Accentuates or inhibits the responses of many cell types to other growth factors; often plays an important role in cell differentiation

specific cell surface receptor that has a shape into which the growth factor fits precisely. Binding of the growth factor to the receptor triggers events within the cell. The cellular selectivity of a particular growth factor depends upon which target cells bear its unique receptor. Some growth factors, like PDGF and epidermal growth factor (EGF), affect a broad range of cell types, while others affect only specific cell types. For example, nerve growth factor (NGF) promotes the growth of certain classes of neurons, and erythropoietin triggers cell division in red blood cell precursors. Most animal cell require a combination of several different growth factors in order to overcome the various controls that inhibit cell division.

If cells are deprived of appropriate growth factors, they stop at the G_1 check point of the cell cycle. With their growth and division arrested, they are said to be in the G_0 phase we discussed earlier. Cells like liver cells that divide only once every year or two spend most of their time in G_0 phase, and mature neurons and muscle cells usually never leave it.

Cancer and the Control of Cell Proliferation

How do growth factors influence the cell cycle? As you have seen, there are two different approaches, one positive and the other negative. PDGF and many other growth factors utilize the positive approach. They trigger passage through the G_1 check point by aiding the formation of cyclins and activating genes that promote cell division. Genes that normally stimulates cell division are sometimes called *proto-oncogenes* because mutations that cause them to be overexpressed or hyperactive convert them into oncogenes (Greek *onco*, "cancer"), leading to the excessive cell proliferation that is characteristic of cancer. Even a single such mutation (creating a heterozygote) can lead to cancer, if the other cancer-preventing genes are nonfunctional. In Mendelian terms, such mutations are said to be dominant.

Some 30 different proto-oncogenes are known. Some act very quickly after stimulation by growth factors. Among the most intensively studied of these are *myc*, *fos*, and *jun*, all of which cause unrestrained cell growth and division when overexpressed. In a normal cell, the *myc* proto-oncogene appears to be important in regulating the G_1 check point because cells in which *myc* expression is prevented will not divide even in the presence of growth factors. A critical activity of *myc* and other genes in this group of immediately responding proto-oncogenes is to stimulate a second group of "delayed response" genes, including those that produce cyclins and Cdk proteins.

Growth factors that utilize a negative approach to cell cycle control block passage through the G_1 check point by preventing the binding of cyclins to Cdk, thus inhibiting cell division. Genes that normally inhibit cell division are called *tumor-suppressor genes*. When mutated, they can also lead to unrestrained cell division, but only if both copies of the gene are mutant. Hence, these cancer-causing mutations are recessive.

The most thoroughly understood of the tumor-suppressor genes is the retinoblastoma (Rb) gene. This gene was originally cloned from children with a rare form of eye cancer that was inherited as a recessive trait, implying that the normal gene product was a "cancer suppressor" that helped keep cell division in check. The Rb gene encodes a protein that is present in ample amounts within the nucleus. This protein interacts with many key regulatory proteins of the cell cycle, but how it does so depends upon its state of phosphorylation. In G_0 phase, the Rb protein is dephosphorylated. In this state, it binds to and ties up a set of regulatory proteins like myc and fos that are needed for cell proliferation, blocking their action and so inhibiting cell division. When phosphorylated, the Rb protein releases its captive regulatory proteins, freeing them to act and so promoting cell division. Growth factors lessen the inhibition imposed by the Rb protein by activating kinases that phosphorylate it. Free of Rb protein inhibition, cells begin to produce cyclins and Cdk, pass the G_1 check point, and proceed through the cell cycle.

Variations in the Cell Cycle

As mentioned already that, eukaryotic cells do not always proceed continuously through predictable cycles of growth and division, with G_1, S, G_2 and M following one another in uninterrupted progression and with every nuclear division accompanied by cytokinesis. Such is often the case, of course, particularly in growing organisms or cultured cells that have not run out of nutrients or space. But many variations are also possible, especially in terms of the relative length of time spent in various phases of the cycle and in the immediately with which mitosis and cytokinesis are coupled.

Variations in Cell Cycle Length

Some of the most common variations in the cell cycle in vivo involve difference in generation time between different cell types. Within the same organism, some cells divide at approximately the same rate as cells in culture, but others differ greatly, depending on their role in organism. Some cells divide rapidly and continuously throughout the life of the organisms as a means of replacing cells that are lost or destroyed during the normal functioning of the organism. Included in this category are the cells that lead to sperm formation and the precursor cells, called *stem cells*, that give rise to blood cells, skin cells, and the epithelial cells that line the inner surfaces of body organs such as the lungs and intestines. Human stem cells may have generations times as short as 8 hours.

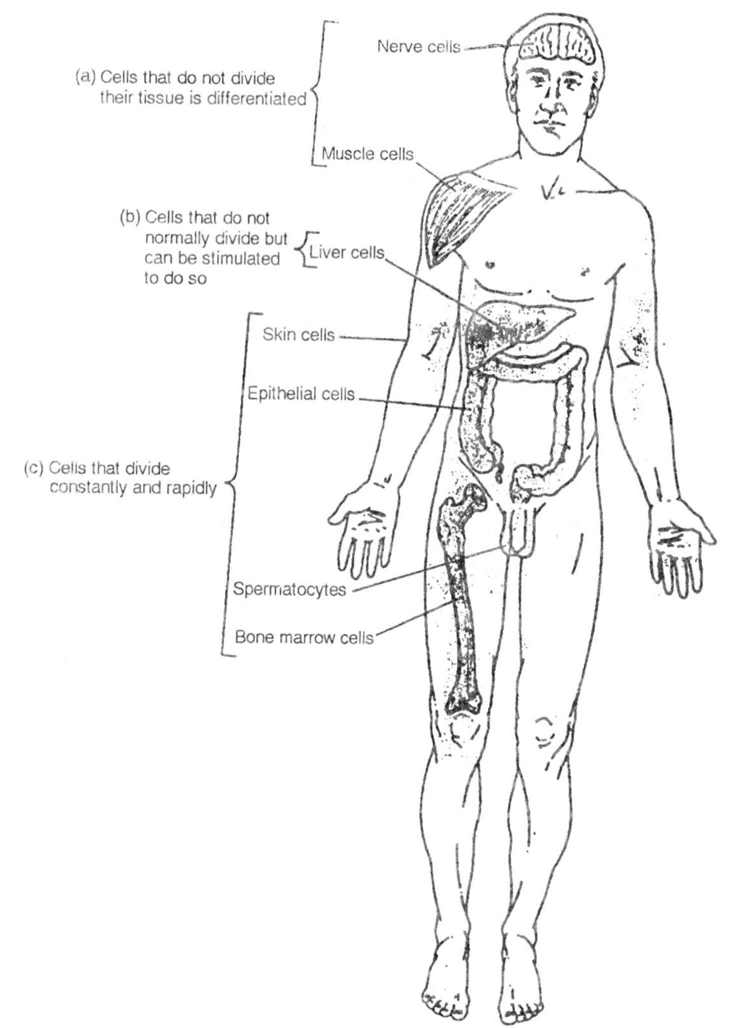

Fig. 10.6. Variations in generation time for cells of different tissues.

Cells of slow-growing tissues, on the other hand, may have generations times of several days or more , and some cells, such as those of nerve or muscle tissue, do not divide at all. Still other cell types do not divide under normal conditions but can be induced to begin dividing again by an appropriate stimulus. Liver cells are in this category; they do not normally proliferate in the mature liver but can be induced to do so if a portion of the liver is removed surgically.

Lymphocytes (white blood cells) are another example; when exposed to a foreign protein, they begin dividing as part of the immune response.

Most of these variations in generation time involve differences in G_1, although S and G_2 can also vary somewhat. Cells that divide very slowly can spend days, months, or even years in the offshoot of G_1 called G_0, whereas cells that divide very rapidly have almost no G_1 phase at all. In fact, some cells even begin DNA synthesis before mitosis is complete, eliminating G_1 entirely.

The embroys of insects, amphibians, and certain other non-mammalian animals are dramatic examples of very short cell cycles, with no G_1 phase and a very short S phase. During early embryonic development in amphibians such as the frog *Xenopus laevis*, for instance, cell division can take less than 30 minutes, even though the normal length of the cell cycle in adult tissues is about 20 hours. Under these conditions, the S phase is completed in less than 3 minutes, at least 100 times faster than in adult tissues. The incredible rate of DNA synthesis needed to sustain such a rapid cell cycle is possible because virtually all replicons are active at the same time, in contrast to the sequential activation seen in adult tissues. In addition, the average replicon length decreases, because new replicons are induced at this time.

Furthermore, these embryonic cells have little or no need to synthesize cellular components other than DNA because the fertilized egg is a very large cell with enough cytoplasm to sustain many rounds of the cell division. Each round of division subdivides the initial cytoplasm into smaller cells, until the cell size characteristic of adult tissues is reached. During the early cleavage divisions of *Xenopus* embryos, for example, not only is G_1 lacking but G_2 is unusually short, so that cells go almost directly from DNA synthesis to mitosis and back to DNA synthesis. In fact, the S phase in such cells begins even before mitosis is complete. From such examples, we know that cell growth during the G_1 and G_2 phases is not an absolute prerequisite for cell division, even though growth and division are usually coupled process.

Variations in Timing of Mitosis and Cytokinesis

For some multinucleate cells, such as the fungal and algal cells already mentioned and the skeletal muscle cells of vertebrates, the multinucleate condition is permanent. In other situations, however, the multinucleate state is only a temporary phase in the organism's development. This is the case, for example, in the development of a plant seed tissue called endosperm in the cereal grains. Here nuclear division occurs for a time unaccompanied by cytokinesis, generating many nuclei in a common cytoplasm. Successive rounds of cytokinesis then occur without mitosis, walling off the many nuclei into separate endosperm cells. A similar process occurs in developing insect eggs. The fertilized egg undergoes mitosis but not cytokinesis and soon consists of hundreds of nuclei in the same cytoplasm; later, cytokinesis catches up.

Regulation of the Cell Cycle

The variability in generation time for cells of the same organism tells us that the cell cycle must somehow be regulated. The molecular basis of this regulation is a subject of intense interest, not only for understanding the life cycles of normal cells but also for understanding how cancer cells manage to escape normal control mechanisms. Now one of the hottest areas of biological research, cell cycle regulation is beginning to reveal its underlying molecular mechanisms. We will begin our discussion with a look at the general concept of cell-cycle checkpoints and some of the early experimental evidence for the nature of their control.

Cell Cycle Checkpoints

Evidence acquired decades ago pointed to a particular point in G_1 as critical for regulation of the mammalian cell cycle. We have already seen that G_1 is the phase that varies most among cell types. Moreover, mammalian cells that have stopped dividing are almost arrested during the G_1 phase. For example, we can stop or slow down the process of cell division in cultured cells by allowing the cells to run out of either nutrients or space or by adding inhibitors of vital processes such as protein synthesis. In all such cases, the cells are arrested in G_1.

These findings suggest that when a cell leaves G_1 and enters the S phase, it is committed to completing the cycle. Therefore, the release of cells from G_1 appears to be a critical control mechanism. More specifically, early researchers identified a point of no return in late G_1, which they called the *restriction point*. Cells that have passed this point are committed to division, whereas those that have not passed this point can remain in G_1 indefinitely, in the resting state called the G_0 state. As the previously mentioned experiments demonstrated, the ability to pass the restriction point can be heavily influenced by factors in the cell's environment.

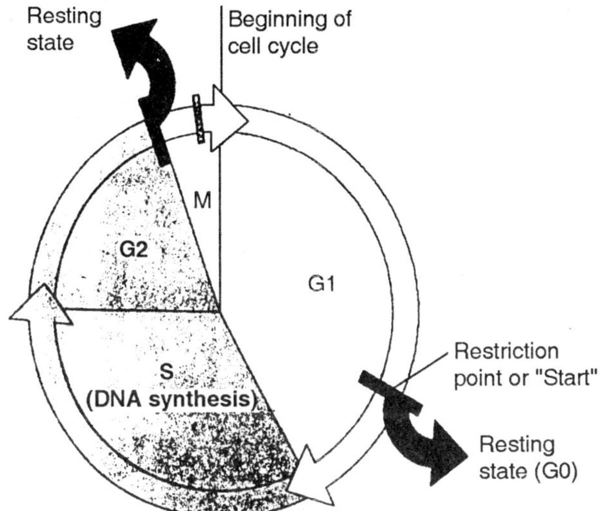

Fig. 10.7. Cell-cycle checkpoints.

Later, research with other types of cells revealed two other points of no return, and all three are now generally termed *cell cycle checkpoints*. At the end of G_2 is a major checkpoint that controls the cell's entry into mitosis (M phase). At the G_2 checkpoint, certain kinds of cells can enter a resting state analogous to G_0. Within M phase, at metaphase, is a third checkpoint, which somehow determines whether all the chromosomes are properly attached to the spindle before allowing anaphase to begin. The relative importance of the G_1 and G_2 checkpoints varies with the organism and cell type. For example, the G_1 checkpoint is the more important checkpoint in the budding yeast *Saccharomyces cerevisiae* (where it is called "Start"), as it is in most cells of multicellular organisms. However, the G_2 checkpoint is the more important one in, for example, the mitotic divisions of a fertilized frog egg and in the yeast *Schizosaccharomyces pombe* (called a *fission yeast* because it reproduces by dividing evenly in two, rather than by budding). A cell's behaviour at a checkpoint is influenced both by preceding events in the cell cycle (such as DNA replication) and by factors in the cell's environment (such as nutrients or hormones). Whatever the influence, its effects are mediated by cellular proteins, activating or inhibiting one another in chains of interactions that can be quite elaborate. However, there is an underlying unity in the molecular strategies of cell cycle regulation.

Early Evidence for Chemical Regulation of the Cell Cycle

As in many areas of scientific inquiry, early attempts to determine how the cell cycle is regulated were hampered by the difficulty of distinguishing between causal relationships and simple correlations. Just because an event usually happens at a specific point in the cell cycle does not necessarily mean it is involved in regulation of the cycle. For example, it was long thought that the critical regulatory factor was simply the ratio of cytoplasmic mass to nuclear mass and that when the cytoplasm reached a certain size, the cell would divide. It is certainly true that cell division is usually correlated with an increase in cytoplasmic mass, but there is no evidence to suggest a necessary causative relationship. Indeed, the cleavage of a fertilized egg into many smaller cells without accompanying cell growth seems to contradict such a suggestion. Moreover, there appears to be no validity to the suggestion that the transition from G_1 to S controlled by the availability of the DNA replication enzymes.

Between 1970 and 1975, it became clear that specific chemical signals present in the cytoplasm were responsible for moving the cell cycle past the G_1 and G_2 checkpoints—that is, for triggering DNA replication (S phase) and mitosis (M phase). Some of the first strong evidence for this came from experiments in which two cultured mammalian cells in different phases of the cell cycle were fused to form a single cell with two nuclei, a *heterokaryon*. If one of the original cells is in S phase and the other is in G_1, the G_1 nucleus in the heterokaryon immediately enters S phase, as though a signal present in the cytoplasm of the first cell triggers the S phase events. Similarly, if a cell undergoing mitosis is fused with another cell in any stage of its cell cycle, even G_1, the second nucleus is immediately driven into the preparatory steps for mitosis, including condensation of dispersed interphase chromatin into visible chromosomes, spindle formation, and fragmentation of the nuclear envelope. If the second cell was in G_1, the condensed chromosomes will be unduplicated.

More direct evidence for a mitosis-including chemical signal came from experiments with frog eggs. In the frog, the oocyte, an egg cell precursor, is arrested in G_2 until hormones stimulate meiosis. (Meiosis is the variation of mitosis that halves the number of chromosomes in egg or sperm production). The oocyte proceeds through most of the phase of meiosis but is arrested in M phase—in metaphase of the second of two meiotic divisions. It is now a "mature" egg cell, capable of being fertilized. Because frog oocytes and eggs are very large, about 1 mm in diameter, it is easy to transfer cytoplasm between them with a fine pipette. In a crucial experiment, it was shown that if cytoplasm taken from a mature egg cell is injected into the cytoplasm of an oocyte, the oocyte immediately begins meiosis. The hypothetical cytoplasmic chemical that induces this oocyte "maturation" was *dubbed maturation-promoting factor* (MPF). It was quickly established that MPF also induces mitosis of fertilized frog eggs (cleavage).

MPF-like activities have since been found in the cytoplasms of a broad range of eukaryotes, including yeasts, marine invertebrates, and mammals. Furthermore, the mitosis inducing factors have proven to be very similar in all these organisms. For example, in yeast cells with a defective or missing MPF gene, the human version of the gene can substitute perfectly well, despite the fact that the last ancestor common to yeasts and humans probably lived about 3 billion years ago! Through these and other kinds of experiments, investigators learned a lot about the MPF activity even before the MPF protein was purified in 1988.

Molecular Basis of Cell Cycle Regulation

The study of cell cycle regulation entered a molecular era in 1988. This new era was brought about by the merging of results from two main lines of research, the physiological/biochemical study of developing frog eggs and the genetic study of yeasts. Their status as single-celled microbes makes yeasts particularly useful model organisms for studying many aspects of eukaryotic cell biology. Intensive research on the genetics of yeast cell cycles had begun in the late 1960s, just a few years before MPF was discovered.

Working with *S. cerevisiae*, geneticist Leland Hartwell undertook a search for mutants that were "stuck" at some point in the cell cycle. Most such mutants would be difficult or impossible to work with, because their blocked cell cycle would prevent them from reproducing. But Hartwell was able to use a powerful strategy of microbial genetics, focusing his search on *conditional mutants*. These are mutants whose defect is apparent only under certain conditions–in this case, at temperatures above the normal range for the organism. A yeast cell with such a *temperature-sensitive mutation* in a gene required for cell cycle operation reproduces normally at 20–30°C but poorly or not at all at 35–37°C. The mutant can thus be grown at the lower ("permissive") temperature for genetic and biochemical study. How can the mutant behave normally under permissive conditions? Presumably the protein encoded by the mutated gene is close enough to the normal gene product to function at the lower temperature, while the increased thermal energy at higher temperatures disrupts its active conformation (the molecular shape needed for function) more readily than that of the normal protein.

In this way, Hartwell and his colleagues identified many genes involved in the cell cycle of *S. cerevisiae* and established the points in the cell cycle at which their products functioned. Predictably, some of these genes turned out to encode DNA replication proteins, but others seemed to function in cell cycle regulation. A breakthrough discovery was made by Paul Nurse and his colleagues, who carried out similar research with the fission yeast *Schizosaccharomyces pombe*. They identified a gene called *cdc2* whose activity was essential for the initiation of mitosis—that is, for passing the G_2 checkpoint. The acronym *cdc* stands for cell division cycle. The *cdc2* gene turned out to be essentially identical to a *S. cerevisiae* gene that Hartwell's group had called *CDC28* and to have counterparts in all eukaryotic cells. (It was Nurse who showed that the human version of the gene could "rescue" mutant yeast cells.) In tribute to the importance of Nurse's discovery, the protein encoded by such a gene is often called a *Cdc2protein*, regardless of the organism where it is found.

This yeast research came together with the frog egg research when it was established that Cdc2 protein was one of two proteins making up MPF. Researchers were now primed to unravel the mysteries of the G2 checkpoint.

The Cdc2 Protein, a Protein Kinase

The Cdc2 protein is a protein kinase, an enzyme that catalyzes the transfer of a phosphate group from ATP to certain other proteins. Phosphorylation by ATP is a major theme in cell biochemistry and is the usual mechanism by which ATP functions to activate molecules, both large and small. In earlier chapters, you have seen that phosphorylation of glucose activates it for glycolysis and that phosphorylation and dephosphorylation of the protein of the sodium-potassium pump causes the shape change that allows Na^+ and K^+ to cross the plasma membrane. The sodium potassium pump protein has its own innate ability to hydrolyze ATP. However, in many other cases the phosphorylation of a protein is catalyzed by a separate protein—that is, a protein kinase. The phosphorylation of proteins by kinases, and their dephosphorylation by enzymes called *phosphatases*, is turning out to be a common cellular mechanism for regulating protein activity. And it is a mechanism that is used many times over in regulating the cell cycle.

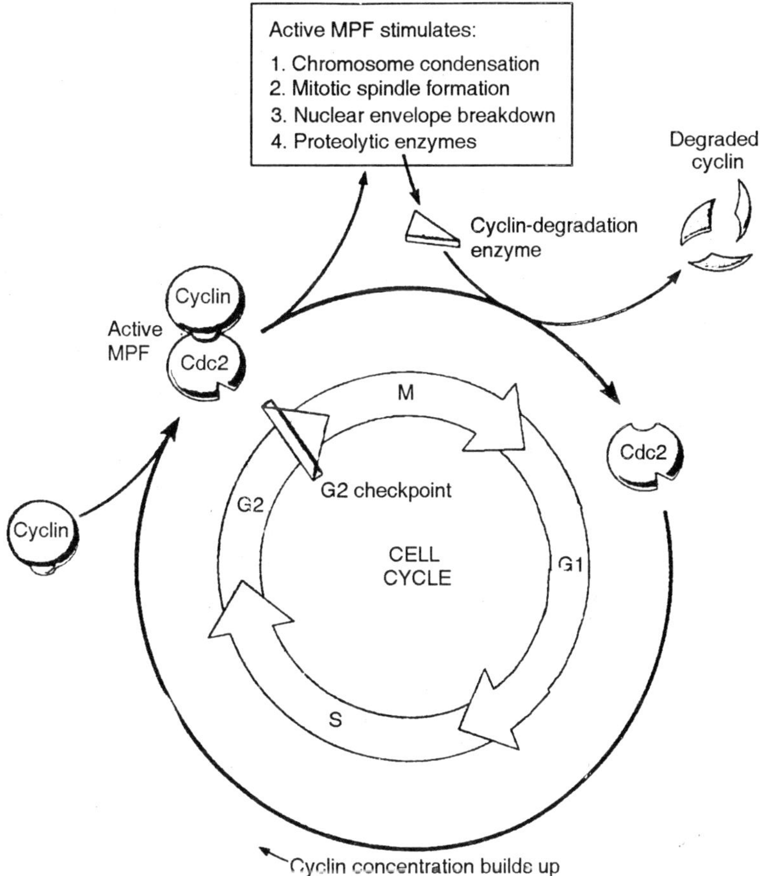

Fig. 10.8. The Cdc2 activity cycle.

The Role of Cyclins

When one looks for the Cdc2 protein at different points in the cell cycle, it is found to be present continuously at about the same concentration. However, it is not continuously active as a trigger for mitosis (or meiosis). Its MPF activity rises rapidly during G_2 phase, peaks during the first half of M phase, and then suddenly drops. MPF's activity is regulated by the second component of MPF, a protein called *cyclin*. As the name suggests, cyclins are a class of protein whose level in the cell oscillates; they are found in all eukaryotic cells. Not coincidentally, the cyclin level in a cell correlates with MPF activity level. MPF activity starts its climb when the cyclin level reaches a critical threshold.

The oscillation of cyclin level is unusual. Most other major cell proteins, like Cdc2, exist at a relatively constant concentration during the cell cycle because synthesis and any degradation occur at a constant rate as the cell grows. Unlike these proteins, cyclin is synthesized at a rate that allows cyclin accumulation to outpace the cell's growth rate—until M phase, when cyclin degradation markedly increases and destroys most of the cyclin present.

The Cdc2-cyclin complex plays a multifaced role in stimulating mitosis—it has all the activities earlier attributed to active MPF. In fact, in the scientific literature. "MPF" or "active MPF" continues to be used to mean the Cdc2-cyclin complex that stimulates mitosis. MPF (the Cdc2 cyclin complex) induces chromosome condensation, the assembly of the mitotic spindle, and the breakdown of the nuclear envelope. Only in the last of these three cases is much known about the molecular mechanism involved: The Cdc2 phosphorylates (and stimulates other kinases to phsophorylate) the *lamin* proteins of the *nuclear lamina*, to which the inner nuclear membrane is attached. phosphorylation causes the lamins to dissociate from each other, and pieces of the nuclear envelope follow suit. By the time mitosis is well under way, yet another activity of the Cdc2-cyclin complex becomes important: It activates proteolytic enzymes that cause its own demise by degrading cyclin, including both cyclin bound to Cdc2 and free cyclin. The Cdc2 protein is recycled.

What about the G_1 checkpoint, the restriction point identified decades ago in mammalian cells? In yeast, in which the G_1 checkpoint is called Start, the go-ahead signal is also given by a Cdc2-cyclin complex, although the cyclin is a different one. In cells of vertebrates, including both frogs and humans, there is a whole family of different cyclins and also a family of proteins more or less similar to the Cdc2 protein. The generic term for a member of the Cdc2 protein family is *cyclin-dependent protein kinase* (Cdk). The various types of Cdk and cyclins act in different combinations at different stages of the animal cell cycle. The details are still begins determined, but current evidence supports the involvement of the animal cell's Cdc2 along with cyclins B and A at the G_2 checkpoint, and Cdk proteins called Cdk2, Cdk4 and Cdk5, along with cyclins E and D (several kinds), at the G_1 checkpoint. Cdk2-cyclin A seems to be important during S phase. The different cyclins are made during different phases of the cell cycle.

You may be wondering about the third checkpoint mentioned earlier, the M-phase checkpoint where the decision is made whether or not to separate the metaphase chromatids and initiate anaphase.

Here neither a new cyclin nor a new Cdk seems to be involved. Instead, the onset of anaphase appears to be triggered by proteolytic enzymes activated by the Cdc2-cyclin complex. However, cyclin breakdown (and the concomitant inactivation of the Cdc2-cyclin complex itself) is, surprisingly, not the anaphase-triggering event. In an experiment using an in vitro system based on from egg extracts a nondegradable from of cyclin B was added, creating a nondegradable, continuously active Cdc2-cyclin complex. Although this complex prevented mitosis from proceeding to completion, sister chromatid separation did occur. This result suggests that the proteolytic enzymes that normally attack cyclin must also attack other key proteins, perhaps including proteins required for holding sister chromatids together.

Regulation of Cdk-Cyclin Complexes by Other Kinases

Unfortunately for students of this subject, there are additional levels of complexity in the regulation of the cell cycle–making up, along with Cdk proteins and cyclins, the chains of activating and inactivating proteins we mentioned earlier. Fortunately, the reactions catalyzed by these proteins have a common theme: phosphorylation and dephosphorylation. To put it another way, most of these other proteins are protein kinases and phosphatases.

Figure indicates the main proteins and the four main reactions involved in the formation of active MPF during G_2, starting with the Cdc2 protein. This scheme is probably similar to what happens at the G1 checkpoint, also. The initial complex formed by the joining of the Cdc2 protein and the MPF (mitotic) cyclin is inactive in the cell; to trigger mitosis, the complex requires the addition of a phosphate group on a particular amino acid of Cdc2 (Thr-161). In the figure, this phosphate is highlighted with yellow. It is added by a specific kinase, which the figure calls "activating kinase." But before that enzyme acts, another *inhibiting* kinase phosphorylates the protein in two other places. (Thr-14 and Tyr-15), such a that its active site is blocked. So the last set pin the activation sequence is actually the removal of the inhibiting phosphates by a phosphatase enzyme. The extra phosphorylations and dephosphorylation steps provide other points in the pathway where the process is subject to control by other factors. In addition, a positive feedback loop is involved: The active form of Cdc2-cyclin activates more and more phosphatase.

At either checkpoint, the Cdk protein and/or the cyclin protein may need to be further modified by additional sequences of reactions before the final Cdk2-cyclin complex is fully active. The details of these process may vary with the organism and, in a multicellular organism, with the cell type. Furthermore, various environmental influences, such as nutrients and hormones, may help determine which cyclins accumulate and at what rate. Most cells have many layers of cell cycle control.

Putting It All Together: The Cell Cycle Regulation Machine

Figure is a generalized and simplified summary of the operation of the molecular machine that regulates the eukaryotic cell cycle, as currently understood. Although much of what we know to date comes from research on the G_2 checkpoint in frogs and yeasts, most cell cycle decisions are probably controlled in a similar way, with the key molecules being protein kinases and cyclins.

The cell cycle machine can be described in terms of two fundamental, interacting mechanisms. One mechanism is an autonomous clock, which on its own goes through a fixed cycle over and over again. The molecular basis of this clock is the synthesis and degradation of cyclins, which occur in a rhythmic fashion. The other mechanism

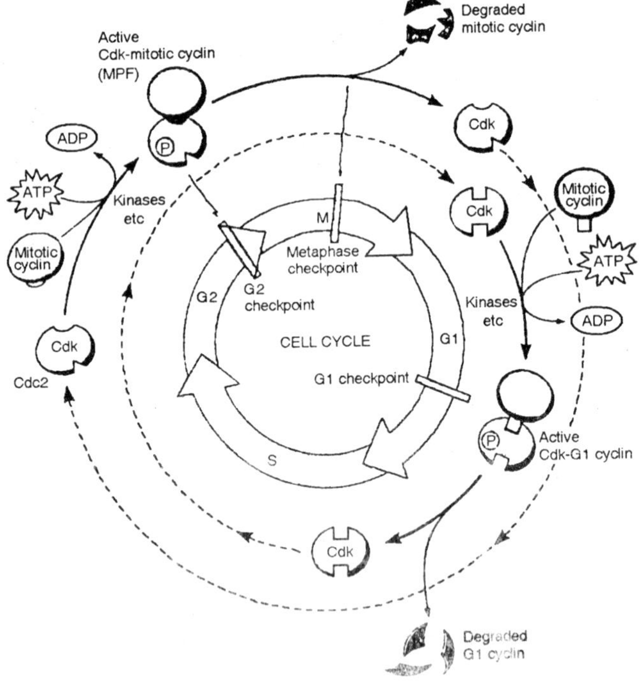

Fig. 10.9 A general model for cell cycle regulation.

adjusts the clock as needed, by providing feedback from the cell's internal and external environments. This mechanism makes use of cyclin-dependent kinases and additional proteins that, directly or indirectly, interact with cyclins. Many of the additional proteins are themselves protein kinases or phosphatases. It is this part of the cell cycle machine that transmits information about the state of the cell's metabolism–including DNA replication–and about conditions outside the cell. Energy required to activate the machine is supplied by ATP.

Even though the Cdk-cyclin core of the cell cycle regulatory machine has been identified, we are still in the dark about many aspects of the cell cycle regulation. How exactly do the Cdk-cyclin complexes influence cell cycle events? That is, what are the actual substrates in vivo for Cdk-cyclin kinase activity? Researchers have a number of candidates, but only lamins have thus far been proven to qualify. Only with more information about substrates will we be able to determine to what extent the different Cdk-cyclins control fundamentally distinct process or, perhaps, cell-type specific versions of the same process. Not only do we need to know more about the cell cycle in the systems that are already under intensive study, such as yeasts and mammalian cells; we also need to learn more about the cells of other organisms—plants, for instance. Such studies are likely to reveal that at least some of the key cell cycle proteins are also involved in regulating other aspects of cell metabolism. Already it is known that yeast has Cdk (called PHO85) that, in combination with various cyclins, participates in both the cell cycle and phosphate metabolism.

At the other end of the chain of cell cycle control is the issue of how growth-promoting or growth-inhibiting signals coming from outside the cell connect with the cell cycle machinery. Hence the study of signal transduction pathways, which we treat intimately interconnected with the study of the cell cycle. In addition, the cancer, which can be described as a genetic disease of the cell cycle. When the normal cell cycle is disturbed by a normal molecules and events, normal cell growth may turn cancerous. More and more, therefore, there is convergence of research on the cell cycle per se and research on the cellular basis of cancer. Thus, we will return to the cell cycle at a number of points in later parts of this book.

What are the Functions of Mitotic Cell Division?

Mitotic cell division plays several roles in the lives of multicellular eukaryotic organisms. First, in conjuction with the differential expression of genes in different cells, it allows a fertilized egg eventually to become an adult consisting of perhaps trillions of individual cells.

Mitotic cell division also allows an organism to maintain its tissues, many of which require frequent replacement. For example, your skin cells live for only about 2 weeks. As dead skin flakes off imperceptibly but constantly, skin cells are continuously replaced by cell division. Your red blood cells become worn out after about 4 months. Through cell division, specialized cells in bone marrow give rise to new red blood cells, which enter the bloodstream at the rate of 3 million per second! Cells of your stomach lining, exposed to acid and digestive enzymes, survive only about 3 days before they must be replaced through the division of underlying cells.

Mitotic Cell Division Forms the Basis of Asexual Reproduction

Mitotic cell division provides the basis of asexual reproduction, in which offspring are formed from a single parent without the uniting of male and female gametes. This mode of reproduction is normal for many unicellular organisms, such as *Tetrahymena*, and yeasts. Many multicellular organisms can also reproduce asexually. Small replicas of the parent grow by means of cell division. Like its relative the sea anemone, a *Hydra* can reproduce by growing a miniature replica of itself as a bud. Eventually the bud separates from its parent, going off to live independently. Because mitosis produces genetically identical cells, these offspring are genetically identical to their parents; they are called clones.

Many plants reproduce both asexually and sexually. The beautiful aspen grooves of Colorado, Utah, and New Mexico develop asexually from shoots growing up from the root system of a single parent tree. The entire groove, although seeming to be a population of separate trees to the admiring visitor, may actually be considered to be a single individual, with its multiple trunks interconnected by a common root system. Recently, biologists at the University of Colorado reported that one of the single largest organisms yet discovered on Earth is a huge aspen groove in Utah, covering 106 acres and including about 47,000 trunks with a total mass of up to 6 million kilograms (13 million pounds). Although individual trunks age and die, the groove lives on; some grooves are thought to be hundreds of thousands of years old. If you plant an aspen tree in your backyard, who knows what you may be starting!

Mitosis also gave rise to the nucleus that produced Dolly. As you will learn in "Scientific Inquiry" Much Ado About Dolly, researchers removed the nucleus of a cell from the udder of a sheep and used it to produce a whole new lamb. This type of asexual reproduction in mammals can occur only in the laboratory!

Autoradiographic Studies on Chromosomal Duplication

Autoradiography is useful technique for cell studies that involve small amounts of materials. Radioactively labeled compounds are used. After the experiment has been performed, the radioactive atoms are localized, by putting a photographic film against the fixed (chemically killed and immobilized) cells. The β rays (electrons) emitted by the radioactive atoms expose the silver grains in the photographic emulsion. Thus by looking at the dark spots on the developed film, one can see the pattern of radioactive compounds in the biological material.

J. Herbert Taylor and his associates studied the transfer of atoms of DNA in the chromosomes of the English broad bean (*Vicia faba*) during mitosis. DNA in the root tips of the broad bean was labeled with tritium (^{3}H), the radioactive isotope of hydrogen, by exposing the growing tips to a solution containing ^{3}H-labeled thymidine. After about one third of a division cycle the seedling were transferred to a growth medium without labeled thymidine but containing colchicine. After periods equal to one or two division cycles, the root tips were fixed and pressed against the photographic film. The electrons emitted by the incorporated tritium are of such low energy that they do not penetrate deeply into the film, and they therefore produce images only at their point of entry into the film emulsion. The chromosomes and their autoradiorgrams can be viewed simultaneously with the light microscope.

The broad bean contains 12 chromosomes (2n =12, n =6). Some nuclei treated in this experiment contained 12 chromosomes, some contained 24, and some contained 48. The chromosomes in cells with 12 metaphase chromosomes have not duplicated following labeling. The chromosomes in cells with 24 and 48 metaphase chromosomes have duplicated once and twice, respectively. The chromosomes in the nuclei containing 12 chromosomes were equally radioactive in the two chromatids. Those chromosomes that had experienced a division and were in the second metaphase after labeling (24 chromosome nuclei) were labeled in one chromatid only. In those cells with 48 chromosomes, two sets of chromosomes were completely unlabeled and the other two sets were labeled like those that had undergone only one division.

Although the actual arrangement of DNA in chromosomes is yet unknown, the transmission of atoms to daughter chromosomes supports the idea that a DNA double helix runs the entire length of the chromosome. For simplicity of presentation the metaphase chromatids in Figure 7.10 have been represented as containing two linear DNA molecules rather than a double helix.

Abnormalities in Mitosis

Under unfavourable conditions the mitotic divisions become defective and thus various abnormalities are formed when exposed to physical and chemical agents like temperature, radiations, necrotics and enzyme inhibitors etc. Some abnormal mitotic divisions are given under the following heads:

1. C-Mitosis (Abnormal Spindle Formation)

Brachet (1975) has described that colchicine inhibits mitosis by disorganizing spindle formation. The results are the formation of polyploid cells, and reduplication of chromosomes. Besides, during mitosis, sometimes cell nucleus is either deformed into a single spheriod compact mass (pycnosis) or becomes broken down (karyorrhexis).

2. Cytasteral Mitosis

Wilson (1901) noticed the formation of numerous asters in the cytoplasm of unfertilized eggs called cytasters by placing them in hypertonic sea water. In the eggs of marine invertebrates, production of many small cytoplasmic asters is of frequent occurrence. The intermixing of nucleoplasm and hyaloplasm seems to be neccesary condition for the aster formation. *Costello* (1940) showed that asters can be produced only if germinal vesicles has broken down.

3. Multipolar and Catenar Mitosis

Mitotic division showing several spindles and centrosomes are common in many protozoans and fish eggs. Multipolarity is usually caused by uneven division of centrosomes as well as irregular distribution of chromatids of the different spindles. It results in the formation of cells as aneuploidy (uneven chromosome number). Catenar mitosis have been described by *Dalcq* and *Simon* (1932) in amphibian eggs. During this, dividing cell forms a large number of asters are capable of dividing in the absence of spindle or nucleus in an autonomous way.

4. Achrosomal Mitosis

Sometimes, mitosis in induced by various agents without use of nucleus or chromosomes. *Briggs et. al.* (1951), in fertilized eggs with

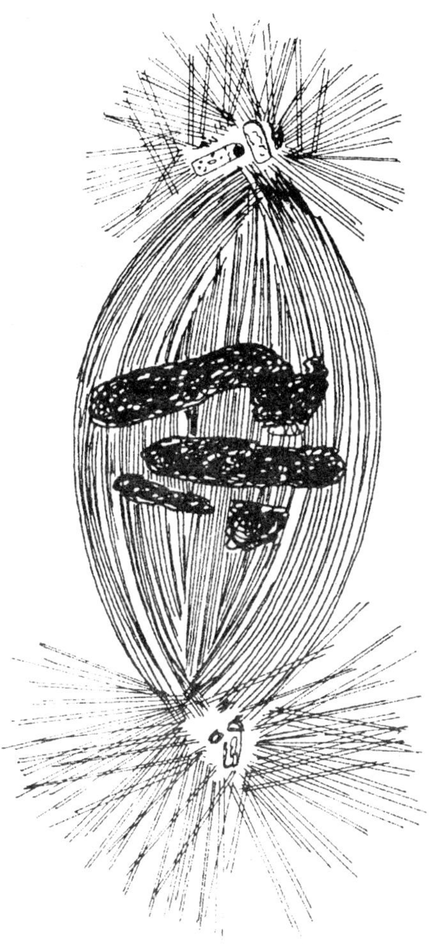

Fig. 10.10. Showing achromatic figure.

heavily X-rayed sperms, removed the egg's maturation spindle by pricking and sucking. In this way, he obained very nice non-nucleate blastulae. Similarly, *Stauffer* (1945) obtained normal non-nucleated Axolotl blastula.

5. Anastral Mitosis

In plant cells and many oocytes, generally asters around the centromeres are absent, thus producing anastral mitosis. *Bataillon and Tchou Su* (1933) described in details the anastral mitosis in amphibian interspecific hybrids.

11

FERTILIZATION

Fertilization is the union of the male and female gametes and the formation of a single group of chromosomes. It is usually irreversible. This fusion establishes in the zygote the diploid condition characteristic of the species involved. The genetic sex of the individual is also determined at this time; the individual is made or female depending on whether the egg is fertilized by a sperm carrying a Y or an X chromosome. When the sperm units with the egg, the egg becomes activated and the zygote begins a series of cleavages that lead to the development of the embryo. The spermatozoon normally contributes the centrosome, which organizes the necessary machinery for cell division. In some cases the point at which the sperm enters the egg establishes the plane of bilateral symmetry in the future embryo. In describing fertilization, the sequence of events leading to the union of the two gametes is usually considered a part of the process and involves the following steps:

1. Activation of the spermatozoon, referred to as *capacitation*.
2. Approach of the spermatozoon to the egg and its contact with the egg membranes.
3. Penetration of the membranes surrounding the ovum.
4. Activation of the egg
5. Syngamy or fusion of the pronuclei, and the establishment of the first cleavage spindle.

Fertilization has greater significance, however, than the union of the sperm with the egg and the production of a new individual. When it involves the union of chromosomes from unrelated groups, it also ensures the distribution of genes throughout the population. It is a method of gene dispersal that introduces variety, offering greater combinations for natural selection. At this level of interpretation, fertilization is a phenomenon that aids in adaptive variation, and is one of a series of nuclear changes that leads to the evolution of the species. Certain marine invertebrates, particularly the sea urchins, are the subjects of most of the studies of fertilization. Their eggs are readily available, relatively large, lack obscuring yolk granules, and can be maintained with ease in their normal physiological medium, seawater. Observation of the steps leading to the fusion of the egg and sperm is less difficult than in other forms.

Among the vertebrates, fish and amphibian eggs provide good investigative material for analytical studies, but there are few extensive descriptions of fertilization of mammalian eggs. Not only are these eggs difficult to obtain but there are also many problems in establishing and maintaining an environment suitable for the continued viability of the gametes (Marx, 1973). The factors involved in the successful fertilization of the egg by the sperm have not all been defined. In fact, the whole subject is somewhat controversial, with no general agreement as to the essential requirements or the step involved in the fertilization reaction. There is a tendency, therefore, to extrapolate and assume that the processes that occur in one form of animal life (marine invertebrates) take place in the mammals as well. This may not be true.

The generalized picture of fertilization presented in this chapter is a composite one and all events may not occur in all animals. If we recognize the danger of overgeneralization, the stepwise pattern of fertilization described offers insight into an extremely complex process. Many features remain unknown, and many species need to be investigated, before a specific picture of fertilization can be detailed for any one group of animals. The understanding of fertilization is further complicated by the fact that although normally the penetration of the egg by the sperm triggers egg activation and the subsequent events leading to development, the same reaction can be induced by other means. In nature, the eggs of a few animals, bees and wasps for example, usually develop without fertilization. Activation of the egg, then, does not depend on some unique property of the spermatozoon, since a variety of agents are effective in initiating changes in the egg cytoplasm. Such a phenomenon (that is, the development of an egg without fertilization) is known as parthenogenesis, and when it occur in nature it is referred to as *natural parthenogenesis*. When experimentally

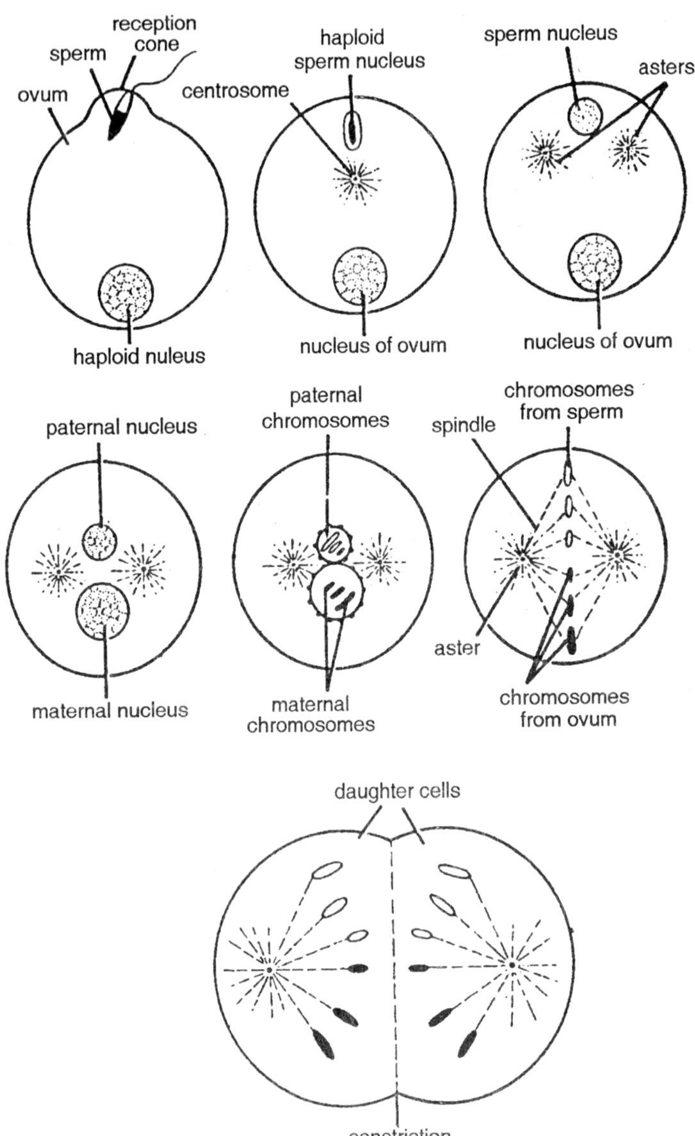

Fig. 11.1. Diagrammatic representation of process of fertilization.

induced in the laboratory, it is *artificial parthenogenesis*. For many years this phenomenon has intrigued biologist trying to gain insight into the problems of fertilization by inducing development through artificial parthenogenesis. By this experimental technique they hope to separate to the egg from those introduced by the sperm.

A. External Fertilization

When the fertilization occurs in the aquatic medium outside the bodies of male and female parents, it is called *external fertilization*. The aquatic medium for the external fertilization may be either sea water or fresh water.

(i) External fertilization in sea water

In marine animals, such as, sea urchins, the communities of sexually mature adults shed eggs and sperms freely into the surrounding water. In such cases, because the developmental hazards are greatest so astronomical numbers of eggs as well as sperms are spawned during any one spwaning period. The adult members of a species, usually become sexually mature depending on the environmental temperatures of the preceding weeks or months, and a rule, one or more ripe females spawn at down or dusk, stimulated by the rapid change in light intensity. Substances liberated with the oviducal fluid the time of sheding of eggs in turn stimulate other ripe females and also the ripe males in the vicinity.

Consequently clouds of eggs and sperms are formed in the sea water at the same time, and mass fertilization occurs. Even so, to reach the eggs, spermatozoa have to travel long distance and their chance of encounter with the eggs may be greatly scarce. The importance of timing (life span of gametes) relates to two factors — (1) the extent of diffusion of the spermatozoa, increasing with the distance they have to travel, and (2) the limited life, with regard to fertilizability of the reproductive cells, especially, the sperm. In the sea, where the complex salt water solution itself is essentially a primeval physiological medium, the eggs remain fertilizable for less than a day, while spermatozoa expand all their potential energy for motility in a few hours at the most.

(ii) External fertilization in fresh water

Among the fresh water animals, the timing of spawning of eggs and shedding of sperms by female and male parents, respectively, becomes more crucial and specific, because, their spermatozoa remain active in fresh water usually for minutes rather than hours. Hence, the common mating procedures of fish, amphibians and fresh water invertebrates, where sperms are delivered directly to the eggs of an individual female at the moment of laying, if not before.

B. Internal Fertilization

In terrestrial forms, particularly where eggs are completely enclosed in impermeable envelopes before being laid (e.g., oviparous animals such as reptiles and birds), or where they are retained within the maternal body throughout development (e.g., ovoviviparous and viviparous animals such as elasmobranchs and mammals), the spermatozoa are delivered internally (in the body of female) by some type of copulatory mechanism or device (*intromittent organ*) of male. In such forms the fertilization may occur either in lower portion of the oviduct near or at the external orifice (e.g., Urodela); in the upper portion of oviduct (e.g., salamanders, reptiles, aves, and most mammals); or in the ovarian follicles (e.g., viviparous fishes such as *Gambusia affinis* and *Heterandria formosa* and certain eutherian mammals such as (*Ericulus*).

On land, in terrestrial animals, there remains no problem of timing or spawning of eggs and shedding of sperms, because the mature sperms are commonly stored in a physiological medium capable of maintaining their life and potential activity for days, weeks, or months, either in moisture conserving capsules or in compartments of the male or female body, to be picked up, transferred, or utilized in one way or another. The mere deposition of eggs and sperms in the general vicinity of each other within a liquid medium (viz., sea or fresh water in case of external fertilization; fluid medium of female reproductive tract in case of internal fertilization) does not insure their meeting, even though spermatozoa possess a propelling tail for active motility. In those forms in which external fertilization occurs, it has been found that the movements of the spermatozoa are entirely at random and the spermatozoa collide with the eggs as a matter of pure chance. Such chance encounters occur regularly in nature partly due to enormous number of spermatozoa produced by the male gland, and partly the result of the eggs being a relatively very large target, so that it can be hit fairly easily. In vertebrates where, the fertilization is internal, the movement of the spermatozoa from the site of deposition to the site of fertilization usually depends little on the active swimming of the spermatozoa themselves. Rather, spermatozoa tend to be transported passively by muscular contractions of the female tract, and also, by the counter currents in the cilia-propelled, backward flowing liquid content of the tract.

Mechanism of Fertilization

The mechanism of fertilization is complicated one and is completed in the following stages:

Approach of the Spermatozoon to the Egg

Whether fertilization is external or internal, the first step is the encounter of spermatozoon and the ovum, which is brought about by swimming movements of spermatozoa. Encounter between sperm and ovum is purely accidental, because there are a few cases in which the sperms are guided towards ovum by chemical substances.

Sperm Viability

There are many critical events intervening between the formation and liberation of mature gametes and their final fusion in fertilization. The immediate result of coitus is the deposition of semen in the vagina (*insemination*). Thence the spermia must make their way through the uterus and into the upper part of the uterine tubes where fertilization ordinarily takes place. In comparison with the size of the spermia, the distance they must travel is great, and the route may be beset with chemical hazards in the form of abnormally strongly acid secretions or mechanical obstacles such as a crooked and compressed cervical canal or uterine tubes narrowed or occluded by disease. The enormous numbers of spermia contained in an ejaculate of semen (on the average in the neighborhood of 200,000,000) makes it probable that some of them will reach the oviduct while they are still capable of penetrating and fertilizing the ovum. There has been, and still is, much misinformation current as to the feats of travel and length of life of spermatozoa.

The present state of our knowledge does not justify any too dogmatic statements as to the exact length of time that human spermia retain their motility—and, more important, their fertilizing power—but both of these periods are certainly much shorter than formerly believed. Persistence of motility used to be regarded as indicative of fertilizing capacity. We now know that motility lasts much longer than the capacity of carrying out fertilization. In the case of the rabbit, for example, we have good experimental evidence that the spermatozoa lose their ability to fertilize after about 30 hours in the female genital tract, while their motility lasts up to about 2 days. Comparable data for human spermia are far less precise. The best-qualified opinion places their retention of fertilizing power at probably about 1 to 2 days, with motility persisting for perhaps double that time. It should be emphasized that these statements refer to ejaculated sperm in the female genital tract.

The length of time sperm cells may remain alive and retain their ability to fertilize varies greatly under different environmental conditions. In the epididymis and vas deferens, where they remain nonmotile, spermatozoa certainly retain their full capacities for many days. Their characteristic power of motility is aroused only when, at the moment of ejaculation, they are mixed with the secretions of the seminal vesicles and the prostate and bulbo-urethral glands. That their length of life thereafter depends in large measure on the rate at which they expend their limited store of potential energy is clearly indicated by recent experimental work in artificial insemination. The motility of the spermatozoa in freshly ejaculated semen can be checked by chilling. Under these conditions they do not immediately dissipate their available store of energy. Taking advantage of this fact, the semen of pedigreed stock has been shipped thousands of miles by airplane and introduced into females by means of a syringe, with the successful production of offspring by what might be called "remote control of paternity."

Sperm Transport

There still remains much to be learned about the manner in which the spermatozoa male their way from the vagina through the uterus and the uterine tubes. The spermatozoa themselves, of course, are actively motile, swimming in a fluid medium, tadpole-fashion, at a rate variously estimated as between 2 and 4 mm. a minute. But without some directive stimuli the course of their locomotion is frequently changed and it seems exceedingly doubtful that their own movement alone would account for the arrival of spermatozoa at the upper end of the uterine tubes as promptly as it is known to occur in the case of certain experimental animals. In the rabbit, for example, spermatozoa have been found at the upper end of the uterine tubes 3 hours after coitus. There is some evidence suggesting that spermatozoa tend to orient themselves so that they move against a gentle current, thus exhibiting what students of animal behaviour call a positive rheotactic response. But even assuming that the downward ciliary current in the uterus is an effective orienting stimulus, as has been maintained by many workers, the time at which spermatozoa reach the ovarian end of the tube is far too short to be accounted for on this basis.

Apparently muscular action of the uterus and uterine tubes plays an important part in the prompt arrival of spermatozoa at their destination. At the height of the sexual orgasm in the female there are spasmodic contractions of the smooth muscle of the vagina and uterus. There is some evidence indicating that these contractions may immediately draw some of the freshly deposited semen from the vagina into the uterus. While this may ordinarily be an accelerating factor in sperm transportation it certainly is not an indispensable one, for there are innumerable well-authenticated cases, both clinical and experimental, of pregnancy occurring in the absence of orgasm on the part of the female. In such instances the entrance and traversing of the uterus must depend primarily on the activity of the spermatozoa themselves. Mention has already been made of the heightened muscular activity of the uterine tubes at the time of ovulation.

On the basis of recent studies it seems probable that this increased activity is important in sperm transportation as well as in the journey of the ova toward the uterus. Careful observation of the activity of surgically exposed tubes in living experimental animals indicates that temporary rings of contraction tend to divide the tube into a series of compartments. At any given moment in any compartment, the downward-beating cilia along the outer walls tend to create also central back eddies. In such currents and countercurrents the spermatozoa in the lumen of the tube would be scattered rapidly throughout the area between two adjacent contraction rings. When the zones of contraction relax at one level and form at another, some spermatozoa would be crowded back toward the uterus but others would find themselves in a new compartment nearer the ovary. The formation and reformation of such compartments by temporary rings of contraction at shifting levels would rapidly disperse the spermatozoa throughout the length of the tube.

Viability of Ovum

When liberated from the ovary an ovum at once begins to undergo certain changes which can be characterized as aging or deterioration. Among other things there is a tendency for its protoplasm to become progressively more coarse. With this loss of the originally finely dispersed phase of its colloidal material the ovum loses vigor. These changes progress rapidly to a point, where the ovum, although technically still alive, can no longer be fertilized. As previously stated, the best information at present available indicates that the human ovum does not retain its capacity to be fertilized much over a day after its discharge from the ovary. If, however, the ovum is fertilized within this period, these deteriorative changes are checked and the protoplasm increases its activity in a way that is often described as "being rejuvenated." The nature of these changes is not as yet fully understood, but they involve increase in permeability and increase in oxidation rate.

There is also an increase in the amount of ammonia excreted. This indicates that there has been an increase in purine metabolism.

which is important in the synthesis of nuclear materials. These changes symbolize, of course, the beginning of the period of tremendously rapid growth which is destined to end in the production of a new individual. Interestingly enough, fertilization in the usual manner by the male sex cell is not the only ay an ovum may have its deterioration checked and be started on its growth phase. A variety of other stimuli may be substituted for the male sex cell. Changes in the ionic concentration of the sea water is effective in initiating development in the eggs of some marine invertebrates. Insect eggs have been started developing by stroking them with a camel's hair brush. Pricking with a needle has been effective in inducing frog's eggs to means other than its union with the male sex cell is known as *artificial parthenogenesis*.

The fact that artificial parthenogenesis is possible emphasizes the fact that all the necessary morphogenetic factors for development are present in the ovum and that the process of fertilization is essentially, as Barth puts it, a sort of "release mechanism." In other words, something from the sperm cell, or in artificial parthenogenesis the chemical or mechanical factor employed, releases potential energy already present in the egg. It should not be overlooked, however, that this release mechanism is far from the whole story. The sperm brings with it its quota of hereditary potentialities, and the mixture of germinal material from two parents produces a vigor of growth not manifested in eggs starting their development parthenogenetically.

Agglutination

In the presence of egg water (water in which eggs have been lying for sometimes), the spermatozoa become "sticky" and adhere to the surface of the egg to its membrane and even to each other. This mutual adhesion of the spermatozoa results in their clumping or agglutination which is easily observed with the sperms of some animals, specially in sea urchin. The agglutination and sticking of sperms to eggs of the same species is found in most animals. The agglutination depends to a large extent on environmental conditions and on certain chemicals such as "*fertilizin*" which is generally present in the surface layer of the egg. The fertilizin is glyco-protein or mucopolysaccharide in chemical composition. The molecules of the fertilizin are quite large having the molecular weight of about 300,000 and each molecule may have more than one "*active group*" by which it may become attached to the surface of the spermatozoa. Another chemical substance present in the surface layer of the cytoplasm of spermatozoa is the "*antifertilizin*", having a low molecular weight than fertilizin. Molecular weight of antifertilizin is about 10,000.

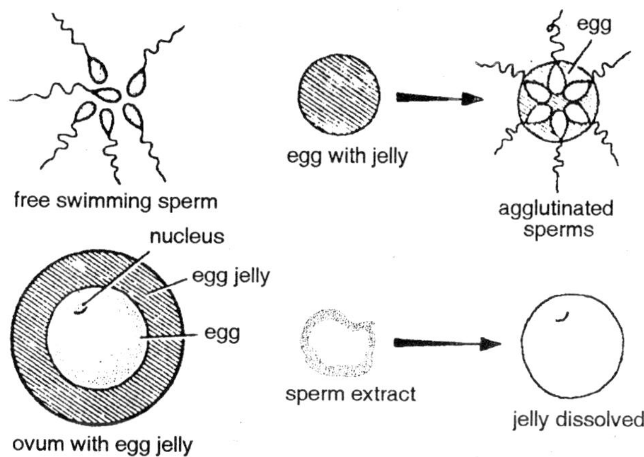

Fig. 11.2. Fertilizin—antifertilizin reaction.

The antifertilizin can be extracted out from the spermatozoa by heating, freezing or acidifying the water. Both fertilizin and antifertilizin are having certain specific peculiarity as they combine in a specific manner i.e., the egg fertilizin of any species reacts best with the sperm antifertilizin of the same species. These can react with other species even, but the rate of reaction may be much weaker, this is possible only in the case when two species are fairly nearly related to one another. The reaction between the fertilizin and antifertilizin molecules accounts for both the agglutination of the spermatozoa by egg water and the adhesion of the spermatozoa to the egg membrane or egg surface. The fertilizin particles have more than one *reactive spots* on their surfaces so that one fertilizin particle may become attached to two or more spermatozoa, thus, binding together. This reaction or adhesion of a spermatozoon to the surface of the egg or to the egg membrane is the result of the establishment of a bond between the antifertilizin molecules embedded in the surface layer of the cytoplasm or the egg membrane.

Sperm Penetration

The actual penetration of the egg by the spermatozoon can be separated into three general steps.

1. The sperm must penetrate the membranes that surround the egg. These vary from the thick tough chorion or vitelline membrane of some fishes, to the jelly layers of the amphibian, and to the zona pellucida and attached corona radiata of the mammals.
2. When the spermatozoon contacts the egg surface, its membrane fuses with the plasma membrane of the egg.

3. The sperm nucleus along with its middle piece is drawn into the cytoplasm of the egg. The tail mayor may not be left outside the membrane or trapped in the perivitelline space.

The egg water of sea urchins not only brings about the agglutination of the spermatozoa, but it also causes the sperm to undergo a structural change known as the *acrosomal reaction*. Whether fertilizin is the responsible agent for all the changes associated with this reaction is not known. The acrosomal reaction takes a variety of forms in different animals, but the end result is the release of materials, usually in the form of the acrosomal filament, and the secretion of lysins. The filament aids the sperm in penetrating the membrane barriers of the egg, and the lysins dissolve away parts of the membrane, providing a pathway for the entering spermatozoon. The solvent action of these enzymes provides the mechanism for sperm penetration.

Capacitation

Before the acrosomal reaction can take place, however, the sperm must undergo some kind of physiological change that increases its ability to penetrate the egg. The general term *capacitation* is given to this change. The egg water initiates this sperm activation in the sea urchin, and a similar process occurs in the amphibian when the spermatozoon comes in contact with the jelly coats. Removal of the jelly coats from the egg before they come in contact with the sperm inhibits fertilization. On the other hand, eggs taken from the body cavity, which lack jelly coats and normally cannot be fertilized, may be penetrated by the spermatozoon if they are fist exposed to jellied eggs. Obviously the spermatozoa and the jelly coat somehow interact and increase the fertilizing capacity of the gamete. The environment of the female genital tract induces capacitation in the sperm of those animals that practice internal fertilization. In mammals freshly ejaculated sperm transferred to the ampulla region or newly ovulated eggs fertilized few eggs. On the other hand, insertion of the sperm into the genital tract before ovulation occurs, activates the sperm in some way and enhances their capacity to fertilize the egg.

Acrosomal Reaction

Membrane fusion

Once the spermatozoa are activated, the series of events described as the acrosomal reaction may be followed by electron microscopy. Prior to the 1960s researches believed that the plasma membrane of the egg elevated and phagocytized the sperm, drawing it inside the

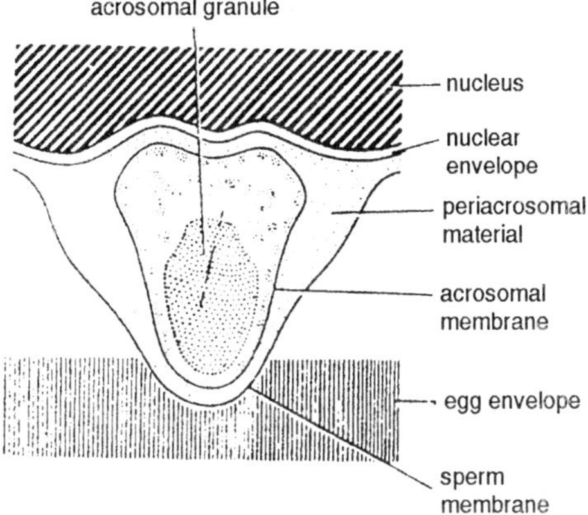

Fig. 11.3. Electron micrographic structure of acrosomal region of spermatozoan of Saccoglossus.

egg. Although this may occur in some instances, electron microscopic studies reveal that in general the penetration of the egg by the sperm involves a fusion of their membranes. In this process the shape of the acrosome is altered. The successive stages in the acrosomal reaction in the invertebrate *Hydroides hexagonus* is depicted. The acrosomal vesicle (the covering over the acrosome) splits, the acrosomal granule disappears (apparently releasing lysin), and the one or more filaments contact the plasma membrane. Invagination occurs in the plasma membrane at the points of contact with the filaments, and fusion of the two membranes takes place at these areas of interdigitation. These and other detailed studies of the acrosomal reaction have been carried out by the Colwins, who investigated this process in the annelid worm *Hydroides* and in the protochordate *Saccoglossus*.

According to the Colwins, "the major role of the acrosome is apparently to deliver the sperm plasma membrane to the egg plasma membrane." A similar series of acrosomal events have been observed in the toad, chicken, hamster, rabbit, guinea pig, and man; so it appears that the *Hydroides-Saccoglossus* pattern of gamete membrane fusion described by the Colwins also occurs in the chordates. Few complete studies, however, have been made on the vertebrates. Mammalian spermatozoa recovered after they have penetrated the zona pellucida lack an acrosome. This loss is usually interpreted as analogous to the splitting of the acrosomal vesicle when the invertebrate sperm contact the egg. The acrosomal granules released apparently, aid the sperm in penetrating the thick pellucida. One of the most detailed studies of sperm penetration in the mammal was made by Szollosi and Ris (1961). They followed later stages in the fertilization process in the rat and described the penetration of the plasma membrane by the sperm of this animal. Their electron micrographs showed that after the sperm penetrated the ovum it had no plasma membrane, although one was present before and during the process of fertilization. They suggested that contact between the sperm head and the plasma membrane of the egg brought about a rupture of the two membranes.

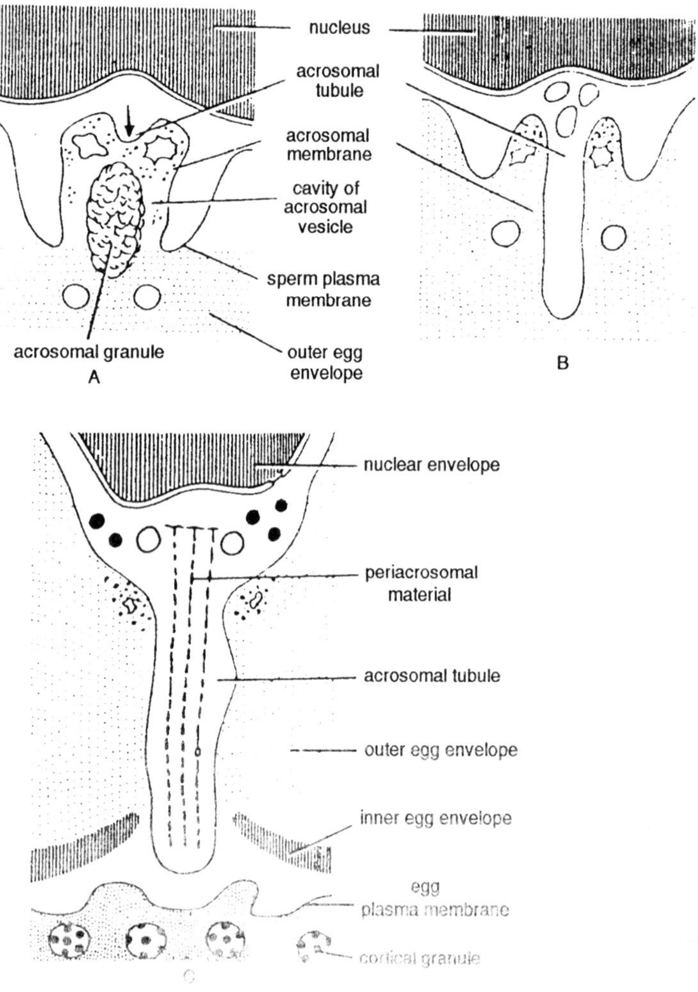

Fig. 11.4. Acrosomal changes during fertilization of Saccoglossus.

As a result, the egg membrane fused with the sperm plasma membrane at the point of contact and formed a continuous membrane around the egg and outer surface of the sperm. At first a deep fold of membrane forms around the sperm. Eventually, as fusion of membranes proceeds toward the tail of the sperm, the entire naked sperm is drawn into the egg, leaving its plasma membrane to be incorporated into the egg membrane. These investigations by the Colwins and by Szollosi and Ris demonstrate the importance of egg and sperm plasma membrane in the actual entrance of the sperm into the egg cytoplasm. It is possible that the acrosome of both invertebrate and vertebrate sperm undergoes similar changes. However, at the present time insufficient evidence on enough species prevents us from making a generalized statement concerning acrosomal structure, sperm activation, and egg membrane penetration. Once the acrosomal filaments contact the plasma membrane, the cytoplasm flows up inside the filament membrane, covering the sperm head, midpiece, and possibly the tail. This cytoplasmic elevation is the *fertilization cone*.

The type of acrosomal filament varies from animal to animal, ranging from one in *Arbacia* to many in the annelid *Hydroides hexagonus*. The shape of the fertilization cone differs according to the form of the acrosome filaments. In mammals, it has been described as a small mound at the site of sperm contact. The fertilization cone may be of short duration, lasting only 20 seconds. In some invertebrate eggs the cone forms before fertilization; thus doubt is cast on its function. In other examples the sperm appears to penetrate the membrane by undulating movements of the tail and no cytoplasmic cone forms at all.

Release of lysins

The spermatozoa of most vertebrates contain a substance that enables them to penetrate the various layers around the egg. The material dissolves a localized pathway through the membranes enabling the acrosomal filament to reach the egg surface. This substance is enzymic in nature and known by the general name of *sperm lysins*. Lysins differ from one species to another and are released when the acrosomal granule disappears. Attempts to extract the lysins and identify them chemically have not been to successful because of the small amount of material available. They are protein in nature according to chemical analysis, but the specific class of enzymes has not been identified. Some investigators feel that the sperm may release more than one kind of enzyme.

According to recent studies, the jelly layers of certain amphibian eggs depend on the presence of disulfide bonds for maintaining their structure. It has been suggested that the lysins of this group of animals may utilize a disulfide bond as a substrate. According to these workers (Gusseck and Hedrick, 1971), the fusion of the egg plasma membrane and sperm membrane occur by a sulfhydryl-disulfide bond interchange. They believe that fertilization should be explained on a molecular basis. The mammalian egg offers a unique problem of sperm penetration, since at ovulation it is surrounded by the zona pellucida, the corona radiata, and various numbers of cumulus cells.

It is very difficult to pull away the cumulus oophorus from a newly ovulated rodent egg although the sperm must penetrate this barrier. Its entrance is made easier by a lysin a cumulus dispersing factor, identified as hyaluronidase, present in living rabbit, rat, and mouse sperm suspensions or extracts. This dispersing factor acts upon the intercellular cement of the follicular cells by depolymerizing and hydrolyzing the *hyaluronic acid* cement that holds the cells together. In vitro studies show that the concentration of the enzyme is proportional to the number of sperm present, since it is associated with the sperm itself rather than the semen. After some hours in the female reproductive tract the spermatozoa undergo capacitation and release their enzymes into the seminal fluid. Researchers assumed that the concentration of the enzyme was high to be effective in denuding the ovum, but they later learned that the sperm of the dog contains no hyaluronidase. This enzyme, then, is not the total answer to sperm penetration.

It is now believed that the sperm probably contains sufficient enzyme to make a pathway for itself through the various layers. Narrow slits in the zona pellucida appear after the sperm penetrates this membrane and offer visual evidence of a lytic substance. Microvilli anchor the cells of the corona radiata to the zona pellucida of the ovum. The two cannot be mechanically separated without injury to one of the membranes. The sperm may release more than one enzyme to act on the two layers. The cells fall apart after contact with sperm or contents of the oviduct for a few hours. Some investigators suggest that possibility that a tubular factor that acts on the cells of the corona radiata is also secreted. Apparently after contact with the contents of the fallopian tube, the microvill are retracted and free the ovum. Possibly the ciliary and muscular movements of the oviduct may mechanically remove the coronal cells as the egg makes its way down the tubes to the uterus.

Activation of the Egg

The process of initiating development in an egg is called *activation*. It is initiated or stimulated by the sperm. The egg responds to the sperm by forming fertilization cone and by undergoing the various surface and internal changes. All these changes collectively constitute *activation*. During activation the following changes occur in the egg:

1. The egg surface produces *fertilization cone*.
2. The vitelline membrane is lifted and is converted into *fertilization membrane*.
3. The cortical granules explode.
4. The cytoplasm exhibits movements.
5. The permeability of plasma membrane increases.
6. The coenzyme NAD is phosphorylated.
7. The rate of protein synthesis increases.
8. Mitosis is initiated.
9. The breakdown of polysaccharide occurs.
10. The enzyme dehydrogenase increases.

Many theories have been proposed to explain how the sperm activates the egg. A few are given below:

(a) The theory of Boveri

The mature egg has no *division centre* (centriole). The egg has all the other factors, except the division-centre for initiating the development. The sperm has an active division-centre. So during fertilization the sperm introduces its active division-centre into the egg. This division-centre activates the egg to divide.

(b) The theory of Loeb

Loeb suggested that the sperm brings in two principles. The first one is a lytic principle. It brings about cortical cytolysis which leads to a sudden increase in the oxidation-process of the egg. The second principle regulates cytolysis and excess oxidation.

(c) The theory of Bataillon

Bataillon believed that the unfertilized egg is inhibited because of the accumulation of metabolic products. Activation or fertilization leads to the release of these substances to the egg's exterior. This leads to the accumulation of perivitelline fluid and the elevation of the fertilization-membrane.

(d) Fertilizin-Antifertilizin theory

F.R. Lillie stated that the egg is activated by the fertilizin-antifertilizin reaction. Fertilizin is a glycoprotein present in the egg. Antifertilizin is an acid protein present in the sperm. Fertilizin activates, attracts and agglutinates the sperm at the egg's surface. As

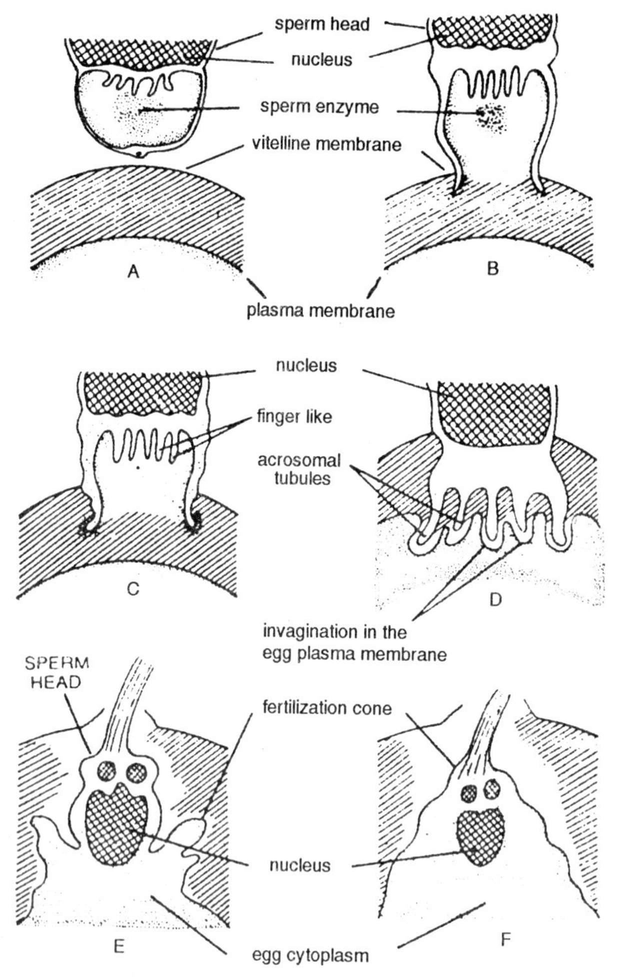

Fig. 11.5. Acrosomal reaction and passage of sperm head into the egg cytoplasm in Hydriodes hexogonus. A—Approach of spermatozoan (with intact acrosome). B—Contact with vitelline membrane; fusion of plasma-acrosome membrane and the release of sperm enzyme over egg surface. C—Sperm head moves through the vitelline membrane. D—Acrosome in the deep invagination of the plasma membrane of the egg. E—Passage of the sperm here into the egg cytoplasm and formation of the fertilization cone.

the sperm touches the egg, it unites with a part of fertilizin molecule. This union releases an activating principle within the egg. The activating principle activates the egg as a whole. The most important change in the egg is the *cortical reaction* including the formation of fertilization-membrane. The fertilization-membrane and fertilizin-antifertilizin reaction prevent *polyspermy*.

(e) Change of Viscosity theory

This theory was postulated by *Heilbrunn* (1915, 28, 43). During activation, calcium is released in the egg-cytoplasm. This leads to an increase in the viscosity of egg-cytoplasm. This change initiates development.

(f) The theory of Tyler

This theory gives a molecular mechanism for the activation of the egg. In sea urchin egg, protein synthesis is initiated immediately after fertilization. In the mature, unfertilized egg, protein synthesis is nil, although it contains the entire machinery for protein synthesis. It has been demonstrated that mRNA in the unfertilized egg is "masked" or inactivated. The masking-substance is supposed to be a protein. At fertilization the masking protein is freed and mRNA is unmasked. Hence they participate in protein synthesis. The dissolution of masking protein is brought about by an enzyme liberated into the egg by the spermatozoon at the time of fertilization.

(g) The theory of Deinhibition

This theory is based on the observations of *Runnstrom* and *Brachet*. According to them, during maturation metabolic *inhibitors* accumulate in the oocyte. This is eliminated and the egg is deinhibited.

Completion of Meiosis

Usually the formation of the second polar body must be completed, since in most vertebrates arrest of the meiotic process occurs while the eggs are still in the ovarian follicle. Ovulation usually begins after the spindle forms for the second meiotic division, and the dyads arrange themselves on the metaphase plate. The penetration of the sperm stimulates the chromosomes on the maturation spindle to pass into the anaphase stage. The completion of nuclear maturation immediately follows the fertilization process. Little information is available concerning the details of the extrusion of the second polar body. We do know, however, that in the rabbit, as long as 15 minutes may elapse between sperm penetration and completion of the second polar body. It may take 2 hours for the mouse, and 4 hours for the rat to complete the meiotic process.

Cortical Reaction

The penetration of the egg by the sperm produces an almost instantaneous reaction in the cortex of the egg. These changes start at the point of sperm contact and pass over the surface of the egg; the exact changes that occur vary from animal to animal. In the past most of our information was based on microscopic examinations with dark-field illumination or polarized light. Studies show that the interference colour changes at the time of fertilization, indicating a dispersion of material at the egg surface, possibly lipids. Often there is streaming of cytoplasm toward the point of sperm entrance and rearrangement of cytoplasmic constituents within the egg. Cortical granules visible at the surface of the egg disappear, and a membrane, the *fertilization membrane*, lifts off the egg surface. Not until the electron microscope became available was it possible to obtain more precise information. These new studies reveal that the surface of the sea urchin egg consists of two membranes, an outer vitelline membrane and an inner plasma membrane.

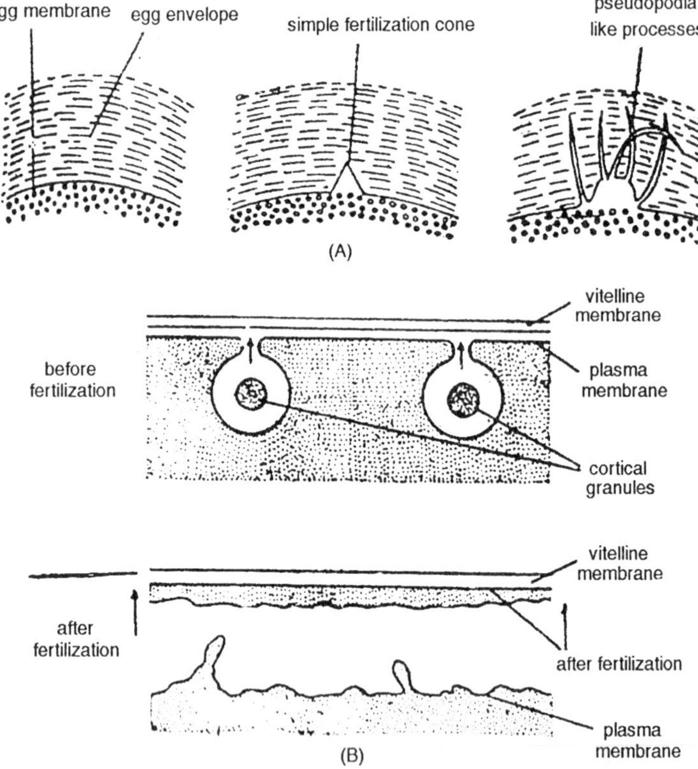

Fig. 11.6. A—Fertilization cone; B—Formation of the fertilization membrane in the egg sea urchin egg.

At fertilization the inner membrane remains on the egg and a space, the *perivitelline space*, develops between the two. Granules enclosed in membranes and closely associated with the egg membrane are located in the cortex of the egg. These cortical granules explode and disappear at the time of fertilization. Electron micrographs reveal that both the granule membrane and the egg plasma membrane rupture at the point of contract and the two membranes then become continuous. As a result the granules are ejected into the newly established perivitelline space where they line up and become attached to the vitelline membrane. The vitelline membrane and the material of the cortical granules contribute to the fertilization membrane in these animals. Cortical granules or vacuoles that disappear after fertilization have been reported in the eggs of teleostean fishes, amphibians, hamsters, and rabbits. The granules of the fishes and amphibians contain a polysaccharide, similar to that identified in the sea urchin egg.

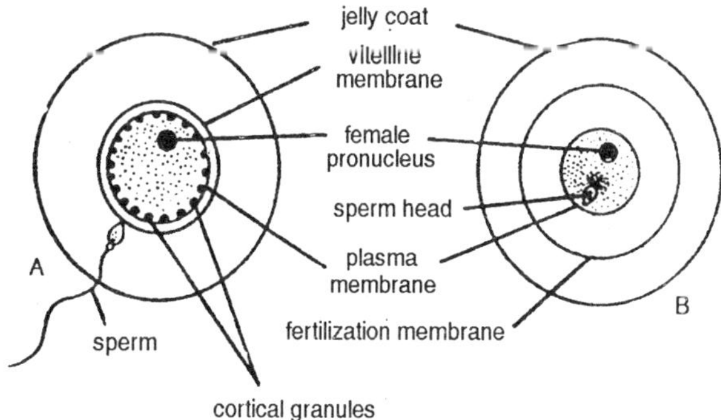

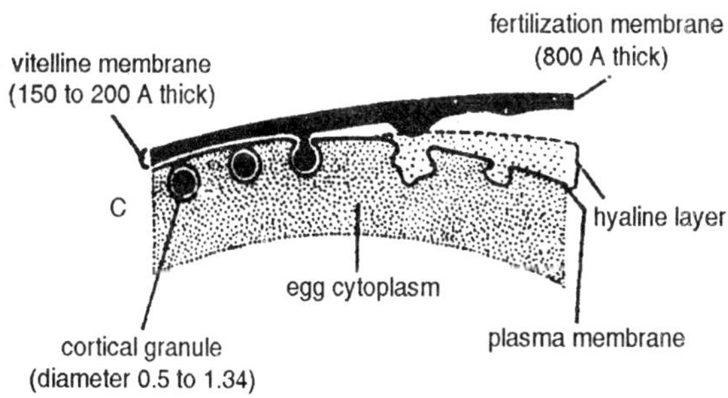

Fig. 11.7. Cortical reaction and formation of fertilization urchin. A—Sea-urchin egg before fertilization with intact cortical granules. B—Sea-urchin egg after fertilization membrane. C—Mechanisms involved in the cortical granule explosion and formation fertilization memrbane.

A lack of sufficient information prevents us from defining their specific role in the fertilization process. However, the inference can certainly be drawn that the activity of the granules at the time of fertilization is an integral part of egg activation. Fertilization membranes similar to those described for the sea urchin have been studied in the protherian mammals, the frog, and the trout. The vitelline membrane contributes to the fertilization membrane in the frog; a similar membrane, the chorion, helps form the fertilization membrane in the trout. Instead of a vitelline membrane or chorion, it is the zona pellucida that surrounds the eggs of higher mammals.

There is little evidence that the mammalian membrane actually elevates at fertilization although the egg shrinks and a perivitelline space is established. However, it does undergo certain structural changes that can be correlated with entrance of the first sperm and that make it less permeable to other spermatozoa. After fertilization, the egg's surface becomes smooth, and the microvilli of the corona radiata are no longer visible. Regardless of the specific type of outer membrane (vitelline, chorion, or zona pellucida), the surface of the fertilized egg and the unfertilized egg differ structurally from one another. We do not understand the mechanisms involved in the formation of the fertilization membrane. It has been suggested that the "exploding" granules release substances into the perivitelline space to cause an influx of water, an osmotic phenomenon that might explain the growth of this space. As the material leaves the cortex of the egg, some shrinkage in ooplasm occurs and this, too, could contribute to the formation of the space. The lifting of the vitelline membrane from the egg surface and the explosion of the cortical granules are energy-requiring reactions and thus can be prevented by inhibitors of oxidative phosphorylation.

Polyspermy Block

When a sperm penetrates an egg, certain physiological changes occur that can be correlated with the structural changes at the egg's surface. Once the sperm enters the egg, the egg surface becomes refractory to other sperm. The condition whereby the egg is penetrated by more than one sperm is known as *polyspermy* and is usually lethal to the cleaving egg. If two sperm with their centrioles enter the egg, a triaster or tetraster forms, which directs the formation of two or more spindles. The chromosomes become distributed unequally on the spindles, and cell division soon comes to a half. Therefore, after the penetration of one sperm a barrier, which restricts the entrance of another sperm, usually develops. In the sea urchin this polyspermy-preventing barrier appears to reside in the fertilization membrane, since its mechanical removal allows multiple sperm entry. In other animal the egg surface acts as the barrier, but in many mammals it is the zona pellucida that becomes impermeable to more than one sperm. This reaction is known as the *zona reaction*. If polyspermy does result, the sperm usually remain in the perivitelline space. The presence of the sperm in the space seems to indicate that the plasma membrane acts as a secondary barrier. In a few cases polyspermy is normal.

More than one sperm enter the eggs of certain insects, amphibians, reptiles, and birds. In these animals, however, only one sperm develops into the male pronucleus and, therefore, only one cleavage spindle forms. The precise polyspermy-blocking reaction is not understood. Since it is correlated with changes in the cortical region of the egg, the molecular rearrangement occurring at the surface of the egg at the time of fertilization may be responsible in some way in preventing entrance of more than one sperm. The perivitelline fluid that is formed, partially at least, from the discharged cortical vacuoles, appears to be effective also in blocking the entrance of more than one sperm. Vacquier et. al. (1973) recently demonstrated the presence of a protease in the cortical granules of sea urchin eggs. The protease hardens the vitelline membrane and lytically releases supernumerary sperm bound to the egg before the cortical reaction. The protease thus prevents polyspermy by this dual action.

Paths of the Pronuclei

The first accurate study of the paths of the pronuclei during the fertilization was made by *Roux* in frog, where he marked the course of the sperm by two compartments:

(i) A penetration path.

(ii) Copulation path.

Penetration path is the path travelled by the sperm (Male pronucleus) towards the female pronucleus (in case when female pronucleus is present in the middle of he egg). It is nearly vertical to the surface while in the *copulation path* the male nucleus moves towards the point of union with the egg nucleus. Here in later case the female pronucleus is generally accentric in position, that is why both these paths form a considerable angle. A third path which is the *cleavage path* may also added, along which the united nuclei move together to the definite position of the first cleavage nucleus. All these paths or

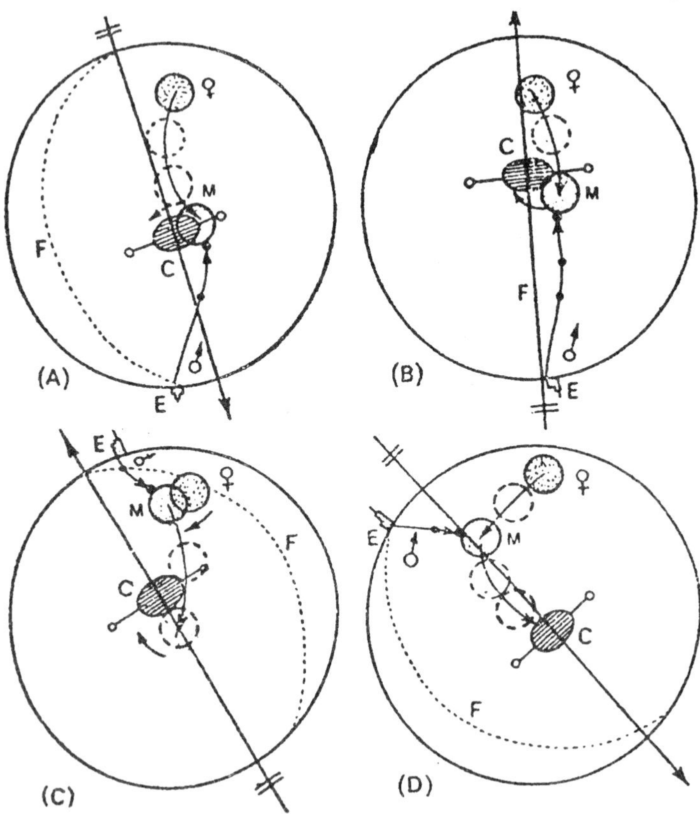

Fig. 11.8. Diagram showing the path of the pronuclei in four different eggs of the sea urchin.

facts can be well traced the sea urchin egg where the egg nucleus at first occupies an accentric position near the point at which the polar bodies are formed, but before fertilization may wander to any position.

Generally the sperm penetrates and enters the egg at any point (but it is supposed to be predetermined), the sperm nucleus generally first moves towards the centre, that shows no constant relation to the position of the egg nucleus. So this much of the path travelled by the male nucleus after penetration is called the *penetration path* (already stated). Then the sperm or male pronucleus moves towards the egg or female pronucleus which is excentrically placed, making *copulation path*. And from the meeting point the opposed pronuclei move slowly along the *cleavage path* to their final position, which is always in the egg axis and slightly eccentric towards the animal pole.

Fusion of the Haploid Pronuclei

After the penetration of the sperm into the ovum, the sperm moves towards the female pronucleus to form *zygote*. Only the head region of the sperm concerns is the fusion with female pronucleus, contains the nucleus and the middle piece along with a centromere. There is no general understanding of how these parts actually reach the anterior of the ovum, although it appears likely they are "drawn" in through some activity of the egg cytoplasm rather than through a mechanical action of the spermatozoon. During the penetration or entrance of the sperm, the tail is ordinarily discarded out side the eggs. But generally in mammals (mouse) it remains attached with the sperm but it soon degenerates and plays no role in subsequent events.

Entry of spermatozoon in the egg of vertebrate incites the second maturation division. And the egg nucleus becomes ready for union after the production of the second polar body. The male pronucleus always moves towards the female pronucleus, while the latter in turn

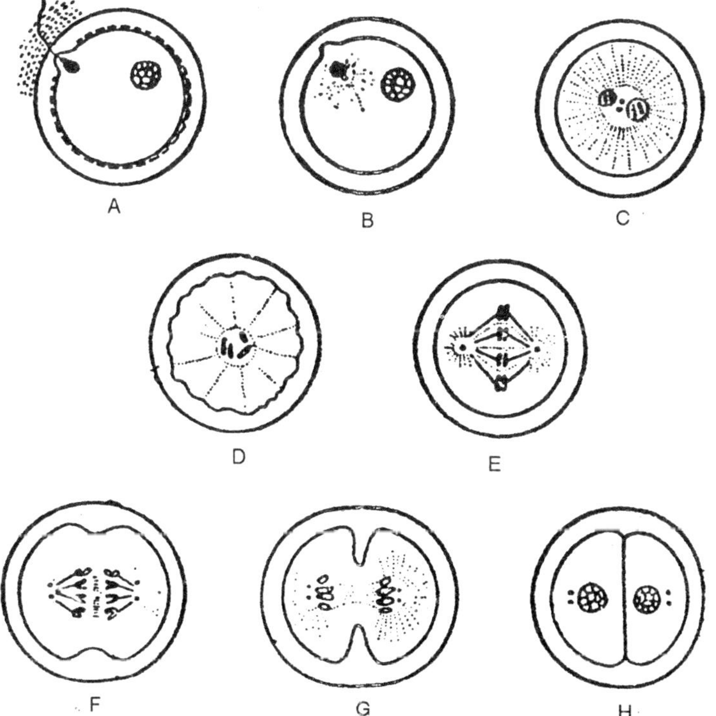

Fig. 11.9. Schematic figures of fertilization and the first cleavage.

often moves to meet the male pronucleus. But what causes them to move and how the movements take their correct course is wholly unknown. As the pronuclei approach each other the centrosome brought in by the spermatozoon subdivides and a spindle system is established. In few animal types, the pronuclei now literally fuse. Ordinarily, however, in mammals and other vertebrates, each pronucleus loses its membrane and concommitantly its chromatin resolves into the haploid set of chromosomes. The two sets of chromosomes than arrange themselves across the spindle. This arrangement, making readiness for the first cleavage division, represents the consummation of fertilization.

KINDS OF FERTILIZATION

In the organisms following types of fertilization occur:

1. Monospermic Fertilization

In most animals, usually only one sperm enters in the egg, this type of fertilization is known as *monospermic fertilization*. The monospermic fertilization is common in the coelenterates, annelids, echinoderms, bony fishes, frogs and mammals.

2. Polyspermic Fertilization

When many sperms enter in the egg, the fertilization is known as the *polyspermic fertilization*. It maybe of two types:

(i) Pathological polyspermy

Under certain abnormal conditions when in a monospermic type of egg, many sperms enter in the egg, the condition is known as the *pathological polyspermy*. This type of egg does not develop further and dies soon.

(ii) Physiological polyspermy

In the animals with large yolky eggs such as molluscs, selachians, urodels, reptiles and birds, the polyspermic fertilization usually occurs. Such polyspermic fertilization is known as *physiological polyspermy*. In these cases, many sperms enter in the egg but the pronucleus of only one sperm units with the pronucleus of the egg and rest are degenerated soon. Such eggs are viable and develop further.

3. Polyandry

When two male pronuclei unite with a female pronucleus, the union is known as *polyandry*, *e.g.*, man and rat.

4. Polygamy

When two egg pronuclei unite with single male pronucleus the phenomenon is known as *polygamy*, e.g., sea urchins, polychaete worm, urodels and rabbits.

5. Gynogenesis

When only sperm activates the egg but its pronucleus does not unite with the egg pronucleus, e.g., planarians and nematodes.

Significance of Fertilization

The results of fertilization are:

1. The entrance of sperm activates the secondary oocyte to complete its second maturation division.
2. Induces the movement of cytoplasm and the pigment granules and marks the fertilization track.
3. Induces the 2nd centriole and initiates spindle formation.
4. Restores the diploid number of chromosomes and recombines the maternal and paternal genetic traits.
5. Induces change in the periphery of egg and this change precludes the entry of other sperms.
6. This causes separation of vitelline membrane which allows the rotation of egg inside.
7. This enhances the metabolic activities and thus renews the vigour and vitality.
8. The amount of cytoplasm lost due to the separation of polocytes is restores.
9. Establishes a new plane of egg axis.
10. Causes rearrangement and organization of egg cytoplasm into distinct '*organ forming areas*.'

POLYSPERMY

Normally the eggs are fertilized each by one sperm, though more than one sperm may enter the egg. So when one egg is fertilized by one sperm the condition *monospermy* occurs as in Echinoderm, nematodes, molluscs or mammals. The term *polyspermy* is applied in those cases where the eggs are penetrated by more than one sperm. This polyspermy mainly confined to eggs heavily laden with yolk (insects, elasmobranchs, amphibians, reptiles, birds etc.). Generally in polyspermy, only one sperm nucleus conjugates with the egg nucleus while the other sooner or later degenerates without conjugation either with the egg nucleus or with one another.

In some cases, the degeneration takes place very early (urodeles, insects). While in still others the supernumerary sperm nuclei may enlarge, assume a vesicular form and divide repeatedly by mitosis producing a number of small nuclei having haploid number of chromosomes. Here in such cases the normal distribution of the chromosomes is affected at each mitosis, hence the resulting embryo contains nuclei of two kinds, diploid ones descended from the original fused nuclei, and haploid ones derived from supernumerary sperm nuclei. Larvae having such abnormalities are abnormal in various degrees and incapable of complete normal development.

Physiological Changes in Fertilization

As the sperm enters the egg, it triggers a number of physiological changes in the egg. They are as follows:

1. Elevation of Fertilization Membrane

The vitelline membrane is lifted off from the surface of the egg. This membrane is now called *fertilization membrane*. It is strengthened by the deposition of cortical granule materials on its inner surface. A fluid called *perivitelline fluid* gradually accumulates in the space between the surface of the egg and the fertilization membrane. The fertilized egg freely rotates inside the perivitelline fluid.

2. Explosion of Cortical Granules

When the sperm enters the egg the cortical granules explode and release their contents. The cortical granules synthesize the *fertilization membrane*, *perivitelline fluid* and the *hyaline layer*.

3. Cytoplasmic Movements

This contact of sperms sets in the egg elaborate cytoplasmic movements. The movement of egg-cytoplasm is reflected in the violent activity of the pigment granules on the surface. The cytoplasmic movement is best illustrated in amphibian eggs. As the sperm penetrates through the cortex of the egg, a trail of dark pigment from the egg's periphery flows in after the *sperm*. This initial path of the sperm constitutes the *penetration path*. Then the sperm begins to travel towards its place of meeting with the female pronucleus. This secondary path is the *copulation path*. On the surface of the egg opposite to the point of sperm entry, the peripheral area of the egg becomes lighter in colour and assumes a grey appearance. This area is crescentic in shape and is known as the *grey crescent*.

4. Permeability of Plasma Membrane

The permeability of plasma membrane increases in the case of the molecules of water, ethylene, glycol, phosphate etc.

5. Phosphorylation of Coenzymes

At fertilization the coenzyme NAD is phosphorylated into NADP and NADPH in the presence of the enzyme NAD *kinase*.

$$NAD + ATP \xrightarrow{\text{NAD kinase}} NADP + ADP$$

6. Rate of Oxygen Consumption

The rate of oxygen utilization may increase or decrease or may not change. In frog and toad there is a pronounced drop in *respiratory quotient*. In sea-urchin and lamprey oxygen consumption is increased during fertilization. In teleost fish, *Fundulus*, there is no change in the rate of oxygen consumption.

7. Rate of Protein Synthesis

In the unfertilized egg of sea-urchin there is no protein synthesis. During fertilization the rate of protein synthesis increases.

8. Initiation of Mitosis

Fertilization initiates mitosis in the egg resulting in cleavage. Mitosis requires the development of mitotic apparatus. It is produced exclusively by the centriole introduced by the sperm. The introduction of sperm centriole is a must for the egg to form a mitotic spindle. Thus the sperm stimulates the first mitotic division (cleavage) of he fertilized egg, by contributing its centriole to the egg.

9. The Breakdown of Polysaccharide

Immediately after fertilization a rapid breakdown of polysaccharide takes place. There is a corresponding increase in lactic acid.

10. Hexose Phosphate

It increases considerably after fertilization.

11. Dehydrogenase

This enzyme increases after fertilization.

12

Gametogenesis

The *germ cells* give rise to the gametes of the individual. They provide the continuity between generations and are segregated early in development from *somatic cells*, which contribute to the formation of the body. The germ cells can be distinguished cytologically from the somatic cells in the differentiating gonad before it is possible to tell whether the embryo is female or male. Certain cells located outside the gonad and even outside the body of the embryo (at earlier stages of development) are believed to be the precursors of the germ cells. These cells are the *primordial germ cells*.

Many embryologists consider them to be the only cells destined to form the future gametes of the individual. They can be identified about 24 days after fertilization in the human embryo and after about 19 hours of incubation in the chick. The fact that they are very early separated in the gonads, especially in the ovary, protects the germ cells from the diseases and injuries that somatic cells suffer, although they, too, can be affected by the poor environment of an unhealthy body. In the gonads, the germ cells develop into the oogonia or spermatogonia and proliferate. Eventually they transform into oocytes or spermatocytes and undergo nuclear and cytoplasmic maturation.

As a result of nuclear maturation, a reduction occurs in the chromosome number in each gamete through the process of meiosis. When the egg cytoplasm matures, there is synthesis of RNA and some proteins—all the essentials for development. The egg stores these materials in its cytoplasm for future use by the embryo. The spermatozoon, on the other hand, discards its cytoplasm in favour of specializing in motality and consequently depends on its surroundings for its nourishment. At the end of the maturation process the egg is ready for *ovulation* and the sperm for *spermiation* (release from the Sertoli cells). Passage through the respective gonadal ducts completes their structural and biochemical changes. The ova or sperm are prepared for a successful union at fertilization, a necessity for species survival in vertebrate animals where sexual reproduction is the rule.

Comparison of Somatic and Germ Cells

When a cell divides mitotically, the chromosomes in the nucleus are distributed equally, qualitatively and quantitatively, between the two daughter cells. As a result each daughter cell is identical to the parent cell as far as genetic composition is concerned. All sexually derived individuals start out as one cell, the fertilized egg, which then divides repeatedly to give rise to a new individual. As a result, all cells of an embryo contain the same number and kind of chromosomes despite the fact that some cells will eventually differentiate into germ cells (ova and sperm), some into muscle cells, and some into skin or nerve cells in the adult body. Each cell carries the same code in the DNA of its chromosomes for all the morphogenetic or physiological activities that go on in the body of a particular species. The genes and the chromosomes of both the somatic and the germ cells are identical. It is not, then, their hereditary material that distinguishes between these two types of cells.

Actually, the capacity of the adult somatic cell to follow the coded instructions contained in the DNA of its genes appears to be limited. A skin cell may carry the code for all cellular activities, but it differentiates and functions only as a skin cell, and not as a germ cell or a muscle cell. Somewhere along the developmental pathway the destiny of the cell became fixed, its possibilities for differentiation were restricted. Embryologists say that it becomes *determined*. Its potentiality is limited or, is *partially repressed*. Despite the fact that the cell contains the code for all activities that go on in the organism's cells, most of these potentialities functions are expressed by particular types of cell. In some instances, the somatic cells can reproduce their own kind. A skin cell from the germinativum layer of the epidermis can undergo mitosis and form a new skin cell. A liver cell can give rise to another liver cell. But many cells cannot form new cells, for example, the highly differentiated nerve cells, for example, the highly differentiated nerve cell. However, none of the somatic cells can become whole individuals. Only certain cells in the body have the ability to develop into new organisms under normal conditions. These are the cells that carry the germ plasm and are segregated from the somatic cells early in development. They divide repeatedly by mitosis, undergo meiosis at their maturity, and differentiate into ova or sperm.

The ova, as opposed to the somatic cells, are said to be harmoniously *totipotent*, since they possess the ability not only of forming the various types of tissues associated with the specific animal's body, but they also are capable of organizing it so that a total, fully formed individual is produced. These cells contain sufficient substrate, the proper mechanisms, and some kind of organization center that allow them to express their total potentially and to give rise to a complete embryo. The germ cells are considered to be highly specialized cells. They not only carry the genetic code, which is passed on to the next generation, but the ova also contain the "ingredients," the cytoplasm of the egg, out of which a new individual begins its development. The cytoplasm of most oocytes is highly basophilic; that is, it stains readily with basic dyes, indicating the presence of deoxyribonucleic and ribonucleic acids. This reaction is primarily from the presence of ribosomal RNA supplied by the nucleolus. However, messenger and transfer RNA is also present in the cytoplasm as well as DNA associated with the mitochondria.

Generally, somatic cells do not have this high RNA content. During oogenesis the egg organizes itself, synthesizes messenger and ribosomal RNA, produces some proteins, and, in general, prepares itself for operating the cell during the early developmental stages. The sperm cannot form a new individual out of its own cytoplasm, since most of it is discarded as spermiogenesis takes place. However, the sperm have their own unique function, which is to add half of the genes (the paternal characteristics) to the individual and to trigger the egg in such a way that physiological mechanisms of the cell are set into operation and development is initiated. Perhaps the most striking difference between the two cell types is the fact that somatic cells divide mitotically but are incapable of undergoing *meiosis* and forming gametes, an essential process if normal development is to occur. These two types of cell divisions are compared in table. The ability to divide *meiotically* is delegated only to a few cells of the embryo, those that become the germ cells.

We do not understand the basic mechanisms causing he members of chromosomal pairs to repel each other as they line up on the spindle during mitosis, but to attract one another during meiosis. The ability to undergo meiosis is a unique characteristic of germ cells. No one has yet been able experimentally to induce this type of division in an animal somatic cell. It is obvious that under normal circumstances the ability to give rise to a new organism is restricted to the egg. The fact that the egg can be activated artificially (without the aid of the sperm) and induced to develop into a total organism (parthenogenetically) indicates that the egg contains all the essential materials necessary for development. If experimental evidence is considered, the distinction between germ cells and somatic cells is not as harp and well defined as it appears to be in the normal developing organism. In fact, under laboratory conditions the somatic cell is revealed to retain many of its potentialities assumed lost when it differentiated.

The work of F.C. Steward and his colleagues (1964) with carrot plants raises some interesting speculations. Normally a carrot grows from a seed, but these investigators have been able to stimulate fully differentiated tissue of a mature carrot into active growth. When a cell of one of these mature plants was freed from its normal cellular (or tissue) environment, both the differentiated nucleus and the cytoplasm were capable of interacting in such a way that a new embryo developed. Small plugs from nongrowing areas of carrot root grown in coconut milk rapidly increased their weight. If individual cells were taken from the plugs and placed in separate fresh flasks of coconut milk, a few of these cells underwent mitosis and organized themselves into carrot embryos. In other words, each somatic cell behaved as if it were a fertilized egg. It passed through various embryonic stages and developed into a plantlet, which became a mature carrot plant when transplanted to soil. There obviously had been no irreversible changes in the nucleus or cytoplasm of the fully differentiated carrot cell.

According to Steward's experimental results, the interrelationship of somatic cells maintains their specialized state. When separated from the environment of other cells, the differentiated somatic cell is capable of producing a new plant, a function under normal circumstances delegated only to the germ cells.

Origin of Primordial Germ Cells

Two types of cell are identified when the developing gonad is sectioned and stained. First there are small, somatic cells that will give rise to follicles, Sertoli cells, interstitial cells, and surface epithelium; and then there are large, round cells with vesicular nuclei considered *primordial germ cells*. It is these latter cells that many embryologists believe are destined to give rise to the eggs or sperm of the adult animal. They generally agree that the mesoderm of the germinal ridge is the source of somatic cells of the gonad. This ridge is a thickened longitudinal strip of tissue located lateral to the dorsal mesentery. However, the primordial cell appear to originate from a different source. One approach to their study has been to trace methodically their presence in the embryo backward in developmental time until they first appear. When this is done, various areas of the embryo outside the gonad reveal the presence of these primordial cells. They migrate from these areas into the germinal ridge either through ameboid movement or by way of the blood vessels.

Weisman's concept of Biological Immortality

The origin of the primordial cells has intrigued biologists for many years. The fact that these cells are set aside from the somatic cells early in development led August Weisman (1834-1914) to hypothesize that the body was composed of two distinct plasms: the somatoplasm, which gives rise to the body proper, and the germ plasm, which is transmitted from one generation to the next. He believed that the germ plasm was located in the nucleus of the cells and was distributed unequally during cell division, with the cells making up the organs receiving specific *determiners*. That is, cells destined to form the heart received heart determiners as opposed to brain or kidney determiners. This qualitative parceling out of nuclear determiners was an orderly process that occurred during divisions of the fertilized egg.

Weisman believed that the determiners in the germ cells were not dispersed as in the soma. He speculated that the germ cells were set aside early in cleavage and were given a full complement of the material, and therefore these cells contained the hereditary determiners for all the cells of the body. As a result of his hypothesis a kind of "biological immortality" was suggested in which molecules of germ plasm were passed unchanged from one generation to another. Weisman believed that the primordial germ cells were not derived from the embryo itself but from substance that could be traced directly to the parent germ cell, the germ plasm. This germ plasm did not contribute directly to the formation of the body of the new individual in each generation, but was set aside for the formation of germ cells of the next generation. He suggested that the germ plasm grew by absorbing new materials, but its constituents remained unchanged from generation to generation.

Weisman's ideas about the physical continuity of the germ plasm and the unequal distribution of determiners during cleavage were postulated before the rediscovery of Mendel's work and, therefore, before genetics had reached its present state of knowledge. He knew nothing about chromosomes and genes but tried to work out some concept by which he could explain the passing of inherited characteristics from parent to embryo. Much of Weisman's work has not been supported by experimental evidence, but it was of value in posing the problems inherent in development. There is no experimental evidence that demonstrates the passage of specific molecules from one generation to another for all vertebrate animals. We do not believe that a stockpile of molecules was set up in the primeval sludge. What is inherited, it is agreed, is the pattern of development followed by the particular individual. This patter is under the control of the genes, and it is the genes that replicate and are passed on to the next generation.

Modern Concept of Germ Plasm Origin

Weisman's theories about the immortality of the germ plasm stimulated extensive investigation as biologist sought to verify or disprove his ideas by experimentation. The origin of the germ plasm is a difficult problem to solve, since a permanent, nontoxic method of marking the plasm is needed before it can be followed through successive generations. This labelling not only must be stable but also must be specific for the germ plasm, differentiating between it and the plasm of the somatic cells. No such technique is available at the present time.

There is evidence (Blackler, 1958) that a specific area of cytoplasm within the frog's egg is set aside early for the formation of the gametes. This cytoplasm located near the vegetal pole in the newly fertilized but uncleaved eggs of *Rana temporaria* and *Rana pipenes* stains with Azure A, a dye that selectively stains nucleic acids. The dye remains in those cells formed from this region during cleavage, labeling them as they take up their position in different locations in the embryo. The RNA-rich cytoplasm, first located in the vegetal region, segregates into cells that move to the middle of the endoderm below the gut cavity. These cells contain the "germinal plasm" since they may be traced from the floor of the gut cavity to its roof, from here of the dorsal mesentery, and then into the germinal ridges.

It is difficult to say whether the Azure A-stained cytoplasm is responsible for the specific quantities that differentiate germ plasm from somatoplasm, but it does indicate that a specific area in the fertilized egg is segregated early for gamete formation in the frog. Another experimental procedure used to study the origin of the primordial germ cells involves the surgical removal of some of the cell layers of the embryo. The embryo of frogs in their early stags consists of an outer ectodermal layer or "tube" and an inner gut "tube" of endoderm; this is the "tube within a tube" body-plan arrangement associated with triploblastic (three germ layered) animals. The mesoderm is sandwiched between these two tubes. Embryologists are able to remove surgically the endodermal layers of cells and leave a shell of ectoderm and mesoderm. If this endodermal tube is removed from the frog embryo about the time the neural tube closes (the neural stage), gonads develop but they are sterile. These results agree with the concept of primordial germ origin suggested by Blackler for the frog—that gonadal somatic tissue develops from the mesoderm.

On the other hand, the cells that give rise to the future gametes are derived from the endodermal cells and migrate into the gonadal primordium. Surgical removal of this endodermal layer excised the primordial germ cells with it; none were left to find their way to the rudimentary ovary or testes. However, the gametes of all amphibians do not originate from this same endodermal source. If the endoderm from another embryo, one that differs in pigmentation, is increased back into the shell, the host cells can be distinguished from the donor cells. The exchange of endodermal types in salamander embryos showed that the germ cells do not develop from the "marked" (pigmented) endoderm but rather from the host's tissue. These experiments and other suggest that the primordial germ cells in amphibians originate from at least two sources. In the frogs, evidence supports the endoderm as the source of the future germ cells, but in the salamanders they originate from the mesoderm. Regardless of the germ source in the amphibian embryo, authorities agree that the germ cells reach the site of the rudimentary gonad by ameboid movement.

In the chick, after about 30 hours of incubation, certain large cells identified as the primordial germ cells appear in a *crescentic* area in front of the head in the extraembryonic endoderm, that is, in tissues located outside the embryo proper. This area may be surgically removed, or destroyed by cauterizing with a hot needle or by irradiation, without disturbing the chick's development. Four days after their first appearance in this crescentic area of a normal chick embryo, the primordial germ cells are found in the rudimentary ovary when it is sectioned and stained.

On the other hand, no primordial cells appear in the developing gonad of the experimental animal (an embryo with this crescentic area removed) despite the fact that the germinal ridge was not disturbed.

Unlike the amphibian the primordial germ cells of the chick do not make their way through the tissues by ameboid movement, but instead they have been observed to penetrate the blood vessels where they travel to the rudimentary gonad by way of the vascular system. The cells have been identified in the vascular system, and although some are lost and degenerate, many find their way to the proper site. The intriguing question of why or how these cells selectively take up their position in the rudimentary gonad belongs to the realm of experimental embryology. In mammalian embryos, including man, the primordial germ cells apparently arise from the endodermal layer near the yolk sac. In the human embryos they have been identified at the posterior end of the primitive streak, the area posterior to the embryo.

Later, they appear in the endoderm of the hindgut when the embryo is only a few millimeters in length. Although no experimental investigations have been carried out on human embryos, in the mouse certain large cells, rich in alkaline phosphatase and believed to be primordial germ cells, can be selectively stained and their migratory path followed. In these animals cinematographic recordings reveal that the primary germ cells migrate through the tissues as in the amphibian, by ameboid movements, possibly aided by their ability to bring about lysis of cells and membranes that block their path. They move from the gut into the dorsal mesentery and then into the germinal ridge. As they migrate, they undergo repeated mitoses and multiply from less than a hundred cells to a few thousand. The fact that in the early stages of development these cells can be traced from some area outside the rudimentary gonad into the developing gonad, does not necessarily indicate that they are the precursors to the egg and the sperm.

There is a reciprocal relationship between a gonad rudiment and gametes. The gametes need the environment of the gonad in order to mature, and in some animals the rudimentary gonad will not develop properly without the gametes. Some authorities reason therefore, that the primordial germ cells function only to induce the ovary or testes to form the gametes. In many cases the primordial germ cells die without progressing further. There are some biologists who believe that all primordial germ cells die once they make their way to the gonadal primordium and induce it to differentiate. These investigators look to the gonadal epithelium as the source of future gametes. They are responsible for the term "germinal epithelium" which refers to the coelomic lining covering the ovary and testis. As the gonad develops, there is a great proliferation of cells. The primordial cells become embedded in the mesoderm of the genital ridge and lose some of their differentiating characteristics (special staning affinities, for example). It is difficult, if not impossible, to tell one cell from another or to determine the origin of any one cell. The proliferating cells may be derived from the primordial germ cells, or from the germinal epithelium (surface epithelium) or from certain mesodermal cells composing the rudimentary gonad, or from a combination of these sources. At this time we cannot proble the question further and should now consider the development of the germ cells within the gonad.

SPERMATOGENESIS

As stated already that the *spermatogenesis* is the formation of sperms from the cells of germinal epithelium. The cells of germinal epithelium are deploid like other body cells and undergo meiosis and form haploid *sperms*. The germ cells are located within the cellular layer along the periphry of the tubules. It is quite possible that all the spermatozoa produced within the testis arise from the primordial germ cells. The other cells within the tubule wall serve either a supportive or a nutritive role and do not form any germinal elements. For our purposes we need not dwell upon thee nongerminal elements of the testis, but can consider the main events of spermatogenesis itself. At some time a primordial germ cell may begin to enlarge and to reveal increased internal activity. As it does so, it tends to move inward from the periphery of the tubule, becomes increasingly basophilic, that

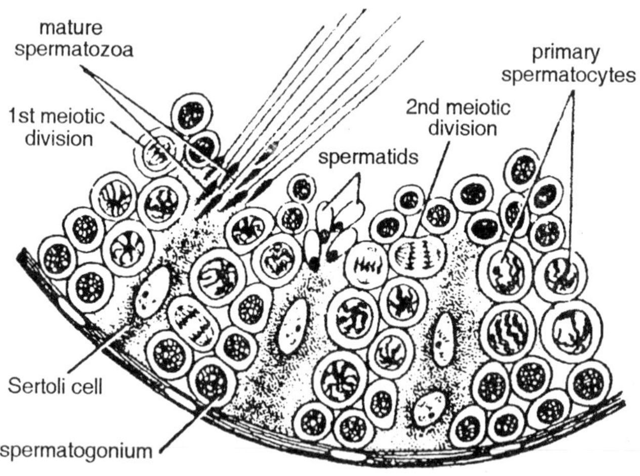

Fig. 12.1. A part of the mammalian testis showing Sertoli cells, spermatocytes and spermatogenesis.

is, stains readily with basic dyes, and eventually undergoes a mitotic division. The daughter cells of this division are known as *spermatogonia.*

A spermatogonium itself may now undergo a division that produces two *spermatocytes*. The division of a spërmatogonium, itself a product of mitotic division to form two primary spermatocytes is another mitotic division. The spermatocytes, however, undergo two divisions that are peculiar to sex cells in a process designated *meiosis*. The distinctive feature of these meiotic divisions is the reduction of the chromosomes to one-half the normal number. Thus the spermatogonium of he human normally contains 46 chromosomes. This is referred to as the *diploid*

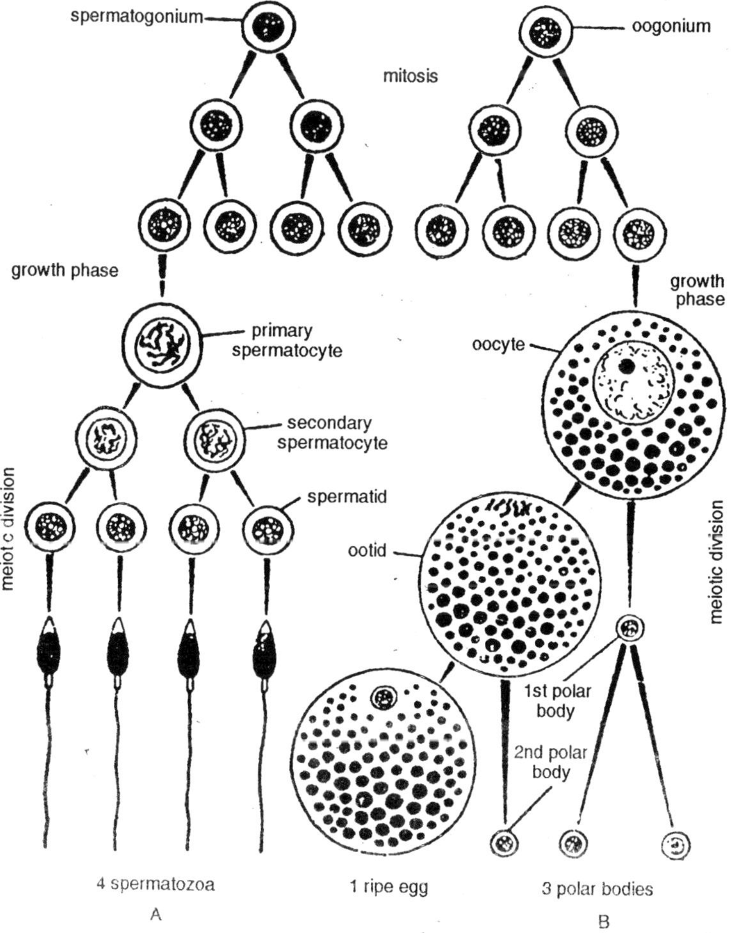

Fig. 12.2. A—Spermatogenesis; B—Oogenesis.

number. In an ordinary mitotic division the two daughter cells originating from the division are like the parent cell in that they contain the diploid number of 46 chromosomes. This is therefore true of the primary spermatocyts derived from the spermatogonium, because this is meiotic division. Following the meiotic divisions of the spermatocytes, however, the resulting *spermatids* contain one half the normal chromosome complement, the *haploid set*. Thus each diploid spermatocyte generates four haploid spermatids. The reduction of chromosome number in gametogenesis obviously is responsible for the constancy of chromosome numbers and kinds in species. When a haploid sperm eventually unites with a haploid ovum, the fertilized egg is diploid cell. An added significance of the division during spermatogenesis is the possibility of modifications of the material transmitting hereditary characteristics through various forms of chromosomal interchange.

SPERMIOGENESIS

A large number of haploid spherical spermatids are formed during spermatogenesis. From these haploid spermatids, sperms are developed by *spermiogenesis*. Each haploid sperm can be divided into three regions, head, collar and tail region, which will be taken in the last of this chapter. Here under this heading, we are taking the formation of head, collar and tail region from the cytoplasmic organelles of spermatids such as Golgi bodies, Mitochondria, Centriole etc.

Formation of Head

Head of the sperm is composed of two regions : *acrosomal region* which is formed by the Golgi body of the spermatid, and the *nuclear region* having the haploid dense chromatin mass of the spermatid. In the formation of acrosome, one can trace a conspicuous change in the Golgi body. Golgi bodies of the spermatid accumulate at a place some what towards the posterior side of the nucleus where the flattened sacs and vacuole dilates in such a precise way that a large vacuole or *acroblast* is developed. Then the acroblast moves towards the anterior side of the nucleus and in the mean time a *granule* is secreted by the wall of acroblast. This granule is called the *acrosomal granule* which increases in size and within a short duration occupies the entire space of acroblast. At this stage it can be labelled as *acrosome*.

No conspicuous changes have been traced within the nucleus until the acroblast and its differentiated acrosome completely for their migration around it. The chromatin substance then advantage itself in a layer against the inside of nucleus membrane. In the mean time the non-chromatic portion of the nucleus gradually diminishes and disappears

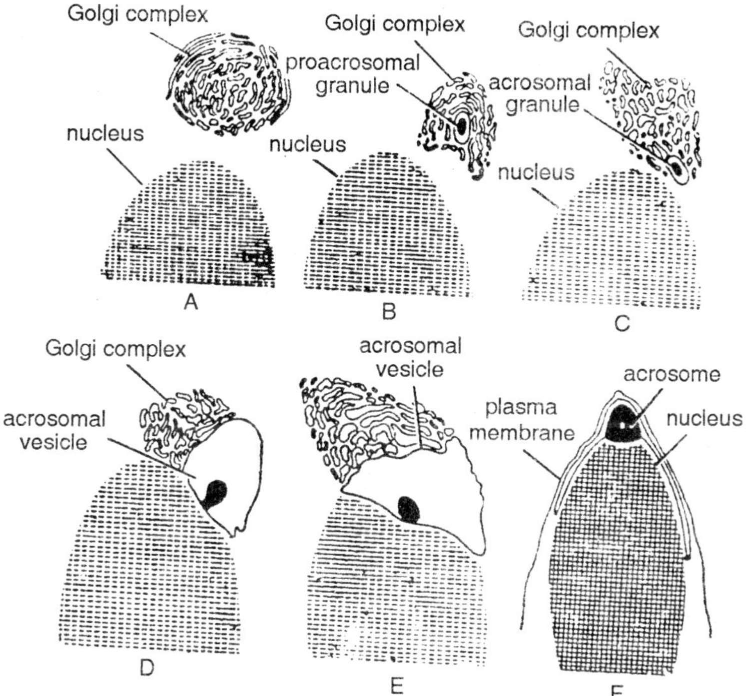

Fig. 12.3. Formation of acrosome of a spermatozoon.

leaving the extreme concentrated chromatic mass in the nuclear or head region of the sperm.

Formation of the Tail

Centrosome

The *centrosome* of a spermatid after the second meiotic division consists of two centrioles which have the structure of two cylindrical bodies, lying at right angle to each other. During early stages of sperm metamorphosis, the two centrioles move to a position just behind the sperm nucleus in the neck region. A depression is formed in the posterior surface of the nucleus and one of the two centrioles becomes placed in the depression with its axis approximately at right angles to the main axis of the spermatozoon. This is *proximal centriole* of the spermatozoon; the other centriole, the *distal centriole*, takes up a position behind the proximal one with its axis coinciding with the longitudinal axis of the spermatozoon. The distal centriole now gives rise to the *axial filament* of the flagellum of the spermatozoon for which it serves as basal granule.

Mitochondria

Most of the mitochondria of spermatids concentrate around the distal centriole and proximal part of the axial filament and form the *middle piece* of the tail of spermatozoon. In mammals, the mitochondria join in one continuous body which becomes twisted spirally around the proximal part of axial filament and the distal centriole. In other animals, the mitochondria fuse together to form massive clumps called *mitochondrial bodies*. Around the periphery of the middle piece the cytoplasm forms a condensed layer known as the *manchette*; the manchette also surrounds the distal part of the head of the spermatozoon, where it is not covered by the cap. A dark ring called "*ring-centriole*", different from the centriole, is sometimes seen at the posterior end of the middle piece. It forms the boundary between the middle piece and the tail-piece. The function of the ring-centriole is now known. The principal piece and tail piece (end piece) of the tail are composed of axial filament only in most animals except the mammals. In mammals, the axial filament of principal piece is accompanied on the outer side by nine much thicker fibres which are wedge-shaped in cross-section. These fibres start in the middle piece but do not reach upto the end-piece of the spermatozoon tail. The fibres of axial filament of a mammalian sperm tail are also surrounded by flattened bands which occur as semi-circular ribs articulating with each other on the opposite sides of the sperm tail (*Telkka*, *Fawcett* and *Christensen*, 1961). The end-piece of sperm tail has only axial filament which remains covered with cytoplasm in and plasma-membrane.

Protein Synthesis during Spermiogeneses

As described by *Brink* (1968) that some amount of protein synthesis take place during spermiogenesis. Because, no m-RNA is synthesized during spermiogenesis, so it is believed that stable m-RNA is transcripted before the mature phase starts.

Factors Controlling Spermatogenesis

The morphological events just described occur in an orderly, regulated matter, and, although there appear to be governing factors intrinsic to the testis, many testicular functions are under the control of influences emanating from a site external to the gonad. Foremost among the external influences upon the testis of vertebrate animals are the endocrine glands in particular the *pituitary gland*, or *hypophysis*. This gland is located at the base of the brain, where it is attached by a stalk to the *hypothalamus*, the ventral most area of the portion of the forebrain known as the diencephalon.

The pituitary gland is composed of two major divisions, an *anterior lobe*, or *adenohypophysis*, and a *posterior lobe*, or *neurophypophysis*. Both divisions of the pituitary secrete a variety of hormones that affect most parts of the organism. An important group of hormones secreted by the anterior lobe (adenohypophysis) is that of the *gonadotrophic hormones.* Among other effects, the gonadotrophins maintain the gonads at a level of optimal function. The onset of spermatogenesis and its completion occur under the influence of the pituitary-produced gonadotrophins. It is of interest that pituitary itself is subject to external influences. It has long been known that light exerts a profound effect upon the pituitary gland and the levels of gonadotrophin activity. It is now clearly recognized that in birds and rodents, among other vertebrates, gonadotrophin secretion and gonadal activity is influenced by the length of day.

Activation of the gonads by increments of light was demonstrated several decades ago by Rowan's experiments with the junco. Juncos were trapped in September during their southward migration and maintained outdoors during the severe temperatures of a Canadian winter. The days were gradually lengthened by artificial illumination of the aviaries, thereby simulating the daily increase in the length of days during early spring. Under this regimen the juncos developed by December gonads approximating in size the normal breeding testes of May. Comparable results have since been obtained in a variety of vertebrates. It may be noted that some invertebrates also reveal an influence of photoperiodicity in those case where light plays a role in the process of gametogenesis and the actual liberation of gametes. In many vertebrate the influence of light gonadal activity is mediated through a series of neural structures, beginning with the retinal layer of the eye. Neuronal relays in the basal parts of the forebrain (*telencephalon* and *diencephalon*), in particular the hypothalamus, culminate in an active process of neurosecretion. Neurohumoral elements liberated from the localized groups of nerve cell bodies termed *hypothalamic nuclei* affect the secretion and release of the gonadotrophic hormones of the adenohypophysis and thus gonadal activity.

The apparent mechanism whereby the hypothalamus regulates pituitary function is discussed in the section of this chapter developed to sexual photoperiodicity. In the seminiferous tubules of mammals, rhythmic "waves" of spermatogenesis pass along the longitudinal axis of the tubule. There thus appears to be an orderlines beyond that immediately apparent, which suggests there are other varieties of regularity and regulation as yet unrecognized. These and other facets of testicular function, which are beyond the scope of this volume, provide splendid topics for additional reading.

Morphology of Mature Spermatozoon

Though the spermatozoa of different groups of animals exhibit a great variety of form, yet the basic morphological plan which relates to the functional aspect of sperm, remains the same. In general, the sperm is divided into head, middle piece and tail with no nutrient material within itself. They are capable of performing active locomotion in liquid or semi-liquid medium to reach the egg and by fusing with the egg, cause the egg to start developing. It introduces its nucleus and centriole in the egg interior.

Structure of Head

The sperm head exhibits a diversity of shapes in different groups of vertebrates. The shape depends on the shape of the nucleus to as a great extent. Its anterior tip is differentiated as *acrosome* which enables the spermatozoon to penetrate through the egg membranes and to establish connection with the egg cytoplasm. It contains protease enzymes and certain polysaccharides (*Cohn* 1969). The major part of the head is occupied by the nucleus containing genes and is thus responsible for the transmission of hereditary characters form the male parent. A thin layer of cytoplasm is present in between the membrane of acrosomal vesicle and the sperm plasma membrane as *peri-acrosomal cytoplasm*.

Neck

The part of the sperm following the head is called the neck. It carries a proximal and a distal centriole. The two lie at right angle to one another. The distal centriole forms and gives attachment to the axial filament of the sperm tail. The proximal centriole initiates cell division (cleavage) in the fertilized egg.

Middle Piece

The middle-piece contains the base of the flagellum and all the mitochondria. In some animals, the mitochondria form compact and isolated clumps through out the middle piece; but in rabbit it forms a tightly coiled spiral of elongated mitochondria around the proximal part of the axial filament and the distal centriole. The mitochondria, being carrier of oxidative enzymes, are responsible for oxidative phosphorylation and supply flagellum with energy (ATP) to be used for the propulsion of the spermatozoon. However, this energy is limited and once utilized cannot be renewed, except in mammals and in those

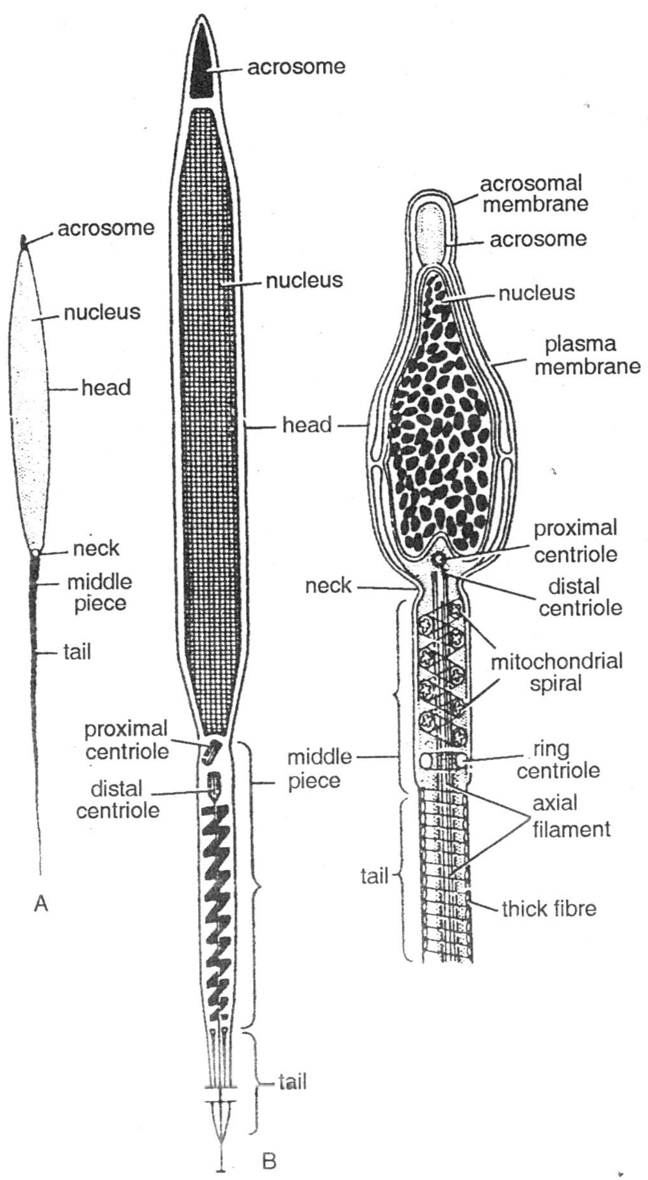

Fig. 12.4. Structure of a mammalian sperm. A—Under light microscope; B—Under electron microscope.

animals where spermatozoa remain active within maternal body because there are energy sources available to the spermatozoa. A dark ring is sometimes seen at the posterior end of the middle piece forming the boundary between the middle piece and the tail. The structure is called the "*ring centriole*" different from the centriole. Its function is not known.

The Tail

(Principal piece and end-piece). The tail of the sperm is composed of a single flagellum. This flagellum has a typical flagellar structure. The whole array of flagellar fibres is called, the *axial filament*. The entire tail is divided into an anterior *principal piece* following the middle piece ad the posterior *tail piece* or the *end piece*. In these regions, the fibre system of tail flagellum is reduced to the axial complex of two central fibres surrounded by the ring of nine peripheral fibres. Throughout the principal piece, there occurs a surrounding fibrous helix which is composed of semi-circular ribs articulating with one another no opposite sides of the sperm tail. The main function of the spermatozoon is to carry the paternal genetic dowry and to activate the ovum.

Types of Sperms

The type of sperm produced varies from species to species. The size of the sperm may be as little as 0.02 mm in crocodile or as

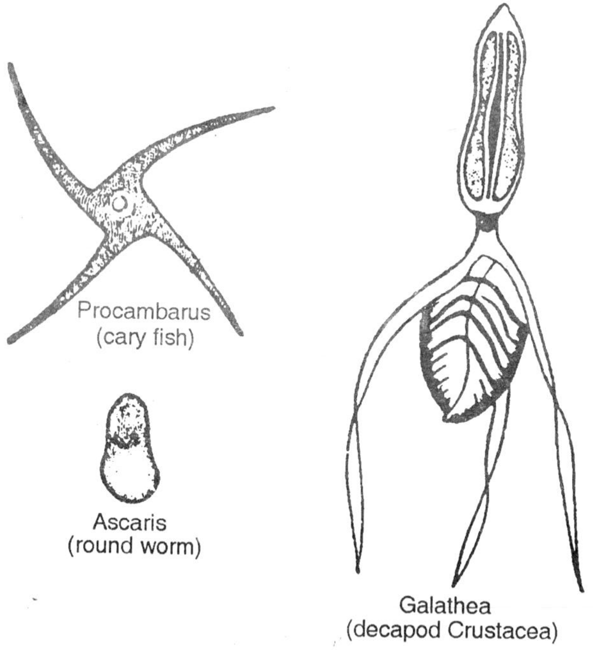

Fig. 12.5. Forms of non-flagellate spermat oa.

large as 2 mm or more in *Balanoglossus*. The sperm shape is, however, species specific. It may be the spheroidal (teleosts), rod or lance-shaped (amphibians), spoon-shaped (man and many other mammals), or hooked (mouse and rat). The sperm types are again divided into two main types found in animals *flagellate spermatozoa* which possess a flagellum or tail-like organelle. They may be *mono flagellate* (in majority of vertebrates) or *biflagellate* (in toad and fish) spermatozoa. The *non-flagellate spermatozoa* lack flagella and are found in *Ascaris*, crab etc.

OOGENESIS

It has been noted that in some characteristics the early formation of the ovum and sperm are comparable. If, however, the formation of the ovum from a primordial germ cell and its chromosomal alterations during meiosis compares with that phase of spermato-genesis, the later history of the unfertilized egg is very different. In female vertebrate animals ovulation involves a seasonal or a rhythmic process in which the egg is liberated from the ovary into the body cavity. From there the ovum is transported into the oviduct and thence, by means of ciliary movement and/or peristaltic motions of the oviduct, to the uterus or the exterior. The preovulatory egg develops in the ovary from a very small oogonium to a large egg, which at ovulation may be in one or another of the stages of maturation, depending upon the species. This maturation process involves, first, a reduction in the number of chromosomes in the egg. Attendant upon this reduction in chromosome number there is, as in the sperm, a segregation of the hereditary units, a phenomenon which assures that eggs of different genetic composition are produced within the same species.

In some species the sex chromosomes segregate during maturation, giving rise to two types of eggs, male-determining and female-determining eggs. In other species this form of segregation occurs in the sperm, resulting in two types of sperm. Growth of the ovum is the most striking aspect of maturation. Most of the primitive germ cells are approximately 10 microns (0.01 millimeter) in diameter, the size of an average body cell. In mammals such cells increase to a size that in some species may reach a diameter of 200 microns. In the frog the increase is up to a diameter of 2000 microns; in birds the diameter of the ovum is as large as 40,000 microns. This tremendous increase in size results primarily from the deposition of yolk, which, because it is rich in fats, carbohydrates, and proteins, constitutes a useful energy source and a source of raw materials for he synthesis of

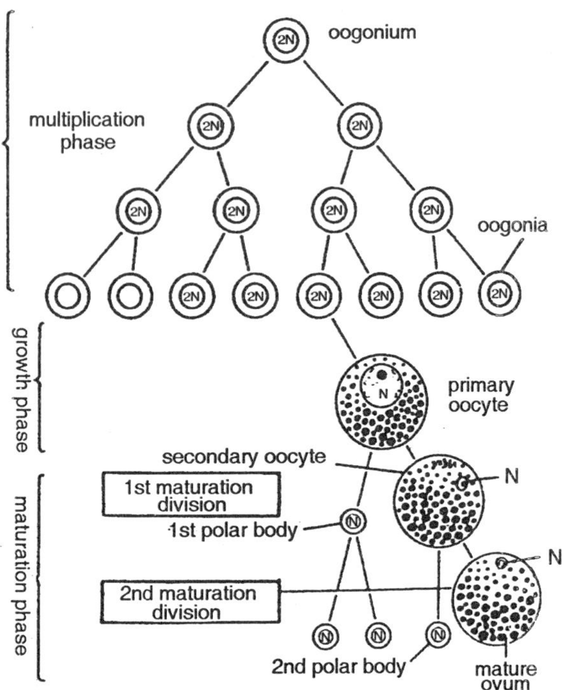

Fig. 12.6. Diagrammatic representation of stages during oogenesis.

protoplasm. The large size of eggs, then reflects not so much an increased amount of protoplasm as in increased amount of stored food materials. At this time only the yolk and its formation will be outlined. Yolk is the usual form of food storage in the egg.

Most eggs contain some yolk, which is similar in composition to that of the hen. Normally in the form of yolk granules or platelets it is composed primarily of proteins, phospholipids, and neutral fats. In the mature amphibian egg, for example, protein yolk represents roughly 45 percent of the dry weight of the egg, lipoids 25 percent, and glycogen approximately 8 percent. Yolk may occur within the cytoplasm of the egg, as in many invertebrates, lower chordates, and amphibians, or it may be more or less segregated from the cytoplasm, as in bony fishes, reptiles, and birds. There is some uncertainty regarding the cellular organelles responsible for yolk formation. In recent years electron microscopy has enabled a more adequate understanding of yolk formation in the oocytes of such diverse animals as insects, mollusks, amphibians, and mammals.

It seems clear from several studies that one variety of yolk granule, perhaps representative for all, forms within or in close association with modified oocyte mitochondria. The yolk itself in some, perhaps all, cases is not synthesized within the oocyte. Yolk components are produced at a site external tot he oocyte and transported in soluble form via the blood stream to the oocyte, where they are converted, through the activity of the mitochondrial enzymes, into insoluble yolk granules. There is good evidence in vertebrates, for example, that egg proteins and phospholipids are synthesized in the liver and then transported to the oocyte. Quantitative radioassay experiments in the bird reveal that the incorporation of radioactive precursors in highest initially in the liver and lowest in the oocyte. Within 12 hours after injection of the labeled compounds, however, the radioactivity of the liver decreases by approximately 40 percent, whereas the radioactivity of the oocytes increases by more than 80 percent, indicating the initial synthetic process in the liver and the later transfer of these compounds to the ooxytes. This scheme is slightly complicated by the close relation between the oocytes and the surrounding follicle cells. In most animals microvill emerge from the surface of the oocyte, interdigitating with microvilli derived from the adjacent follicle cells. The latter represent

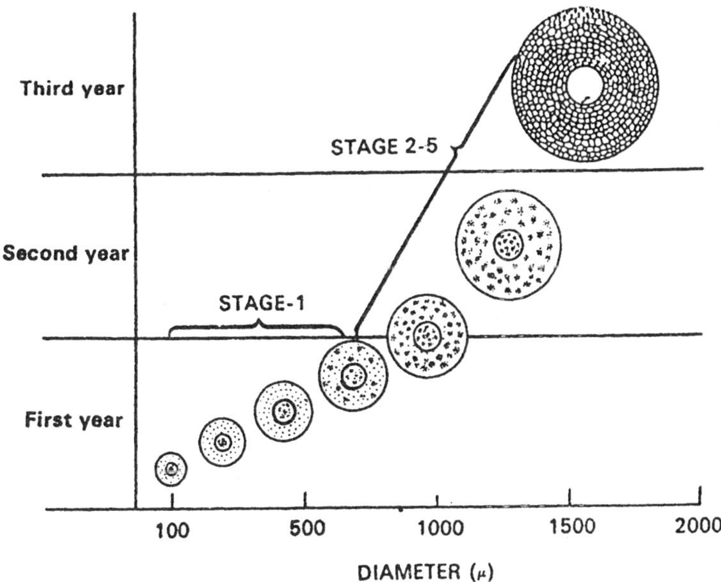

Fig. 12.7. Growth of frog's oocyte showing increase in its diameter in three sucessive generations.

an intermediary whereby intercellular transfer of materials may occur. In some invertebrates (some insects, annelids, and mollusks) special *nurse cells*, acting in conjunction with follicle cells, play an important role in providing nutrition for the growing oocyte. Various building materials pass into it from the nurse cells and follicle cells. These cells should, then, be considered an integral part of the metabolic apparatus of the oocyte.

Changes in the Nucleus

No conspicuous changes have been traced upto the formation of primary oocyte. After its formation a sequence of changes have been observed. When the oogonial cells enlarge in size to enter the *phase of growth* or *vegetative phase* and form the primary oocytes, the chromatin material assumes definite chromosomes. The free ends of all the chromosomes then arrange themselves in such a precise manner that they face towards one pole. This stage is called the bouquet stage. The chromosomal threads which constitute the bouquet arrangement are also known as *leptotene threads*. The leptotene threads now conjugate to give rise haploid number of bivalents. At the same time numerous side branches or side loops are developed by the

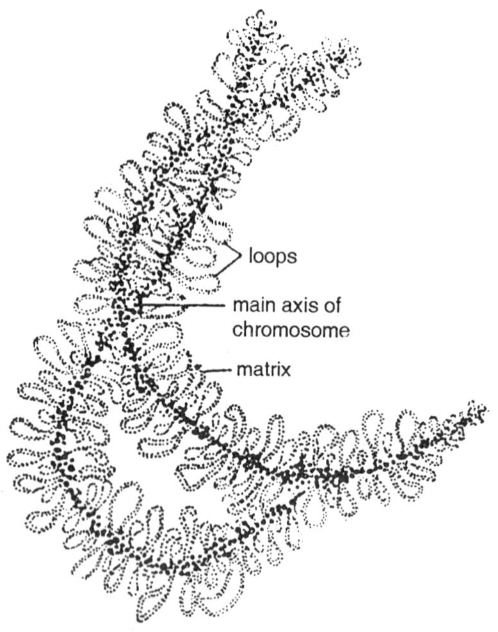

Fig. 12.8. A lampbrush chromosome from oocyte of newt, Triturus after meiotic pairing.

chromosomes. Such chromosomes bearing side loops are called *lampbrush chromosomes*. Nucleolus also plays an important role in the synthetic activity taking place in the nucleus. The small nucleus may give rise to several nucleoli by fragmentation and budding. All these nucleoli come to lie near the nuclear membrane. Due to these changes the outline of nucleus becomes irregular which shows sac like protrusions into which lie nucleolar fragments from where they pass out into the cytoplasm.

Changes in the Cytoplasm

An early oocyte is spherical in outline having a nucleus in the middle, while the remaining portion of the oocyte is filled with cytoplasm along with a number of cytoplasmic organelles such as Mitochondria, Golgi bodies, Cell center etc. All these organelles take an important role in *vitellogenesis*. Cytocentrum or cell center or centrosome is situated in the vicinity of nucleus enclosing one or two centrioles. The word *archoplasm* or *idiosome* can be applied for the denser cytoplasm in which centrioles are embedded in centrosome.

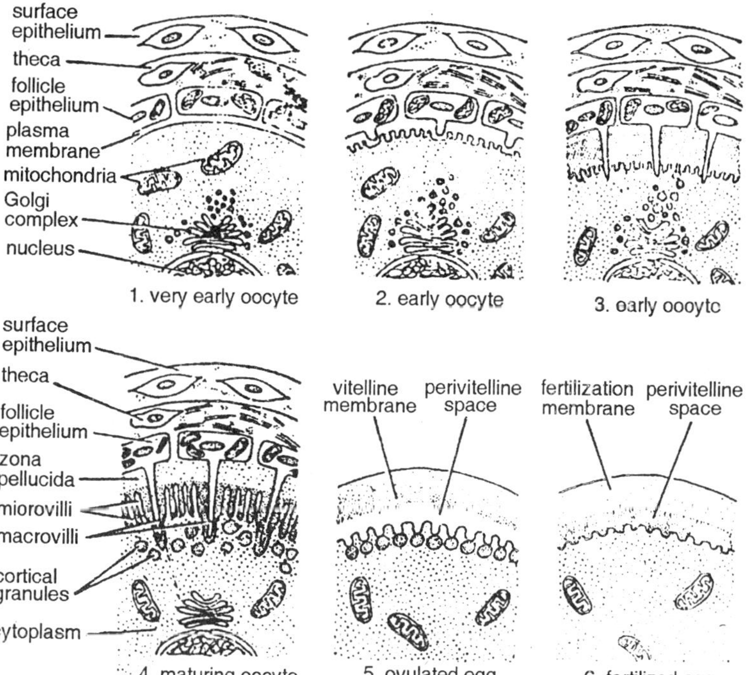

Fig. 12.9. Formation of cortical granules from small vesicles of the Golgi complex.

Then soon the nucleus which is haploid in nature is surrounded by ring or circles developed by the arrangement of Golgi bodies, mitochondria and centrosome in circles. The entire circular rings thus formed can be labelled as *Balbianic vitelline rings* or *yolk nucleus*. Yolk nucleus may either surrounded the original nucleus of the developing ovum containing chromosomes, or may lie adjacent to it. The presence of yolk nucleus can be observed in young oocyte. Then the entire organelles of yolk nucleus such as Golgi bodies, mitochondria, centrosome etc. disperse through the cytoplasm and disappear leaving a number of granules at their places. These granules or globules are the *yolk granules* or *yolk globules*.

Physio-chemical Nature of Yolk

Yolk is a complex of variably assembled components, rather than a definite chemical substance. The principal components are *proteins*, *phospholipids* and *fats* in different combinations. Depending on which of these components predominate, the yolk is distinguished as "*protein yolk*" or "*fatty yolk*". These two kinds of yolk are present side by side in the eggs of many animals. The avian yolk as a whole contains 48.7% water, 16.6% proteins, 32.6% phospholipids and fats and 1% carbohydrates. The fatty portion of avian yolk is mainly neutral fat (50% of the dry weight), the remaining being phosphatides and cholesterol. In animals, yolk is found in three forms as given here under:

Granular Yolk

Protein yolk of many invertebrates like echinoderms and of lower chordates (*Amphioxus*, Tunicates) consists of fine yolk granules which are fairly evently distributed in the cytoplasm of the eggs.

Yolk Platelets

In *amphibians* eggs, the yolk is found in the form of large granules called *yolk platelets*. The yolk platelets are oval and flattened in one plane. They contain two main proteinaceous substances: *phosphovitin* and *lipovitellin*. Phosphovitin is a highly phosphorylated protein (phosphorus 8.4%), whereas lipovitellin contains a considerable amount of bound lipid (17.5%). In the yolk platelets 2 molecules of phosphovitin are associated with 1 molecule of lipovitellin in a structural unit. Electron micrographs of amphibian yolk reveal that these units are arranged in the platelet in a crystalline lactic work with regular hexagonal packing (*Wallace*, 1963). In addition to the yolk platelets the amphibian egg contains lipid and glycogen. Lipid is found in the cytoplasm in the form of *lipochondria*, which consists of an internal core of lipid surrounded by a thin protein layer. *Cyclostomes*, *elasmobranchs*, *ganoids* and the *lungfishes* have eggs with a distribution of food reverses much the same as in amphibians.

Yolk Spheres

The yolk of birds, reptiles and bony fishes lies in a compact mass in the interior of the egg. The cytoplasm is restricted to a thin layer on the surface, with a thickened cap on the upper side. Most of the yolk is liquid but about 23% is in the form of solid "*yolk spheres*".

Functions of Yolk

1. Yolk is the most usual form of food storage in the egg.
2. It influences the differentiation of ooplasm and the patterns of cleavage.
3. The size of the egg is determined by the amount of yolk present in it.
4. Yolk exercises an important influence on the morphogenetic movements of blastomeres during gastrulation.
5. The nature of development whether *indirect* with larval forms or *direct* with juvenile stages is governed by the amount of yolk present in the egg.

Role of Follicle/Nurse Cells in Oogenesis

The growing oocytes are surrounded by special nutritive cells which immersely help their growth in various ways. There are two main types of nutritive cells, viz., *follicle cells* and *nurse cells*.

Follicle Cells

In mammals particularly and some other vertebrates, the oocytes are surrounded during growth and maturation phases by special cells of the ovary, the *follicle cells*. These are derived from the germinal epithelium of the ovary. Initially, the young oocyte is surrounded by a single layer of follicle cells but later the number of follicle cells increases greatly, the cells becoming arranged in several rows. In a mammals, the follicle cells and the developing oocyte together constitute a *grafian follicle*. As the egg approaches maturity, and eccentric cavity called *antrum* appears in the mass of the follicle cells. This cavity is filled with a fluid known as *liquor folliculi* which is secreted presumably by the cells of the follicle.

In the beginning, there is a simple apposition of the follicle cells and the oocyte. The cytoplasmic membranes of the adjoining cells remain separated by a narrow gap of about 80Å. The plasma membrane of oocyte and that of follicle cells show close connections at some points in the form of *desmosomes*. At a later stage a wider space appears between the follicle cells and the oocyte. However, the follicle cells maintain their contact with the oocytes at the points where the desmosomes were observed in the earlier stage. The surface of a young oocyte is drawn out into numerous finger-like *microvilli* which project into the space between the oocyte and follicle cells. These microvilli interdigitate with *cytoplasmic processes* of the follicle cells. The presence of the microvilli greatly increases the surface area of the oocyte. This increase in area facilitates metabolic turnover between the oocyte and the surrounding cells. It is believed that the follicle cells actively help in the growth of the oocyte by secreting substances which are taken up by the oocyte.

The individual microvilli cannot be seen with the optical microscope and the zone of microvilli appears as a radially striated layer known as the *zona radiata*. The presence of small in pocketing of the oocyte cytoplasm at the base of the microvilli points out that the oocyte takes in fluid and dissolved substances from the space between itself and the follicle cells by way of "cell drinking" or *pinocytosis*.

Nurse Cells

In some invertebrates like annelids, insects and molluscs the oocyte is surrounded, in addition to follicle cells, by special nurse cells. Derived from the egg cell, the nurse cells supplement the function of follicle cells in providing nutrition to the growing oocyte. In *Drosophila* an oogonial cell divides by four successive mitotic divisions into 16 cells. One of these cells becomes an oocyte whereas the other 15 become nurse cells and nourish the oocyte. Nutrients from the cytoplasm of the nurse cells pass into the oocyte through gaps developed in the cell membranes two cell types. This type of relationship is different from that found between oocyte and follicle cells because in this case no microvilli or cytoplasmic processes are developed at the interface between the oocyte and the nurse cell. In some insects and annelids the nurse cells are gradually consumed during the growth of the oocyte. In molluscs e.g., the snail *Helix*, the entire nurse cells are engulfed in the cytoplasm of the oocyte.

Architecture of the Mature Egg

All eggs are surrounded by a cell membrane, or *plasmalemma*. With very few exceptions, they bear an additional membrane, produced in the ovary, which is known as the *vitelline membrane*; in mammals it is known as the *zona pellucida*. Secondary membranes, secreted by ducts, such as the chorion of insects or the jelly coats of amphibian eggs, also occur but are not important to this discussion. The cytoplasm of the egg contains, of course, various organelles, yolk granules, and often large amounts of pigment. Of considerable importance to the progress of development is a vaguely defined layer of gelated cytoplasm, approximately 2 to 3 microns in thickness, immediately below the cell membrane. This layer, including the cell membrane, is referred to as the *cortex*, or the *cortical layer*, of the egg. Its importance will be discussed later. In most animals the cortex contains granules, of mucopolysaccharide nature, which range in size from less than 1 to approximately 2 microns. The cortex may also contain varying amounts of pigment. While the egg is still in contact with the follicular cells, follicular processes may penetrate the cortical layer; this may be of importance in determining the specific character of the cortical layer in some animals.

Some organization within the egg is indicated by its *polarity*. All animal eggs have a polar structure. The two opposite poles that can be distinguished are referred to as the *animal* and *vegetal poles* of the egg. An imaginary line connecting the poles defines the main axis of the egg, the *animal vegetal axis*. The polarity of the egg is often apparent in the arrangement of its cytoplasmic inclusions. In many eggs the yolk is not evenly distributed; often its density increases from the animal toward the vegetal pole with corresponding structural changes.

In some cases there are substantial differences in the degree of pigmented; in many amphibians, for example, the animal region of the egg surface is heavily pigmented, whereas the vegetal region is essentially unpigmented. In addition to an obvious polarity, many animal eggs passes a *bilateral symmetry*. This may be expressed in the shape of the unfertilized egg, as in insects; in other cases the symmetry is not apparent until after fertilization. There is reason to believe that in many cases the polarity of eggs originates during their growth phase within the ovary. It is of some relevance, them, to inquire to what extent polarity or other evidence of organization is expressed within the unfertilized egg and to what extent it is indicative of development potentialities or predestination.

Pigment, particularly in amphibians, is an easily recognized marker of cytoplasmic asymmetry. Yet it is not clear that the pigment distribution within amphibian eggs predelineates developmental fates. The pigment is localized most heavily at the very periphery of the

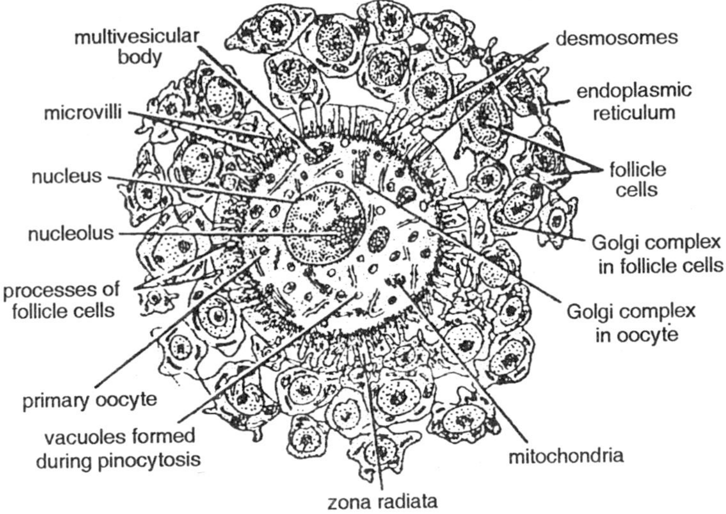

Fig. 12.10. Young oocyte of a mammal surrounded by follicle cells.

animal hemisphere of the egg, within the deepest layer of the cortex, and it does not extend into the vegetal hemisphere. There is no apparent corresponding differential of other cytoplasmic components of the frog egg; interestingly, however, during the developmental stages just prior to the deposition of yolk granules within the oocyte, the greatest concentration of ribonucleic acid coincides with the localization of heavy pigment. The distribution of pigment in some mollusc and sea urchin eggs has some predictive value which will be discussed later. It may be worthwhile to review briefly other evidences of organization within the unfertilized eggs of animals.

Selective localization of cytoplasmic components, indicating some organization of the egg, is best examplified by molluscs, annelids, and ascidians. In most mollusks the superficial part of the egg cells is formed by a thin, yolk-free layer of cytoplasm. Local thickenings of this layer may occur near the animal and vegetal poles, forming *pole plasms*. There are evidences of internal organization also. In certain gastropod mollusks, for example, movements of various egg substances occur during prefertilization phases of maturation of the eggs, as a result of which they are concentrated at certain places within the ovum. These processes, termed *ooplasmic segregation*, establish a condition in which different parts of the egg differ more or less in their cytoplasmic composition. Thus glycogen tends to shift and concentrate toward the animal pole of the egg; ribonucleic acid also si of higher concentration in the pole plasm relative to the rest of the cytoplasm. Vitamin C, presumably bound to the Golgi bodies, tends to concentrate into an annular band near the equator of the egg. The displacements and selective accumulations of cytoplasmic components are continued during the early development stages, but it is noteworthy that these processes, important for later development, are well underway in the unfertilized egg.

There is little evidence for asymmetric distribution of cytoplasmic components within the eggs of higher animals. It may be noted that in the mammalian egg there is evidence for a heavy concentration of RNA at one pole of egg. There is, however, no reason to believe that pattern of pigment distribution and perhaps other suggestive distribution patterns represent a form of preorganization in most animal eggs. It is clear, nonetheless, that the animal egg is not to be regarded as a completely homogenous system. Polarity and symmetry alone are difficult to explain without assuming local differences in the composition within the egg, which are apparent earlier in some species than in others.

Organization of the Egg

There are two extreme possibilities relative to the functional organization of the egg. Either each organ in the adult is represented in the egg by some special physical or chemical composition, or the egg contains unorganized protoplasm that is gradually changed into the organized structures of the formed embryo. The first concept (*preformation*) involves a mosaic, or a pattern of organ-forming substance, which are special substances that determine each and every organ. The second concept (*epigenesis*) depicts an unorganized protoplasm that requires the action and interaction of various agents to convert it into the various structures of the adult organism. Before considering the additional implications of these two possibilities, it will be valuable to review conditions in the sea urchin egg.

One local race of a mediterranean species was found to display a definite polarity indicated by a band of pigment composed of many small red granules. The parts of this egg essential to the following analysis are the thin outer cortex, the fluid, inner endoplasm, and the red band of pigment granules, the pigment band. The nucleus may be in any position in this cell. The pigment band provides a natural marker for a specific region of the unfertilized egg; by observing this band during development, it is possible to determine what develops from the protoplasm of this specific region. The pigment band is just below the equator of the egg, toward the vegetal pole. The first cleavage along the animal-vegetal axis bisects the pigment band; during all the cleavage stages this band keeps its same position relative to the animal and vegetal poles.

At the later, eight-cell, stage, the pigment band is still visible. It has been cut off into the four lower cells in the vegetal hemisphere. It maintains its position just below the equator during the blastula stage, which consists of a single layer of cells arranged to form the walls of a liquid-filled sphere. Figure shows a section of the blastula through the pigment band and also outlines the fate of the pigment band through the process of gastrulation. For present purposes this process may be defined as a folding process that converts the single-layered blastula into a double-layered gastrula and forms the primitive gut, or *archenteron*. During the surroundings into the cytoplasm of the developing oocyte may account for its polarity. In most cases the polarity of the egg is probably determined while it is still within the ovary. Whether it occurs through a kind of group effect, differential chemical gradients within the ovary itself, the transmembranal passage of materials into the oocyte, or a combination of these and other unrecognized mechanisms is subject to further investigation.

Egg Membranes

By the time the vertebrate egg reaches maturity, egg develops or membranes, which protect it from chemical or physical injury, develop. In some animals they act as barriers to multiple sperm penetration. Not all vertebrates have the same type of egg membranes. They vary according to the class of animal and reflect the adaptation made by the animal in order to ensure development of the young in its particular environment. There are several ways of classifying these membranes, but the simplest way is to group them according to their origin. Those membranes formed in the ovary and laid down between the plasmalemma and the follicular cells are considered to be *primary membranes*. The follicular cells produce *secondary membranes*. However, it is difficult if not impossible always to determine whether the egg cytoplasm, the follicular cells, or the cooperative efforts of both produce the membranes. *Tertiary membranes* are secreted by the cells of the oviduct as the egg travels down the duct toward the cloaca.

Membranes produced by Ovary or Follicular cells

Eggs, like all living cells, have a plasma membrane around their surface that holds the yolk and cytoplasm together as an entity and functions osmotically to control the egg contents. The membrane is the *plasmalemma*. A noncellular, transparent *vitelline membrane* forms on the outside of the plasmalemma, but is given different names in different animals. In amphibia and birds it is in close contact with the ooplasmic surface until the egg is fertilized, at which time it separates from this surface, forming a touch fertilization membrane. In fish this membrane is referred to as the *chorion*, and in reptiles and mammals it is given the name *zona pellucida*. It usually remains intact through several stages of cleavage where it appears to help hold the dividing cells together.

External to the primary membrane are the follicle cells. Microvilli from the follicle cells and from the plasmalemma surface of the oocyte often interdigitate at the zona pellucida giving it the appearance of a radially striated zone under the light microscope. This striated zone is known as the *zona radiata*. When the graafian follicle of the mammals ruptures and releases the mature ovum, the egg carries with it, for some distance down the follopian tube, a layer of follicular cells. These cells are columnar in shape and arranged radially in a single layer around the ovum. They are known as the *corona radiata* and should not be confused with the unfortunate similar term, zona radiata, which refers to the interdigitating microvilli.

Membranes produced by Oviduct

The tertiary membranes involve albumen layers, shell membranes, and the shell itself. As the egg of the amphibian spirals down the oviduct, three rather uniform layers of albumen (jelly) are deposited around it. The inner layer is a thin one and most viscous; the outer, wide and more fluid; the middle layer, intermediate. The jelly envelopes hold the eggs together in masses or strands, protect the eggs from infections, insulate the eggs, make them unappetizing to predators since they are tasteless, and anchor the eggs to twigs and plants. Besides these physical functions, the jelly coats apparently also help to make the frog's fertilizable, since up to now no egg taken directly from the body cavity has been induced to develop into an embryo.

Five membranes make up the envelopes of the chick egg. External to the vitelline membranes are added the white of the egg (albumen), two shell membranes, and a porous shell. As the egg begins its spiral pathway down the oviduct, albumen is secreted around the vitelline membrane of the egg. The rotation of the egg in the oviduct twists the albumen that projects from the yolk and forms what is known as the *chalaza*. As the egg proceeds down the duct, concentric layers of egg white are added around the yolk. The chalaza helps anchor the egg in the center of the albumen, which is an additional nutritional reserve for the developing embryo and which has bactericidal qualities. Inner and outer shell membranes are secreted around the egg white and are in contact with one another except at the blunt end of the egg. In this area one can see that the inner membrane retains with the egg white, while the outer membrane becomes associated with the shell of the egg.

Significance of Extraneous Envelopes of Egg

Regardless of their form, egg envelopes appear to be initially secretions of either the oocyte or the surrounding follicle cells, mainly as by-products of cell activity or as a basement membrane typical or epithelial tissue as such, each chemically peculiar to the tissue and species concerned. Any material or structures once present may be exploited secondarily to serve other functions. Thus, material from either the oocyte or the surrounding follicle cells or some oviducal tissue, readily serves the eggs as protective structure and it is commonly augmented for this purpose, particularly in relatively large, yolky eggs and in all eggs that are laid out of water. Even in mammalian egg-small, almost yolkless, and existing in a nutrient liquid medium when shed from the ovary—the *zona pellucida* surrounding the ovum, has been considered (1) as a protective device to prevent polyspermy, i.e., fertilization by more than one spermatozoon; (2) as a means of preventing egg fusion; and (3) as a necessary means of maintaining normal cleavage of the egg following fertilization. Further, in ascidians, particularly solitary ascidians, not only does the basement membrane of the follicle cells survive as the chorion, which plays a role in preventing self-fertilization of the egg, but the follicle cells themselves persist attached to the chorion and, by virtue of vacuoles in their cytoplasm, function collectively to increase buoyancy.

Types of Eggs

Some eggs are small while others are larger. Eggs of certain birds are supposed to be the largest in size. Eggs are the modified and largest animal cells. The large size is due, not to a general exaggeration of all the parts normally found in an animal cell, but to the large quantity of cytoplasm that is present. In eggs small or good amount of yolk particles, synthesized by Golgi body, mitochondria or endoplasmic reticulum, are present. The *yolk* or *deutoplasm* serves as a source of nourishment for the young organism until it can tend for it

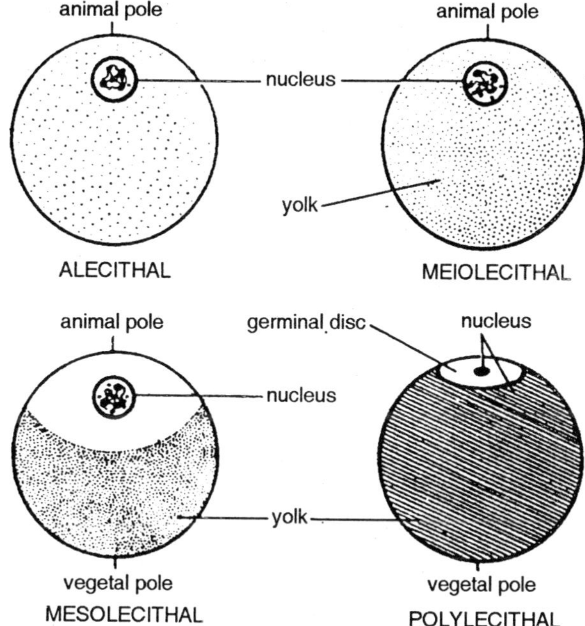

Fig. 12.11. Types of chordate ova.

self or alternatively, exploit the food provided by the parent. On the basis of presence or absence and amount of yolk particles, the eggs can be classified as follows:

Alecithal Type

When the yolk particles are entirely lacking as in placentals.

Oligolecithal Type

Here the yolk particles are present but in the little amount as in Echinodermata.

Isolecithal Type

When yolk particles are distributed evenly throughout the cytoplasm as in fishes.

Centrolecithal Type

In insects the yolk particles are restricted to the centre of the egg.

Teololecithal Type

When the yolk increases in quantity and becomes accumulated at one end or pole of the egg as in frog.

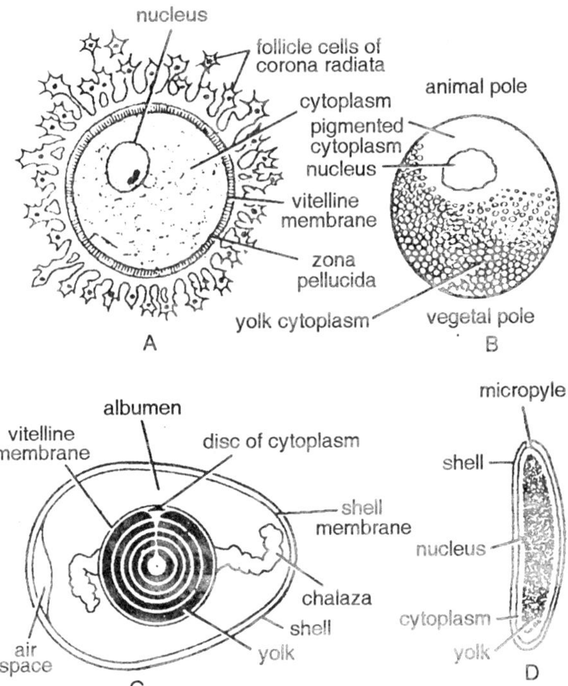

Fig. 12.12. Different types of egg. A—Microlecithal; B—Mesolecithal; C—Macrolecithal; D—Centrolecithal.

Macrolecithal Type

In birds and reptiles, the yolk particles are in good amount. Here, in such cases the size of nucleus and cytoplasm reduce and lie in the form of a small germinal disc.

The yolk present in the eggs of chordates is, as a rule, aggregated cheifly towards one pole of the cell, the *vegetative pole*, whilst the egg nucleus lies near the other pole, the *animal pole*, in a region relatively, or completely, free from yolky substance.

Comparison of the Egg and the Sperm

Both gametes are morphologically complete cells. Each has a nucleus and a cytosome containing representatives of the centrosomes, mitochondria, and Golgi bodies. Each has a plasma membrane. Yet neither is capable of independent, continued existence, for physiologically they are unbalanced. The egg is large, inert, contains a vast store of metaplasm, is protected by egg envelope, and has host the power of continued division. The sperm is small, highly motile contains little cytoplasm and no metaplasm, is devoid of protective membranes, and in itself has lost the power of continued division.

The Influence of Yolk on early Development

As already stated that the eggs are supposed to be the largest cells in the body and are provided with little or good amount of yolk or deutoplasm, which plays important part in determining the type of cleavage undergone by the fertilized egg. *Yolk* or *deutoplasm* is an inert material and when present in quantity has a noticeable effect in damping down the rate at which the cleavage planes pass through the egg. If yolk was evenly distributed, then its presence would merely slow down division, but its uneven distribution in telolecithal eggs causes the cleavage planes to be impeded chiefly in the vegetative hemisphere. This leads to the production of blastomeres of unequal size. Those nearer the animal pole being smaller (because they divide more rapidly) than those nearer the vegetative pole. In such cases the blastocoel becomes excentric in position and lies nearer the animal pole. In fishes, reptiles and birds the large eggs are having great quantities of yolk and in every egg the yolk particles are separated from the cytoplasm which is confined to a small cap, the *blastodisc*, at the animal pole. Here in such cases only the cytoplasmic blastodisc being capable of cell division, whilst the yolky portion remains as such (undivided). This type of cleavage in which the furrows do not pass completely through the egg, is spoken of as *partial* or *meroblastic* in contrast to the *total* or *holoblastic* cleavage experienced by eggs having a smaller concentration of yolk as in amphioxus, amphibians and most mammals.

13

ENERGY PRODUCTION IN CELL

Thermodynamics are important in many areas of biology. Many texts in this field, however, offer relationships between various thermodynamics entities without explaining fully what those entities re nor how the relationships are derived. The reader is often left with little real understanding. In this text we have elected to give a fuller discussion of the principles underpinning thermodynamics. This we believe will prove to be a greater value to the reader's subsequent studies and work than a collection of half understood truisms. As a consequence this chapter is rather a long one. Do not attempt to study it all in one setting.

VALUES OF THERMOCYNAMICS

The value of thermodynamics to the biotechnologist lies in the type of information it can provide.

This may be concisely summarized as follows:

1. Relationships between quantities of heat and work in biological systems and to systems at equilibrium. The information we derive from these relationships is vital to understanding metabolism and for the design and operation of bioreactors. It forms a basis for predicting the influence of physical and chemical parameters on various processes.
2. For systems at equilibrium the effect of changes in temperature, composition etc on a variety of physio-chemical and biological phenomena can be predicted by applying the first and second laws of thermodynamics.

   The ability to predict the position of equilibrium is fundamental to the manipulation of biological systems to optimize yields of desired products in biotechnology. It is also basic to the understanding of biochemical processes.

3. Non-equilibrium processes involving temperature, electromotive force (emf), or concentration gradients and the flow (or flux) of heat, mass and electricity can be analyzed by non-equilibrium or irreversible thermodynamics. This extension of classical thermodynamics gives a unified method of treating the transport processes which lie at the heart of all living organisms and all bioreactors and other chemical engineering plants.

Macroscopic and Microscopic Perspectives

Two contrasting but ultimately complementary approaches have characterized the development of the science of biology. One approach involves the study of large populations whilst the other is concerned with the behaviour of individual entities, organisms, cells or even atoms and molecules. We may distinguish these two approaches as the macroscopic and microscopic perspectives.

Definition of a system

In all sciences, analysis begins with conceptually (or even physically) separating a defined region of space or a finite portion of matter, termed a system, from its surroundings. The surroundings contain everything outside the system which has a direct bearing upon the properties of the system. The system is then described using prameters related to the behaviour of the system, and to its interactions with its surroundings.

Macroscopic properties

The macroscopic description of a system involves the specification of a small number of fundamental measurable properties.

Volume, temperature, pressure and composition are examples of the macroscopic properties which may be used to characterize a physical or chemical system.

Macroscopic properties useful for the scientific description of systems are characterized by:

(i) Being few in number;

(ii) Involving no special assumptions concerning the structure of matter;

(iii) Generally being measurable directly.

Pressure is a typical macroscopic property and was exploited for the successful description and understanding of physical systems long before the development of the atomic, molecular and kinetic theory concepts upon which our modern understanding of pressure is based.

Microscopic properties

The microscopic description of a system in contrast requires assumptions to be made about the structure of matter. The existence of atoms and molecules is assumed for example and postulates are developed relating to their motion, structure, energy states and interactions. Characteristically it is necessary to specify a number of quantities which can not be directly measured and which are not immediately suggested by our sense perceptions.

From a microscopic viewpoint, a system could be regarded as being an assemblage of a huge number N of molecules which individually can exist ina large number of discrete states of energies, E_1, E_2 ... E_n. Interactions between molecules involve collisions and electrostatic and other field forces and for their description probability concepts are applied. The equilibrium state of a system is taken as being the state of highest probability with each energy state containing a definite numerical population of molecules under a given set of conditions.

The two view points are not incompatible because macroscopic properties are simply time averages of microscopic characteristics. Our perception of macroscopic characteristics tends to remain unchanged as it is, after all, the perception of reality through our senses. In contrast the microscopic viewpoint is constantly being changed in the light of advances in our theoretical understanding. The basis for the justification of our theoretical assumptions lies in the comparison of the conclusions reached from the microscopic viewpoint with the deductions made from the macroscopic perspective.

Thermodynamic Approaches

Max Planck in his classic 'Treatise on Thermodynamics' noted that the subject developed as a result of three distinct methods of investigation.

He wrote that the most fruitful approach starts from a few very general empirical facts, mainly the two fundamental principles (laws) of thermodynamics. This approach gave us two key properties needed to describe systems, the thermodynamic energy (U) and the entropy (S). This macroscopic approach exploiting U, S and a few other fundamental properties such as mass, volume etc is the basis of classical thermodynamics and has been widely applied in chemistry, engineering and biology.

The two other approaches to thermodynamics outlined by Planck are of much less general application. They are the approach of

Helmholtz which confines itself to the initial hypothesis that heat is due to motion and the detailed kinetic theory treatments of Clausius, Maxwell and Boltzmann. The latter approach treats heat as being due to the definite motions of molecules and considers atoms as discrete masses. This has been exploited in statistical mechanics or statistical thermodynamics.

Basic Concepts

Thermodynamics are concenred with systems and in particular with the energetics of systems. They are concerned with the bulk properties of matter rather than with the molecular properties.

The study of thermodynamics evolved from attempts to understand steam engines but the interrelationships between useful work, energy and equilibria hold for all systems including biological ones.

Types of Systems

A system is any specified part of the universe such as on organism, a fermenter or a test tube. It is separated from its surroundings, the rest of the universe, by a boundary the characteristics of which define the type of system.

Isolated system/adiabatic process

An isolated system has a boundary which is impermeable to both matter and all forms of energy so that it exchanges neither heat nor matter with its surroundings. Any process which occurs in such a system is termed an adiabatic process. Perfectly isolated systems do not exist but the concept is useful and a reaction in a Dewar (Vacuum) flask is a close enough approximation for many purposes.

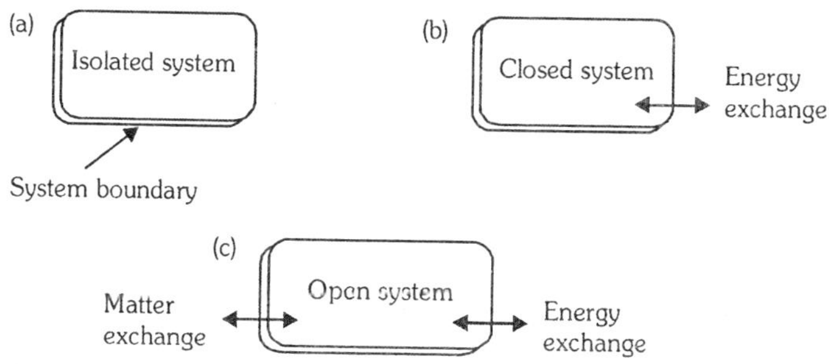

Fig. 13.1. Various systems: (a) isolated system; (b) closed system and (c) open system.

Closed and isothermal system

In a closed system the boundary is permeable to energy but ther is no transfer of matter between the system and its environment. If the temperature is kept constant we have an isothermal system.

Open system

An open system is one which can exchange both energy and matter with its surroundings.

Work and Energy Interconversion

Energy is defined as the capacity to do work. When a system does work its energy content falls. When work is done upon a system its energy content is increased.

Work is organized motion and mechanical work is defined as force times distance. Although in a biochemical reaction mechanical work may be done against the pressure of the atmosphere if there is an increase in volume due to gas evolution, we normally think of work in a different way in relation to biological processes. Work can take many forms in biological systems and involve displacement against electrical, mechanical or chemical potential forces. These various forms of energy are interconvertible.

If F is a generalized force and dy is a generalized displacement then the work done on the system is:

$$dW = Fdy$$

We can use this generalized equation to apply it to different types of work and forces.

We must stress here that dW has a negative value when the energy content of the system decreases (= work is done by the system on the environment) while dW has a positive value when the energy content of the system increases (= work done by the environment on the system).

Table 13.1. The relationship between work done on a system and different forms of pressure and displacements.

Type of work	*Work done on the system dW*
Volume change (mechanical work)	$P \times dV$ where P is the external pressure and dV the volume change
Electrical work	$E \times dZ$ where dZ is the electrical charge transferred and E the potential
Work of contraction of a fibre	$F \times dl$ where F is the force exerted and dl the change in length

Work and energy are interconvertible and heat is a measure of the kinetic energy of the constituents of a system. The random movements of the atoms and molecules and their internal vibrations increase when heat is transferred to the system. Work is done when the motion induced by the transfer of energy is organized and not chaotic. For example the movement of ions or electrons in an organized way across a membrane constitutes work. In contrast if there is merely an increase in random motion no work is being done.

Types of Work and Energy

It is necessary to distinguish between intensive factors and extensive factors. Intensive or potential factors as they are also called, are independent of the size of the system. Extensive factors (also called capacity factors) do depend on the size of the system; they are doubled when the size of the system is doubled.

Energy is the product of pairs of associated intensive and extensive factors a number of which are given in Table 13.2.

Table 13.2. Pairs of energy factors.

Types of energy	*Intensive (potential) factor*	*Extensive (capacity) factor*
Mechanical (PV)	Pressure (P)	Volume (V)
Electrical (EZ)	Electrical potential (E)	Electrical charge (Z)
Thermal (TS)	Temperature (T)	Entropy (S)
Chemical ($M_i\mu$)	Chemical potential (μ)	Mass (M) or number of moles (N) of the ith species

The direction of change when two systems are brought into contact, with no barrier between them, is determined by the difference in potential factors. The systems will change in such a way as to equalize the magnitude of the potential factors throughout the combined system. A system reaches a state of complete equilibrium when no localized differences in any potential factors exist within the system. Equilibrium is thus a time-invariant state and a system in equilibrium will show no tendency to change.

Let us consider what happens when two vessels filled with gas at different pressures are connected to each other. Pressure is an intensive (potential) factor and will equalize until it is the same in both vessels. If the vessels are rigid the pressure only will change but if we have joined together two balloons the volumes will alter to equalize the pressures. In this second case the extensive (capacity) factor volume has changed but it was the potential factor gradient which determined the direction of change and equilibrium was attained when the potential gradient had been eliminated. The potential factor here is temperature. In the system described there is a gradient of the potential factor.

Thus heat will flow from the hotter to the colder body until both are at the same temperature.

The chemical potential μ is the intensive factor for chemical energy and the extensive (capacity) factor is the amount of the chemical species present which can be expressed as number of particles of the particular species, the number of moles (N) or the mass (M). Chemical potential determines the direction of chemical and physical processes which tend to continue until the chemical potential is equalized throughout the system. In both types of change there is a spontaneous movement from higher to lower chemical potential and systems are in equilibrium with each other when their chemical potentials are identical.

Living systems can be in a state of true and complete equilibrium but a state of apparent or dynamic equilibrium may be transiently attained for example during steady state metabolism or growth in a fermenter. Classical equilibrium thermodynamics can fortunately be applied without serious problems to many processes in living systems but irreversible thermodynamics must sometimes be used.

State and Path Functions

If we consider the intensive property temperature, we are considering a property which is part of the description of a particular state. It is independent of the path by which the system reached that particular state. For this reason it may be termed a 'state function' in contrast to a 'path function'. The work which has gone into the attaining of a particular state and which depends upon the path taken to reach that state is an example of a path function.

Now that we have introduced some of the terms used in thermodynamics, we can examine the laws of thermodynamics and their application to biochemical systems.

Beginnings of Biochemical Thermodynamics

The foundations of modern biochemical thermodynamics can be traced back to 12 minutes past eight on the morning of February 3rd 1783 when a Gunea pig was placed in an ice calorimeter. This was in effect an adiabatic container surrounding a closed vessel containing the Guinea pig and the amount of heat transferred was measured by the amount of ice melted. These studies by Lavoisier and Laplace linked heat production with oxygen consumption and carbon dioxide formation. It was subsequently established that the heat evolved by a small mammal metabolizing carbohydrate to carbon dioxide and water was, within the limits of experimental error, the same as the heat evolved when the same substance was completely burnt in air or oxygen.

Biological oxidation was perceived as being simply equivalent to a slow form of combustion. It would appear, therefore, that biological processes follow the same set of thermodynamic rules (laws) as normal chemical processes. Thus in order to apply thermodynamic principles to biological systems, we need to consider the laws of thermodynamics.

Zeroth Law of Thermodynamics

Definition: If two systems A and B are each in thermal equilibrium with a third system C, then A and B are also in equilibrium with each other.

The temperature of a system gives an indication of the potential a system has to transfer heat to another system. Experience teaches us that when two closed systems A and B, able to exchange energy but not matter with each other, are in thermal equilibrium with a third system C they are also in thermal equilibrium with each other.

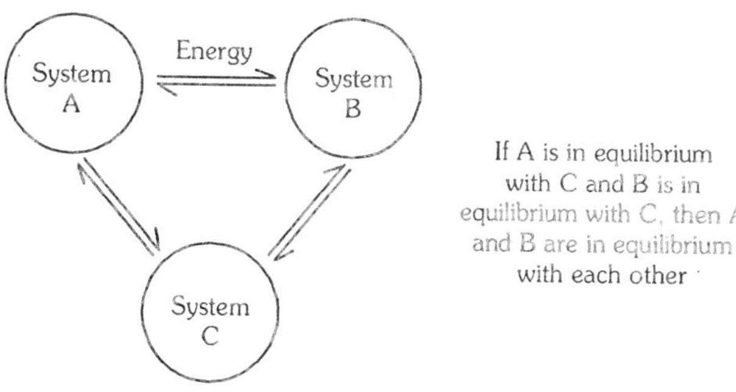

If there is no net flow of heat from A to C or from B to C then there will be no net flow of heat between A and B. This empirical fact is the zeroth law of thermodynamics. Its odd name indicates that logically it should precede the other laws of thermodynamics.

Like all the laws of thermodynamics it rests on observation, experiment and experience and not upon theory.

First Law of Thermodynamics

Definition: Changes in a body inside an adiabatic enclosure from a given initial state to a given final state involves the same amount of work independently of how the change is brought about.

The experimental studies of Joule in particular established that mechanical work could be transformed into heat and that when the same amount of work was performed the same rise in temperature was produced in a given quantity of water in an adiabatic enclosure. The adiabatic enclosure prevented exchange of heat or matter with the surroundings but work could be performed on the system. It was observed that all forms of work produced an equivalent amount of heat no matter what the form of the work was.

This led to the formulation of the first law of thermodynamics which states that the change of a body inside an adiabatic enclosure from a given initial state to a given final state involves that same amount of work independently of how the change is brought about.

Since energy is defined as the capacity to do work, we might consider the first law of thermodynamics in another way. The amount of energy released or adsorbed by a body to change from a given initial state to given final state is the same irrespective of how the change is brought out.

There are a lot of important consequences that arise from the first law of thermodynamics so let us investigate these in more detail.

Internal Energy

A system is taken from state A to state B by the performance of a quantity of work W_{ad} on the system. The process is adiabatic. The first law implies that W_{ad} is independent of the path. W_{ad} depends on the states of the system only. We can therefore consider that the system has a property, a state function, U such that:

$$W_{ad} = U_B - U_A \qquad ...(1)$$

The function U is termed the internal energy. The change in internal energy ΔU when the system goes from state A to state B under adiabatic conditions is:

$$\Delta U = U_B - U_A$$

If the system changes under non-adiabatic conditions so that it is in thermal contact with its surroundings the work involved in the process of changing from state A to state B may not be the same as it was under adiabatic conditions. The change in internal energy ΔU will however be the same this is a state function and independent of the path. Therefore where ΔQ is the heat absorbed by the system from its surroundings during the process and W is the work done on the system by its surroundings we may write:

$$\Delta U = \Delta Q + W \qquad ...(2)$$

The sum $\Delta Q + W$ represents the mechanical equivalent of all the thermal and mechanical operations of the surroundings upon the system. ΔQ is of course dependent upon there being a temperature difference between the system and its surroundings. If there is no temperature difference then $\Delta Q = 0$.

Principle of conservation of energy

In other words the change in the internal energy is the algebraic sum of the mechanical equivalents of the effects produced within the environment when a system is transformed from state A to state B. This, in fact, is a statement of the Principle of Conservation of Energy. The first law of thermodynamics is nothing more than the principle of conservation of energy applied to phenomena involving the production or absorption of heat.

This is of course an important concept. We will begin to relize its relevance to biological systems in general and cell in particular.

Now let us broaden Equation (2) to apply it to other forms of work.

You should have come to the following conclusions:

1. Hydrostatic (mechanical work) $\Delta U = \Delta Q - PdV$ and U is a function of P, V and T (since ΔQ is a function of temperature).
2. Contracting/relaxing fibre $\Delta U = \Delta Q + Fdl$ and U is therefore a function of T, F and l.
3. Electrical cell $\Delta U = \Delta Q + EdZ$ and U is therefore a function of T, E and Z.

All three equations have the same general form. Note however the signs (+ and -), these are important. You should remember these, or better still, understand why these are positive in some cases and negative in others.

Let us consider (1) first. When the system expands (that is dV is positive), then work has been done on the surroundings in the expansion. Therefore PdV (the work done) is lost from the system and PdV has a negative value. In case (2), work has to be done to stretch a fibre. Thus in increasing the length of a fibre (that is dl is positive), all work (Fdl) is done on the fibre and has therefore a positive value.

Sign Conventions

Thermodynamics consider energy changes from the point of view of the system. Energy expended by the system in doing work on its surroundings is lost from the system and therefore is given a minus sign.

When $W = +8$ kJ this means 8 kJ of energy have been supplied to the system by doing work on it. When $\Delta Q = -8$ kJ this means that 8 kJ of energy have left the system as heat and when $W = -8$ kJ this means that the system has done 8 kJ of work on its surroundings.

Enthalpy

In biology we are interested not in the actual internal energy change ΔU but in how much of this energy is available for biological purposes such as growth, biosynthesis etc. Most biological reactions occur at constant pressure and under these conditions work done associated with volume changes such as gas absorption or evolution is not available for biological purposes. It is therefore convenient to identify another function of state (H) the enthalpy. Enthalpy is also called the heat content or heat of formation.

The change in enthalpy (heat content) is given by:

$$\Delta H = \Delta U + P\Delta V \qquad ...(3)$$

or if the increase in volume is due to the formation of n moles of gas:

$$\Delta H = \Delta U + nRT$$

The enthalpy, H, is a function of state because it involves only U, P and V which are themselves functions of state.

The enthalpy change, ΔH is the quantity of heat absorbed by a closed isothermal system at constant pressure when it changes from one thermodynamic state to another without performing any work other than that associated with the volume change.

Volume changes during reactions in solution are negligible. What then is the relationship between ΔH and ΔU for an isothermal biochemical reaction in solution in which no gas is evolved?

If you think about this carefully when $\Delta V = 0$ then substituting in to (3) gives:

$$\Delta H = \Delta U$$

Experimentally ΔU and ΔH are obtained by measuring the heat of reaction using an adiabatic calorimeter in which the temperature change of the calorimeter during a reaction can be measured and this enables us to calculate ΔQ and thus ΔU. If there is no volume or pressure change then $\Delta Q = \Delta U$.

Two major types of calorimeters are used. The constant volume adiabatic calorimeter uses a constant volume reaction vessel surrounded by a water bath. The calorimeter is insulated to prevent heat loss from the system. The temperature change ΔT produced by the reaction initiated in the vessels enables the heat of reaction at constant volume ΔQ_v, to be calculated from a knowledge of the heat capacity C of the calorimeter.

$$\Delta Q_v = C\Delta T$$

The second type of clorimeter is the constant pressure calorimeter which is similar but operates at constant pressure.

Terminology

An *exothermic reaction* is one in which the system gives out heat to its surroundings so that the enthalpy of the system falls (ΔH is negative).

An *endothermic reaction* is one in which the system absorbs heat from its surroundings (ΔH is positive). For biochemical reactions the main contribution to ΔH comes from energy changes associated with the formation or breaking of chemical bonds.

For carrying out energy calculations, a standard reference value is chosen and the energy of all other states can be calculated from this reference value (this is analogous to using sea level as a reference value in geography). For thermodynamic calculations, the chosen standard conditions are: 298.15 K and 1 atm and all substances in their standard states (pure substance as it exists at 298.15 K and 1 atm). According to this convention, the enthalpy of the elements at 298.15 K and 1 atm = 0. The energy of compounds can be calculated from this reference value by taking into account the energy effects during their formation. For compounds in solution of course both formation of the compound and its dissolution have to be taken into account.

The standard enthalpy of formation is the enthalpy change associated with the formation of a compound from its elements in their standard states at 298.15 K.

If you know that acetic acid is a liquid at 298.15 K and it has the formula $C_2H_4O_2$ and that oxygen and hydrogen are gases at this temperature and carbon is a solid in the form of graphite write down an equation for the formation of acetic acid to which the term standard enthalpy of formation applies.

The equation is:

$$2C_{(graphite)} + 2H_{2(g)} + O_{2(g)} \rightarrow C_2H_4O_{(l)}$$

(note that subscript g = gas, l = liquid).

Thus the standard enthalpy of formation of acetic acid refers to the enthalpy change associated with converting two moles of graphite, two moles of gaseous hydrogen, two moles of gaseous oxygen to one mole of liquid acetic acid at 298.15 K and 1 atm.

Of course, if we use non-standard conditions, or we change the physical state of the reactants or products (for example use a different allotrope of carbon), this will influence the enthalpy change. In this case we would have to define the conditions in describing the enthalpy change.

Hess's Law

Definition: Whether a reaction is performed in several stages or in a single step the overall heat change will be the same.

Hess's law of constant heat summation

The first law of thermodynamics is often applied in the form of Hess's law of constant heat summation. This states that whether a reaction is performed in several stages or in a single step the overall heat change will be the same, i.e. the heat change of the single step will equal the algebraic sum (taking account of +/– signs for heat absorbed or evolved) of all the heat changes for the individual stages.

We have available the following information. The heat of combustion (enthalpy change for complete oxidation) at 293 K and standard atmospheric pressure, for ethanol is –1371 kJ mol^{-1} and the corresponding values are –1168 kJ mol^{-1} and –876 kJ mol^{-1} for acetaldehyde (CH_3CHO) and for acetic acid (CH_3COOH) respectively. Thus we can write:

for alcohol oxidation:

1. $C_2H_5OH_{(l)}+O_{2(g)}\rightarrow 2\ CO_{2(g)}+3H_2O_{(l)}$ $\quad \Delta H=-1371$ kJ mol^{-1}

for acetaldehyde oxidation:

2. $CH_3CHO_{(l)}+2^1/_2\ O_{2(g)}\rightarrow 2\ CO_{2(g)}+2H_2O_{(l)}$ $\quad \Delta H=-1168$ kJ mol^{-1}

and for acetic acid oxidation:

3. $CH_3COOH_{(l)}+2\ O_{2(g)}\rightarrow 2\ CO_{2(g)}+2H_2O_{(l)}$ $\quad \Delta H=-876$ kJ mol^{-1}

Subtracting (2) from (1) gives us:

$CH_2H_5OH_{(l)}-CH_3CHO_{(l)}+{}^1/_2\ O_{2(g)}\rightarrow H_2O_{(l)}$ $\quad \Delta H=(-1371-(-1168))$ kJ mol^{-1}

which gives us:

$C_2H_5OH_{(l)}+{}^1/_2\ O_{2(g)}\rightarrow CH_3CHO_{(l)}+H_2O_{(l)}$ $\quad \Delta H=-203$ kj mol^{-1}

Thus for the oxidation of alcohol to acetaldehyde: $\Delta H=-203$ kJ mol^{-1}.

Subtracting (3) from (2) we get:

$CH_3CHO_{(l)}+{}^1/_2\ O_{2(g)}\rightarrow CH_3\ COOH_{(l)}$ $\quad \Delta H=(-1168-(-876))$ kJ mol^{-1} $=-292$ kJ mol^{-1}

Thus for the oxidation of acetaldehyde to acetic acid: $\Delta H=-292$ kJ mol^{-1}.

These values of ΔH apply only for the stated conditions. This example shows how we can predict the heat output from a simple bioreaction using thermochemical data.

If we consider the oxidation of amino acids derived from protein during nutrition we will see how Hess's law can be applied to a rather more complex biological problem.

We will use alanine as an example. Alanine may be metabolized to urea and carbon dioxide by a process of biological oxidation. Starting from protein consumed during the digestive process we may regard solid alanine as our starting point for purposes of this calculation.

The equation for the complete oxidation of alanine is:

4. $CH_3CHNH_2COOH_{(s)} + 3^3/_4\ O_{2(g)} \rightarrow 3\ CO_{2(g)} + 3^1/_2\ (H_2O)_l + 1/2N_{2(g)}$
$\Delta H° = -1620$ kJ mol^{-1}

Here we have used the superscript ° to represent standard enthalpy (that is enthalpy changes under standard conditions). This is useful shorthand.

For the complete combustion of urea:

5. $CO\ (NH_2)_{2(s)} + 1^1/_2\ O_{2(g)} \rightarrow CO_{2(g)} + 2H_2O_{(l)} + N_{2(g)}$ $\Delta H° = -632$ kJ mol^{-1}

Every two alanine molecules will give rise to one urea so we may obtain the equation for the partial oxidation of alanine to carbon dioxide and urea by subtracting (0.5) × Equation (5) from Equation (4). This will give us Equation (6). Try this on a piece of paper for yourself. (Note each of the two urea nitrogens will have come from an alanine molecule which only contains one nitrogen atom).

6. $CH_3CHNH_2COOH_{(s)} + 3\ O_{2(g)} \rightarrow 2^1/_2\ CO_2 + 2^1/_2H_2O_{(l)} + ^1/_2\ CO(NH_2)_{2(s)}$ $\Delta H° = (-1620 - (^1/_2) \times (-632)$ kJ mol$^{-1} = -1304$ kj^{-1}

However the urea will not be in the form of solid urea and allowance must be made for the fact that it will be in solution.

The equation for the dissolution of urea in water to give for example a concentration of 0.1 mol^{-1} is:

7. $CO(NH_2)_{2(s)} \rightarrow CO(NH_2)_2$ (aq 0.1 mol^{-1}) $\Delta H° = -15.0$ kJ mol^{-1}

so to convert $^1/_2CO(NH_2)_{2(s)}$ to $^1/_2CO(NH_2)_2$ (aq 0.1 mol^{-1}) then the energy change = -7.5 kJ mol.

Thus if we add this to Equation (6) we can then write:

$CH_3CHNH_2COOH_{(s)} + 3O_{2(g)} \rightarrow 2^1/_2CO_2 + 2^1/_2H_2O_{(l)} + ^1/_2CO(NH_2)$ (aq 0.1 mol^{-1}) DH° = -1304 + (-7.5) kJ mol = -1311.5 kJ mol^{-1}

To have ignored the heat of solution would have lead to a 0.6% error in DH for the biological oxidation of alanine, for a smaller amino acid such as glycine the error would be greater (1.2%) as glycine contains a higher proportion of nitrogen.

A similar calculation can be made for ammonia as the end-product.

It is important to remember that when we are considering the energetics of chemical reactions we must not only remember enthalpy changes arising from the chemical changes but also take into account the energy changes resulting from the change in physical states.

Entropy and the Second Law of Thermodynamics

It is a well established empirical observation that there is a natural direction of change: heat flows from a hot body into its cooler surroundings, a solute will diffuse from a concentrated solution to a less concentrated one, hydrogen and oxygen react together to form water.

These are all examples of thermodynamically 'spontaneous' processes and they can only be reversed if work is done on the system. In controlled circumstances spontaneous change can be made to perform useful work.

A moment's thought will have enabled you to answer 'not necessarily'; consider the reaction between hydrogen and oxygen. When the two gases are mixed any change is at an undetectable slow rate in the absence of a catalyst or a stimulus such as a spark. Similarly glucose does not rapidly become oxidised to CO_2 and H_2O in the presence of oxygen. 'Spontaneous' refers to the direction not the rate of a process.

The first law of thermodynamics states that the total energy is conserved in any process. It follows from this that total energy does not determine the direction of spontaneous change. Any loss of energy by a system will be balanced by an increase in the energy of its surroundings. Yet spontaneous change occurs only in one direction.

Second Law of Thermodynamics

Clausius, in the 1860s, recognized the existence of a further function of state which relates to the capacity of a system to undergo transformation and which gives a measure of this capacity. We can get an understanding of what this function is by considering the second law of thermodynamics. This is an empirical generalization like the first law and has been stated in a number of ways, many of which are more useful to engineers and physicists than to biochemists. J.A.V Butler has stated the second law in the form, 'spontaneous processes (those which may occur of their own accord) are those which when carried out under proper conditions can be made to do work'. He also added that if carried out reversibly they will yield a maximum amount of work; in the natural irreversible way the maximum work is never obtained. We will explore exactly what he meant in the following section.

It is always convenient to remember a simple definition of a law.

"Spontaneous processes are those which when carried out under proper conditions can be made to do work."

Thermodynamic Reversibility

This term must be confused with physical or *biochemical reversibility* which simply means that a process or transformation can be reversed or that a reaction proceds at a measurable rate in both directions.

The term 'thermodynamically reversible' refers to a change so infinitesimally small that both the system and its immediate surroundings can be restored to their initial states without producing changes in the rest of the universe. Any process which was thermodynamically reversible would be infinitely slow and always very close to equilibrium.

All natural processes are in fact thermodynamically irreversible.

Table 13.3. Some thermodynamically irreversible processes in biochemistry and biology.

Mechanical	*Thermal*	*Chemical*
Snapping of a stretched fibre; free expansion of a gas (into a space at lower pressure); collapse of a surface film	Conduction or radiation of heat to cooler surro-undings	Chemical reactions; diffusion and mixing; osmosis; dissolution

The first law of thermodynamics tells us how much energy there is in 'total' in a system and if we can establish how much of this is unavailable we can determine how much is left to do useful work. A thermodynamically reversible process is one which is carried out in such a way as to develop the maximum work.

Reactions will only proceed spontaneously if they can perform work and hence this maximum work gives us a true measure of the tendency for a reaction to occur. The ability to perform work does not however, tell us anything about the rate at which a reaction will proceed.

Entropy and Change

If we consider the melting of ice to give water at 0°C (273.15 K) there is a great increase in the number of microscopic states available to the system when the highly ordered solid is replaced by the more disordered liquid at the same temperature. The capacity for transformation is thus increased. In an ice-water mixture at 273.15 K the two phases are in equilibrium and reversible melting and thawing take place. If an infinitesimal amount of heat (dQ) is absorbed by an infinitesimal amount of ice, the ice will melt but the temperature will not significantly change. The change in thermal energy for the ice will be temperature multiplied by the capacity factor for thermal energy (TdS). The capacity factor for thermal energy is called entropy (S)

We may thus write:

$$TdS = dQ$$

rearranging gives:

$$dS = \frac{dQ}{T} \qquad ...(4)$$

for the entropy change for the ice.

The water will however have lost an infinitesimal amount of heat dQ and will have undergone an equivalent entropy change.

If we regard the ice as the system and the water as its surroundings we see that for an infinitesimal, reversible change:

$$\Delta S_{surrounding} + \Delta S_{system} = 0 \qquad ...(5)$$

$$\Delta S_{total} = 0 \qquad ...(6)$$

In irreversible changes, the total entropy of the system and the surroundings increases (in other words there is a tendency to increase disorder). We may, therefore, write:

$$\Delta S_{surroundings} + \Delta S_{system} > 0 \qquad ...(7)$$

i.e. has a positive value.

We may in fact write for all changes:

$$\Delta S_{total} \geq 0 \qquad ...(8)$$

and indeed:

$$\Delta S_{universe} \geq 0$$

It is impossible to diminish the entropy of a system of bodies without thereby leaving behind changes in other bodies. Every process in nature takes place in such a way as to increase the sum of the entropies of all the bodies taking part in the process. In the limiting case of reversible processes the sum of the entropies remains the same.

Earlier we gave a definition of the second law of thermodynamics in terms of 'spontaneous processes are those which when carried out under proper conditions can be made to do work.' We can now describe the second law of thermodynamics in another way.

"The entropy of a system increases in a thermodynamically irreversible process and remains unchanged in a reversible process. It can never decrease."

Thus either ΔS_{system} or $\Delta S_{surroundings}$ can be a negative quantity for a particular process, but their sum can never be less than zero.

Entropy at the Molecular Level

Entropy is the capacity factor for thermal energy. It is a function of state. Entropy, as a function of state, is a product of the macroscopic viewpoint. The microscopic viewpoint enables us to see entropy as a consequence of the number of microstates in which the system could find itself due to the arrangement of the atoms into groups and molecules and the way in which energy is distributed into kinetic motion, vibrations and rotations. It is in effect a function of the degree of disorder in the system.

A system with a high degree of disorder has a high S value. Likewise a system with a low degree of disorder has a low S value.

Boltzmann has related the thermodynamic probability of a particular microstate (Ω) to entropy in the following way:

$$S = k \ln \Omega \qquad \text{...(9)}$$

where k is the Boltzmann constant.

The thermodynamic probability describes the number and relative importance of the possible microstates of a microscopically specified system. Ω is a measure of the disorder of a system and Equation (9) above gives us a simple relationship between entropy and disorder. From information theory, the information increases as the number of choices for the arrangement of a system decreases (that is as the degree of disorder decreases). Thus we may regard entropy either as being a measure of the degree of disorder or as a measure of the lack of information about the exact state of a system.

Care is needed when thinking about order in biological systems. For example the assembly of viruses from their subunits in aqueous solution might be regarded as an increase in order (that is a decrease in entropy). This seems to be the reverse of our previous argument that in all natural processes there is an increase in entropy. The explanation for this apparent paradox is as follows. Clearly the assembly of the virus itself involves an increase in order but the component subunit would be solvated if assembly did not occur. As the subunits associate to form the viruses, then water molecules are released leading to an increase in the entropy of the solution. The net result is an increase in the entropy of the system as a whole.

Gibbs and Helmholtz Functions

Chemical and biochemical reactions move towards an equilibrium with both reactants and products being present. At equilibrium there is no tendency for any net change to occur.

Consider a system, not in chemical equilibrium, undergoing an infinitesimal irreversible process involving transport of matter between phases in a heterogeneous system, or a chemical reaction in a homogeneous system, or both. These systems transfer heat dQ to or from a reservoir at temperature T.

If dS is the entropy change of the system and dS_R the entropy change to the reservoir then by the second law of thermodynamics:

$$dS_R + dS > 0$$

Therefore the change in entropy could be thought of a being produced by the transfer of heat (dQ) from a reservoir at temperature T to the system at the same temperature. In this situation, the reservoir would lose energy and the system would gain it, thus we could write:

$$-\frac{dQ}{T} + dS > 0$$

or multiplying by T and changing the signs:

$$dQ - TdS < 0$$

(Notice the change from >0 to <0 because we have changed the signs).

As a result of the energy (heat) transfer to the system, the internal energy of the system will have changed by dU and if there has been any volume change the amount of work performed will be PdV. This may be expressed by:

$$dQ = dU + PdV$$

so application of the second law of thermodynamics to a system and its reservoir (surroundings) ultimately leads to the expression for the system:

$$dU + PdV - TdS < 0$$

For a system at constant temperature and volume, PdV = 0 and so the inequality becomes:

$$dU - TdS < 0$$

or:

$$d\,(U - TS) < 0$$

As U, T and S are all functions of state we have a new function of state (U – TS) which is called the Helmholtz function, A.

We may write:

$$dA < 0$$

A in systems of constant temperature and volume has its minimum value at the final equilibrium state.

If we take T and P as constant the inequality becomes:

$$d(U + PV - TS) < 0$$

But earlier (Equation (3) we showed that $\Delta H = \Delta U + P\Delta V$ or:

$$dH = dU + PdV$$

thus:

$$d(H - TS) < 0$$

Again H, T and S are all functions of state so we can write:

$$dG < 0.$$

where G is another new function of state called the Gibbs function. For a system at constant temperature and pressure, G decreases during an irreversible process and has a minimum value at the final equilibrium point.

We can write for a system changing from one thermodynamic state to another:

$$\Delta G = \Delta H - T\Delta S \quad ...(10)$$

where ΔG is the Gibbs function change for the transition characterized by an enthalpy change ΔH and an entropy change ΔS.

The Gibbs function change (ΔG) for any chemical reaction provides a measure of the capacity to do work. In other words, it is the energy which is made available to perform useful work during a reaction. For this reason the Gibbs function is also referred to as the Gibbs free energy. (Note that in biological texts ΔG is simply referred to as the free energy of a reaction). It is important that you realise that the Gibbs function applies to processes which occur at constant temperature and pressure.

By analogy, the Helmholtz function (A) refers to processes which operate at constant temperature and volume.

Gibbs Function and Equilibrium

We have so far learnt that the Gibbs function change (ΔG) for any chemical reaction provides a measure of the capacity to do work. We have also learnt from Equation (10) that the change in Gibbs function arises from a change in enthalpy (ΔH) and the thermal energy ($T\Delta S$) in the system. In this section we will explain the relationship between product and reactant concentration and ΔG.

At equilibrium there is of course no net forward or backward reactions and there will be no net change in enthalpy or entropy. Thus at equilibrium $\Delta G = 0$.

When a reaction proceeds spontaneously there is of course a change in both enthalpy and entropy and thus a change in the Gibbs function. As the reaction approaches equilibrium, ΔG decreases. We therefore visualize a situation in which the further a system is away from equilibrium, the greater its ΔG value and, therefore, the greater its capacity to do work. In other words the value of ΔG is related to the actual concentrations of reactants and products and their distance from the equilibrium position.

The standard Gibbs function change which we will give the symbol $\Delta G°$ can be defined as the Gibbs function change when all reactants and products at standard concentrations (1.0 mol 1^{-1}) are allowed to reach equilibrium under standard conditions (298.15° K and 1 atm). Clearly the size of $\Delta G°$ will be dependent upon the final equilibrium position. The relationship between $\Delta G°$ and the equilibrium position can be written as:

$$\Delta G° = -RT\ln K_{eq} \qquad \text{...(11)}$$

Remember that $\Delta G°$ refers only to standard conditions (that is, all reactants and products are at standard concentrations, temperature and pressure).

$\Delta G°$ as such is of limited direct use in biological systems because these systems usually operate at the physiological pH = 7. pH 7 means that the hydrogen ion concentration is 10^{-7} mol 1^{-1}, therefore in biological systms often the term $\Delta G°'$ is used. $\Delta G°'$ is the standard Gibbs function change at pH 7. Thus $\Delta G°'$ signifies the change in Gibbs function when reactants and products at a concentration of 1.0 mol 1^{-1} are allowed to proceed to equilibrium at pH 7.0.

Thus we can write:

$$\Delta G°' = -RT\ln K_{eq} \qquad \text{...(12)}$$

where $\Delta G°'$ is the standard Gibbs function change (standard free energy change) at pH7.

Converting to logarithms to the base ten we can write:

$$\Delta G°' = -2.303\ RT\log_{10} K_{eq} \qquad \text{...(13a)}$$

or:

$$\log_{10} K_{eq} = -\frac{\Delta G°'}{2.303RT} \qquad \text{...(13b)}$$

At 25° (298K) and R 8.314 JK^{-1} mol

then 2.303 RT = 2.303 × 8.314 × 298 = 5706 J mol^{-1} = 5.706 kJ mol^{-1}

Thus for 25°C we can re-write Equation (13b) as:

$$\log_{10} K_{eq} = \frac{-\Delta G^{\circ\prime}}{5.7}$$

Now let us turn our attention to non-standard conditions.

The relationship between product and reactant concentrations and ΔG may be written as:

$$\Delta G = \Delta G^{\circ\prime} + RT \ln \frac{[\text{product of initial product concentration}]}{[\text{product of initial reactant concentrations}]} \quad \ldots(14a)$$

or at pH 7:

$$\Delta G = \Delta G^{\circ\prime} + RT \ln \frac{[\text{product of initial product concentrations}]}{[\text{product of initial reactant concentrations}]} \quad \ldots(14b)$$

or:

$$\Delta G = \Delta G^{\circ\prime} + 2.303\, RT \log_{10} \frac{[\text{product of initial product concentrations}]}{[\text{product of initial reactant concentrations}]}$$

Thus for the reaction A + B ⇄ C + D we can write:

$$\Delta G = \Delta G^{\circ\prime} + 2.303\, RT \log_{10} \frac{[C][D]}{[A][B]} \text{ at pH7.}$$

where [A], [B], [C] and [D] are the initial concentrations of reactants and products.

We will use Equation (13) and (15) in some examples.

The enzyme phosphoglucomutase at pH7.0 and 298 K catalyses the following reaction in the presence of magnesium ions.

glucose-6-phosphate ⇄ glucose-1-phosphate

An initial concentration of 0.20 mol l^{-1} glucose-6-phosphate falls to 0.19 mol l^{-1} at equilibrium.

Calculate:

1. K_{eq} for this reaction;
2. $\Delta G^{\circ\prime}$ for the conversion of glucose-6-phosphate to glucose-1-phosphate;
3. $\Delta G^{\circ\prime}$ for the reverse reaction when glucose-1-phosphate is converted to glucose-6-phosphate.

In answering this remember that:

[G-1-P] + [G-6-P] = 0.20 mol^{-1}

The change in Gibbs function for forward and back reactions differs only in sign.

$$\Delta G_{\text{forward reaction}} = -\Delta G_{\text{back reaction}}$$

As the Gibbs function is a function of state the values of $\Delta_f G$ etc are additive, where subscript $_f$ signifies 'formation'. Thus $\Delta_f G$ is the standard free energy of formation.

It follows that for a chemical reaction:

$$\Delta G^\circ = \Sigma\, \Delta_f G^\circ \text{ products} - \Sigma\, \Delta_f G^\circ \text{ reactants}$$

(The symbol Σ means 'the sum of the values of ').

We remind you that when considering reactions in aqueous solution, water may be regarded as:

(i) A pure liquid in which case its standard state is unit activity;

(ii) An aqueous solution of pure water has a concentration of 55.5 mol kg^{-1}. Note that this is not quite the same as 55.5 mol l^{-1}. It is conventional in biochemistry to use an activity of 1 for water in dilute aqueous solutions.

You should note that strictly speaking, standard Gibbs function change only applies to standard conditions (298.15° K, 1 atm). However, we often have to consider energy changes at temperatures other than 298.15 K (most commonly 310 K = 37°C). Just as we noted above that in biochemistry we often consider standard Gibbs function changes at pHs other than at standard pH (=pH 0), we can also consider Gibbs function changes at temperatures other than at 298.15° K. Just as with pH, we must, however, state the temperature. Here we will use the convention $\Delta G'$ to symbolize changes in Gibbs function when the reaction takes place at a stated temperature, pH and pressure other than standard conditions, but with reactants and products in their standard state.

The Gibbs function change for the synthesis of the dipeptide DL leucylglycine can be calculated from glycine and DL leucine at physiological temperatures and pH conditions from the data in Table given below:

Table 13.4. Gibbs function of formation values in aqueous solution at pH 7.0 at 37°C.

Substance	$\Delta_f G'$ *kJ mol*$^{-1}$
Glycine	-367
DL leucine	-330
DL leucylglycine	-448
Water	-235

The reaction is:

glycine + DL leucine $\rightleftarrows$ H_2O + DL leucylglycine

$$DG = -448 + (-235) - [(-367) + (-330)] \text{ kJ mol}^{-1}$$
$$= -683 + 697 \text{ kJ mol}^{-1}$$
$$= +14 \text{ kJ mol}^{-1} \text{ at pH 7.0 and } 37°C$$

It follows from the additive nature of ΔG values that Gibbs function data referring to substances in their pure standard states (gas, solid, liquid) can be related ΔG data for the substances in solution and in ionized or non-ionized states.

$\Delta G°$ of solution refers to the Gibbs function change associated with the concentration change to unit activity.

$\Delta_f G°$ in solution = $\Delta_f G°$ in standard state + $\Delta G°$ of solution; where $\Delta_f G°$ in solution and $\Delta G°$ of solution refer to unit activity in aqueous solution.

Likewise we can write $\Delta_f G°$ of ionized form in aqueous solution= $\Delta_f G°$ of non-ionized form in aqueous solution + $\Delta G°$ of ionization.

Effect of pH and Temperature upon Gibbs Function and Equilibria

Changes in pH may alter the degree of ionization of substrates and if a specific form of the molecule (for example the unionized state) is involved as a product or reactant, the equilibrium constant and ΔG value will vary with pH. If $[H^+]$ is a reactant or product of the reaction in question then there will be a change in pH as the reaction proceeds which for an enzyme catalyzed reaction will often mean a change in enzyme activity. It is therefore normal in biochemistry to carry out reactions in buffered solution.

If we consider a reaction:

$$A + B \rightleftarrows C + D + H^+$$

then

$$\Delta G = \Delta G° + RT \ln \frac{[C][D][H^+]}{[A][B]}$$

If we take all the reactants and products as being in their standard states under standard state conditions with the exception of $[H^+]$ we may write:

$$\Delta G°' = \Delta G° + RT \ln [H^+]$$

$([A] = [B] = [C] = [D] = 1)$

$$= \Delta G° + 2.303 \text{ RT} \log [H^+]$$

we may write:

$$\Delta G°' = \Delta G° - 2.303 \text{ RT pH}$$

We can see from this relationship that the change in Gibbs function is dependent upon pH.

Temperature may also be expected to influence the equilibrium position of a reaction.

Let us consider an exothermic reaction (one which generates heat). We could write the equation as:

$$A + B \rightleftarrows C + D + \text{heat}$$

We might anticipate that by raising the temperature we would push the equilibrium to the left. Thus we might anticipate that the value of DG´ will be influenced by temperature. This is indeed so.

The relationship between temperature and DG´ is described by the Gibbs-Helmholtz equation which may be conveniently expressed in its integrated form as:

$$\frac{\Delta G'_2}{T_2} = \frac{\Delta G'_1}{T_1} - \Delta H^\circ\left(\frac{T_2 - T_1}{T_1 T_2}\right)$$

The assumption has been made in deriving this equation that over a modest temperature range when you change the temperature from T_1 to T_2 the value of ΔH° does not change significantly. Experience shows this would be a reasonable assumption.

Table 13.5. The effect of temperature and ionic, strength on the value of $\Delta G^{\circ\prime}$ ($\Delta G'$) for ATP hydrolysis at pH 7.0 25°C, 37°C and variable [Mg^{2+}].

25°C		37°C	
Ionic strength (I)	$-\Delta G'$ (kJ mol^{-1})	Ionic strength (I)	$-\Delta G'$ (kJ mol^{-1})
0.00	33.51	0.00	34.00
0.10	32.72	0.10	33.15
0.15	32.91	0.15	33.28
0.20	33.17	0.20	33.59

The data demonstrated the need to specify conditions closely for biochemical reactions as a change of one pH unit or a 100 fold change in magnesium ion concentration can produce an almost 10 fold change in the equilibrium constant for ATP hydrolysis.

Nomenclature, Units, Symbols and Functions

Nomenclature

Correct use of symbols and terminology is the key to avoiding confusion in thermodynamics.

Do remember also that in older literature in particular symbols, units and nomenclature often differ from modern practice.

Units, Symbols and Conventions

SI units are used (eg. g, m) but for reasons of convenience one atmosphere is retained as the standard value for pressure rather than expressing the standard state value in Pascals (1 atm = 101.325 k Pa).

The bar (10^5 Pa) has been recommended for reporting standard state data but is not universally used. Most, if not all, biochemical data tabulations refer to 1 atm and for solutions and solids (ie. most biological cases) the differences are small enough to neglect for most purposes.

Physical states are represented as follows:

g-gaseous; l-liquid; s-solid; c-crystalline; aq-dissolved in water.

The subscript f and the term formation are used for the formation of a substance from its elements. The physical form (allotrope) of solids must be specified as must be the physical conditions under which the substance was formed. Thus $\Delta_f H$ would be an enthalpy of formation under the specified conditions ($\Delta_f H$ and not ΔH_f is used because the f modifies the operator Δ not the H, which is the symbol for a physical quantity.

Thermodynamic Standard Functions

These refer to standard reaction conditions which are defined as:

(i) Temperature = 298.15 K;

(ii) Pressure, 1 atmosphere (101.325 k Pa);

(iii) Composition, all components in their standard states.

The standard state of a substance is the pure substance (not in solution!) as it exists at 298.15 K and standard atmospheric pressure e.g. gaseous carbon dioxide, solid glucose and liquid water.

For substances in solution the standard state of a solute or solvent is normally defined as unit activity.

In the literature a superscript '$\ominus$' or 'o' is used to indicate thermodynamic functions relating to reactions under standard conditions and Δ to signify the difference between the values of a function for two states of a system. For convenience, we have adopted what has become the more common practice of using superscript 'o'.

G is the Gibbs function and ΔG° is the change in Gibbs function for a reaction taking place under thermodynamic standard conditions

(298.15 K, a pressure of one atmosphere and all the components in their standard states).

$\Delta G^{\circ\prime}$ is used to specify the change in Gibbs function for a reaction in solution under standard conditions with all components in their standard states with the exception of hydrogen ion activity. Hydrogen ion concentration is usually 10^{-7} mol l^{-1} (pH7) unless otherwise specified.

$\Delta G'$ is the change in Gibbs function when the reaction takes place at a stated temperature, pH and pressure other than standard conditions but with reactants and products in their standard states.

ΔG is the change in Gibbs function when the reaction takes place at constant pressure and temperature under arbitrary but stated conditions (often corresponding to physiological or 'test tube' concentrations). In principal we can use similar conventions for other thermodynamic functions, for example enthalpy (H).

We point out that in the literature you may find the use of 'f' in thermodynamic functions for formation located after the physical quantity symbol, as in ΔH_f $(=\Delta_f H)$. Non SI units are frequently to be found in older literature, particularly the use of the thermochemical calorie (1 calorie = 4.184) instead of the Joule to express energy.

Symbols for Functions

There has also been a lack of consistency in the terminology and symbols used for thermodynamic functions. In this text we have used the following symbols:

U is the thermodynamic energy (internal energy, frequently given the symbol E) in Joules (J).

H is the enthalpy (heat of formation or heat content) in Joules (J).

S is the entropy in J K^{-1}.

G is the Gibbs function (free energy, net work-function or Gibbs free energy, frequently given the symbol F in older literature) in Joules (J).

A is the Helmholtz function (maximum work function, available energy or Helmholtz free energy, also sometimes given the symbol F) in Joules (J).

Q is heat absorbed in Joules (J).

T is the thermodynamic (absolute) temperature in K.

Equilibrium Constants

Strictly speaking, K_{eq} is the thermodynamic or true equilibrium constant calculated from the activities of the components at equilibrium.

Activities are concentrations corrected for deviations from ideal behaviour, which is only found in very dilute solutions where:

$$\text{activity} \rightarrow \text{concentration}$$

K_c is the equilibrium constant calculated from the stoichiometric concentrations of the components at equilibrium.

Because of the degree of uncertainty over physiological concentrations due to experimental error etc and because of the lack of knowledge of activity coefficients for substances in the intracellular environment it is normal to use stoichiometric concentrations and to assume K_{eq} = approximately K_c in biochemical thermodynamic calculations. The error in the assumption is not usually large.

For our purpose it is usually sufficient to assume $K_{eq} = K_c$ and we use the common biochemical notation of K_{eq} to represent the equilibrium constant calculated from the stoichiometric concentrations of the components at equilibrium.

State Functions and the Δ Notation

We have used the symbol Δ to represent a change in particular functions. Remember however that changes in state functions are dependent only on the initial and final states. We should therefore signify the state. For example the state may be solid or liquid or solution. Thus we should use a notation to indicate this. Thus $X_{(s)}$ signifies the value of a state function when the system is a solid. Likewise the $X_{(l)}$ signifies the value of a state function when the system is a liquid, and $\Delta_{(s-l)}X = (X_{(s)} - X_{(l)}$ the change in X on melting.

We can use the notation $D_{l \rightarrow g}$ X to signify a change in state function when the state is changed from a liquid to a gas.

This is however rather cumbersome. In most circumstances it is usually self evident which states a ΔX refers to so it is customary to simply write ΔX.

Applications of the Gibbs Function and Entropy to Biological Systems

We may now move on to look at some of the ways in which thermodynamic data may be used to shed light upon biochemical processes. In particular we will look at some applications of the Gibbs function and of entropy.

Steady State Equilibria

So far we have considered individual reactions in isolation. *In vivo* reactions are more usually part of a metabolic pathway.

A metabolic sequence such as a biochemical pathway A → B → C → D → E may achieve a steady state flux through the pathway so that the concentration of substrates, for example [C] and [D] remain constant.

Static and dynamic equilibrium

This leads to a dynamic equilibrium for which the mass action ratio γ of products over reactants ([D]/[C]) is an 'apparent equilibrium constant'. This mass action ratio is not a 'true' thermodynamic equilibrium which corresponds to a 'static' equilibrium. A 'static' equilibrium would result from mixing a fixed amount of substrate with enzyme and allowing the reaction to proceed until no further increase in product concentration was observed.

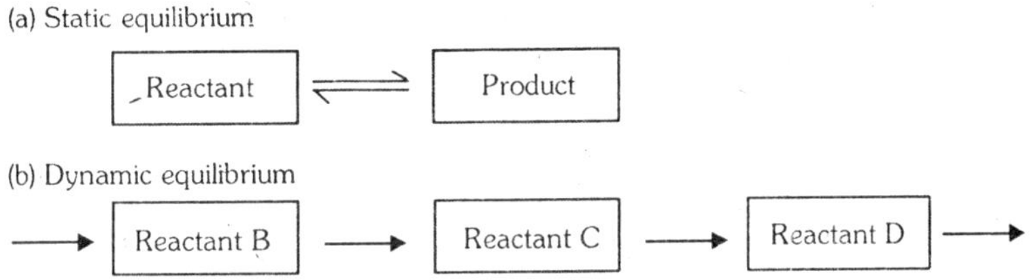

(a) Static equilibrium

Reactant ⇌ Product

(b) Dynamic equilibrium

→ Reactant B → Reactant C → Reactant D →

Fig. 13.2. Static and dynamic equilibrium.

A system of the static type of equilibrium corresponds more to *in vitro* than *in vivo* conditions.

For a system in static equilibrium, the rate of the forward and back reactions are equal so that there is no net reaction and under these conditions $\Delta G = 0$.

We know that:

$$\Delta G^{\circ\prime} = -RT \ln K_{eq} \qquad ..(12)$$

We also know that:

$$\Delta G = \Delta G^{\circ} + RT \ln \frac{[\text{product of initial concentration of products}]}{[\text{product of initial concentration of reactants}]}$$

Now let us turn our attention to the dynamic equilibrium

Is $\Delta G = 0$ for a dynamic equilibrium?

The answer is no. In this case there is a continued flux through the pathway, C is being continually formed and used. For the reaction C → D we can write:

$\Delta G = \Delta G^{\circ} + RT \ln [D]/[C]$ where [C] and [D] are the steady state concentrations of reactant C and product D.

But [D]/[C] is the mass action ratio (γ) so we can write: $\Delta G = \Delta G° + RT\ln \gamma$.

We may write for a reaction at 298 K:

$$\begin{aligned}\Delta G &= -RT \ln K_{eq} + RT \ln \gamma \\ &= -RT (\ln K_{eq} - \ln \gamma) \\ &= -RT \ln\left(\frac{K_{eq}}{\gamma}\right) \\ &= -2.303\, RT \log\left(\frac{K_{eq}}{\gamma}\right) \\ &= -5.7 \log \frac{K_{eq}}{\gamma}\end{aligned}$$

If the *flux* (or flow of material) through an *in vivo*, metabolic sequence leads to a mass action ratio (γ) far removed from the 'static' or 'true' equilibrium constant (K_{eq}) then the term 'non-equilibrium reaction' is used to describe the reaction. Such 'non-equilibrium reaction' represent potential control points in metabolic sequences and it is in fact possible to define a regulatory enzyme as one which catalyzes a non-equilibrium reaction.

Table 13.6. Mass-action ratios (γ) and equilibrium constants (K_{eq}) of reactions in the glycolysis pathway for ascites tumour cells at 25°C (298 K).

Enzyme	K_{eq}	(γ)
Hexokinase (HK)	4.7×10^3	2.6×10^{-2}
Phosphoglucoisomerase (PGI)	0.41	0.23
Phosphofructokinase (PFK)	1×10^3	0.63
Aldolase (ALD)	8.9×10^{-5}	2.9×10^{-5}
Triosephosphate-isomerase (TPI)	4×10^{-2}	1.5
Glyceraldehyde-3-phosphate dehydrogenase plus phosphoglycerate kinase (G3P/PGK)	0.8×10^3	17.8
Phosphoglycerate (PGM)	0.15	0.43
Enolase (ENO)	3.7	1.6
Pyruvate kinase (PK)	9×10^3	2.8

Some examples of mass action ratios (γ) and equilibrium constants (K_{eq}) for reactions in a common metabolic pathway (glycolysis) are given in Table 13.6. You need not worry about the exact chemical changes being brought about by each of the stages.

It can be seen from Table 13.6 and 13.7 that many of these reactions are not far removed from equilibrium and hence are likely to be kinetically reversible *in vivo* (i.e. ΔG is small).

Table 13.7. ΔG value for glycolytic enzymes catalyzed reactions in ascites tumour cells.

Reaction	K_{eq}	$\Delta G\ J\ mol^{-1}$
HK	$\frac{4.7\times10^{3}}{2.6\times10^{-2}}=1.8\times10^{5}$	-30.0
PGI	$\frac{0.41}{0.23}=1.8$	-1.5
PFK	$\frac{1\times10^{3}}{0.63}=1.6\times10^{3}$	-18.3
ALD	$\frac{8.9\times10^{-5}}{2.9\times10^{-5}}=3.1$	-2.8
TPI	$\frac{4\times10^{-2}}{1.5}=2.7\times10^{-2}$	+8.9
G3P/PGK	$\frac{0.8\times10^{3}}{17.8}=44.9$	-9.4
PGM	$\frac{0.15}{0.43}=0.35$	+2.6
ENO	$\frac{3.7}{1.6}=2.3$	-2.01
PK	$\frac{9\times10^{3}}{2.8}=3.2\times10^{3}$	-20.0

Entropy, Gibbs Function and Structure

The third law of thermodynamics may be stated in the form: "Taking the entropy of element, in its most stable form, as zero at a temperature of absolute zero then every substance will have a positive entropy which becomes zero for all perfect crystalline substances (including compounds) at a temperature of absolute zero."

This is clearly consistent with our idea that entropy is a measure of disorder because, for a perfect crystalline solid at absolute zero, when there is no movement, we have complete information about the exact state of the system. Under such conditions there is no disorder.

The value of the third law is that it enables standard entropies ($S°m$) and standard reaction entropies ($\Delta_r S°$) to be obtained.

When we compare the $S°_m$ values in Table 13.8 we see that entropy increases, as we would expect, with increasing disorder in simple substances such as carbon, water and carbon dioxide.

Table 13.8. Standard entropies ($S°_m$) at 298 K.

Substance	$S°_m$ $J\ K^{-1} mol^{-1}$	*Substance*	$S°_m$ $J\ K^{-1} mol^{-1}$
C (diamond)	2.4	Methanol (gas)	239.8
C (graphite)	5.7	Ethanol (liquid)	160.7
H_2O (liquid)	69.9	Ethanol (gas)	282.7
CO_2 (gas)	213.7	Acetic acid (liquid)	159.8
Sucrose (solid)	360.1	Acetic acid (aqueous)	178.7
Methanol (liquid)	126.8	Acetate ion (aqueous)	86.6

When we consider solid diamond with its highly ordered structure we see it has a lower entropy than graphite. Sucrose, a more complex solid, has a much higher entropy which reflects the rotations and vibrations within the molecule.

In the molecular biology area, entropy changes are of particular interest with regard to changes in the three dimensional shape of macromolecules. Such changes are often associated with profound changes in the biological activity of the molecules.

A classical 1934 study by Anson and Mirsky involved the reversible thermal denaturation of the enzyme trypsin.

$$Tr_{native} \rightleftarrows Tr_{denatured} \quad K_{eq} = \frac{[Tr_{denatured}]}{[Tr_{native}]}$$

They found that $\Delta H°$ for the denaturation was +282,800 J mol^{-1} over the temperature range studied and that the enzyme was 50% inactivated at 317 K.

Since:

$$\Delta G = \Delta H - T\Delta S'$$

or for a defined set of conditions:

$$\Delta G' = \Delta H° - T\Delta S'$$

We know that:

$$\Delta G' = -2.303 \text{ RT} \log_{10} K_{eq}$$

$$K_{eq} = \frac{[\text{inactive enzyme}]}{[\text{active enzyme}]}$$

Thus for 50% inactivation $K_{eq} = 1$:

therefore:

$$\Delta G' = 0 \text{ at } 317 \text{ K.}$$

Substituting for $\Delta G'$ and $\Delta H°$:

$$0 = +282{,}800 - 317\ \Delta S' \text{ at } 317 \text{ K}$$

therefore:

$$\Delta S' = \frac{282{,}800}{317}$$

hence:

$$\Delta S = +892 \text{ JK}^{-1} \text{ mol}^{-1}$$

This large increase in entropy can be explained in terms of an unfolding of the protein molecule with a consequent increase in disorder and a fall in information about the exact state of the molecule.

Enzyme activity, particularly for enzymes which regulate metabolic activity is frequently modified by the binding of allosteric effectors. These are molecules which bind at a site removed from that at which the normal substrate binds. They alter enzyme activity by altering the conformation of the protein molecule. If the change in shape is large this should be revealed by an entropy change.

Exergonic and Endergonic Processes

In this section we attempt to distinguish between two pairs of terms which are applied to reactions. These are:

(i) Exergonic and endergonic processes;

(ii) Endothermic and exothermic process.

In essence:

(i) An exergonic reaction is one in which ΔG is negative and which can drive other processes and is therefore capable of doing useful work;

(ii) An endergonic reaction is one in which ΔG is positive and which must be driven;

(iii) An exothermic reaction is one which releases (evolves) *heat* (i.e. ΔH is negative);

(iv) An endothermic reaction is one which absorbs *heat* (i.e. ΔH is positive).

The condition for a process to occur spontaneously is that for a system at constant temperature and pressure ΔG must be negative. Such a process is termed exergonic and represents the system moving towards equilibrium.

The value of ΔG is an indication or function of the displacement of the system from equilibrium. When a process moves away from equilibrium and ΔG is positive the process is termed endergonic.

It is clear that if a specific process in a biochemical or biological system is endergonic then the cell must find a way to make the overall process exergonic. This can be done by coupling thermodynamic process to an exergonic process. Thus in nature the occurrence of an endergonic process implies it must be linked to an exergonic process.

It must also be recognized that if a process is exergonic it only means that the process can occur spontaneously, not that it will proceed at a measurable rate. The ΔG for a reaction gives no indication of the speed of the reaction. This is determined by kinetic, as against thermodynamic, factors.

The reaction why evolution of heat (ΔH is negative) in a reaction does not determine spontaneity is because ΔG depends upon two factors one of which is the $T\Delta S$ contribution which can in some circumstances balance out the ΔH change [recall Equation (11)

$$\Delta G = \Delta H - T\Delta S$$

Equation (11) contains terms derived from both the first law (ΔH) and the second law ($T\Delta S$) of thermodynamics.

Both S and H are functions of state as are G and U. Being functions of state all depend solely upon the initial and final states of the system and hence the value of ΔG will be independent of the pathway between the initial and final states. This means that the value of ΔG for a complex series of transformations can be obtained from the algebraic summation of the ΔG changes for each component reaction in the series. This is a Hess's law-type relationship and can tempt one into the error of regarding the Gibbs function as an energy term to which the law of conservation of energy applies. The use of terms such as 'free energy' for the Gibbs function, 'energy releasing' for exergonic processes and 'energy consuming' for endergonic processes can reinforce this error and indeed this is the reason why some modern texts tend to speak of Gibbs function rather than Gibbs 'free energy'.

The expression **$\Delta G = \Delta H - T\Delta S$ can** suggest that the tendency of systems to move to lower G values is due to a tendency to go states of lower enthalpy and higher entropy. The true driving force for change is the tendency of the universe, the system and its surroundings, to move to a state of higher entropy. The sum of the entropy of the system and its surroundings is maximized. Heat which enters the surroundings as a result of an exothermic reaction ($\Delta H < 0$) increases the entropy of the surroundings. It may puzzle you that spontaneous endothermic reactions do occur with $\Delta H > 0$. In these cases the positive ΔH term is balanced out by a large increase in the entropy of the system.

An important characteristics of ΔG is that changing the relative concentrations of products and reactants can change not only its magnitude but also its sign.

Consider the case where an enzyme catalyzes the reaction:

$$A + B \rightleftarrows C + D$$

and $\Delta G^{\circ\prime}$ is found to be –5.7 kJ mol^{-} at 298 K at pH7.

It is essential to recognize that ΔG not $\Delta G^{\circ\prime}$ determines if a reaction is spontaneous under a given set of conditions. It is the concentration of reactants and products which determines if ΔG is smaller than, greater than or equal to $\Delta G^{\circ\prime}$

It can be seen from the above that substrate and reactant concentrations directly affect the value of ΔG. It is not possible to set a value of ΔG for a reaction *in vivo* in the absence of knowledge of the cellular concentrations of the substrates and reactants. ΔS is concentration related in the same way as ΔG.

ΔG is a state function so its value depends not on how work is done but only on the values of G for the defined initial and final states.

Changes in enthalpy (ΔH) are the source of energy to perform work unless ΔG is greater than ΔH when heat or energy is absorbed from the surroundings.

In 'biology', metabolism involves using chemical energy (internal energy) for carrying out the work of the cell and ΔH sets an upper limit on how much work can be done.

Photosynthesis is the basis of sustained life because the radiant energy absorbed does work in the biological system compensating for the unfavourable entropy changes in the reactions taking place in the living cell.

Coupling of Reactions

If we consider the following reaction, catalyzed by the enzyme pyruvate kinase, which occurs in the glycolytic pathway we see that two molecular transformations have taken place. The overall reaction:

Reaction A phosphoenol pyruvate + ADP $\rightleftarrows$ pyruvate + ATP

may be looked at as involving the following two reactions:

Reaction B phosphoenol pyruvate + H_2O $\rightleftarrows$ pyruvate + Pi

$\Delta G°' = -55.6 \text{ kJ mol}^{-1}$

Reaction C ADP + Pi $\rightleftarrows$ ATP + H_2O

$\Delta G°' = +32.2 \text{ kJ mol}^{-1}$

If we add together reactions B and C, we get reaction A.

Likewise by adding together the energy changes the overall change in Gibbs function is:

$$\Delta G°' \text{ is } -55.6 + 32.2 = -23.4 \text{ kJ mol}^{-1}.$$

The net process is exergonic and could be expected to proceed spontaneously.

It should be recognized that the enzyme pyruvate kinase is a complex protein, a tetramer of 55 kD subunits, which can exist in three forms and that reaction A is the net reaction which takes place when the substrates react with the enzyme. The two reactions B and C do not actually take place as written. Indeed the steps in the conversion of reactants to products in reaction A involve enzyme-bound species so that the equation written for reaction A represents only the net reaction.

However the Gibbs function is a function of state and $\Delta G°'$ for the net reaction will depend only on the initial and final states. It is independent of the actual pathway so that the thermodynamics of the process may be analyzed without need for knowledge of the intermediate reaction complexes.

It is clear that the large negative ΔG associated with the loss or transfer of the phosphate group from phosphoenol pyruvate is the exergonic process which drives the endergonic process of transferring a phosphate group to ADP.

We may describe the two processes as being coupled and the concept of 'coupled' reactions enables us to understand the energetics of many biochemical reactions.

'High Energy' Phosphates

This term is misleading but it is still widely encountered. Its origins lie, in the observation that $\Delta G°'$ for the hydrolysis of ATP and certain other phosphate esters (such as creatine phosphate, phosphoenol pyruvate and 1,3-diphosphoglycerate) was much higher than, for example, that of glucose-6, and glucose-1-phosphate or glycerol monophosphate.

The phosphates with high, negative values for $\Delta G°'$ of hydrolysis appeared to be generally associated with metabolic pathways and processes involved in yielding useful energy for biological purposes.

Erroneous concept of 'high energy' phosphate

The use of the symbol for the 'high energy' phosphate link as in ADP ~ P (ATP) gave the mistaken impression that unusual amounts of energy are associated with a specific bond in the molecule. The term 'bond energy' is used in chemistry to mean the amount of energy needed to break a chemical bond. Thus a high energy bond should be one which is hard to break. A moment's thought will reveal that the term is used in the opposite sense when talking about a high energy bond in biology. A further misconception is that the energy of a molecule is located in specific bonds as against being associated with the whole molecule.

It should be remembered also that:

$$\Delta G = \Delta H - T\Delta S$$

so that the Gibbs function change depends both on changes in enthalpy and changes in entropy. If the entropy change is relatively large than the Gibbs function change will be sensitive to temperature.

In the case of ATP hydrolysis at 310 K, the approximate values of the thermodynamic function changes are:

$$\Delta G' = \text{approximately } -30 \text{ kJ mol}^{-1}$$
$$\Delta H' = \text{approximately } -20 \text{ kJ mol}^{-1}$$
$$\Delta S' = \text{approximately } -34 \text{ J mol}^{-1}$$

The enthalpy change reflects the fact that there are greater electrostatic repulsions between the negative changes in the ATP molecule than in reaction products, the products of hydrolysis have higher enthalpies of solvation than ATP and that there is resonance stabilization of the reaction product molecules. The release of the phosphate group on hydrolysis contributes a relatively large entropy change for ATP hydrolysis, but ΔS is negative because of the increased ordering of water molecules around the products of hydrolysis.

The use of term like 'high energy' phosphate bond, 'energy rich' bond are thus erroneous as the whole molecule rather than a single isolated bond determines the energetics of the system. Nevertheless the use of the term 'high energy phosphate bond' is a convenient shorthand providing the explanations given here are clearly understood.

A further misconception is to view ΔG for the hydrolysis of ATP as exceptionally high by comparison with other phosphate ester in biological systems. The misconception was initially caused by early estimates of ΔG°′ for the hydrolysis of ATP of –50 kJ mol^{-1} whilst much lower values were (correctly) obtained for glucose-6-phosphate and glycerol-1-phosphate.

Substances of High Group Transfer Potential

Table 13.9 below lists the ΔG°′ values for the hydrolysis of a number of substances involved in the transfer of groups in biosynthetic reactions and includes a value for ΔG°′ for ATP which is commonly accepted for biological systems. The ΔG°′ values for ATP hydrolysis are dependent upon temperature, ionic and magnesium concentration as well as pH.

Table 13.9. ΔG°′ values for biologically important substances of high groups transfer potential.

Donor molecule	*Group activated for transfer*	*ΔG°′ kJ mol^{-1}*
ATP	Phosphate	–32.2
1,3-diphosphoglycerate	Phosphate	–56.9
Phosphoenol pyruvate	Phosphate	–55.6
Creatine phosphate	phosphate	–42.7
Acetyl phosphate	Acyl and phosphate	–42.3
Acetyl-S-coenzyme A	Acyl	–33.5
UDP glucose	Glucose	–30.5
Valyl tRNA	Valyl	–35
N^{10} formyl tetrahydrofolate	Formyl	–26

It can be seen from an examination of Table 13.10 that ATP is in fact a compound of intermediate group transfer potential with a ΔG°′ of hydrolysis intermediate between the very high values for substances like phosphoenolpyruvate and the very low values such as for glycerol-1-phosphate.

Measurement of ΔG

We have seen that ΔG values can be obtained from equilibrium data. To illustrate potential problems in obtaining ΔG values let us examine a specific example and consider the likely accuracy of the ΔG value which would be obtained.

Table 13.10. Gibbs function changes for the hydrolysis of some biologically important phosphates.

Substance	*ΔG°′ (pH7)*
Glycerol 1-phosphate	-9.6
Glucose 6-phosphate	-13.8
Glucose 1-phosphate	-20.9
Phosphodiesters	-25.1
ATP	-32.2
Acetyl phosphate	-42.3
Creatine phosphate	-42.7
Phosphoenolpyruvate	-55.6

The value of $\Delta G°'$ for the reaction A ⇄ B is –57 kJ mol^{-1} at 298 K. It can be shown that:

$$\log_{10} K_{eq} = -\frac{\Delta G°'}{5.7}$$

thus:

$$K_{eq}\, 10^{\left(-\frac{\Delta G°'}{5.7}\right)} \text{ with } \Delta G°' \text{ in kJ mol}^{-1}$$

so that:

$$K_{eq} = 10^{-\left(-\frac{57}{5.7}\right)} = 10^{10}$$

The equilibrium will be such that the concentrations of reactants at equilibrium will be so small as to be impossible to measure them with any accuracy (if they can be measured at all!)

Other methods for determining $\Delta G°$ include:

1. Substituting known values of $\Delta H°$ and $\Delta S°$ into the equation:
   $\Delta G° = \Delta H° - T\,\Delta\, S°$
2. From the difference between the algebraic sum of the standard Gibbs function of formation of the products and reactants:
   $\Delta G° = \Sigma\Delta_f G°_{products} - \Sigma\Delta_f G°_{reactants}$
3. Using $\Delta G°$ values for reactions whose net outcome is the reaction for which a $\Delta G°$ value is desired.

   Note that methods (2) and (3) require knowledge for the appropriate $\Delta G°$ and $\Delta_f G°$ values.

4. In the case of oxidation-reduction reactions ΔG° may be obtained from electrode potential measurements.

   ΔS° values may also be obtained if the appropriate data are available using the equation:

   $\Delta S^\circ = \Sigma \Delta S^\circ_{products} - \Sigma \Delta S^\circ_{reactants}$

   ΔH values may be obtained by calorimetry or from heat of combustion data for the reaction components or the application of Hess's law to other appropriate data.

ΔH° values may also be obtained by using the relationships for a reaction at constant pressure.

$$\Delta G^\circ = -RT \ln K_{eq}$$

and

$$\Delta G^\circ = \Delta H^\circ - T\Delta S^\circ$$

so that:

$$\Delta H^\circ - T\Delta S^\circ = -RT \ln K_{eq}$$

hence:

$$RT \ln K_{eq} = T\Delta S^\circ - \Delta H^\circ$$

$$\therefore \ln K_{eq} = \frac{\Delta S^\circ}{R} - \frac{\Delta H^\circ}{RT} \text{ or } \log K_{eq} = \frac{\Delta S^\circ}{2.303R} - \frac{\Delta H^\circ}{2.303RT}$$

but R and ΔS° are constants, then

$$\log K_{eq} = \text{constant} - \frac{\Delta H^\circ}{2.303RT}$$

ΔH° may thus be obtained from the slope of a plot of $\ln K_{eq}$ against 1/T.

Biochemical Role of ATP

It is useful to view ATP and ADP as acting as a donor- acceptor pair for phosphoryl group transfer reactions, accepting phosphate groups from substances of higher group transfer potential and donating them to substances of lower group transfer potential.

The ability to transfer a phosphoryl group to water as indicated by $\Delta G^{\circ\prime}$ for hydrolysis of the phosphate compound gives a measure of group transfer potential.

This view of the role of ATP would be consistent with a rapid interconversion of ATP/ADP within the cell and relatively low ATP concentrations.

The concentrations of ATP found in living cells are in fact of the order of 10^{-3} to 10^{-2} mol l^{-1} of cell water and it has been estimated that the half-time for turnover of the terminal phosphate group is a minute or two in animal cells but only a matter of seconds in bacterial cells.

The hydrolysis of ATP is exergonic ($\Delta G' < 0$) under standard physiological conditions so that about 30 kJ mol^{-1} is available to drive other reactions through coupling. This is a biologically important characteristic of the substance.

Protein biosynthesis is a highly endergonic process not only because of the energy accounted for by the enthalpy change in the formation of a large number of peptide linkages but also because of the large entropy decrease. This decrease is due to the assembly of a large number of amino acids into the protein chain in a precisely ordered sequence. The effects upon entropy of the formation of protein secondary, tertiary and quaternary structure and changes associated with solvation must also be taken into account.

Protein sysnthesis is driven by linking it to ATP via a complex sequence involving transfer RNA as a carrier of the amino acids

Thus the exergonic hydrolysis of ATP is used to drive the endergonic peptide bond formation which has an average $\Delta G°'$ of about +17 kJ mol^{-1} but because of the indirect nature of the process about 3 ATPs are used per peptide link formed.

Glucose oxidation under aerobic conditions produces 38 ATP molecules per glucose molecule and for a modestly sized protein molecule with about 150 peptide links (about the size of myoglobin); peptide bond formation alone will use about 450 ATP molecules. This means about 12 glucose molecules are needed per 1 protein molecule as a minimum. ATP is involved in cellular transport processes across membrans so that more ATP (and more glucose) may be required to transport the glucose and amino acids into the cell before synthesis can begin.

The cell may produce ATP via a number of mechanisms apart from the oxidation of organic substrates. In particular photosynthesis is a major route whilst oxidation of inorganic substrates is used by some bacteria. Anaerobic processes such as the conversion of glucose to lactate in glycolysis are also linked to ATP production.

$$\text{Glucose} + 2Pi^- + 2ADP \rightarrow 2\ \text{lactate}^- + 2ATP + 2H_2O$$

At 310K $\Delta G'$ is about –218 kJ mol^{-1} for the conversion of glucose to two lactate molecules. The standard reaction enthalpy for this reaction is –120 kJ mol^{-1}.

A large increase in entropy due to the breaking of the glucose molecule accounts for the exothermicity being exceeded by the exergonicity. In the production of two ATPs $\Delta G'$ is about +60 kJ mol^{-1} so that the whole process of lactate and ATP production via glucose fermentation has a value of $\Delta G'$ of about –158 kJ mol^{-1}. The process is thus a spontaneous one with the equilibrium strongly in favour of ATP and lactate formation.

Knowledge of $\Delta G'$ for ATP hydrolysis can be exploited in many ways as shown by this final example.

Nitrite is converted to nitrate by micro-organisms which contain an enzyme system able to catalyze the reaction.

NO_2^- (aq) + $^1/_2Q_2 \rightarrow NO_3^-$ (aq)

Note also that D_fG' for NO_2^- (aq) is –34.5 kJ mol^{-1} and for NO_3^- (aq) is –110.5 kJ mol^{-1} we can answer the question, 'Is it thermodynamically possible for the organism to grow aerobically using nitrite as an energy source?'

$\Delta G'$ for the reaction ADP + Pi $\rightarrow$ ATP + H_2O is about + 32 to 33 kJ mol^{-1}.

The oxidation of nitrite to nitrate is thus sufficiently exergonic to drive the endergonic biosynthesis of at least one ATP per molecule of nitrite oxidized.

All living organisms appear to use ATP so nitrite is certainly a potential substrate, on thermodynamic grounds, for the growth of micro-organisms under aerobic conditions.

INDEX

R